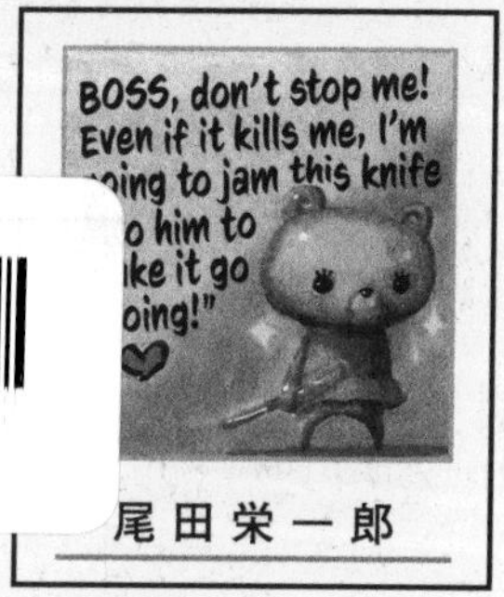
BOSS, don't stop me!
Even if it kills me, I'm
oing to jam this knife
o him to
ke it go
oing!"
尾田栄一郎

I hate cutesy stuff. You have to watch out for people who try to say the following...

"One of a kind" -> "One of a kiiind! ♡"
"Monument!" -> "Monuuuument! ♡"
"Open year round" -> "Open year roooooouuund! ♡"
"Barley Tea" -> "Baaaaarley Teeeeaa! ♡"

Cut it out!
And now, it's time for the manga without Honor or Humanity, *One Piece*! Volume 61! Let's do this!

-Eiichiro Oda, 2011

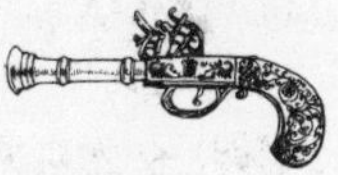

Eiichiro Oda began his manga career at the age of 17, when his one-shot cowboy manga **Wanted!** won second place in the coveted Tezuka manga awards. Oda went on to work as an assistant to some of the biggest manga artists in the industry, including Nobuhiro Watsuki, before winning the Hop Step Award for new artists. His pirate adventure **One Piece**, which debuted in **Weekly Shonen Jump** in 1997, quickly became one of the most popular manga in Japan.

ONE PIECE VOL. 61
PARAMOUNT WAR PART 5 &
NEW WORLD PART 1

SHONEN JUMP Manga Edition

This graphic novel contains material that was originally published in English in SHONEN JUMP #104–107. Artwork in the magazine may have been slightly altered from that presented here.

STORY AND ART BY EIICHIRO ODA

English Adaptation/Lance Caselman
Translation/Laabaman, HC Language Solutions, Inc.
Touch-up Art & Lettering/Vanessa Satone
Design/Fawn Lau
Editor/Alexis Kirsch

ONE PIECE © 1997 by Eiichiro Oda. All rights reserved.
First published in Japan in 1997 by SHUEISHA Inc., Tokyo.
English translation rights arranged by SHUEISHA Inc.

The rights of the author(s) of the work(s) in this publication to be so identified have been asserted in accordance with the Copyright, Designs and Patents Act 1988. A CIP catalogue record for this book is available from the British Library.

Printed in the U.S.A.

Published by VIZ Media, LLC
P.O. Box 77010
San Francisco, CA 94107

10 9 8 7 6 5 4 3 2 1
First printing, March 2012

PARENTAL ADVISORY
ONE PIECE is rated T for Teen and is recommended for ages 13 and up. This volume contains fantasy violence and tobacco usage.
ratings.viz.com

www.viz.com

THE WORLD'S MOST POPULAR MANGA
www.shonenjump.com

SHONEN JUMP MANGA

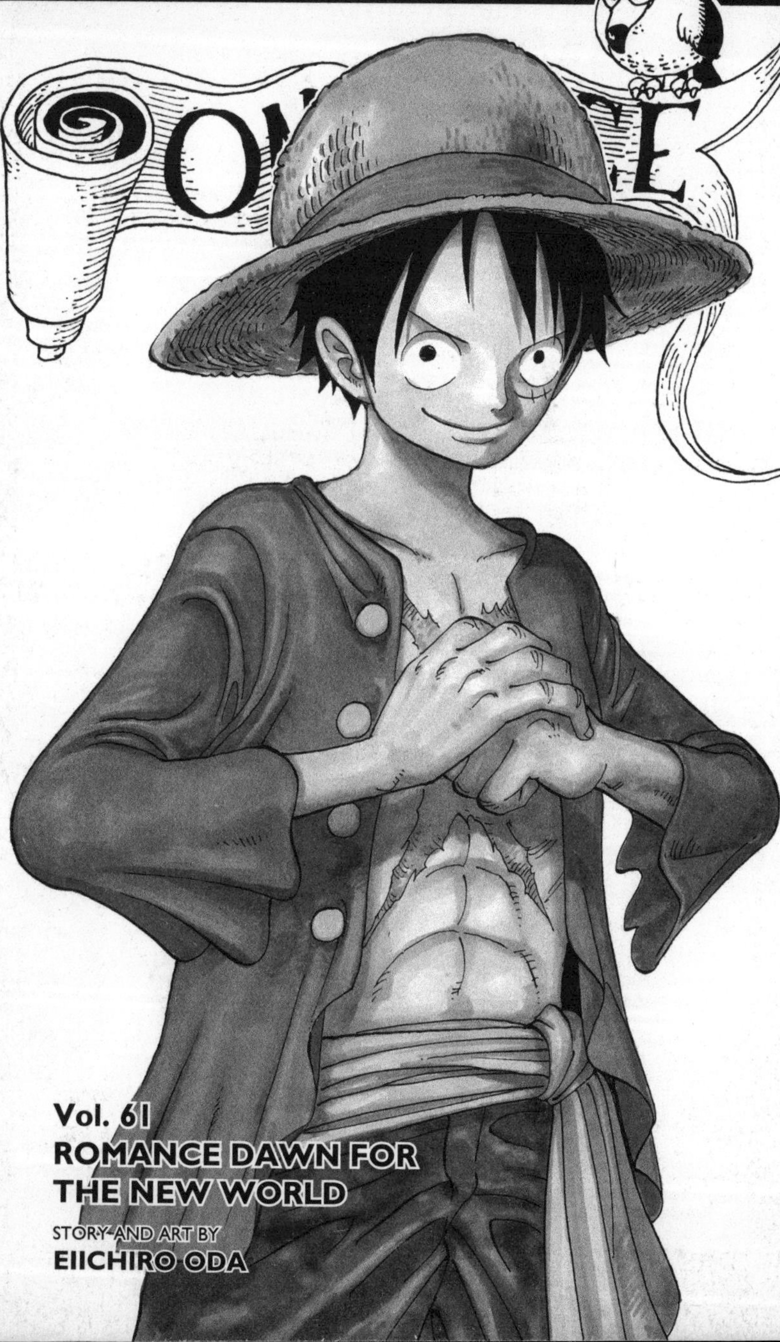

Vol. 61

ROMANCE DAWN FOR THE NEW WORLD

STORY AND ART BY

EIICHIRO ODA

The Straw Hat Crew

Monkey D. Luffy

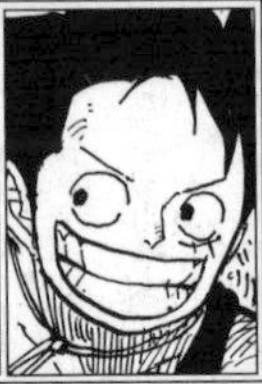

A young man who dreams of one day becoming the Pirate King. He's training with Rayleigh after sending a message to his crew.

Captain, Bounty: 300 million berries

Roronoa Zolo

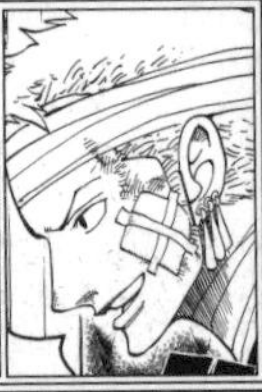

He was sent off to the ruins of the Muggy Kingdom on Gloom Island. He is currently with Perona.

Fighter, Bounty: 120 million berries

Tony Tony Chopper

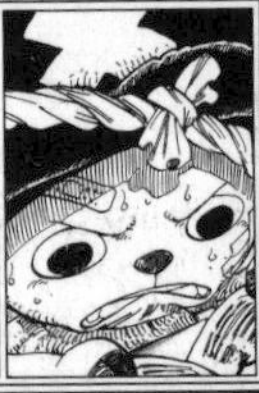

Currently in the Birdie Kingdom, where birds rule over the people. Some say this island is a Treasure Island.

Ship's Doctor, Bounty: 50 berries

Nami

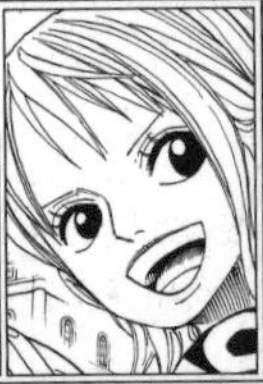

She is currently in Weatheria, a country on a small sky island, where people study the science of weather.

Navigator, Bounty: 16 million berries

Nico Robin

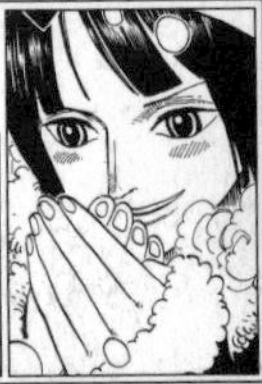

Currently in the country on a bridge called Tequila Wolf. She was enslaved but later freed by the Revolutionary Army.

Archeologist, Bounty: 80 million berries

Usopp

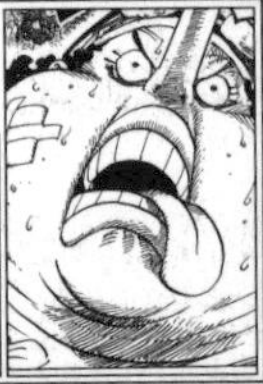

He is currently with Heracles in the bandit forest of Glinston in the Bowin Islands.

Sniper, Bounty: 30 million berries

Franky

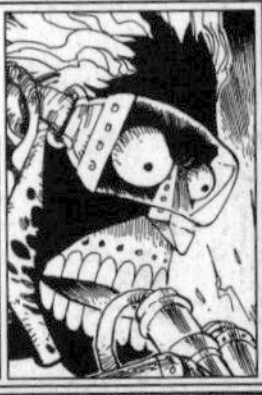

Currently on the Mechanical Island, birthplace of the genius Dr. Vegapunk, in the Future Land Baldimore.

Shipwright, Bounty: 44 million berries

Sanji

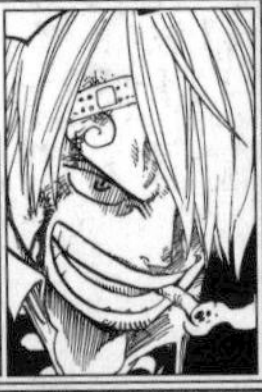

He is on dreamy Peachy Island, known as the second "Island of Women." Is he now a maiden in the infamous Kamabakka Kingdom?!

Cook, Bounty: 77 million berries

Brook

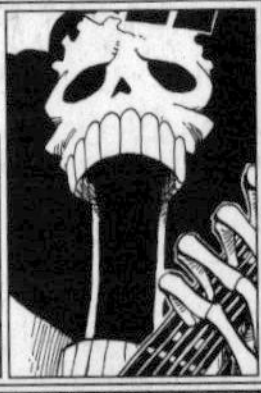

In Hungeria, the impoverished country of Lazy Bones Island. He is currently worshipped by locals as the devil lord.

Musician, Bounty: 33 million berries

Shanks

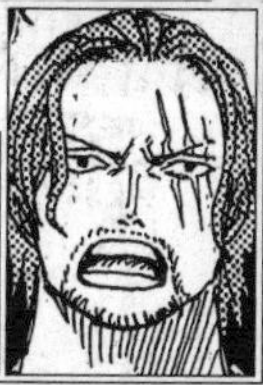

One of the Four Emperors. He continues to wait for Luffy in the second half of the Grand Line called the New World.

Captain of the Red-Haired Pirates

Dracule Mihawk

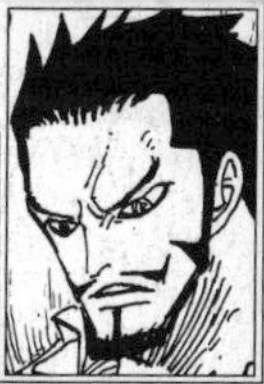

The world's strongest swordsman. He currently lives in the old castle in the Muggy Kingdom where Zolo is.

Member of the Seven Warlords of the Sea

Monkey D. Dragon

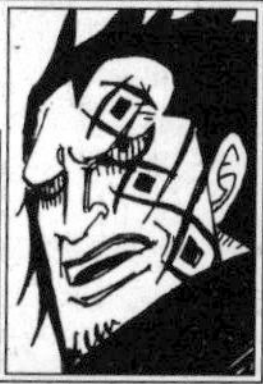

Luffy's father. He is currently on the island of white sand, Baltigo, somewhere in the Grand Line.

Leader of the Revolutionary Army

Monkey D. Garp

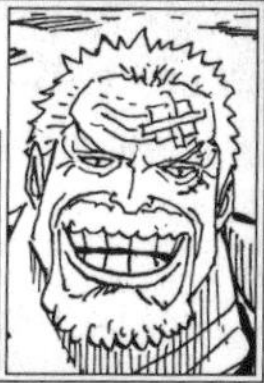

Luffy's grandfather. He resigned from his post after losing Ace in the Paramount War.

Navy Headquarters Vice Admiral

Jimbei

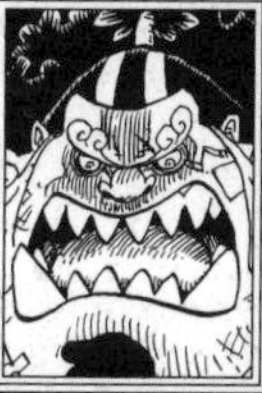

He saved Luffy from near death in the Paramount War and is currently with him on the Island of Women.

Former member of the Seven Warlords of the Sea

Emporio Ivankov

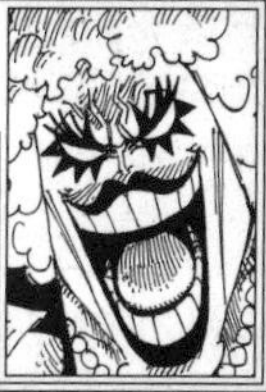

An executive of the Revolutionary Army. He was in the Paramount War with Luffy. Afterward, he met Sanji in his own kingdom, but...

Kamabakka Kingdom Queen (forever vacant)

Silvers Rayleigh

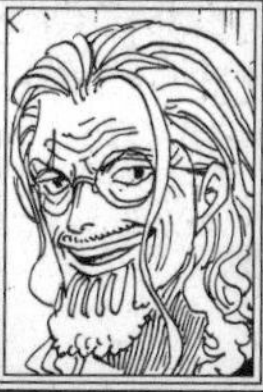

He suddenly appeared on the Island of Women and made Luffy a certain offer...

Former first mate of the Roger Pirates

Boa Hancock

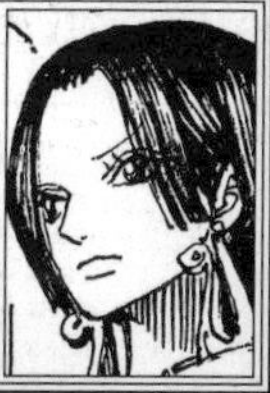

Empress of Amazon Lily. She is hiding Luffy on her island while he recovers from his injuries.

Member of the Seven Warlords, Kuja Pirates Captain

Story

The public execution of Luffy's brother, Ace, sparked the war between the Whitebeard Pirates and the Navy. This battle that Luffy took part in was later called the Paramount War. This battle came to a close with the deaths of Ace and Whitebeard. After escaping, Luffy was wallowing in sorrow on the Island of Women. He then remembered what happened ten years ago with Ace and his other brother, Sabo. Understanding his own weakness, Luffy reconfirmed how important his friends were for him in order to move forward. That was when Rayleigh appeared before Luffy and made him a certain offer. Luffy agreed and sent out a message only his crew would understand...

Vol. 61
Romance Dawn for the New World

CONTENTS

ONE PIECE

Hereafter, volume 61 will start.

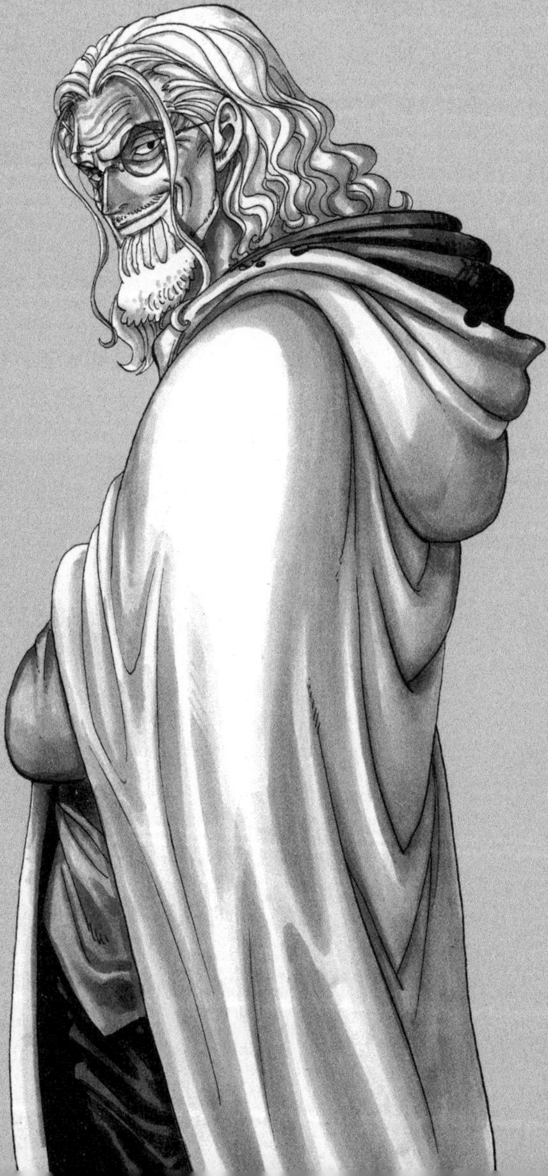

Chapter 595: THE PLEDGE

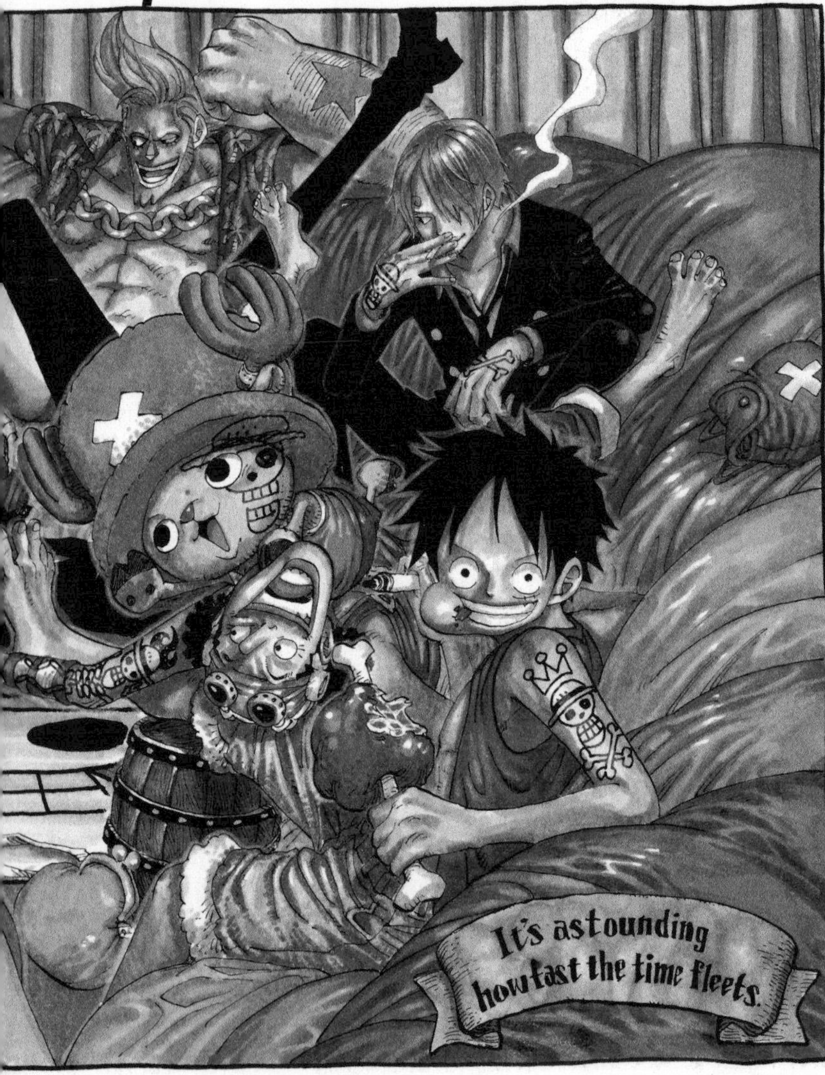
It's astounding how fast the time fleets.

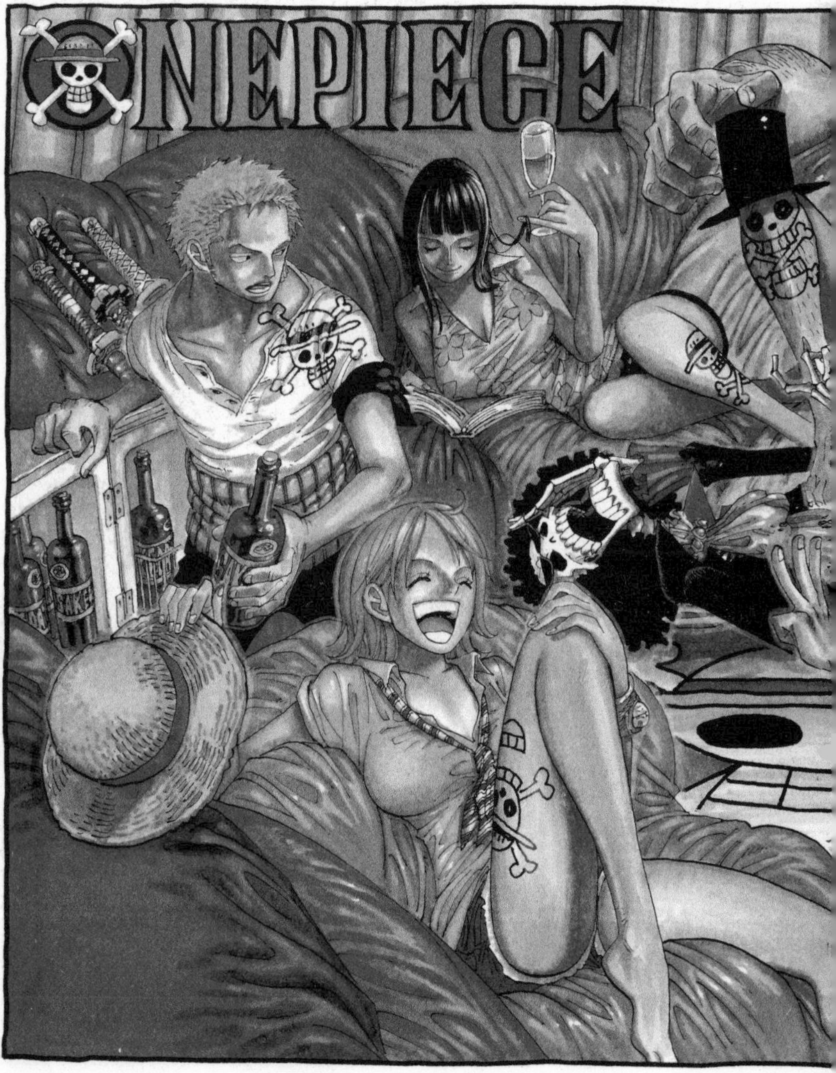
ONE PIECE

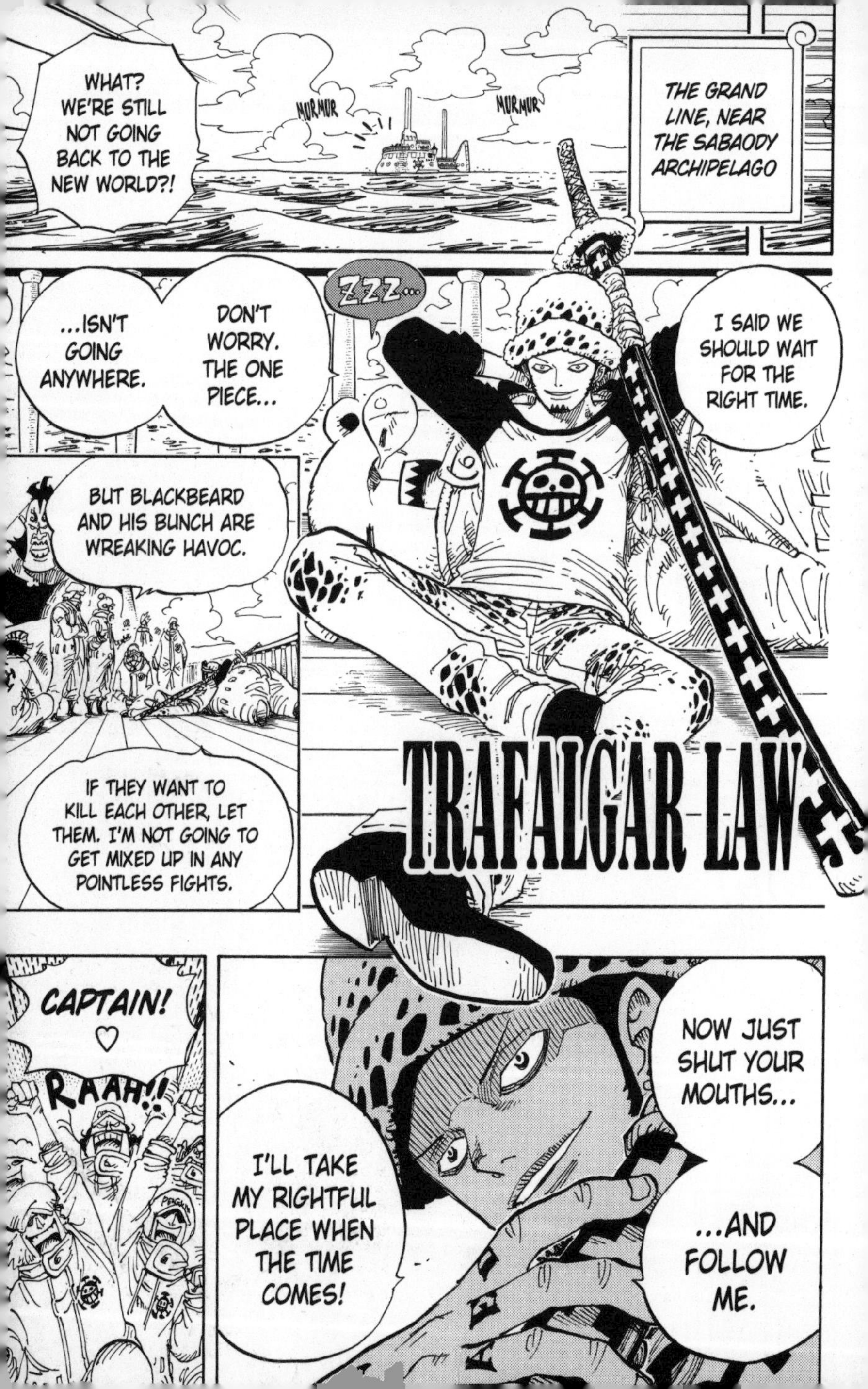
THE GRAND LINE, NEAR THE SABAODY ARCHIPELAGO
MURMUR
MURMUR
WHAT? WE'RE STILL NOT GOING BACK TO THE NEW WORLD?!
I SAID WE SHOULD WAIT FOR THE RIGHT TIME.
ZZZ...
DON'T WORRY. THE ONE PIECE...
...ISN'T GOING ANYWHERE.
BUT BLACKBEARD AND HIS BUNCH ARE WREAKING HAVOC.
IF THEY WANT TO KILL EACH OTHER, LET THEM. I'M NOT GOING TO GET MIXED UP IN ANY POINTLESS FIGHTS.
TRAFALGAR LAW
NOW JUST SHUT YOUR MOUTHS...
...AND FOLLOW ME.
I'LL TAKE MY RIGHTFUL PLACE WHEN THE TIME COMES!
CAPTAIN! ♡
RAAH!!

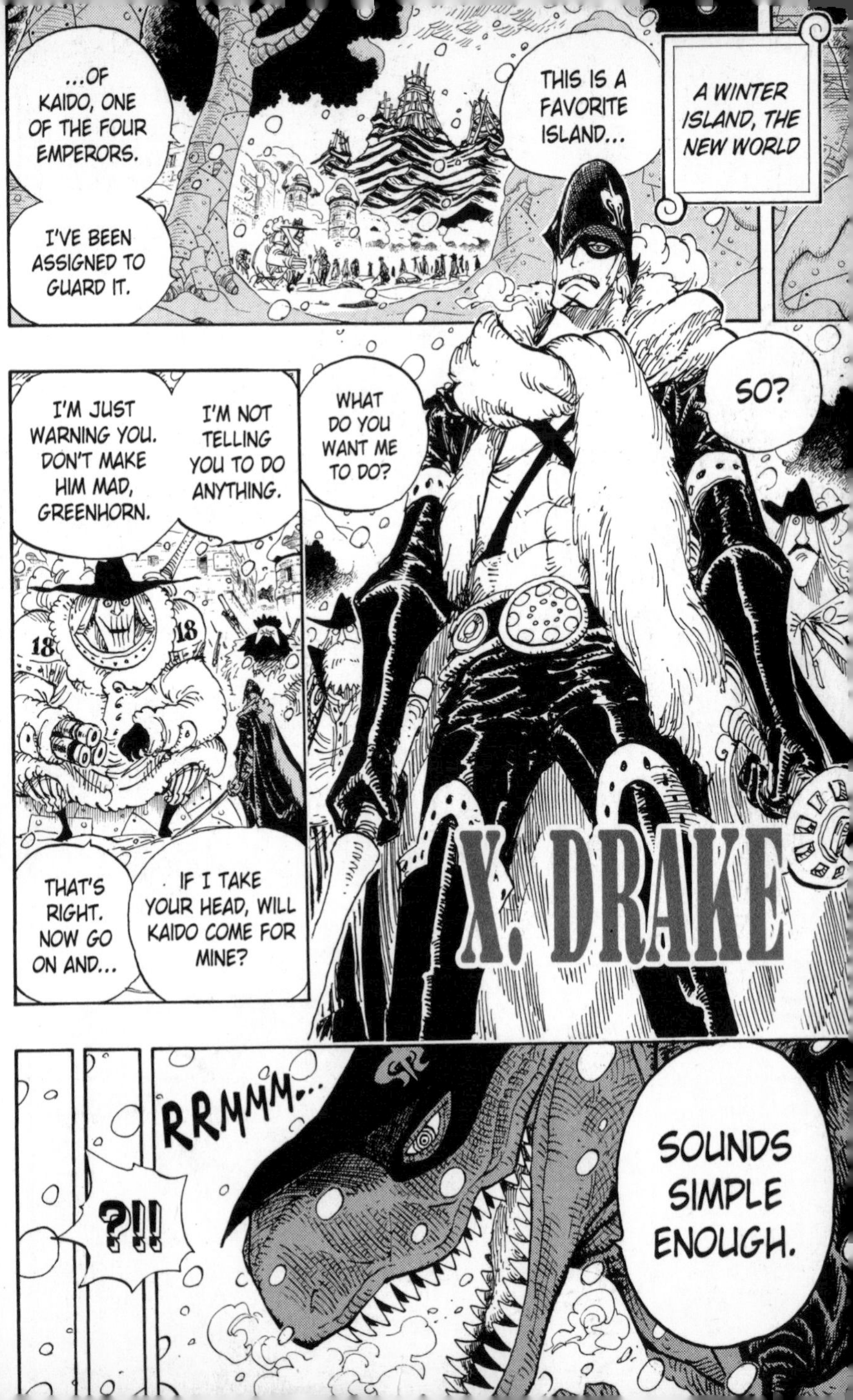
A WINTER ISLAND, THE NEW WORLD
THIS IS A FAVORITE ISLAND...
...OF KAIDO, ONE OF THE FOUR EMPERORS.
I'VE BEEN ASSIGNED TO GUARD IT.
SO?
WHAT DO YOU WANT ME TO DO?
X. DRAKE
I'M NOT TELLING YOU TO DO ANYTHING.
I'M JUST WARNING YOU. DON'T MAKE HIM MAD, GREENHORN.
IF I TAKE YOUR HEAD, WILL KAIDO COME FOR MINE?
THAT'S RIGHT. NOW GO ON AND...
SOUNDS SIMPLE ENOUGH.
RRMMM...
?!!

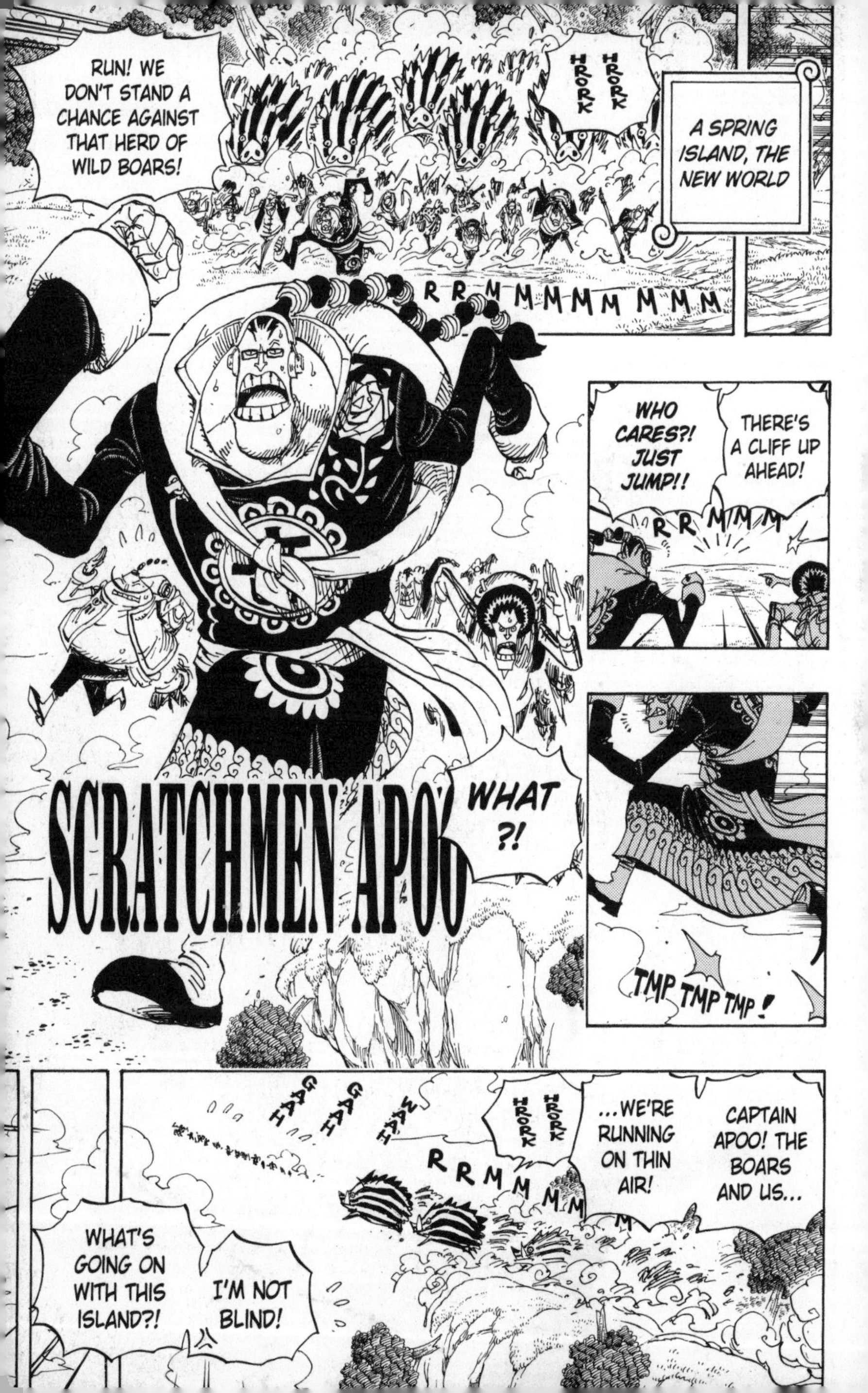
A SPRING ISLAND, THE NEW WORLD
HRORK HRORK
RUN! WE DON'T STAND A CHANCE AGAINST THAT HERD OF WILD BOARS!
RRMMMMMMMMMM
THERE'S A CLIFF UP AHEAD!
WHO CARES?! JUST JUMP!!
RRMMM
TMP TMP TMP!
WHAT ?!
SCRATCHMEN APOO
CAPTAIN APOO! THE BOARS AND US...
...WE'RE RUNNING ON THIN AIR!
HRORK HRORK
WAAH GAAH GAAH
RRMMMMM
I'M NOT BLIND!
WHAT'S GOING ON WITH THIS ISLAND?!

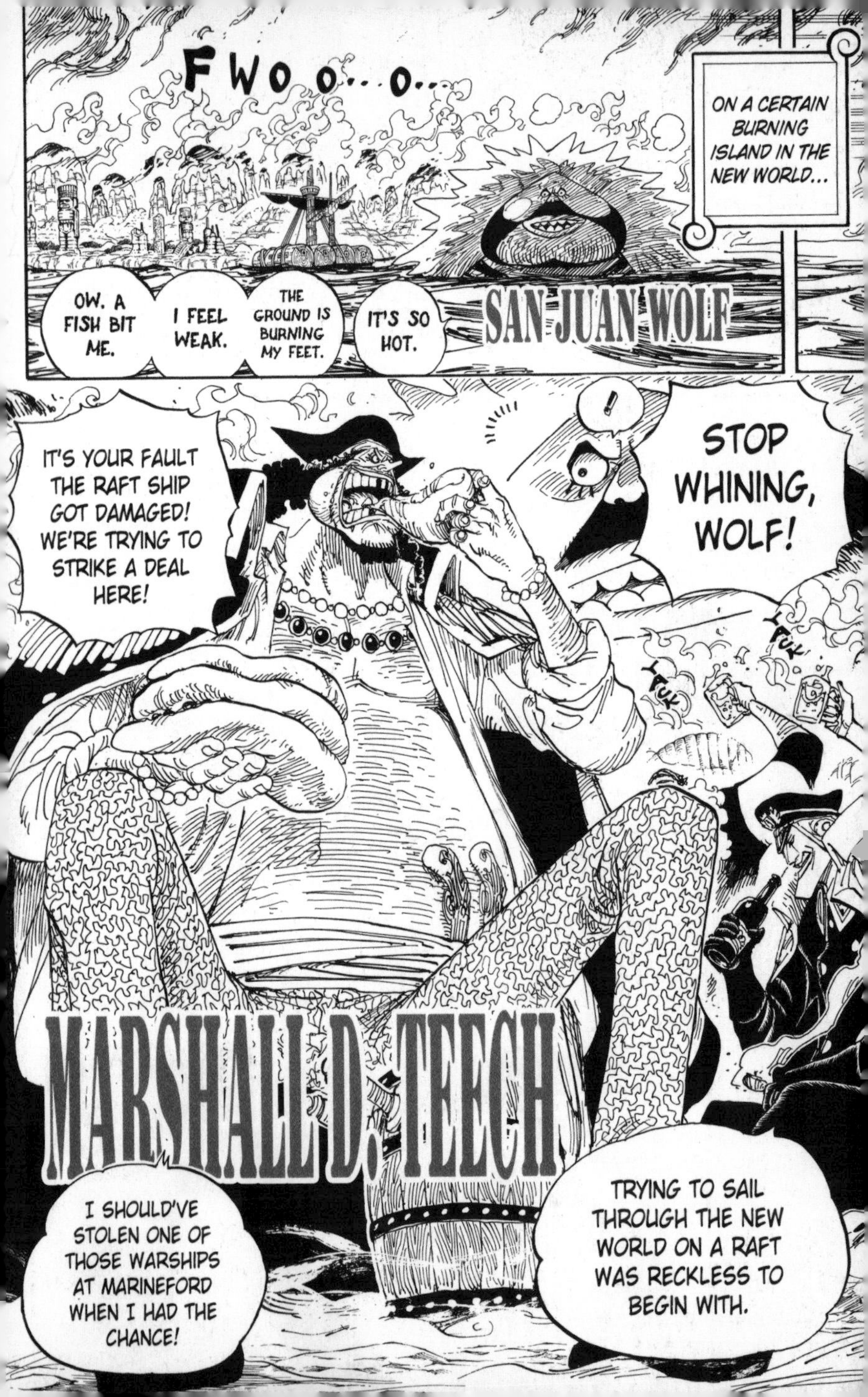

ON A CERTAIN BURNING ISLAND IN THE NEW WORLD...
FWOO...O...
SAN JUAN WOLF
IT'S SO HOT.
THE GROUND IS BURNING MY FEET.
I FEEL WEAK.
OW. A FISH BIT ME.
!
STOP WHINING, WOLF!
IT'S YOUR FAULT THE RAFT SHIP GOT DAMAGED! WE'RE TRYING TO STRIKE A DEAL HERE!
MARSHALL D. TEECH
TRYING TO SAIL THROUGH THE NEW WORLD ON A RAFT WAS RECKLESS TO BEGIN WITH.
I SHOULD'VE STOLEN ONE OF THOSE WARSHIPS AT MARINEFORD WHEN I HAD THE CHANCE!

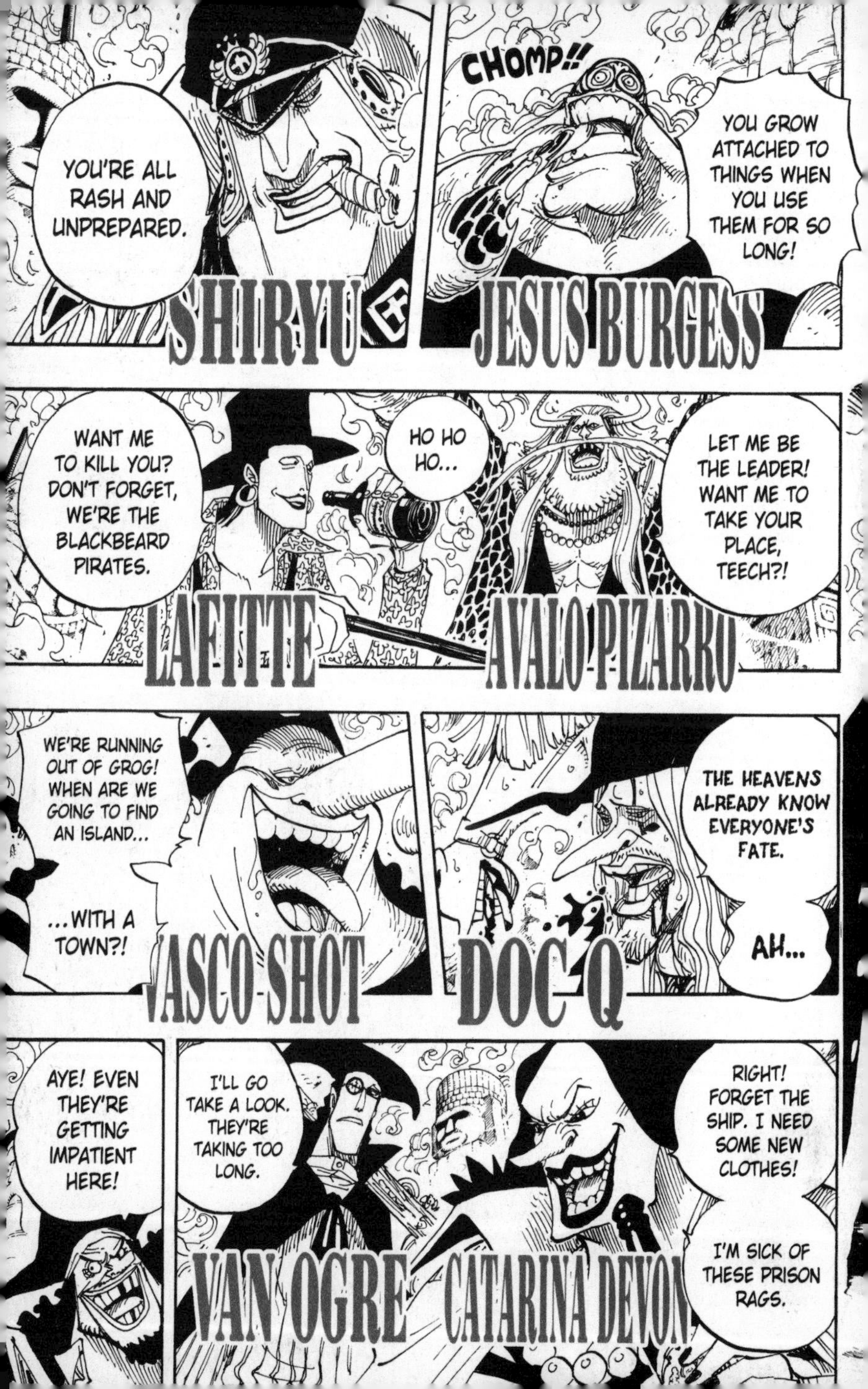
CHOMP!!
YOU GROW ATTACHED TO THINGS WHEN YOU USE THEM FOR SO LONG!
JESUS BURGESS
YOU'RE ALL RASH AND UNPREPARED.
SHIRYU
LET ME BE THE LEADER! WANT ME TO TAKE YOUR PLACE, TEECH?!
AVALO PIZARRO
HO HO HO...
WANT ME TO KILL YOU? DON'T FORGET, WE'RE THE BLACKBEARD PIRATES.
LAFITTE
THE HEAVENS ALREADY KNOW EVERYONE'S FATE.
AH...
DOC Q
WE'RE RUNNING OUT OF GROG! WHEN ARE WE GOING TO FIND AN ISLAND...
...WITH A TOWN?!
VASCO SHOT
RIGHT! FORGET THE SHIP. I NEED SOME NEW CLOTHES!
I'M SICK OF THESE PRISON RAGS.
CATARINA DEVON
I'LL GO TAKE A LOOK. THEY'RE TAKING TOO LONG.
VAN OGRE
AYE! EVEN THEY'RE GETTING IMPATIENT HERE!

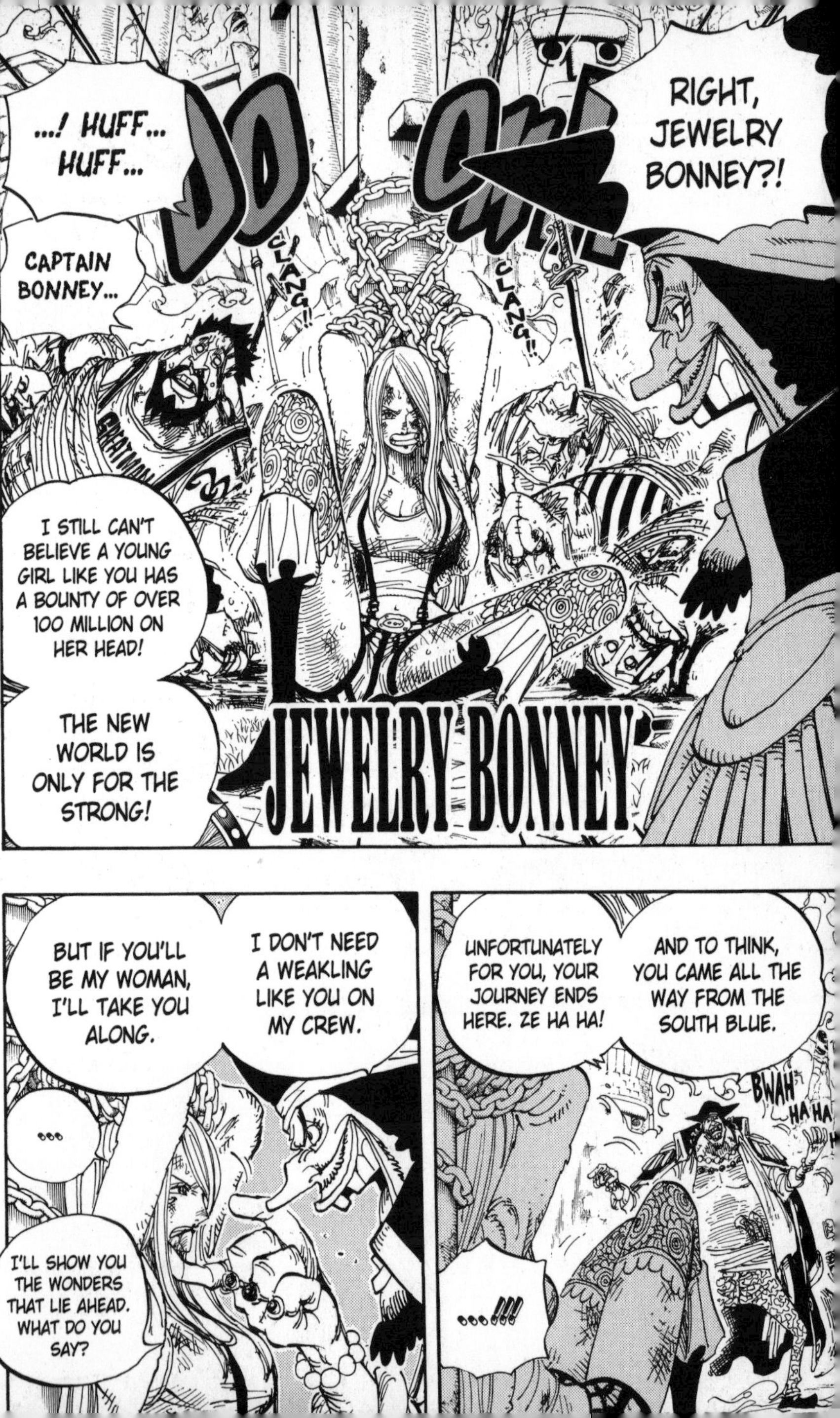
RIGHT, JEWELRY BONNEY?!
CLANG!!
CLANG!!
...! HUFF... HUFF...
CAPTAIN BONNEY...
I STILL CAN'T BELIEVE A YOUNG GIRL LIKE YOU HAS A BOUNTY OF OVER 100 MILLION ON HER HEAD!
THE NEW WORLD IS ONLY FOR THE STRONG!
JEWELRY BONNEY
AND TO THINK, YOU CAME ALL THE WAY FROM THE SOUTH BLUE.
UNFORTUNATELY FOR YOU, YOUR JOURNEY ENDS HERE. ZE HA HA!
BWAH HA HA
...!!!
I DON'T NEED A WEAKLING LIKE YOU ON MY CREW.
BUT IF YOU'LL BE MY WOMAN, I'LL TAKE YOU ALONG.
...
I'LL SHOW YOU THE WONDERS THAT LIE AHEAD. WHAT DO YOU SAY?

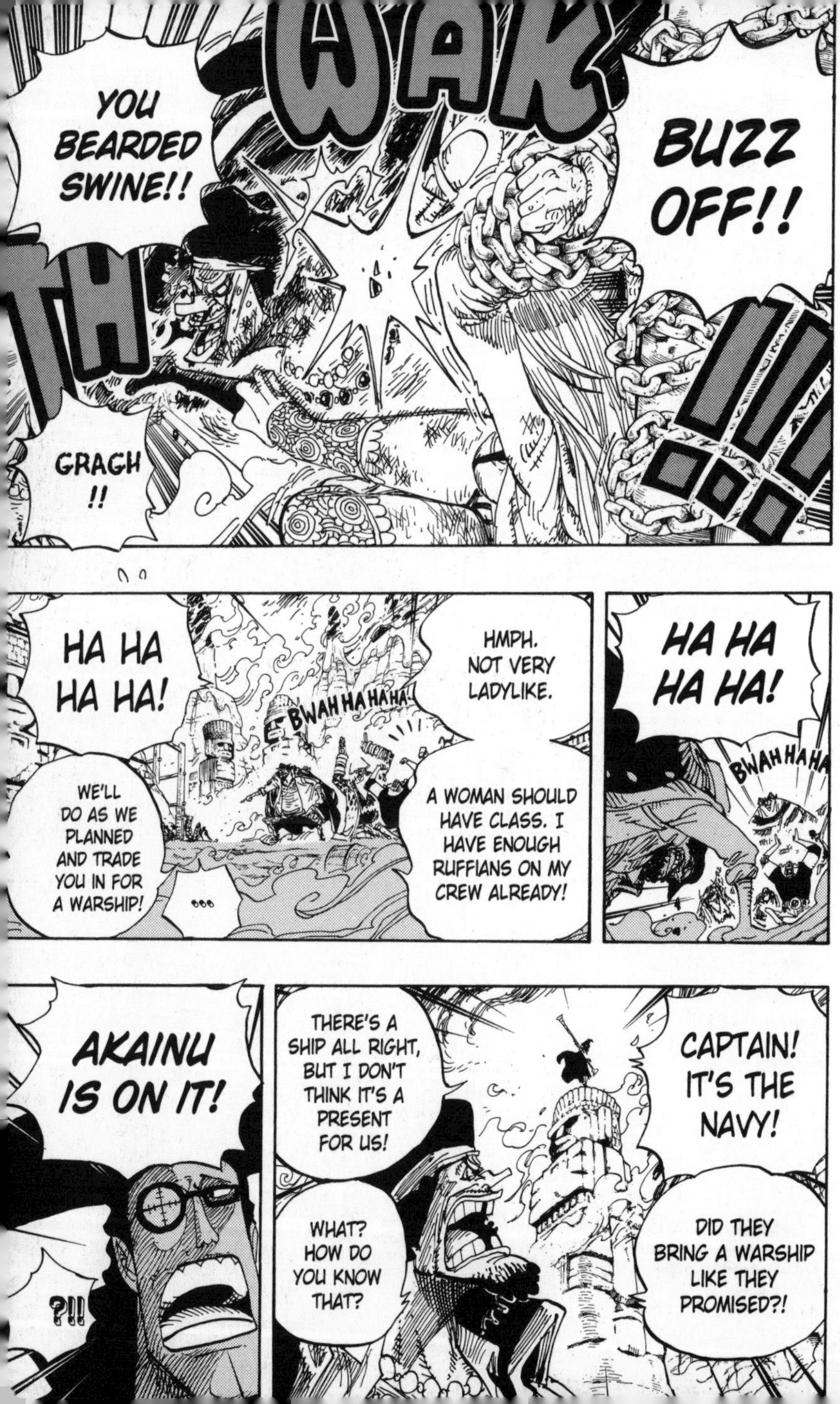
BUZZ OFF!!
WAK
YOU BEARDED SWINE!!
GRAGH !!
HA HA HA HA!
BWAHHAHA
HMPH. NOT VERY LADYLIKE.
A WOMAN SHOULD HAVE CLASS. I HAVE ENOUGH RUFFIANS ON MY CREW ALREADY!
BWAHHAHAHA
HA HA HA HA!
WE'LL DO AS WE PLANNED AND TRADE YOU IN FOR A WARSHIP!
...
CAPTAIN! IT'S THE NAVY!
DID THEY BRING A WARSHIP LIKE THEY PROMISED?!
THERE'S A SHIP ALL RIGHT, BUT I DON'T THINK IT'S A PRESENT FOR US!
WHAT? HOW DO YOU KNOW THAT?
AKAINU IS ON IT!
?!!

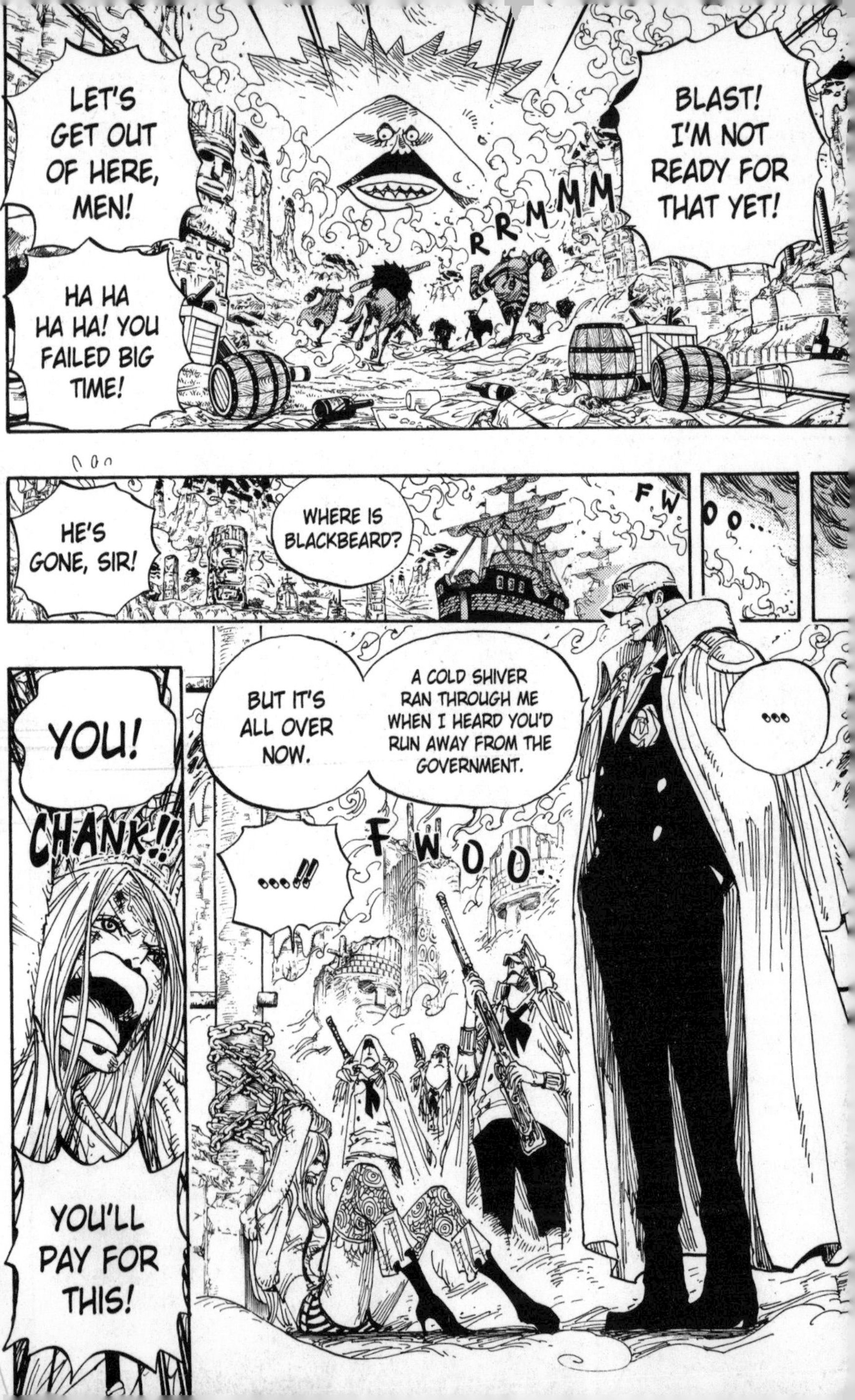
BLAST! I'M NOT READY FOR THAT YET!
RRRMMMM
LET'S GET OUT OF HERE, MEN!
HA HA HA HA! YOU FAILED BIG TIME!
FWOO...
WHERE IS BLACKBEARD?
HE'S GONE, SIR!
...
A COLD SHIVER RAN THROUGH ME WHEN I HEARD YOU'D RUN AWAY FROM THE GOVERNMENT.
BUT IT'S ALL OVER NOW.
FWOO...
...!!
YOU!
CHANK!!
YOU'LL PAY FOR THIS!

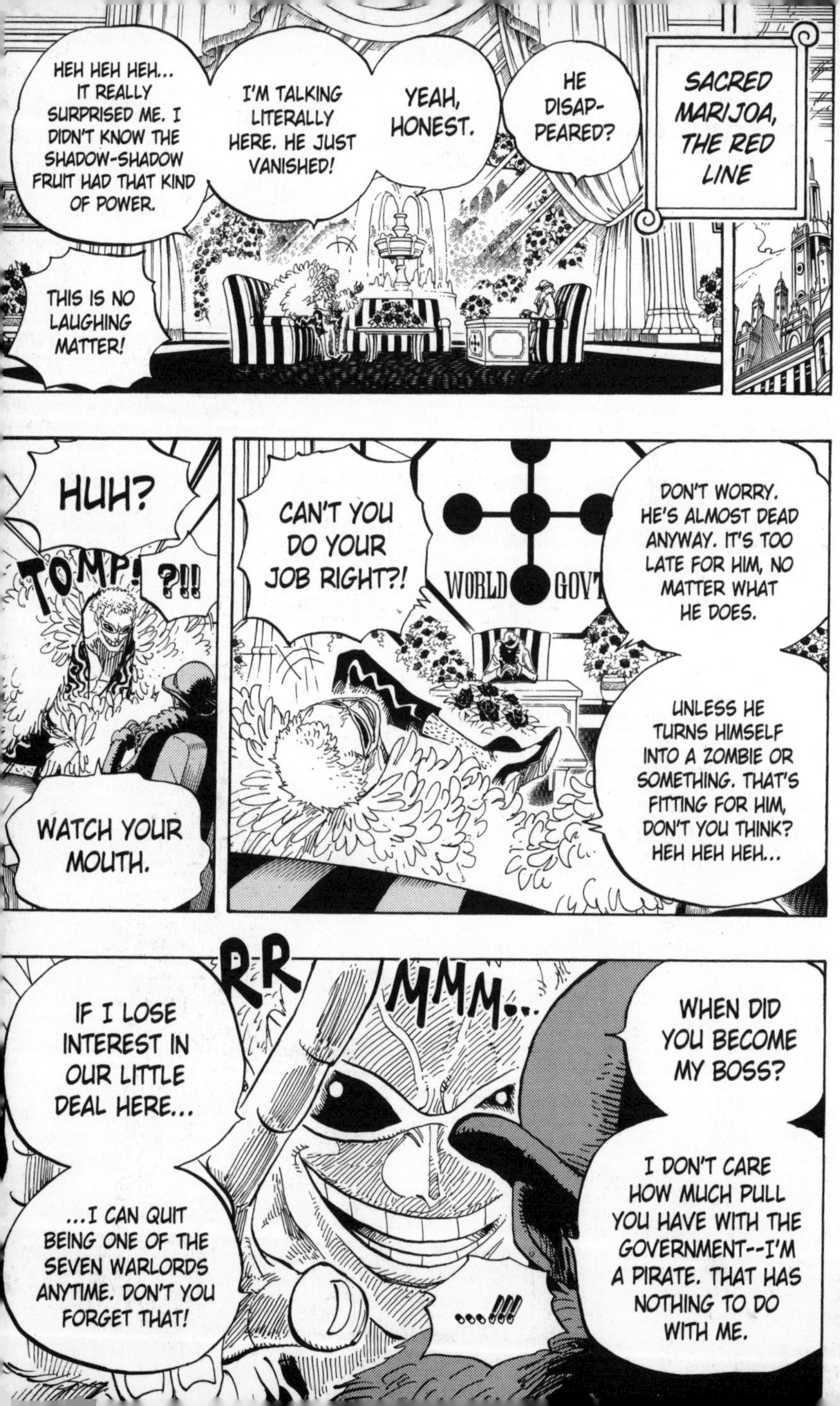
SACRED MARIJOA, THE RED LINE
HE DISAP-PEARED?
YEAH, HONEST.
I'M TALKING LITERALLY HERE. HE JUST VANISHED!
HEH HEH HEH... IT REALLY SURPRISED ME. I DIDN'T KNOW THE SHADOW-SHADOW FRUIT HAD THAT KIND OF POWER.
THIS IS NO LAUGHING MATTER!
CAN'T YOU DO YOUR JOB RIGHT?!
WORLD GOVT
DON'T WORRY. HE'S ALMOST DEAD ANYWAY. IT'S TOO LATE FOR HIM, NO MATTER WHAT HE DOES.
UNLESS HE TURNS HIMSELF INTO A ZOMBIE OR SOMETHING. THAT'S FITTING FOR HIM, DON'T YOU THINK? HEH HEH HEH...
HUH?
TOMP!
?!!
WATCH YOUR MOUTH.
RRMMM...
WHEN DID YOU BECOME MY BOSS?
I DON'T CARE HOW MUCH PULL YOU HAVE WITH THE GOVERNMENT--I'M A PIRATE. THAT HAS NOTHING TO DO WITH ME.
IF I LOSE INTEREST IN OUR LITTLE DEAL HERE...
...I CAN QUIT BEING ONE OF THE SEVEN WARLORDS ANYTIME. DON'T YOU FORGET THAT!
...!!!

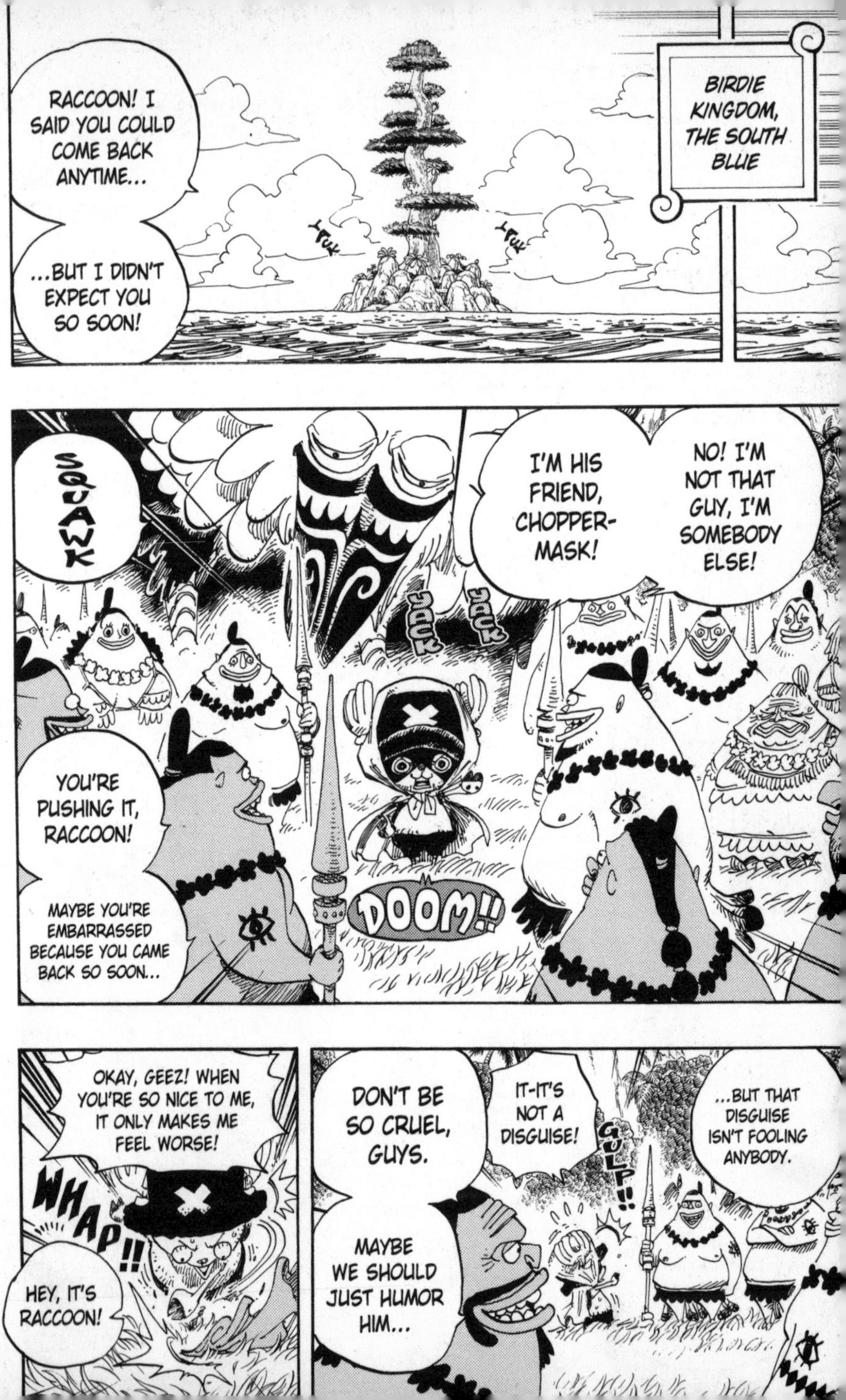
BIRDIE KINGDOM, THE SOUTH BLUE
RACCOON! I SAID YOU COULD COME BACK ANYTIME...
...BUT I DIDN'T EXPECT YOU SO SOON!
NO! I'M NOT THAT GUY, I'M SOMEBODY ELSE!
I'M HIS FRIEND, CHOPPER-MASK!
YACK YACK
SQUAWK
YOU'RE PUSHING IT, RACCOON!
MAYBE YOU'RE EMBARRASSED BECAUSE YOU CAME BACK SO SOON...
DOOM!!
...BUT THAT DISGUISE ISN'T FOOLING ANYBODY.
IT-IT'S NOT A DISGUISE!
GULP!!
DON'T BE SO CRUEL, GUYS.
MAYBE WE SHOULD JUST HUMOR HIM...
OKAY, GEEZ! WHEN YOU'RE SO NICE TO ME, IT ONLY MAKES ME FEEL WORSE!
WHAP!!
HEY, IT'S RACCOON!

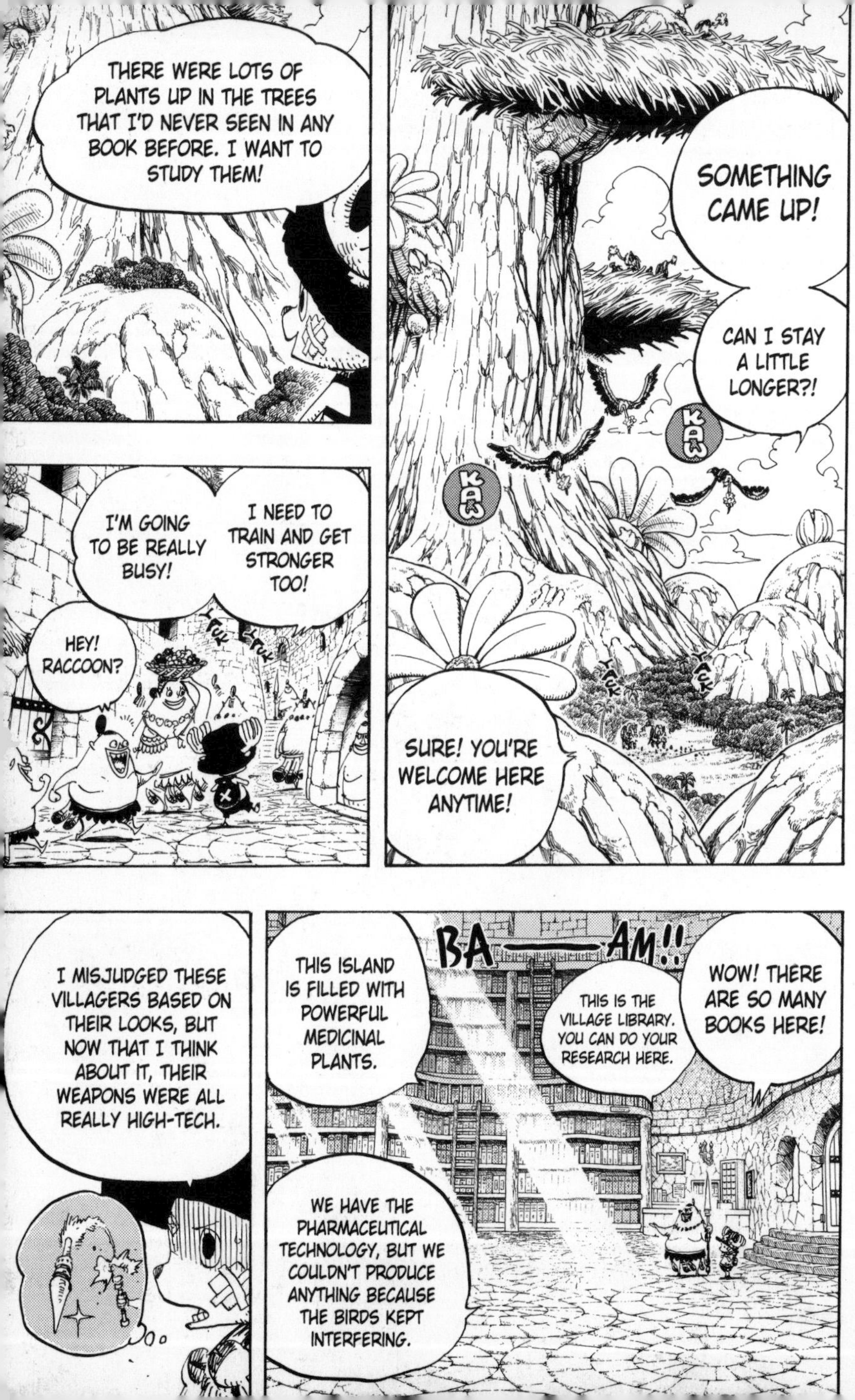
SOMETHING CAME UP!
CAN I STAY A LITTLE LONGER?!
KAW
KAW
YACK
YACK
SURE! YOU'RE WELCOME HERE ANYTIME!
THERE WERE LOTS OF PLANTS UP IN THE TREES THAT I'D NEVER SEEN IN ANY BOOK BEFORE. I WANT TO STUDY THEM!
I NEED TO TRAIN AND GET STRONGER TOO!
I'M GOING TO BE REALLY BUSY!
HEY! RACCOON?
WOW! THERE ARE SO MANY BOOKS HERE!
BA—AM!!
THIS IS THE VILLAGE LIBRARY. YOU CAN DO YOUR RESEARCH HERE.
THIS ISLAND IS FILLED WITH POWERFUL MEDICINAL PLANTS.
WE HAVE THE PHARMACEUTICAL TECHNOLOGY, BUT WE COULDN'T PRODUCE ANYTHING BECAUSE THE BIRDS KEPT INTERFERING.
I MISJUDGED THESE VILLAGERS BASED ON THEIR LOOKS, BUT NOW THAT I THINK ABOUT IT, THEIR WEAPONS WERE ALL REALLY HIGH-TECH.

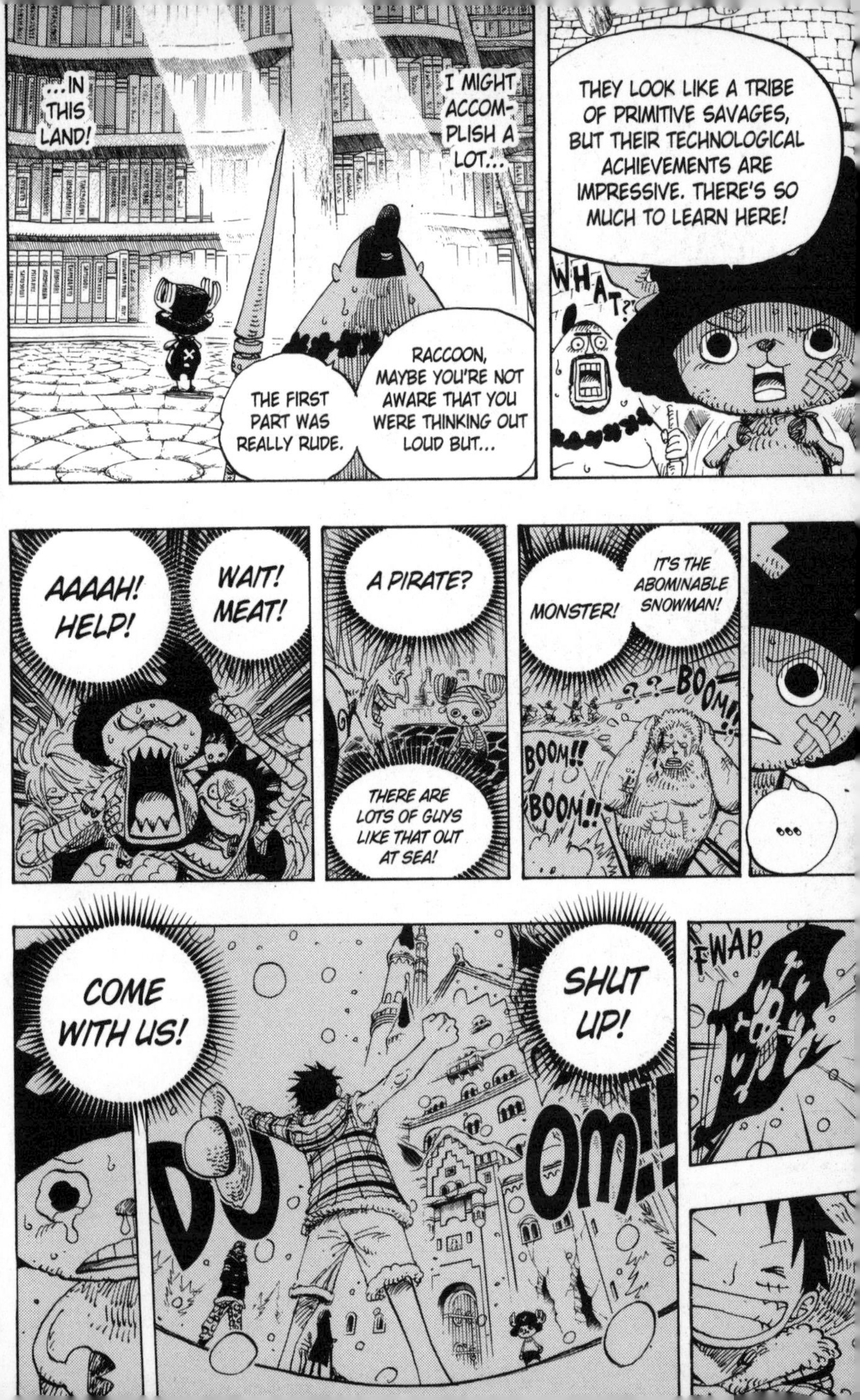
THEY LOOK LIKE A TRIBE OF PRIMITIVE SAVAGES, BUT THEIR TECHNOLOGICAL ACHIEVEMENTS ARE IMPRESSIVE. THERE'S SO MUCH TO LEARN HERE!
WHAT?
I MIGHT ACCOMPLISH A LOT...
...IN THIS LAND!
RACCOON, MAYBE YOU'RE NOT AWARE THAT YOU WERE THINKING OUT LOUD BUT...
THE FIRST PART WAS REALLY RUDE.
...
IT'S THE ABOMINABLE SNOWMAN!
MONSTER!
BOOM!!
BOOM!!
BOOM!!
A PIRATE?
THERE ARE LOTS OF GUYS LIKE THAT OUT AT SEA!
WAIT! MEAT!
AAAAH! HELP!
FWAP
SHUT UP!
COME WITH US!
DOOM!!

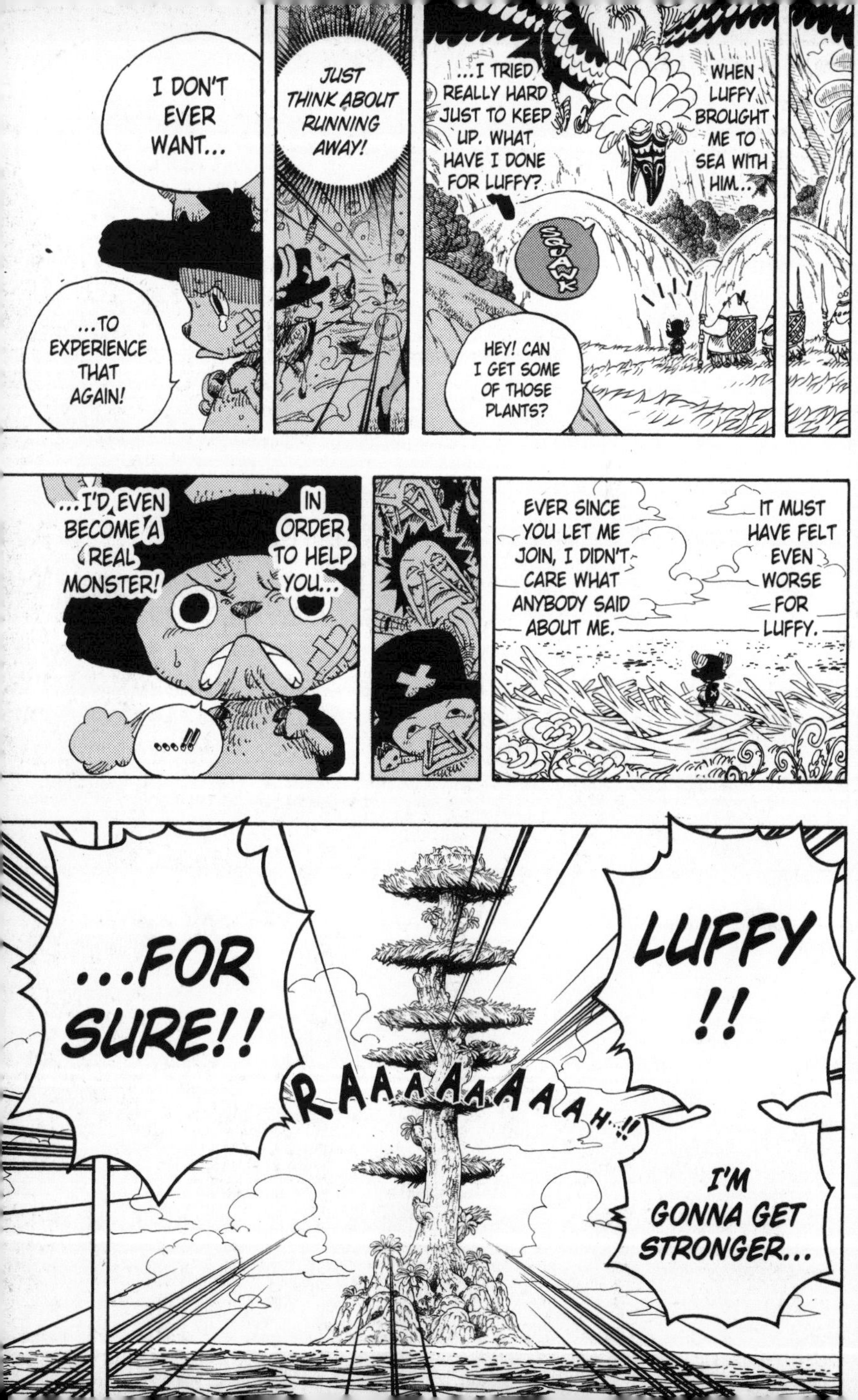
WHEN LUFFY BROUGHT ME TO SEA WITH HIM..
...I TRIED REALLY HARD JUST TO KEEP UP. WHAT HAVE I DONE FOR LUFFY?
SQUAWK
HEY! CAN I GET SOME OF THOSE PLANTS?
JUST THINK ABOUT RUNNING AWAY!
I DON'T EVER WANT...
...TO EXPERIENCE THAT AGAIN!
IT MUST HAVE FELT EVEN WORSE FOR LUFFY.
EVER SINCE YOU LET ME JOIN, I DIDN'T CARE WHAT ANYBODY SAID ABOUT ME.
IN ORDER TO HELP YOU...
...I'D EVEN BECOME A REAL MONSTER!
...!!
LUFFY!!
I'M GONNA GET STRONGER...
RAAAAAAAAAH!!
...FOR SURE!!

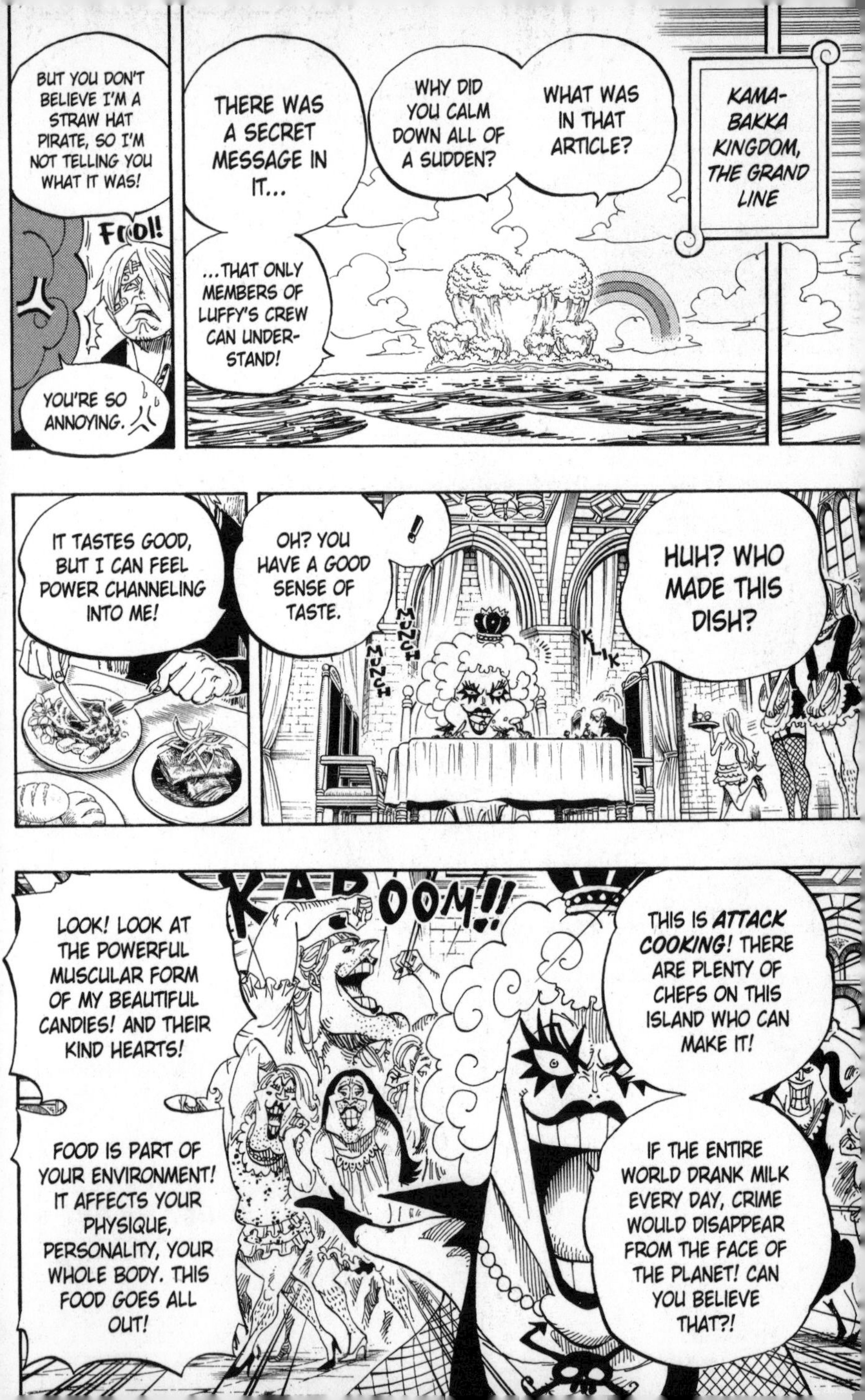
KAMA-BAKKA KINGDOM, THE GRAND LINE
WHAT WAS IN THAT ARTICLE?
WHY DID YOU CALM DOWN ALL OF A SUDDEN?
THERE WAS A SECRET MESSAGE IN IT...
...THAT ONLY MEMBERS OF LUFFY'S CREW CAN UNDERSTAND!
BUT YOU DON'T BELIEVE I'M A STRAW HAT PIRATE, SO I'M NOT TELLING YOU WHAT IT WAS!
FOOL!
YOU'RE SO ANNOYING.
HUH? WHO MADE THIS DISH?
KLIK
!
OH? YOU HAVE A GOOD SENSE OF TASTE.
MUNCH
MUNCH
IT TASTES GOOD, BUT I CAN FEEL POWER CHANNELING INTO ME!
KABOOM!!
THIS IS ATTACK COOKING! THERE ARE PLENTY OF CHEFS ON THIS ISLAND WHO CAN MAKE IT!
IF THE ENTIRE WORLD DRANK MILK EVERY DAY, CRIME WOULD DISAPPEAR FROM THE FACE OF THE PLANET! CAN YOU BELIEVE THAT?!
LOOK! LOOK AT THE POWERFUL MUSCULAR FORM OF MY BEAUTIFUL CANDIES! AND THEIR KIND HEARTS!
FOOD IS PART OF YOUR ENVIRONMENT! IT AFFECTS YOUR PHYSIQUE, PERSONALITY, YOUR WHOLE BODY. THIS FOOD GOES ALL OUT!

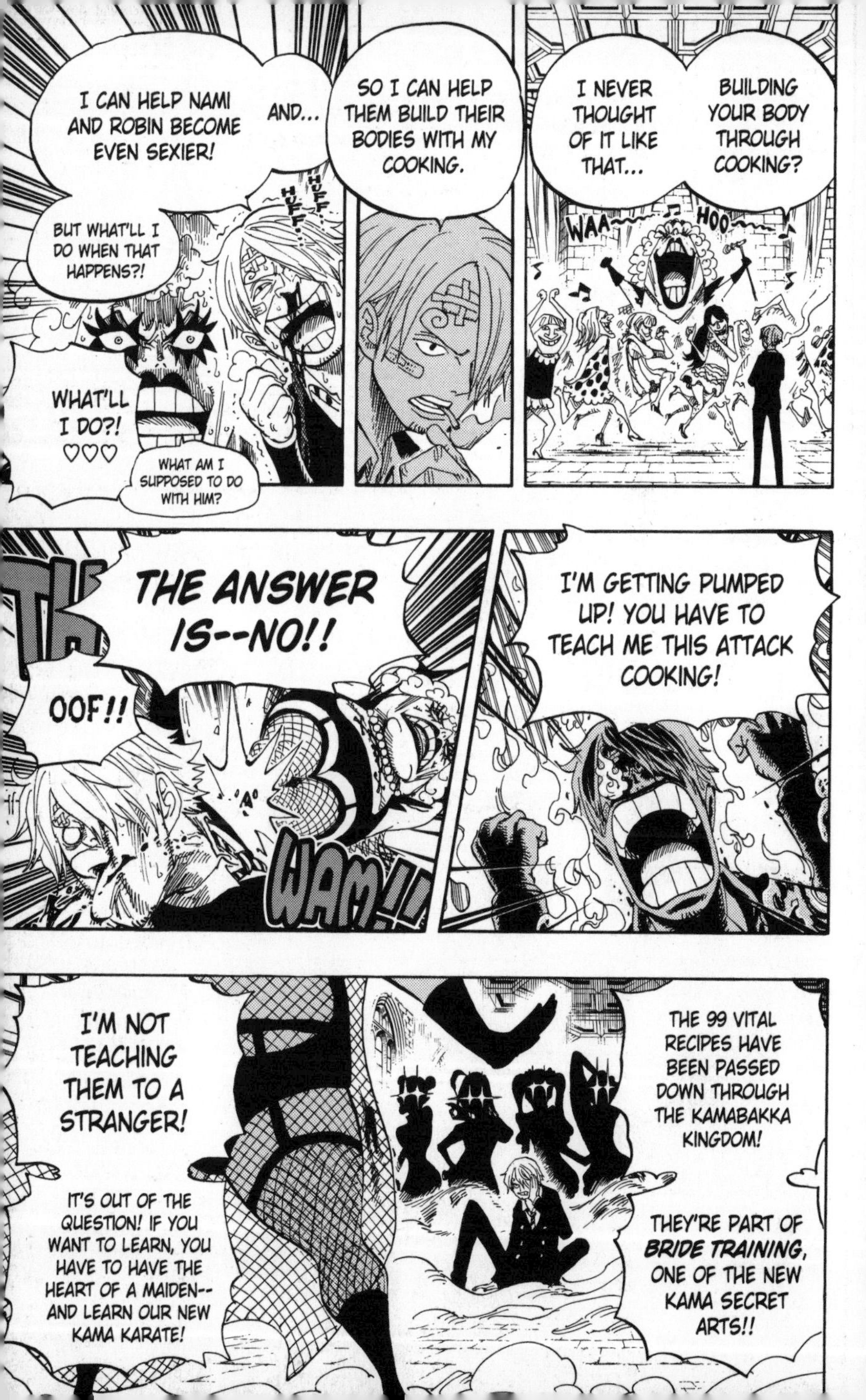
BUILDING YOUR BODY THROUGH COOKING?
I NEVER THOUGHT OF IT LIKE THAT...
WAA~~ HOO~~
SO I CAN HELP THEM BUILD THEIR BODIES WITH MY COOKING.
AND...
I CAN HELP NAMI AND ROBIN BECOME EVEN SEXIER!
HUFF HUFF
BUT WHAT'LL I DO WHEN THAT HAPPENS?!
WHAT'LL I DO?! ♡♡♡
WHAT AM I SUPPOSED TO DO WITH HIM?
I'M GETTING PUMPED UP! YOU HAVE TO TEACH ME THIS ATTACK COOKING!
THE ANSWER IS--NO!!
OOF!!
WAM!!
THE 99 VITAL RECIPES HAVE BEEN PASSED DOWN THROUGH THE KAMABAKKA KINGDOM!
I'M NOT TEACHING THEM TO A STRANGER!
THEY'RE PART OF ***BRIDE TRAINING***, ONE OF THE NEW KAMA SECRET ARTS!!
IT'S OUT OF THE QUESTION! IF YOU WANT TO LEARN, YOU HAVE TO HAVE THE HEART OF A MAIDEN--AND LEARN OUR NEW KAMA KARATE!

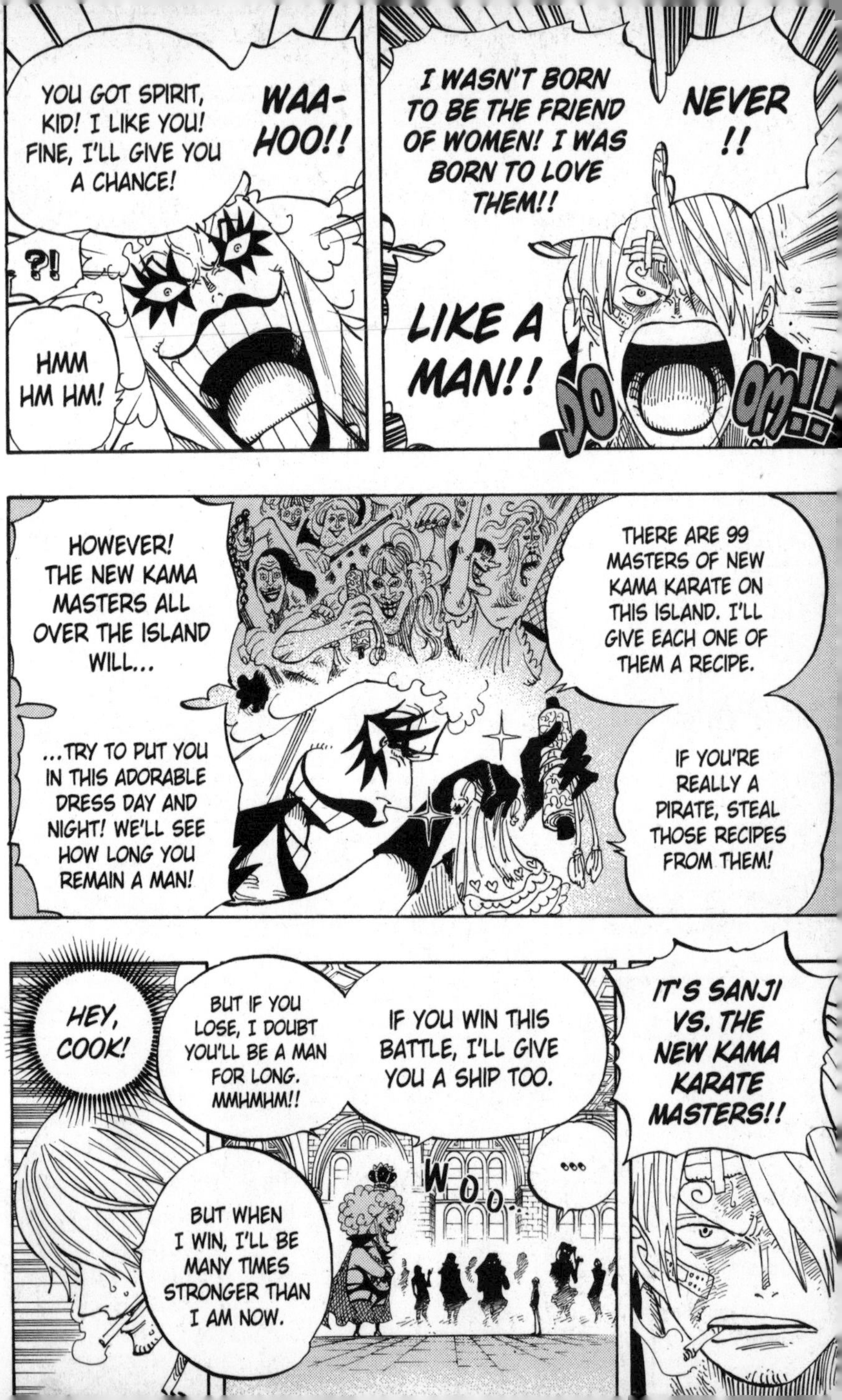
NEVER!!
I WASN'T BORN TO BE THE FRIEND OF WOMEN! I WAS BORN TO LOVE THEM!!
LIKE A MAN!!
DO
OM!!
WAA-HOO!!
YOU GOT SPIRIT, KID! I LIKE YOU! FINE, I'LL GIVE YOU A CHANCE!
?!
HMM HM HM!
THERE ARE 99 MASTERS OF NEW KAMA KARATE ON THIS ISLAND. I'LL GIVE EACH ONE OF THEM A RECIPE.
IF YOU'RE REALLY A PIRATE, STEAL THOSE RECIPES FROM THEM!
HOWEVER! THE NEW KAMA MASTERS ALL OVER THE ISLAND WILL...
...TRY TO PUT YOU IN THIS ADORABLE DRESS DAY AND NIGHT! WE'LL SEE HOW LONG YOU REMAIN A MAN!
IT'S SANJI VS. THE NEW KAMA KARATE MASTERS!!
...
IF YOU WIN THIS BATTLE, I'LL GIVE YOU A SHIP TOO.
BUT IF YOU LOSE, I DOUBT YOU'LL BE A MAN FOR LONG. MMHMHM!!
WOO..
HEY, COOK!
BUT WHEN I WIN, I'LL BE MANY TIMES STRONGER THAN I AM NOW.

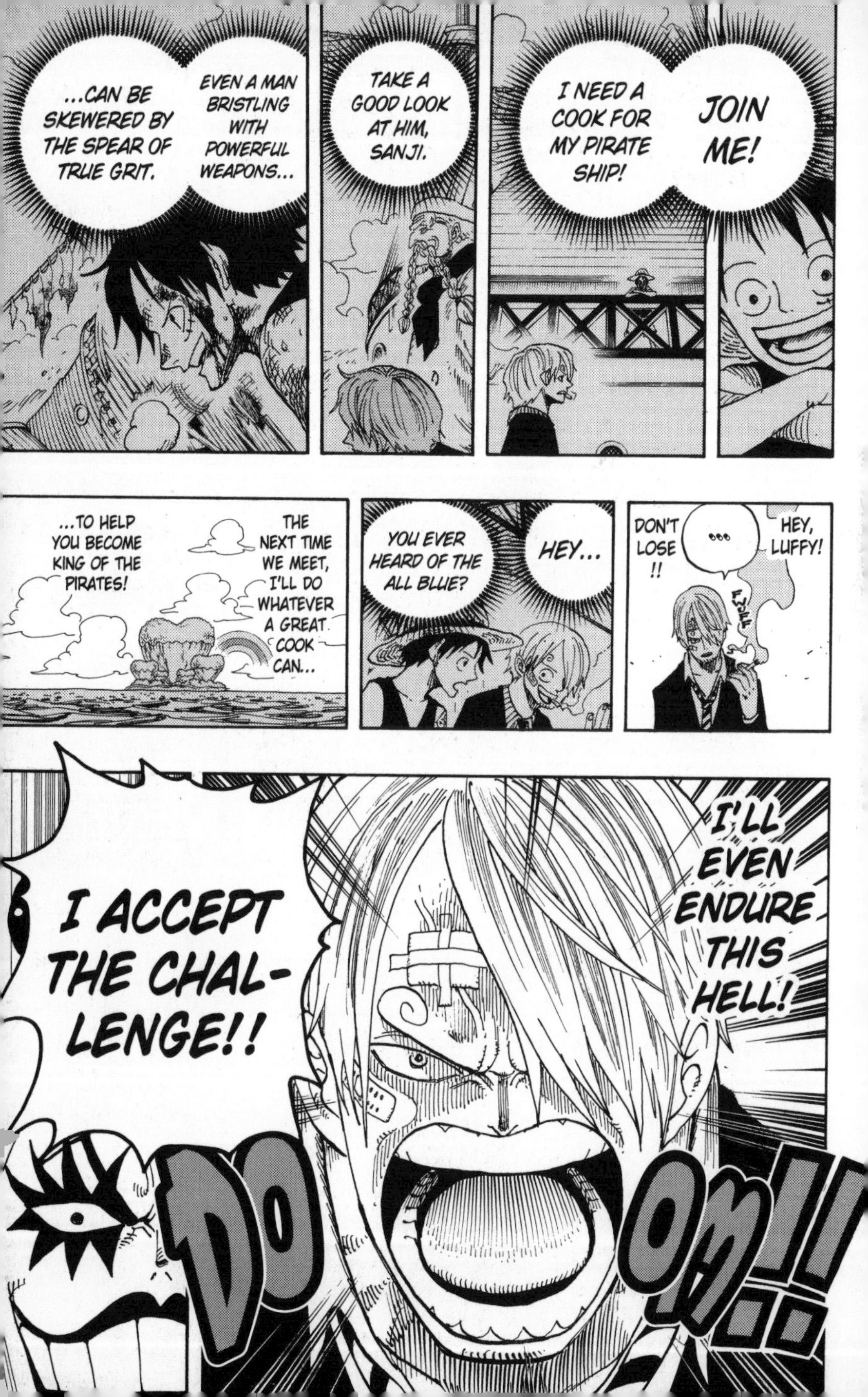
JOIN ME!
I NEED A COOK FOR MY PIRATE SHIP!
TAKE A GOOD LOOK AT HIM, SANJI.
EVEN A MAN BRISTLING WITH POWERFUL WEAPONS...
...CAN BE SKEWERED BY THE SPEAR OF TRUE GRIT.
HEY, LUFFY!
...
DON'T LOSE !!
FWUFF
HEY...
YOU EVER HEARD OF THE ALL BLUE?
THE NEXT TIME WE MEET, I'LL DO WHATEVER A GREAT COOK CAN...
...TO HELP YOU BECOME KING OF THE PIRATES!
I'LL EVEN ENDURE THIS HELL!
I ACCEPT THE CHAL-LENGE!!
DOOM!!

SBS Question Corner

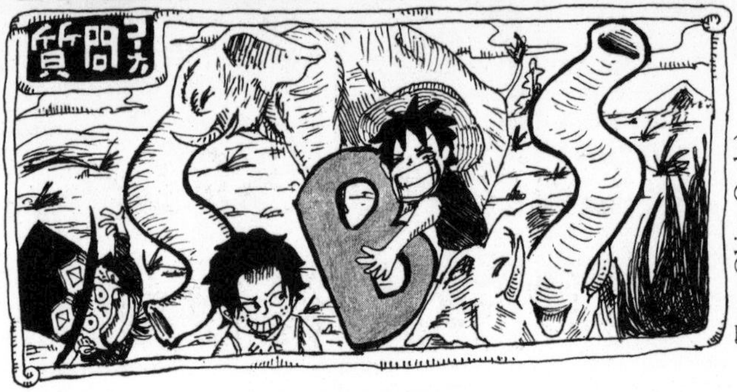

(Toma Ohira, Osaka)

Reader (Q): Oh, I changed my pseudonym.

--Let's Start SBS

Oda (A): Hey! (←Just realized it started.)
Oh... (←Realized he couldn't start it again.)
Aww... (←Depressed.)

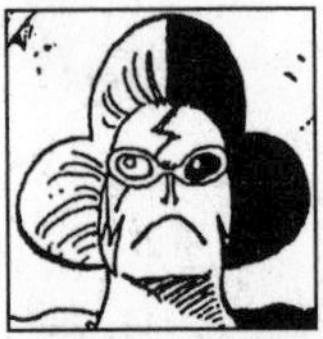

Q: I really REALLY want to become Inazuma.
--31-Year-Old Housewife

A: Sure.

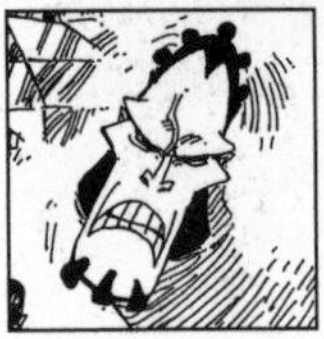

Q: Odacchi, I have a question! It's about the 3rd Division Commander of the Whitebeard Pirates, Diamond Jozu. Is his crotch made of diamond too? I want to know.
--Kintama Negio

A: Yes. Jozu's crotch is made of diamond. It's a diamond crotch.

Q: Question 1: It's started to get boring and tedious so I'm going to end SBS.
--PATAN

A: Don't end it! What do you mean by boring?! Look at the question above! Of course it'll get like this! How else am I supposed to answer?!
Oh, PATAN sent in another question...

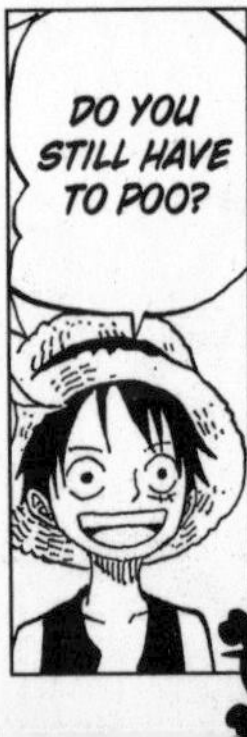
DO YOU STILL HAVE TO POO?

Q: Question 2: Do you poo, Mr. Oda?
--PATAN

A: Well, I'm an idol so I don't!♡ Tee hee!♡
Who're you calling an idol?!
Huff! Huff! Sorry, that was immature of me. I played along with your joke, but I ended up snapping at you... This is all my fault. Pinch!

Chapter 596: SPECTRUM

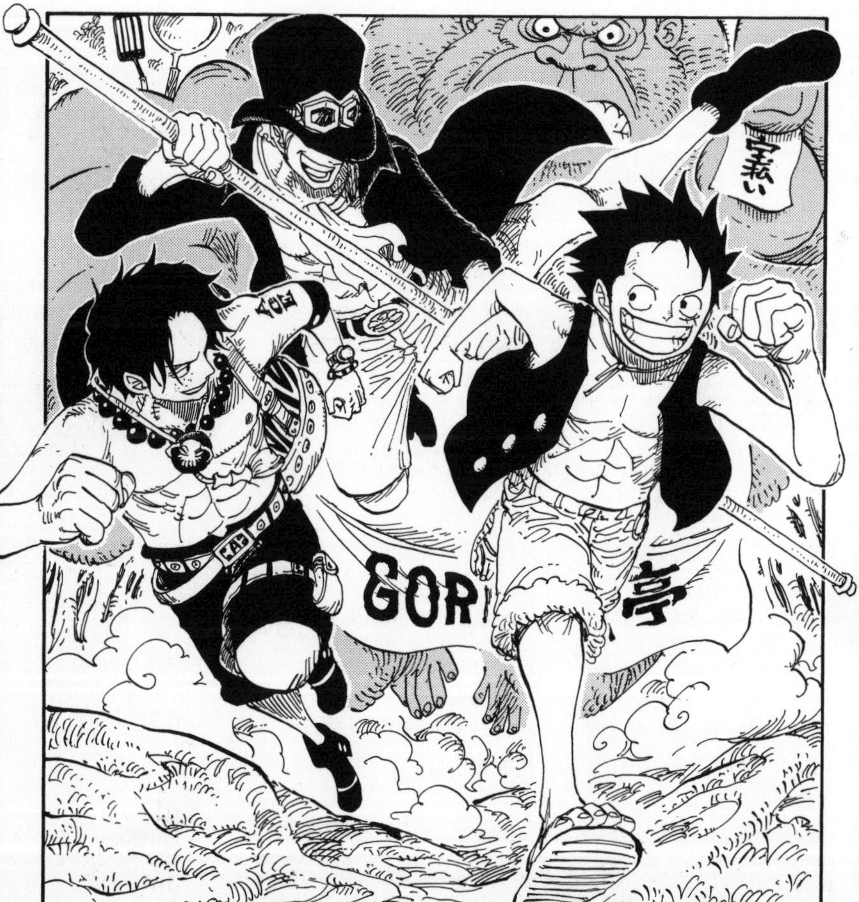
GORI 亭
宝払い

*IOU TREASURE

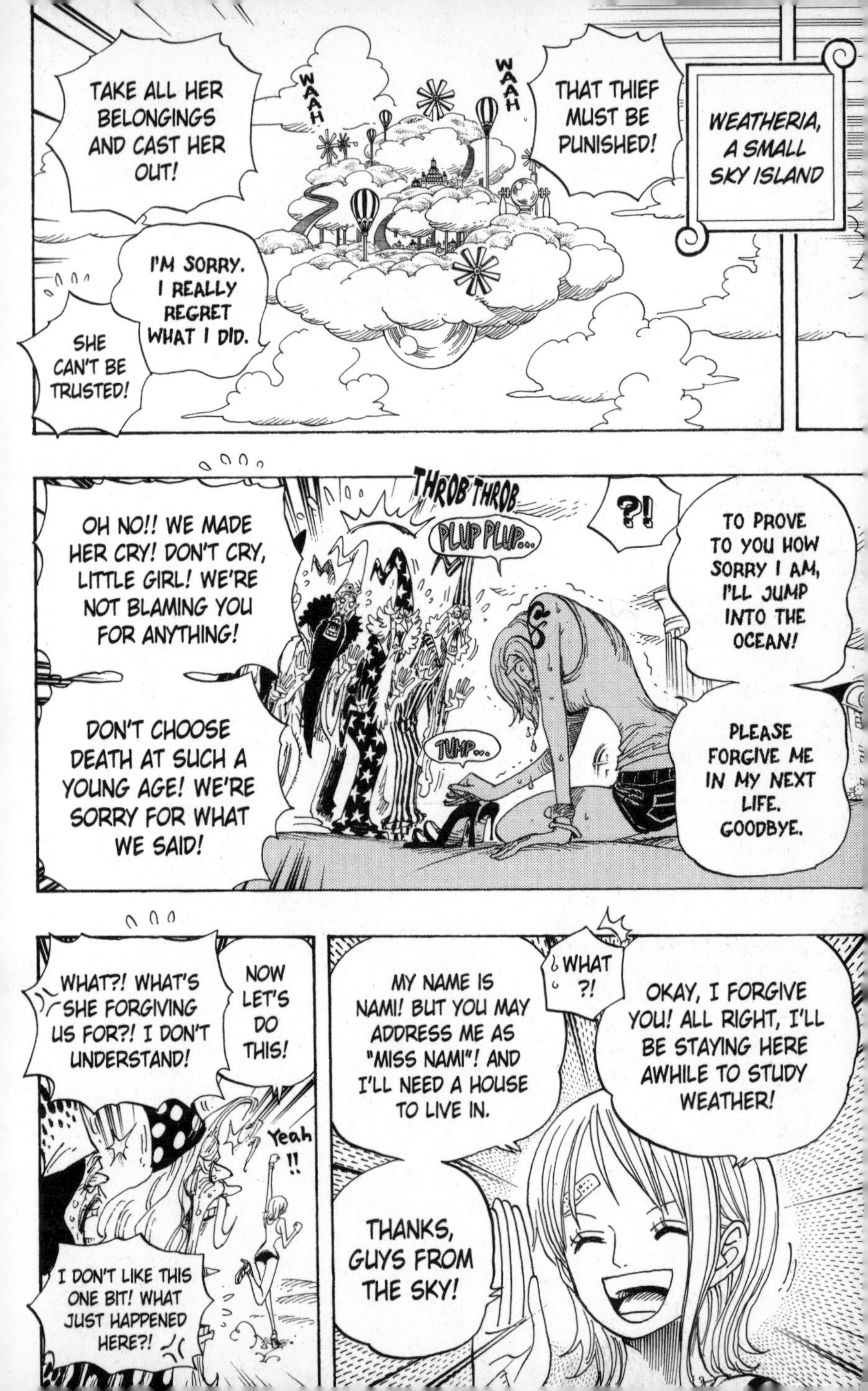
WEATHERIA, A SMALL SKY ISLAND
THAT THIEF MUST BE PUNISHED!
WAAH
WAAH
TAKE ALL HER BELONGINGS AND CAST HER OUT!
I'M SORRY. I REALLY REGRET WHAT I DID.
SHE CAN'T BE TRUSTED!
TO PROVE TO YOU HOW SORRY I AM, I'LL JUMP INTO THE OCEAN!
PLEASE FORGIVE ME IN MY NEXT LIFE. GOODBYE.
?!
THROB THROB
PLUP PLUP...
TUMP...
OH NO!! WE MADE HER CRY! DON'T CRY, LITTLE GIRL! WE'RE NOT BLAMING YOU FOR ANYTHING!
DON'T CHOOSE DEATH AT SUCH A YOUNG AGE! WE'RE SORRY FOR WHAT WE SAID!
OKAY, I FORGIVE YOU! ALL RIGHT, I'LL BE STAYING HERE AWHILE TO STUDY WEATHER!
WHAT ?!
MY NAME IS NAMI! BUT YOU MAY ADDRESS ME AS "MISS NAMI"! AND I'LL NEED A HOUSE TO LIVE IN.
THANKS, GUYS FROM THE SKY!
NOW LET'S DO THIS!
WHAT?! WHAT'S SHE FORGIVING US FOR?! I DON'T UNDERSTAND!
Yeah !!
I DON'T LIKE THIS ONE BIT! WHAT JUST HAPPENED HERE?!

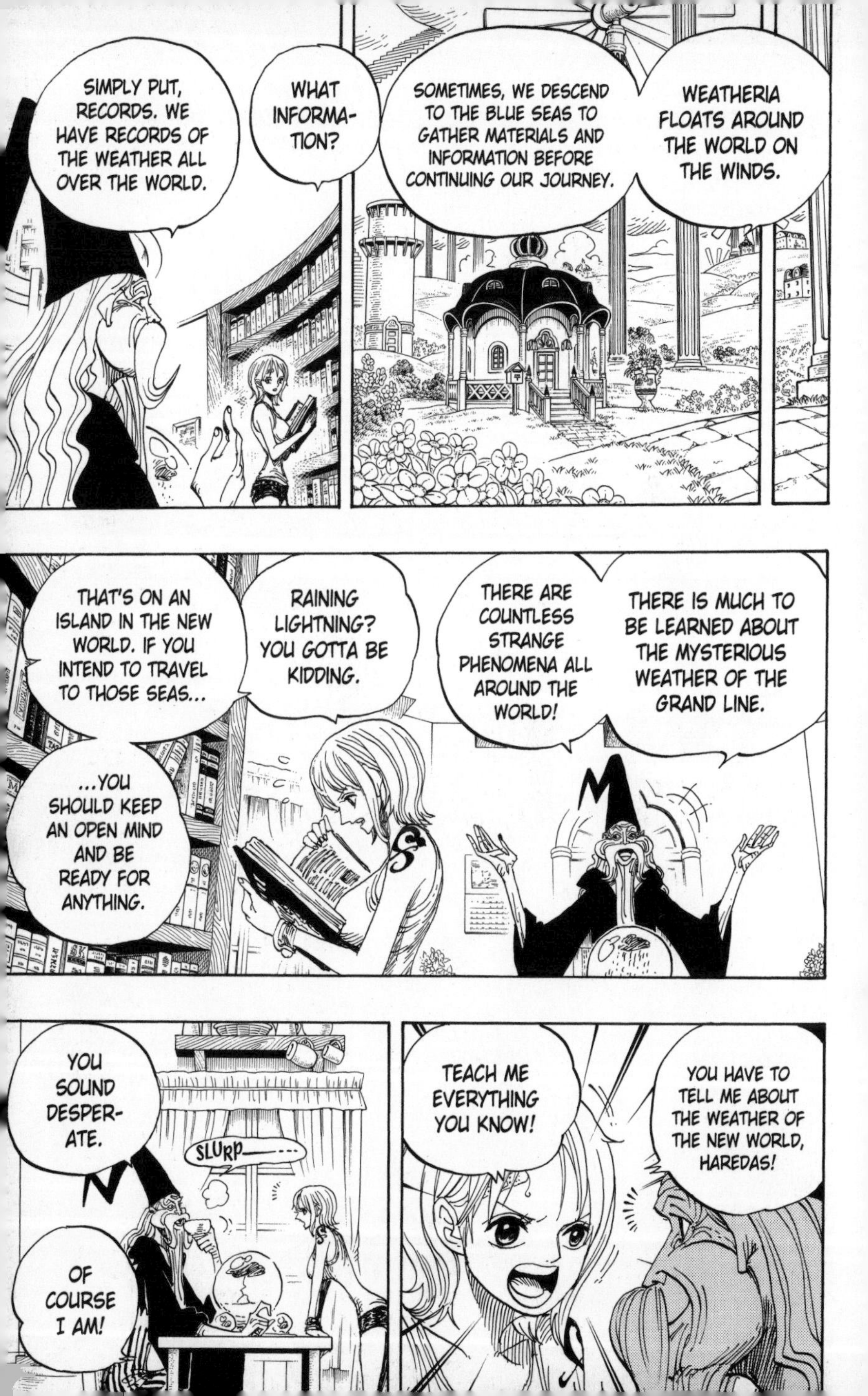
WEATHERIA FLOATS AROUND THE WORLD ON THE WINDS.
SOMETIMES, WE DESCEND TO THE BLUE SEAS TO GATHER MATERIALS AND INFORMATION BEFORE CONTINUING OUR JOURNEY.
WHAT INFORMATION?
SIMPLY PUT, RECORDS. WE HAVE RECORDS OF THE WEATHER ALL OVER THE WORLD.
THERE IS MUCH TO BE LEARNED ABOUT THE MYSTERIOUS WEATHER OF THE GRAND LINE.
THERE ARE COUNTLESS STRANGE PHENOMENA ALL AROUND THE WORLD!
RAINING LIGHTNING? YOU GOTTA BE KIDDING.
THAT'S ON AN ISLAND IN THE NEW WORLD. IF YOU INTEND TO TRAVEL TO THOSE SEAS...
...YOU SHOULD KEEP AN OPEN MIND AND BE READY FOR ANYTHING.
YOU HAVE TO TELL ME ABOUT THE WEATHER OF THE NEW WORLD, HAREDAS!
TEACH ME EVERYTHING YOU KNOW!
YOU SOUND DESPERATE.
SLURP
OF COURSE I AM!

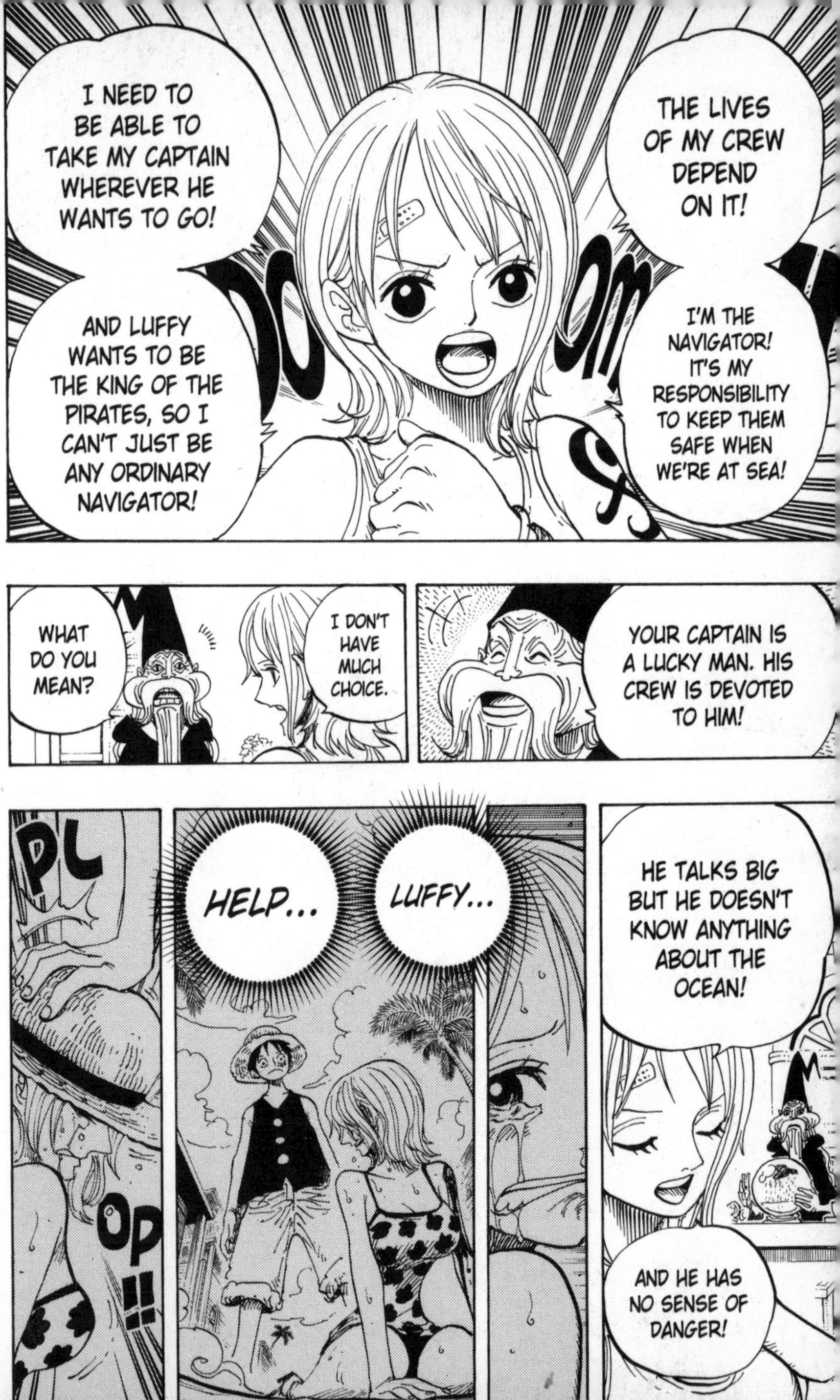
THE LIVES OF MY CREW DEPEND ON IT!
I'M THE NAVIGATOR! IT'S MY RESPONSIBILITY TO KEEP THEM SAFE WHEN WE'RE AT SEA!
DOOM
I NEED TO BE ABLE TO TAKE MY CAPTAIN WHEREVER HE WANTS TO GO!
AND LUFFY WANTS TO BE THE KING OF THE PIRATES, SO I CAN'T JUST BE ANY ORDINARY NAVIGATOR!
YOUR CAPTAIN IS A LUCKY MAN. HIS CREW IS DEVOTED TO HIM!
I DON'T HAVE MUCH CHOICE.
WHAT DO YOU MEAN?
HE TALKS BIG BUT HE DOESN'T KNOW ANYTHING ABOUT THE OCEAN!
AND HE HAS NO SENSE OF DANGER!
LUFFY...
HELP...
PLOP!!

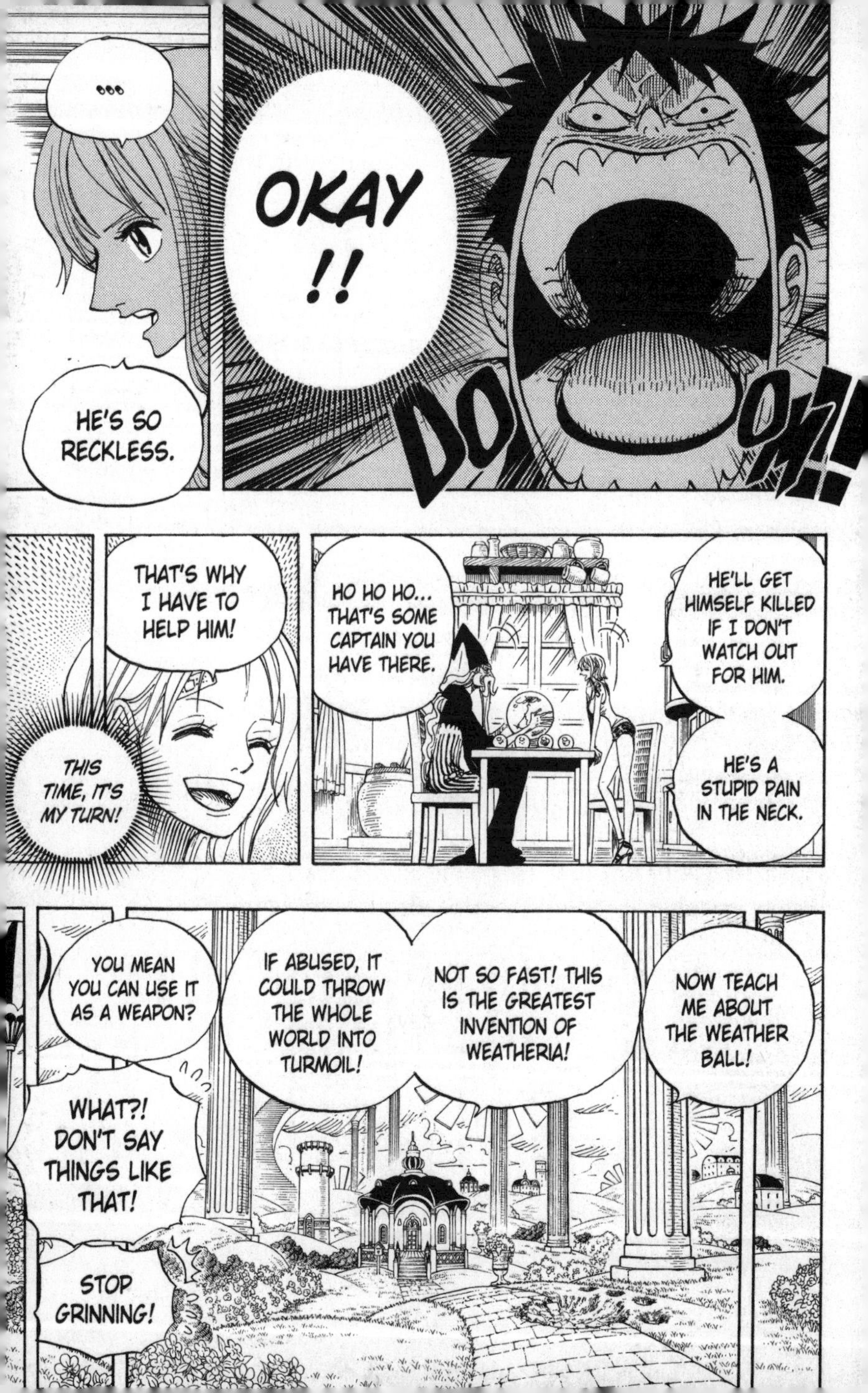
OKAY !!
...
HE'S SO RECKLESS.
HE'LL GET HIMSELF KILLED IF I DON'T WATCH OUT FOR HIM.
HE'S A STUPID PAIN IN THE NECK.
HO HO HO... THAT'S SOME CAPTAIN YOU HAVE THERE.
THAT'S WHY I HAVE TO HELP HIM!
THIS TIME, IT'S MY TURN!
NOW TEACH ME ABOUT THE WEATHER BALL!
NOT SO FAST! THIS IS THE GREATEST INVENTION OF WEATHERIA!
IF ABUSED, IT COULD THROW THE WHOLE WORLD INTO TURMOIL!
YOU MEAN YOU CAN USE IT AS A WEAPON?
WHAT?! DON'T SAY THINGS LIKE THAT!
STOP GRINNING!

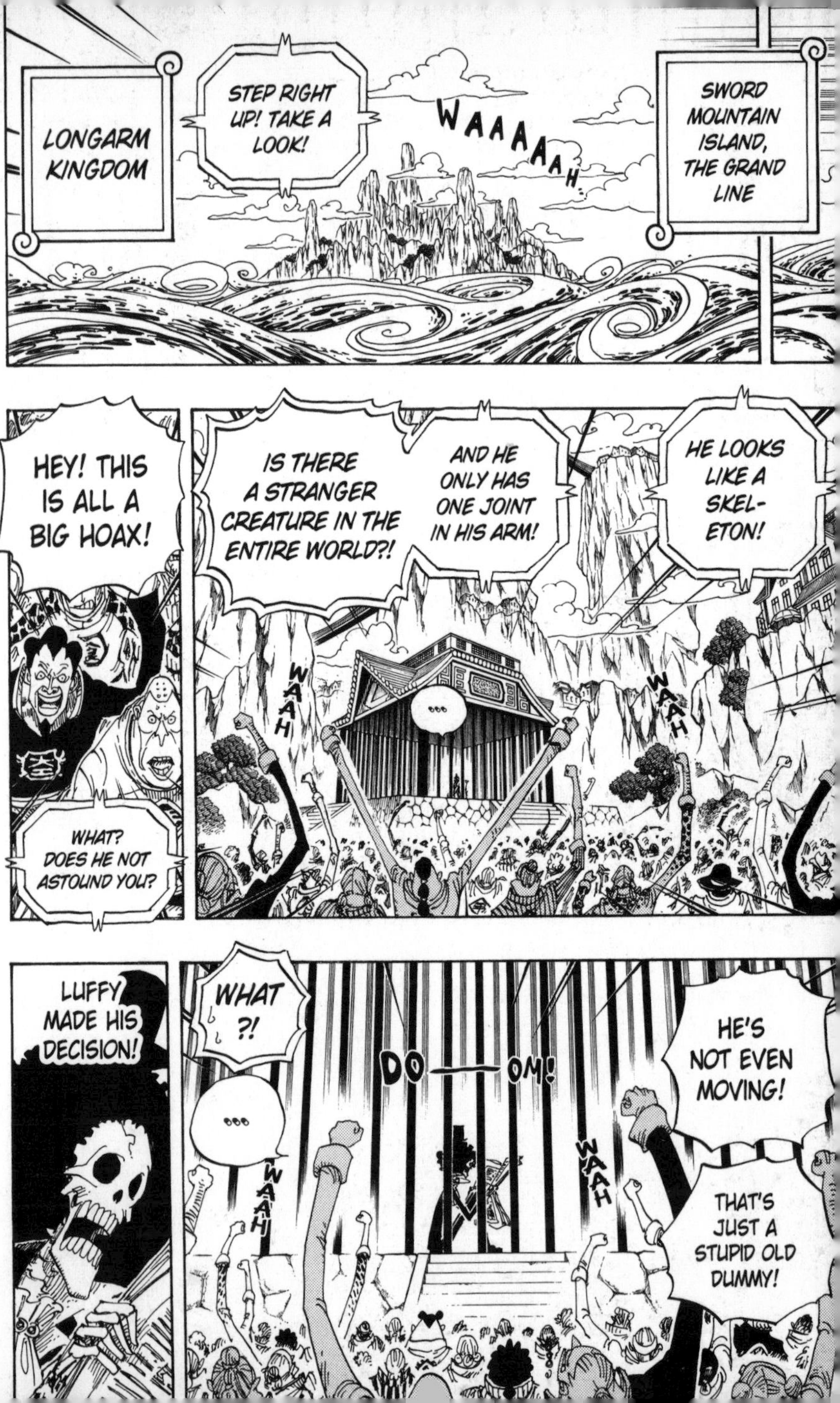
SWORD MOUNTAIN ISLAND, THE GRAND LINE
WAAAAAH
STEP RIGHT UP! TAKE A LOOK!
LONGARM KINGDOM
HE LOOKS LIKE A SKEL-ETON!
AND HE ONLY HAS ONE JOINT IN HIS ARM!
IS THERE A STRANGER CREATURE IN THE ENTIRE WORLD?!
WAAH
...
WAAH
HEY! THIS IS ALL A BIG HOAX!
WHAT? DOES HE NOT ASTOUND YOU?
HE'S NOT EVEN MOVING!
WHAT ?!
DO——OM!
WAAH
THAT'S JUST A STUPID OLD DUMMY!
...
WAAH
LUFFY MADE HIS DECISION!

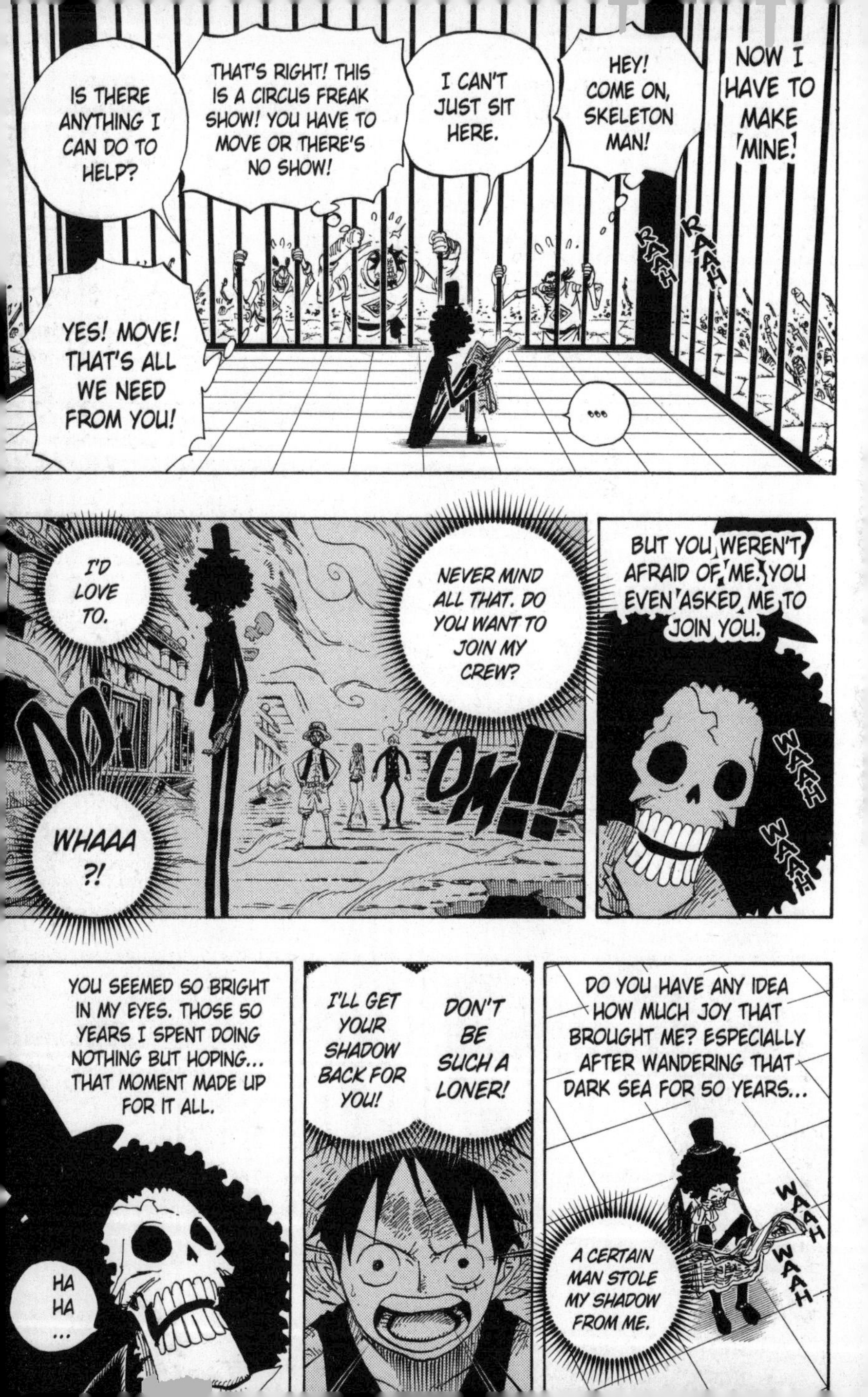

NOW I HAVE TO MAKE MINE!
HEY! COME ON, SKELETON MAN!
I CAN'T JUST SIT HERE.
THAT'S RIGHT! THIS IS A CIRCUS FREAK SHOW! YOU HAVE TO MOVE OR THERE'S NO SHOW!
IS THERE ANYTHING I CAN DO TO HELP?
RAAH RAAH
...
YES! MOVE! THAT'S ALL WE NEED FROM YOU!
BUT YOU WEREN'T AFRAID OF ME. YOU EVEN ASKED ME TO JOIN YOU.
WAAH WAAH
NEVER MIND ALL THAT. DO YOU WANT TO JOIN MY CREW?
I'D LOVE TO.
OH!!
WHAAA ?!
DO YOU HAVE ANY IDEA HOW MUCH JOY THAT BROUGHT ME? ESPECIALLY AFTER WANDERING THAT DARK SEA FOR 50 YEARS...
WAAH WAAH
A CERTAIN MAN STOLE MY SHADOW FROM ME.
DON'T BE SUCH A LONER!
I'LL GET YOUR SHADOW BACK FOR YOU!
YOU SEEMED SO BRIGHT IN MY EYES. THOSE 50 YEARS I SPENT DOING NOTHING BUT HOPING... THAT MOMENT MADE UP FOR IT ALL.
HA HA ...

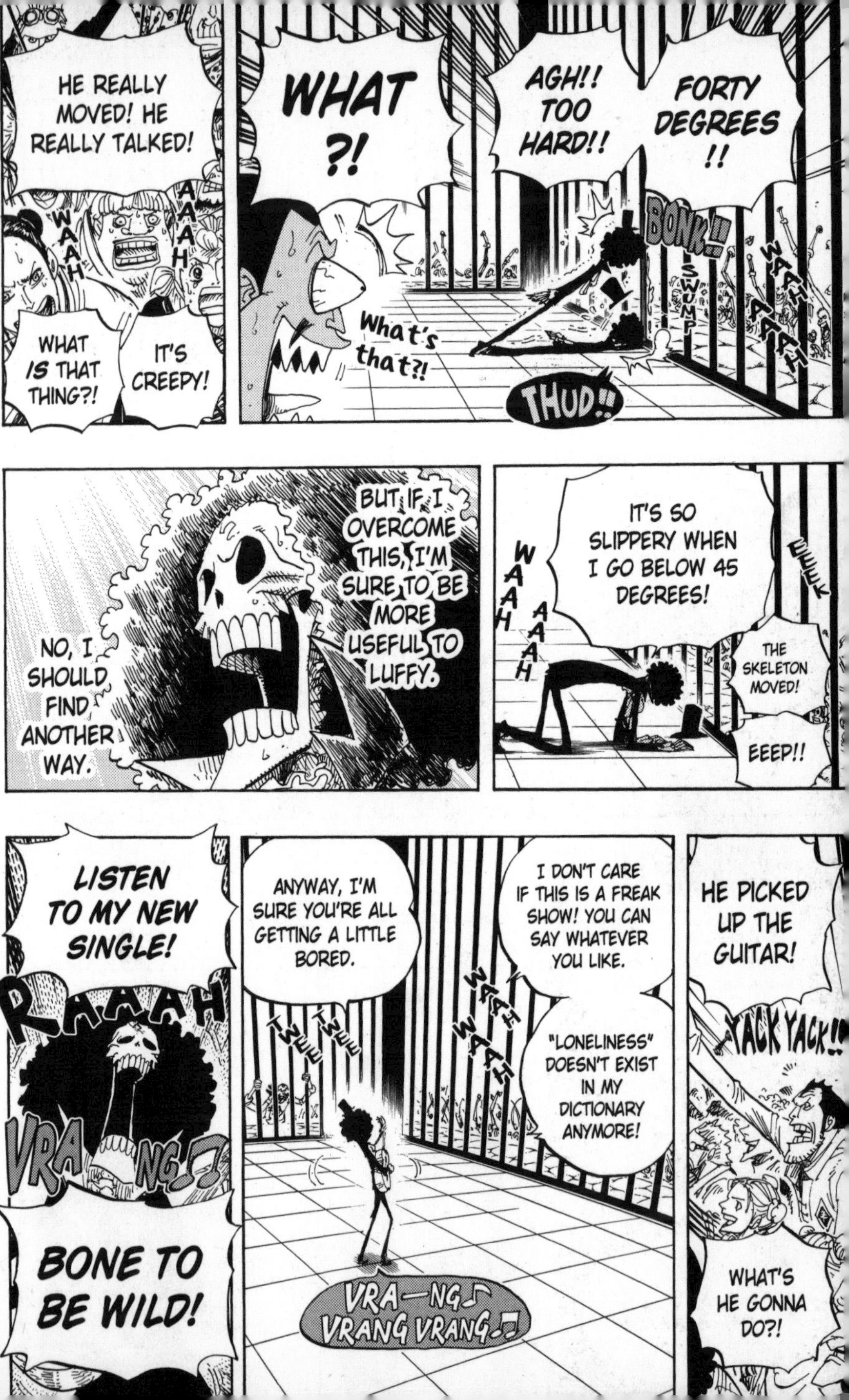
FORTY DEGREES!!
AGH!! TOO HARD!!
WHAT?!
BONK!!
WAAAAH
SWUMP
What's that?!
THUD!!
HE REALLY MOVED! HE REALLY TALKED!
AAAH
WAAH
IT'S CREEPY!
WHAT *IS* THAT THING?!
WAAAH
IT'S SO SLIPPERY WHEN I GO BELOW 45 DEGREES!
EEEK
AAAAH
THE SKELETON MOVED!
EEEP!!
BUT IF I OVERCOME THIS, I'M SURE TO BE MORE USEFUL TO LUFFY.
NO, I SHOULD FIND ANOTHER WAY.
HE PICKED UP THE GUITAR!
YACK YACK!!
WHAT'S HE GONNA DO?!
I DON'T CARE IF THIS IS A FREAK SHOW! YOU CAN SAY WHATEVER YOU LIKE.
ANYWAY, I'M SURE YOU'RE ALL GETTING A LITTLE BORED.
WAAH WAAH
TWEE TWEE
"LONELINESS" DOESN'T EXIST IN MY DICTIONARY ANYMORE!
VRA—NG VRANG VRANG
LISTEN TO MY NEW SINGLE!
RAAAAH
VRA NG
BONE TO BE WILD!

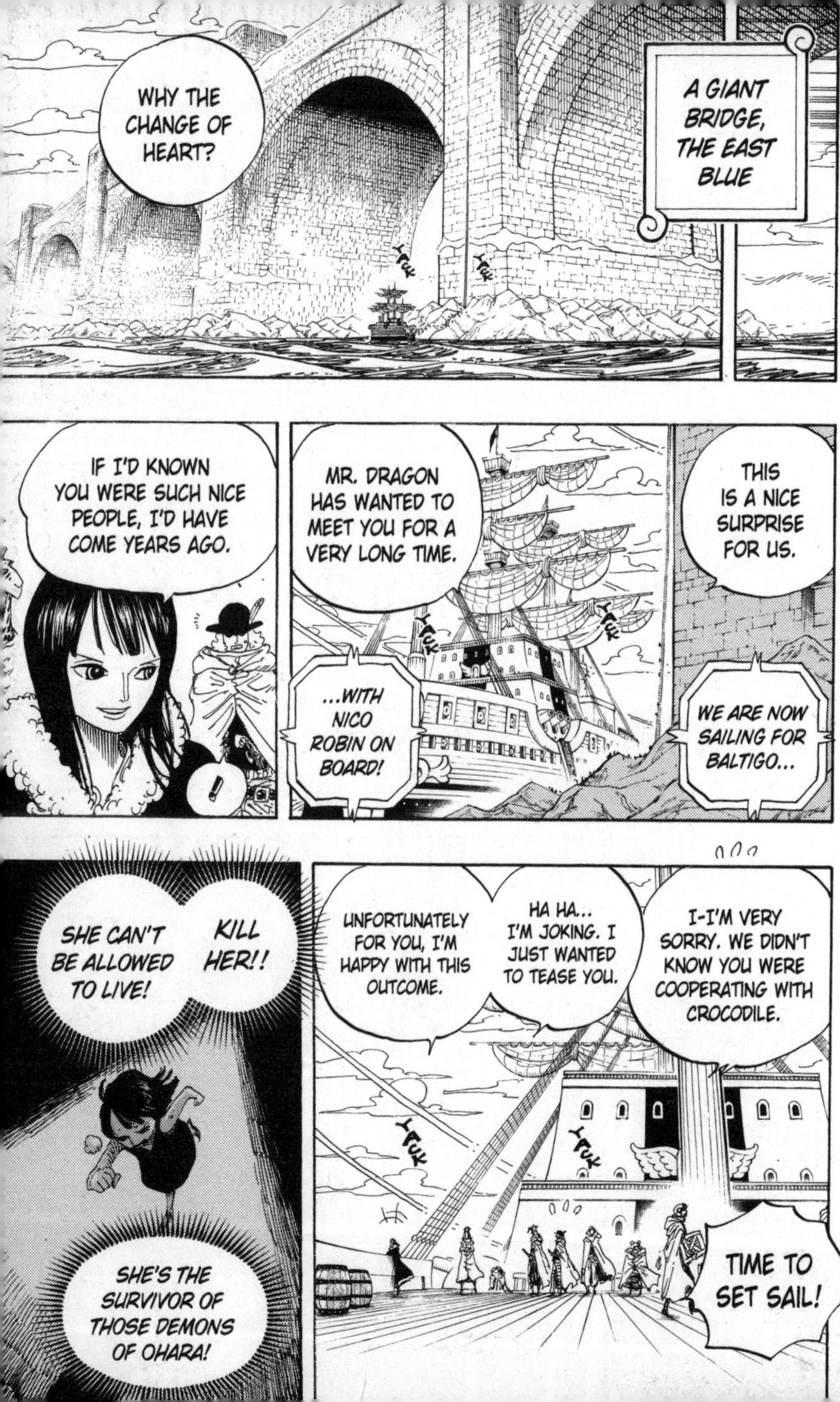
A GIANT BRIDGE, THE EAST BLUE
WHY THE CHANGE OF HEART?
THIS IS A NICE SURPRISE FOR US.
WE ARE NOW SAILING FOR BALTIGO...
MR. DRAGON HAS WANTED TO MEET YOU FOR A VERY LONG TIME.
...WITH NICO ROBIN ON BOARD!
IF I'D KNOWN YOU WERE SUCH NICE PEOPLE, I'D HAVE COME YEARS AGO.
!
I-I'M VERY SORRY. WE DIDN'T KNOW YOU WERE COOPERATING WITH CROCODILE.
HA HA... I'M JOKING. I JUST WANTED TO TEASE YOU.
UNFORTUNATELY FOR YOU, I'M HAPPY WITH THIS OUTCOME.
TIME TO SET SAIL!
KILL HER!!
SHE CAN'T BE ALLOWED TO LIVE!
SHE'S THE SURVIVOR OF THOSE DEMONS OF OHARA!

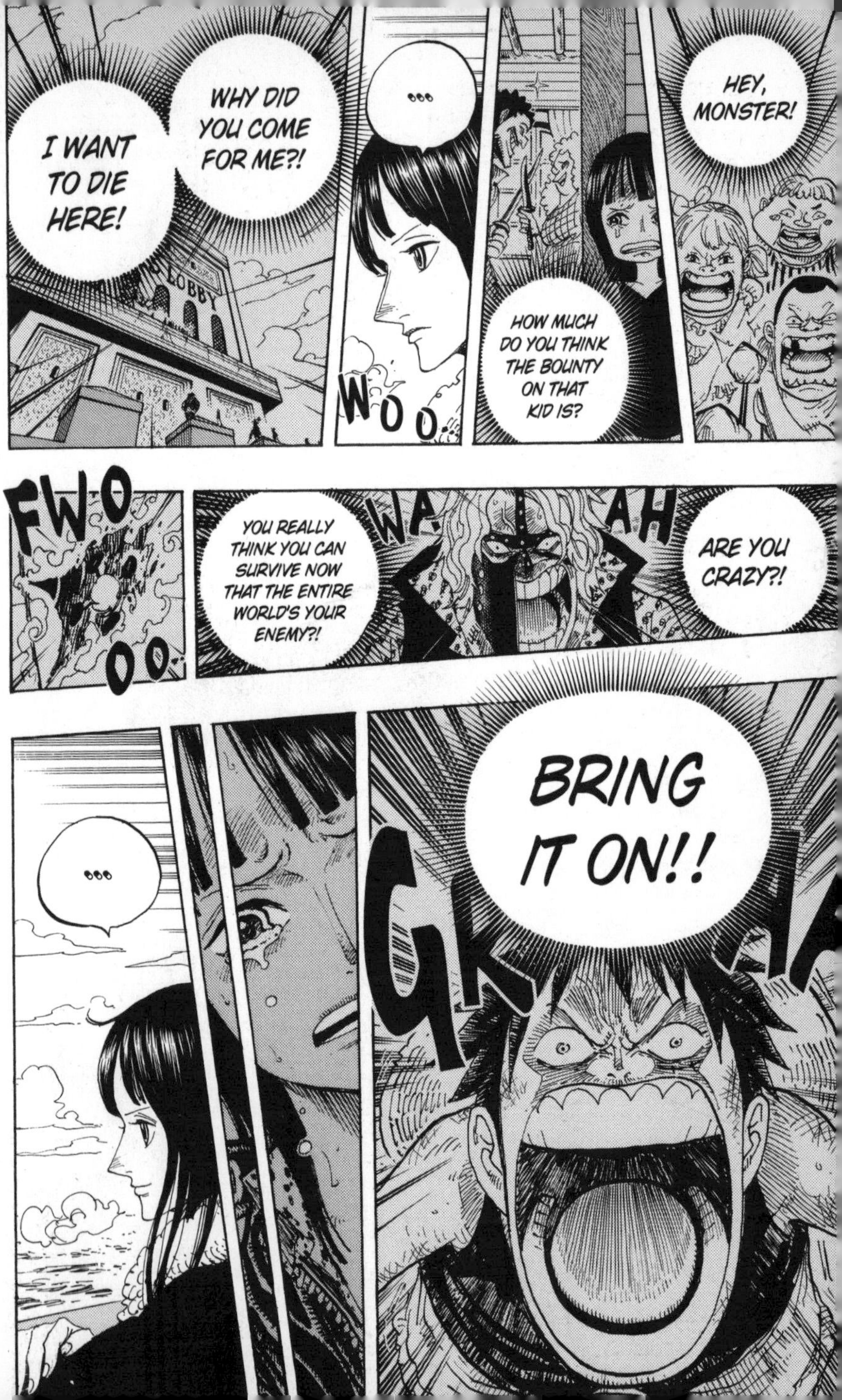
HEY, MONSTER!
HOW MUCH DO YOU THINK THE BOUNTY ON THAT KID IS?
...
WOO
WHY DID YOU COME FOR ME?!
I WANT TO DIE HERE!
ARE YOU CRAZY?!
WA AH
YOU REALLY THINK YOU CAN SURVIVE NOW THAT THE ENTIRE WORLD'S YOUR ENEMY?!
FWO
OO
BRING IT ON!!
...

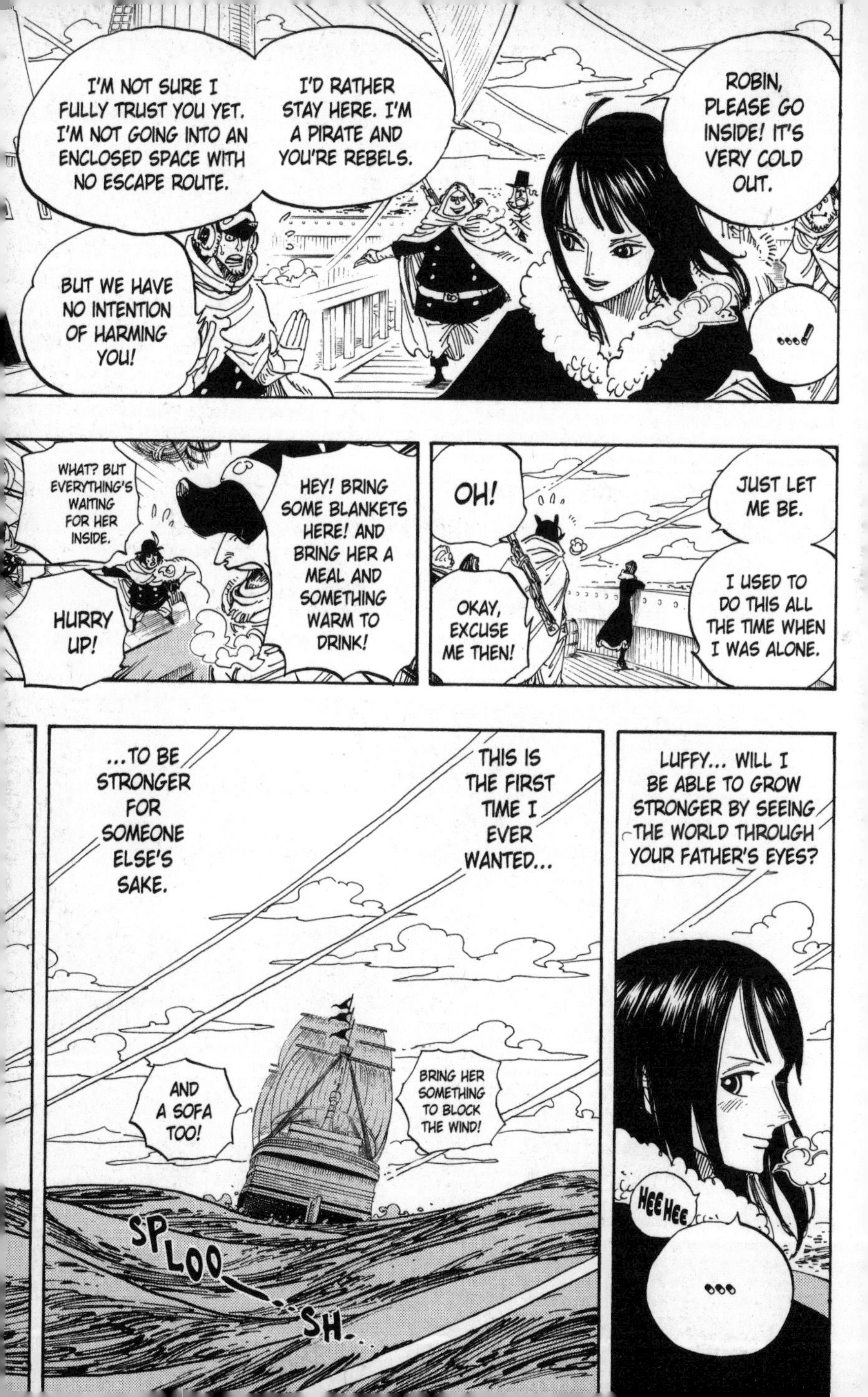
ROBIN, PLEASE GO INSIDE! IT'S VERY COLD OUT.
...!
I'D RATHER STAY HERE. I'M A PIRATE AND YOU'RE REBELS.
I'M NOT SURE I FULLY TRUST YOU YET. I'M NOT GOING INTO AN ENCLOSED SPACE WITH NO ESCAPE ROUTE.
BUT WE HAVE NO INTENTION OF HARMING YOU!
JUST LET ME BE.
I USED TO DO THIS ALL THE TIME WHEN I WAS ALONE.
OH!
OKAY, EXCUSE ME THEN!
HEY! BRING SOME BLANKETS HERE! AND BRING HER A MEAL AND SOMETHING WARM TO DRINK!
WHAT? BUT EVERYTHING'S WAITING FOR HER INSIDE.
HURRY UP!
LUFFY... WILL I BE ABLE TO GROW STRONGER BY SEEING THE WORLD THROUGH YOUR FATHER'S EYES?
HEE HEE
...
THIS IS THE FIRST TIME I EVER WANTED...
...TO BE STRONGER FOR SOMEONE ELSE'S SAKE.
BRING HER SOMETHING TO BLOCK THE WIND!
AND A SOFA TOO!
SPLOO—SH

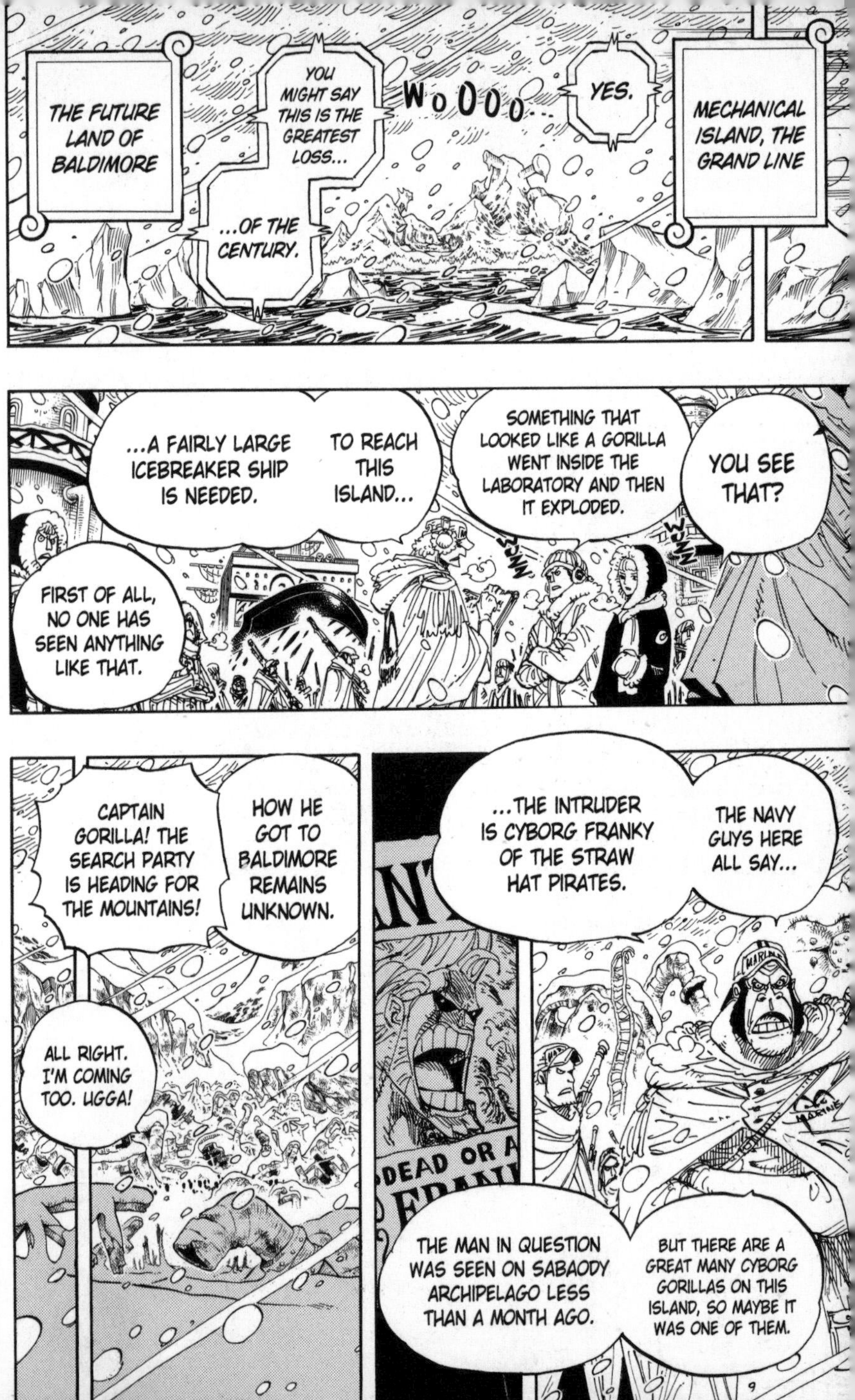

MECHANICAL ISLAND, THE GRAND LINE
YES.
WOOOO...
YOU MIGHT SAY THIS IS THE GREATEST LOSS...
...OF THE CENTURY.
THE FUTURE LAND OF BALDIMORE
YOU SEE THAT?
WUNN
SOMETHING THAT LOOKED LIKE A GORILLA WENT INSIDE THE LABORATORY AND THEN IT EXPLODED.
WUNN
TO REACH THIS ISLAND...
...A FAIRLY LARGE ICEBREAKER SHIP IS NEEDED.
FIRST OF ALL, NO ONE HAS SEEN ANYTHING LIKE THAT.
THE NAVY GUYS HERE ALL SAY...
...THE INTRUDER IS CYBORG FRANKY OF THE STRAW HAT PIRATES.
DEAD OR A
BUT THERE ARE A GREAT MANY CYBORG GORILLAS ON THIS ISLAND, SO MAYBE IT WAS ONE OF THEM.
THE MAN IN QUESTION WAS SEEN ON SABAODY ARCHIPELAGO LESS THAN A MONTH AGO.
HOW HE GOT TO BALDIMORE REMAINS UNKNOWN.
CAPTAIN GORILLA! THE SEARCH PARTY IS HEADING FOR THE MOUNTAINS!
ALL RIGHT. I'M COMING TOO. UGGA!

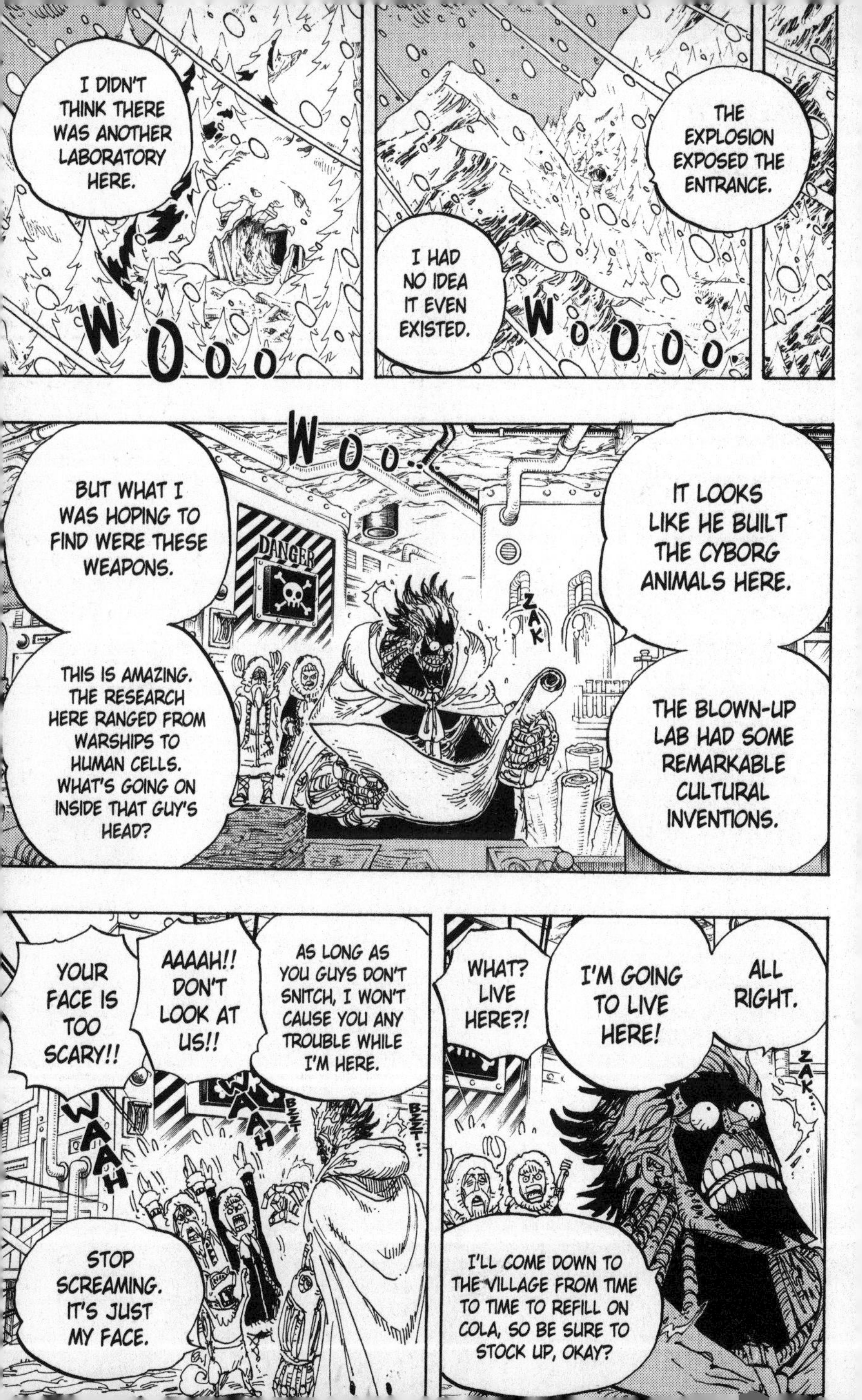
THE EXPLOSION EXPOSED THE ENTRANCE.
I HAD NO IDEA IT EVEN EXISTED.
WOOOOO
I DIDN'T THINK THERE WAS ANOTHER LABORATORY HERE.
WOOOO
IT LOOKS LIKE HE BUILT THE CYBORG ANIMALS HERE.
THE BLOWN-UP LAB HAD SOME REMARKABLE CULTURAL INVENTIONS.
WOO...
ZAK
BUT WHAT I WAS HOPING TO FIND WERE THESE WEAPONS.
THIS IS AMAZING. THE RESEARCH HERE RANGED FROM WARSHIPS TO HUMAN CELLS. WHAT'S GOING ON INSIDE THAT GUY'S HEAD?
ALL RIGHT.
I'M GOING TO LIVE HERE!
WHAT? LIVE HERE?!
ZAK...
I'LL COME DOWN TO THE VILLAGE FROM TIME TO TIME TO REFILL ON COLA, SO BE SURE TO STOCK UP, OKAY?
BZZT...
AS LONG AS YOU GUYS DON'T SNITCH, I WON'T CAUSE YOU ANY TROUBLE WHILE I'M HERE.
BZZT
AAAAH!! DON'T LOOK AT US!!
WAAH
YOUR FACE IS TOO SCARY!!
WAAH
STOP SCREAMING. IT'S JUST MY FACE.

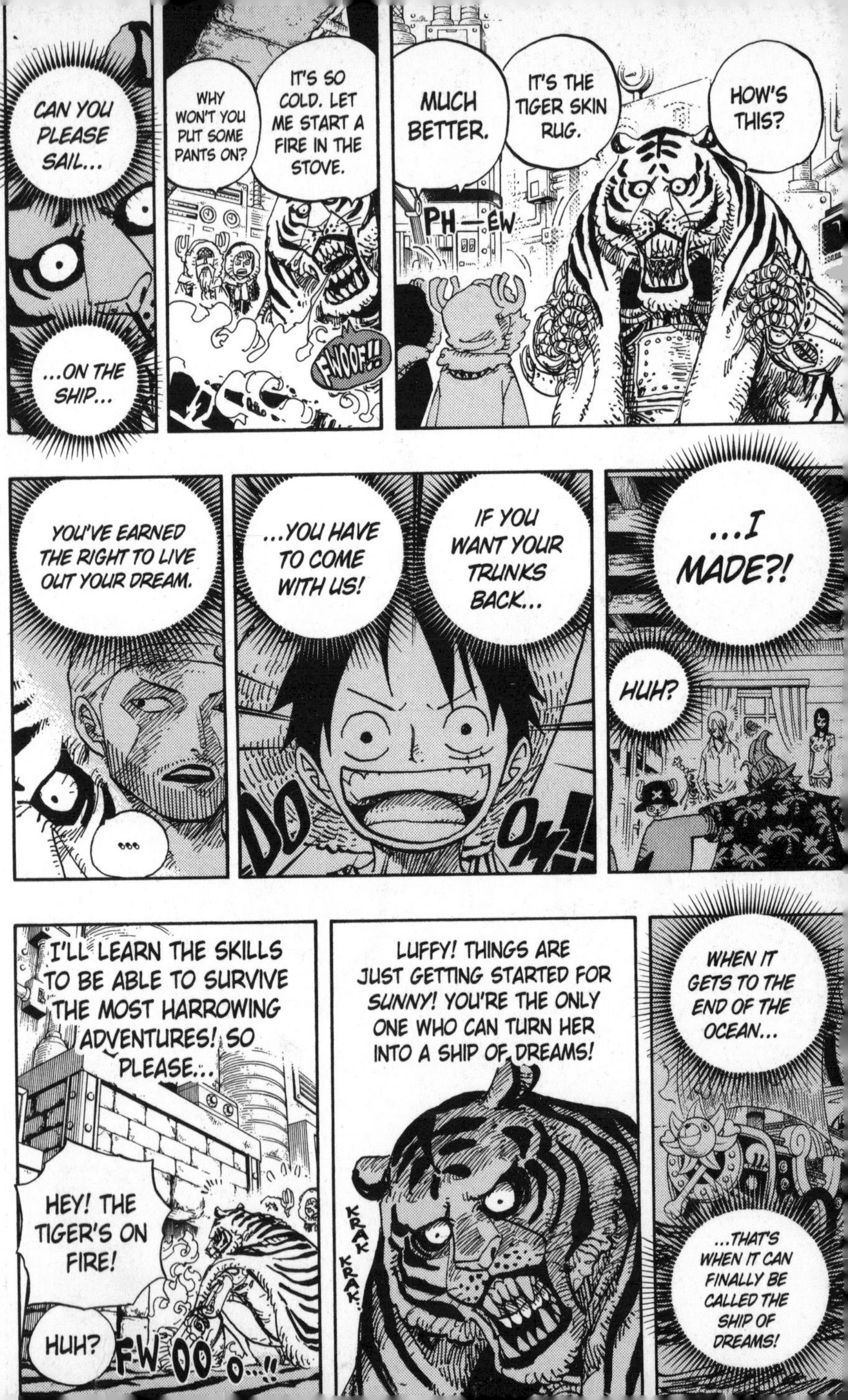
HOW'S THIS?
IT'S THE TIGER SKIN RUG.
MUCH BETTER.
PH—EW
IT'S SO COLD. LET ME START A FIRE IN THE STOVE.
WHY WON'T YOU PUT SOME PANTS ON?
FWOOF!!
CAN YOU PLEASE SAIL...
...ON THE SHIP...
...I MADE?!
HUH?
IF YOU WANT YOUR TRUNKS BACK...
...YOU HAVE TO COME WITH US!
DOOM!!
YOU'VE EARNED THE RIGHT TO LIVE OUT YOUR DREAM.
...
WHEN IT GETS TO THE END OF THE OCEAN...
...THAT'S WHEN IT CAN FINALLY BE CALLED THE SHIP OF DREAMS!
LUFFY! THINGS ARE JUST GETTING STARTED FOR SUNNY! YOU'RE THE ONLY ONE WHO CAN TURN HER INTO A SHIP OF DREAMS!
KRAK
KRAK
I'LL LEARN THE SKILLS TO BE ABLE TO SURVIVE THE MOST HARROWING ADVENTURES! SO PLEASE...
HEY! THE TIGER'S ON FIRE!
HUH?
FWOOo...!!

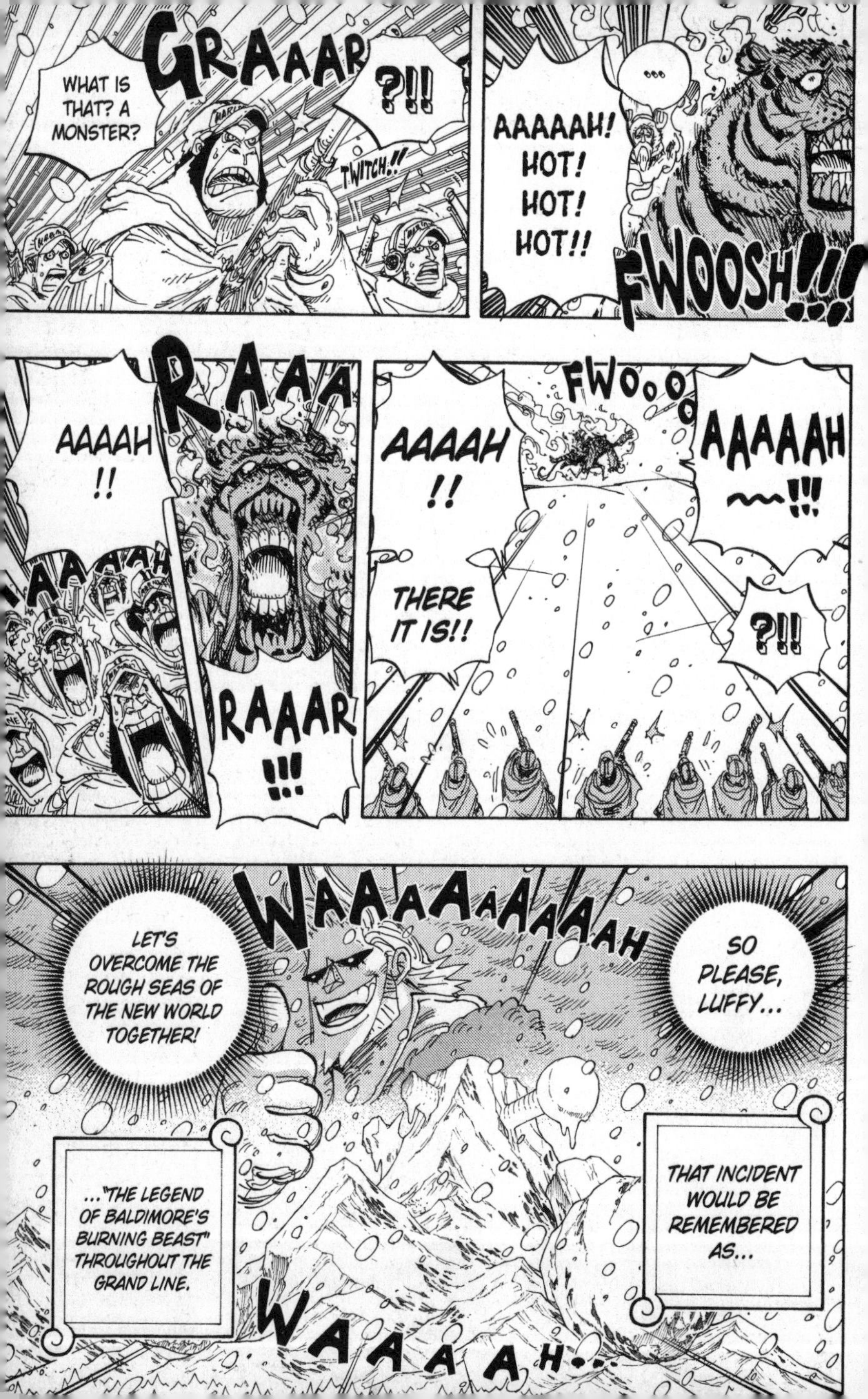
...
AAAAAH! HOT! HOT! HOT!!
FWOOSH!!!
GRAAAR
?!!
WHAT IS THAT? A MONSTER?
TWITCH!!
AAAAAH ~~!!!
FWOOOO
AAAAH!!
THERE IT IS!!
?!!
RAAA
AAAAH!!
RAAAR!!!
SO PLEASE, LUFFY...
WAAAAAAAAAH
LET'S OVERCOME THE ROUGH SEAS OF THE NEW WORLD TOGETHER!
THAT INCIDENT WOULD BE REMEMBERED AS...
..."THE LEGEND OF BALDIMORE'S BURNING BEAST" THROUGHOUT THE GRAND LINE.
WAAAAH...

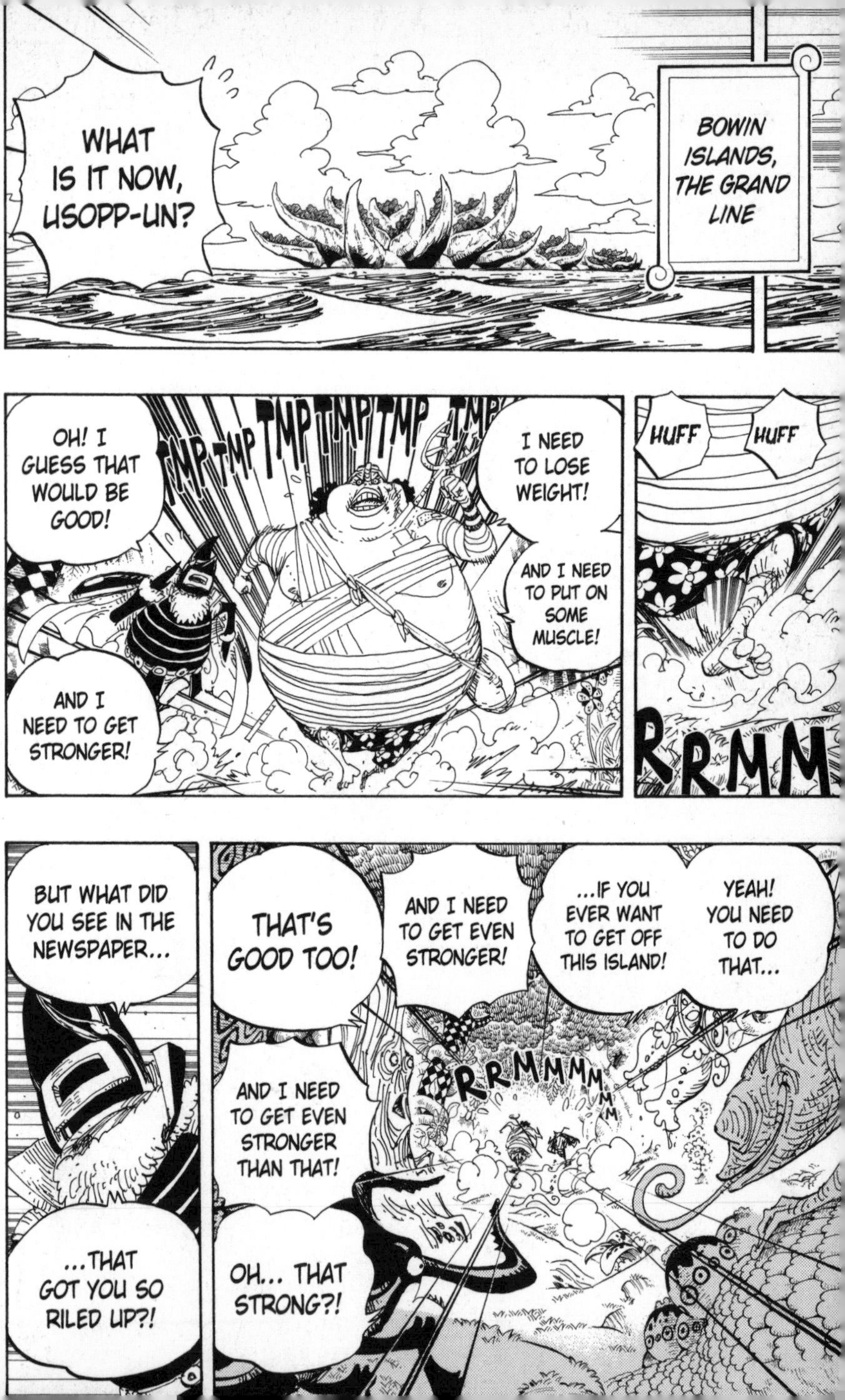
BOWIN ISLANDS, THE GRAND LINE
WHAT IS IT NOW, USOPP-UN?
HUFF
HUFF
RRMM
TMP TMP TMP TMP TMP TMP TMP
I NEED TO LOSE WEIGHT!
AND I NEED TO PUT ON SOME MUSCLE!
OH! I GUESS THAT WOULD BE GOOD!
AND I NEED TO GET STRONGER!
YEAH! YOU NEED TO DO THAT...
...IF YOU EVER WANT TO GET OFF THIS ISLAND!
AND I NEED TO GET EVEN STRONGER!
THAT'S GOOD TOO!
RRMMMMMM
AND I NEED TO GET EVEN STRONGER THAN THAT!
OH... THAT STRONG?!
BUT WHAT DID YOU SEE IN THE NEWSPAPER...
...THAT GOT YOU SO RILED UP?!

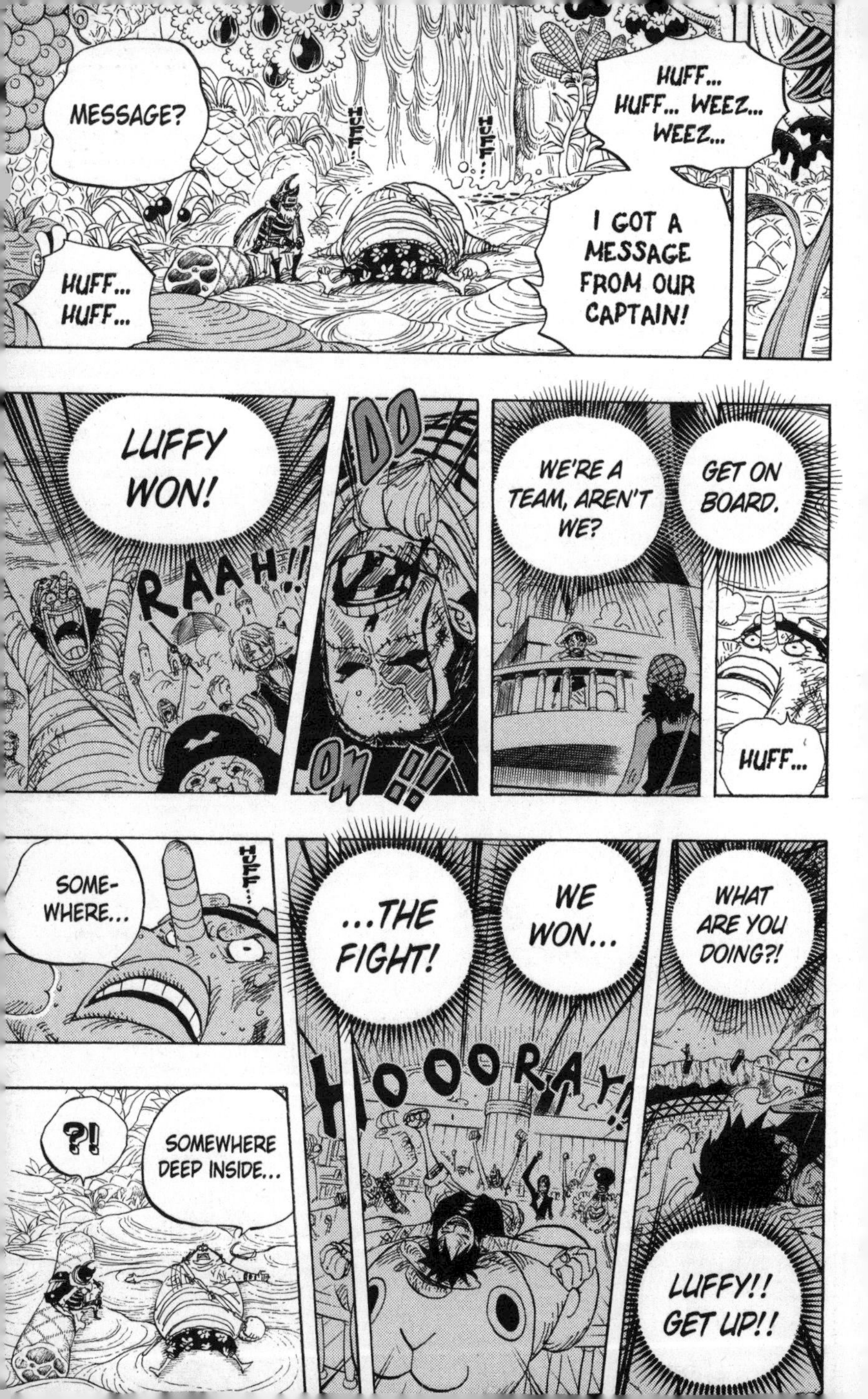
HUFF... HUFF... WEEZ... WEEZ...
HUFF!..
HUFF!..
MESSAGE?
I GOT A MESSAGE FROM OUR CAPTAIN!
HUFF... HUFF...
GET ON BOARD.
HUFF...
WE'RE A TEAM, AREN'T WE?
DOOM!!
LUFFY WON!
RAAH!!
WHAT ARE YOU DOING?!
LUFFY!! GET UP!!
WE WON...
...THE FIGHT!
HOOORAY!!
HUFF...
SOME-WHERE...
SOMEWHERE DEEP INSIDE...
?!

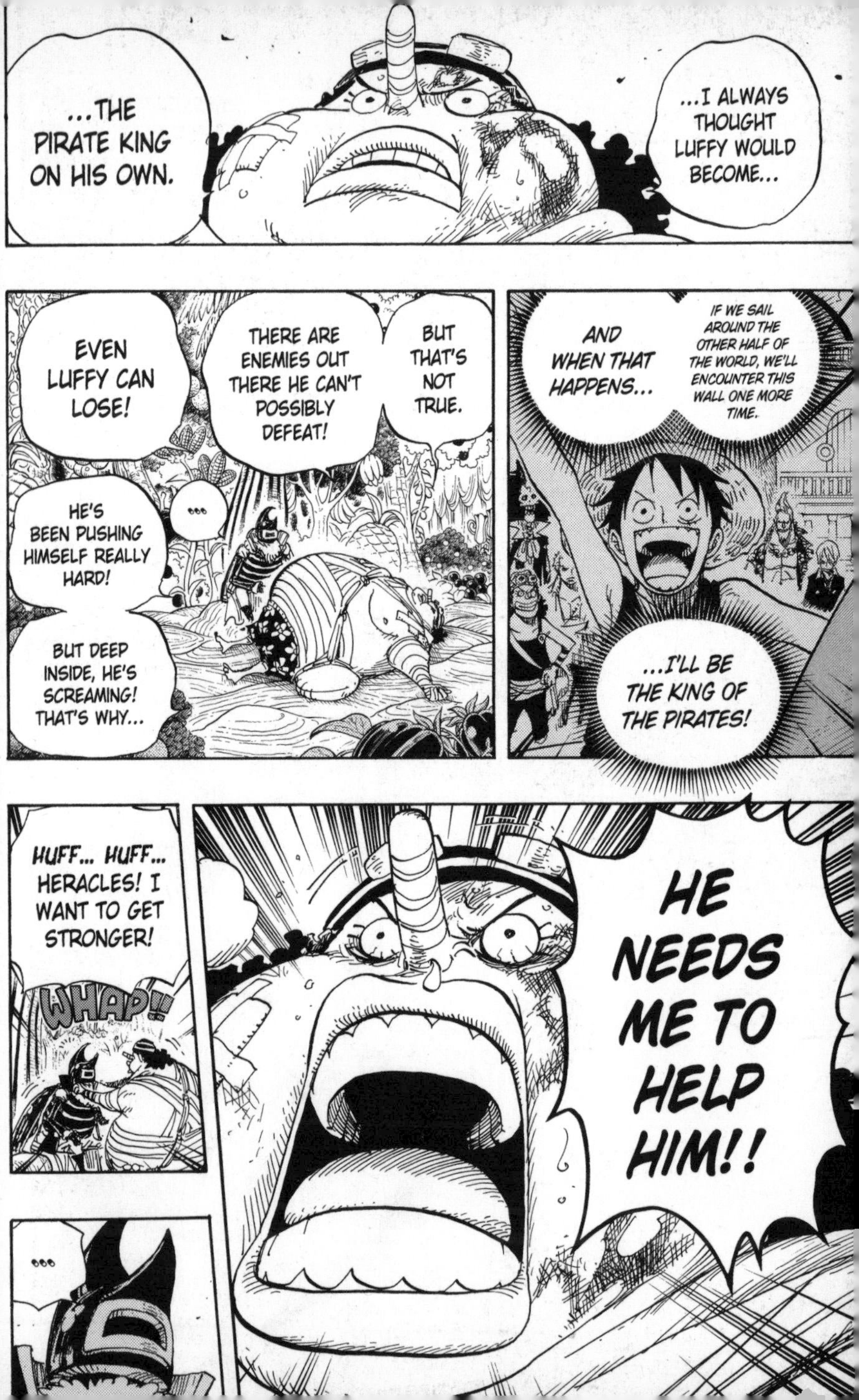
...I ALWAYS THOUGHT LUFFY WOULD BECOME...
...THE PIRATE KING ON HIS OWN.
IF WE SAIL AROUND THE OTHER HALF OF THE WORLD, WE'LL ENCOUNTER THIS WALL ONE MORE TIME.
AND WHEN THAT HAPPENS...
...I'LL BE THE KING OF THE PIRATES!
BUT THAT'S NOT TRUE.
THERE ARE ENEMIES OUT THERE HE CAN'T POSSIBLY DEFEAT!
EVEN LUFFY CAN LOSE!
...
HE'S BEEN PUSHING HIMSELF REALLY HARD!
BUT DEEP INSIDE, HE'S SCREAMING! THAT'S WHY...
HE NEEDS ME TO HELP HIM!!
HUFF... HUFF... HERACLES! I WANT TO GET STRONGER!
WHAP!!
...

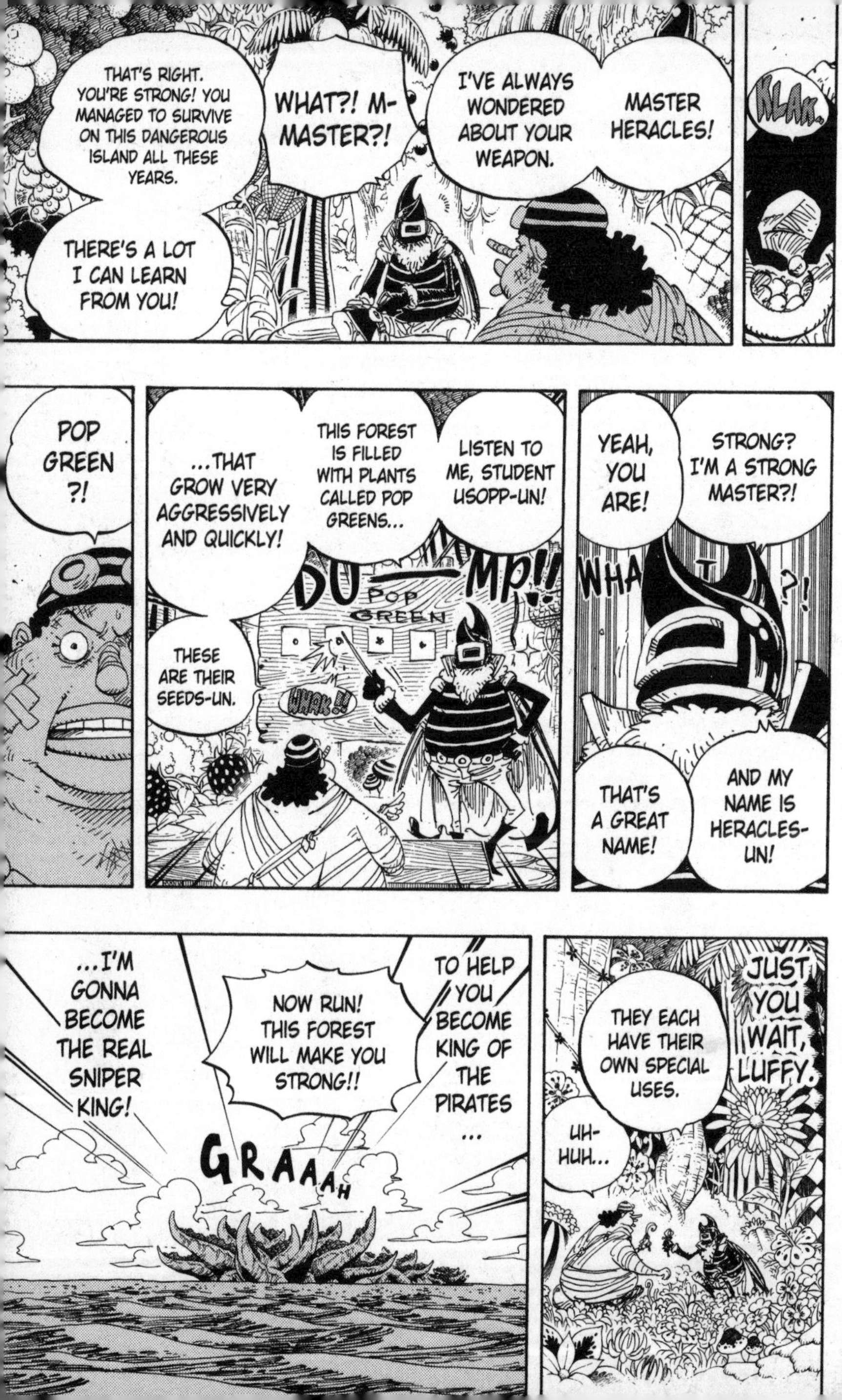
KLAK.
MASTER HERACLES!
I'VE ALWAYS WONDERED ABOUT YOUR WEAPON.
WHAT?! M-MASTER?!
THAT'S RIGHT. YOU'RE STRONG! YOU MANAGED TO SURVIVE ON THIS DANGEROUS ISLAND ALL THESE YEARS.
THERE'S A LOT I CAN LEARN FROM YOU!
STRONG? I'M A STRONG MASTER?!
YEAH, YOU ARE!
WHAT?!
AND MY NAME IS HERACLES-UN!
THAT'S A GREAT NAME!
LISTEN TO ME, STUDENT USOPP-UN!
THIS FOREST IS FILLED WITH PLANTS CALLED POP GREENS...
...THAT GROW VERY AGGRESSIVELY AND QUICKLY!
DU—MP!!
POP GREEN
WHAK!!
THESE ARE THEIR SEEDS-UN.
POP GREEN ?!
JUST YOU WAIT, LUFFY.
THEY EACH HAVE THEIR OWN SPECIAL USES.
UH-HUH...
TO HELP YOU BECOME KING OF THE PIRATES...
NOW RUN! THIS FOREST WILL MAKE YOU STRONG!!
...I'M GONNA BECOME THE REAL SNIPER KING!
GRAAAAH

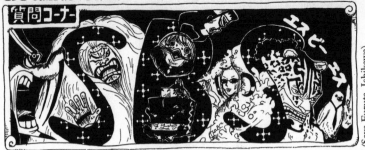

SBS Question Corner

質問コーナー
エスビーエス
(Saya Furuta, Ishikawa)

Q: If Sanji becomes president, how will he govern?

--Kennichi (from Aichi)

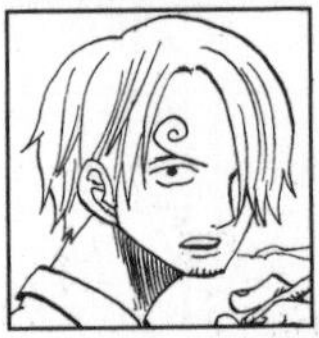

A: Let's see. First, he'll set up some legislation that will give preferential treatment to women. He'll create government bodies that are populated only by beautiful women. He'll probably make laws that say only women can eat good food, or how the movie theaters will have Ladies Day six days a week. Society will definitely be bad for all men. After the men revolt, his rule will come to an end.

Q: Hello, Mr. Oda. No matter how much I look at the cover of volume 57, I can't find the 8th Division Leader, Namule. What happened to him?! You have to give him some screen time on SBS!

--Jozu

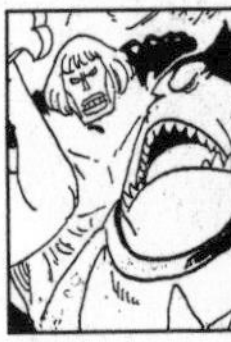

A: Oh, you're right. But I actually did draw him. He got cut off because of the printing. He's still there in the original drawings I made. I'll be sure to display him in an artbook someday. I'm so sorry, Namule!

Q: If you took "cuteness" away from Chopper, what would he be like? Please draw him like that! O-Oh, what do your curtains smell like?

--Our Curtains Stink

A: Well, the curtains at my workplace smell like lavender... Or floral... Or rosy... Or like crap...

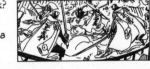

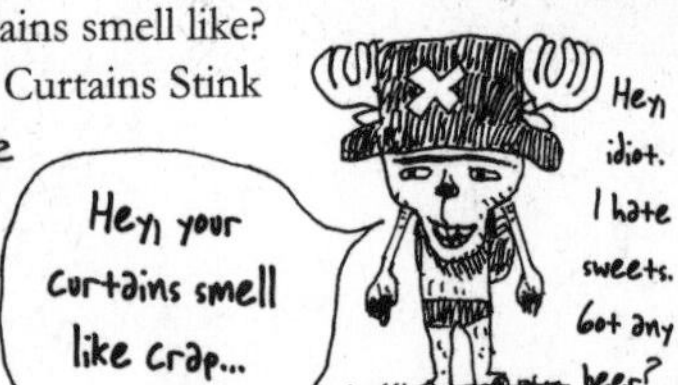

Hey, your curtains smell like crap...
Hey, idiot. I hate sweets. Got any beer?

Q: I want to ask about the coats that Naval officers wear. You know, the ones that say "Justice" on them. They always manage to stay on their shoulders no matter how much they move around. Do they snap on or something? Or glue? My husband insists that they're held down with rubber bands, but what do you think?

--Koteni

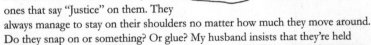

A: Unfortunately, it's nothing like that. It's a coat with "Justice" inscribed on the back. The reason it never falls off is because "Justice" will always stand firm! As long as they have that in their hearts, the coats WILL NOT FALL!

Chapter 597:
~~3D~~2Y

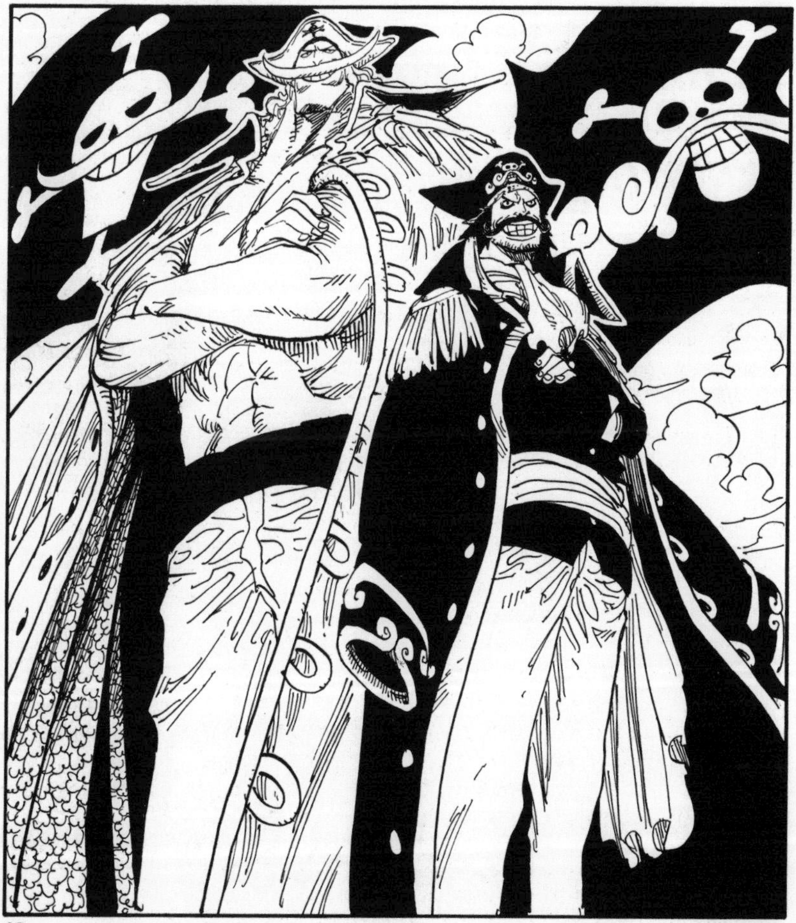

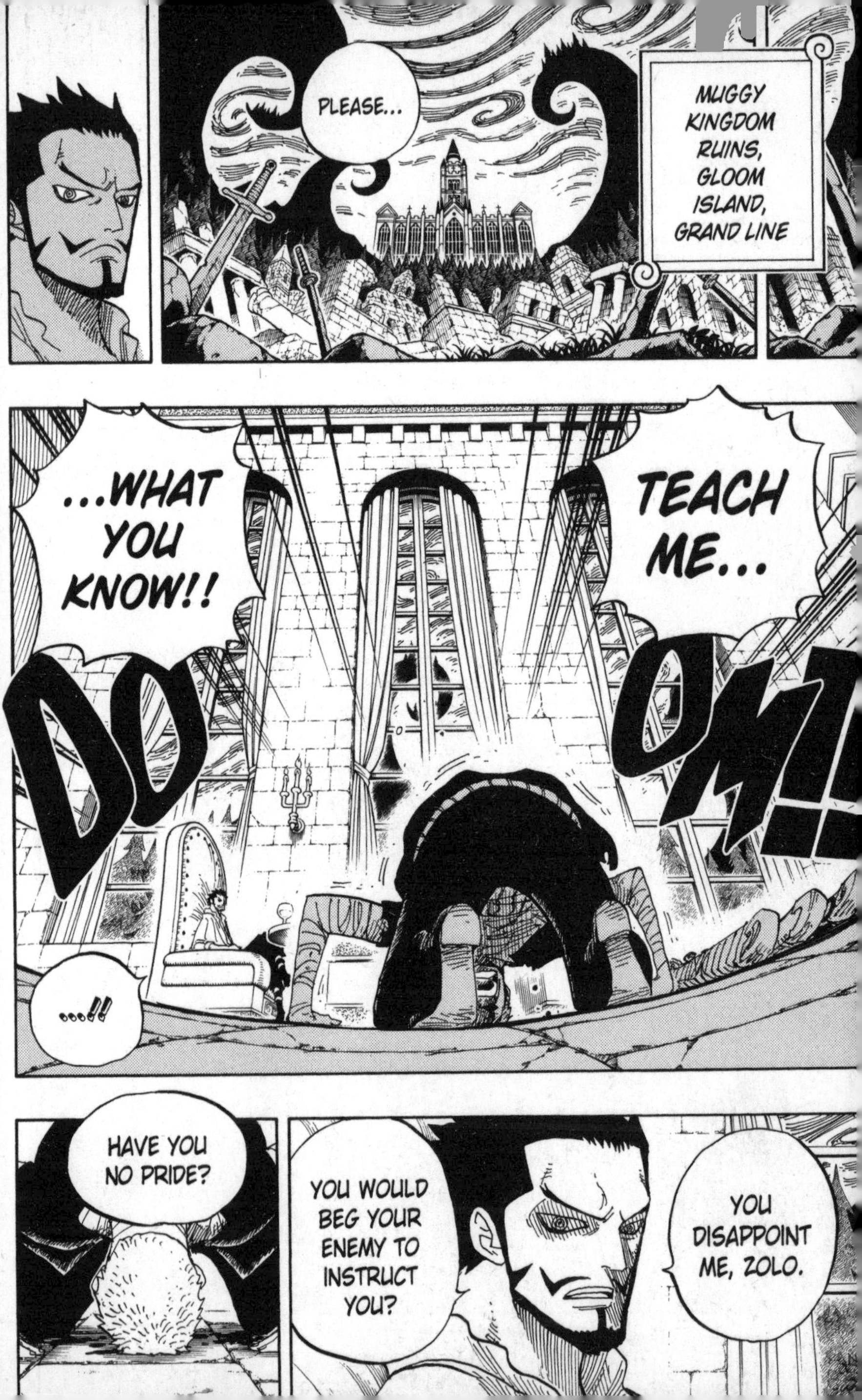
MUGGY KINGDOM RUINS, GLOOM ISLAND, GRAND LINE
PLEASE...
TEACH ME...
...WHAT YOU KNOW!!
DOOM!!
...!!
YOU DISAPPOINT ME, ZOLO.
YOU WOULD BEG YOUR ENEMY TO INSTRUCT YOU?
HAVE YOU NO PRIDE?

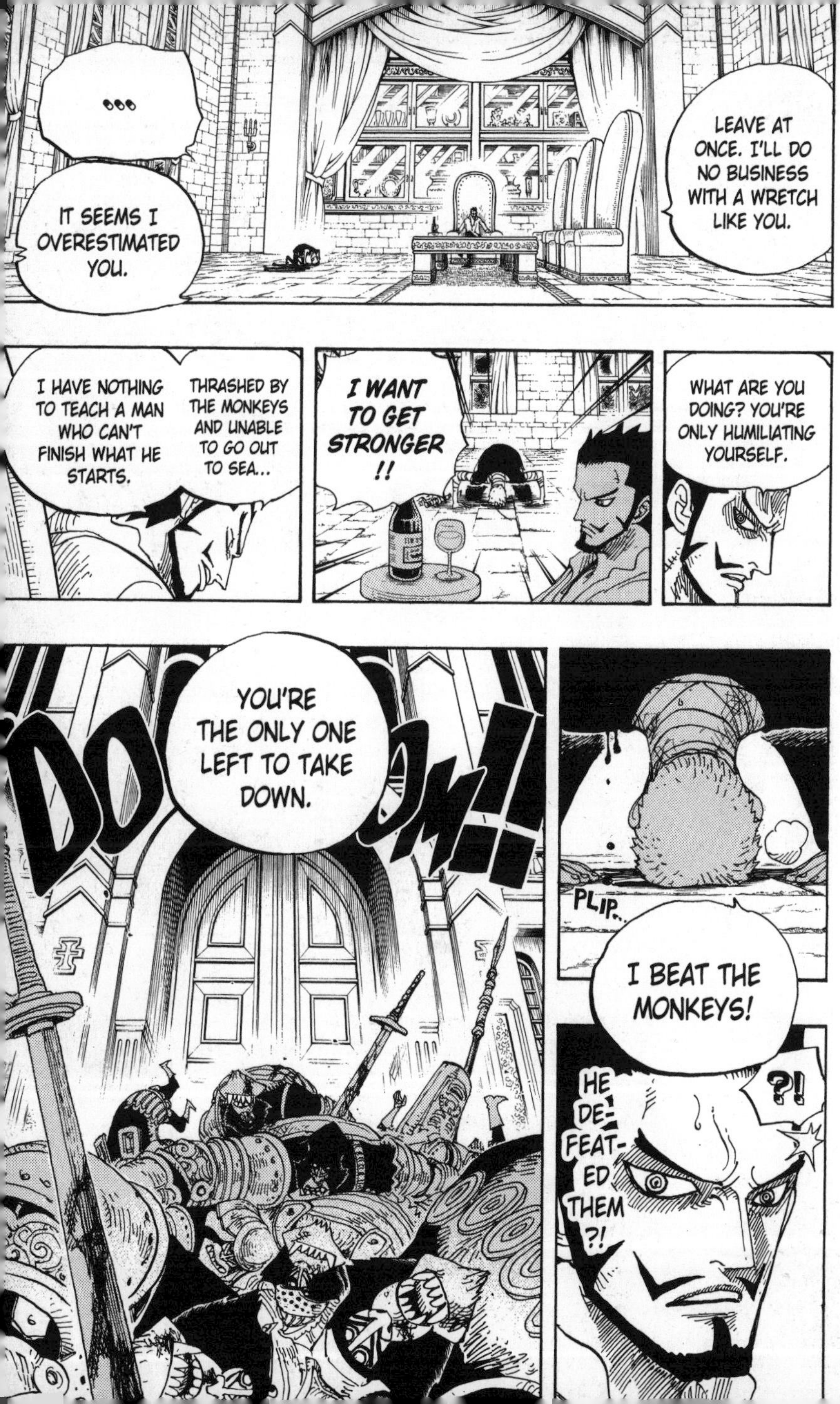
LEAVE AT ONCE. I'LL DO NO BUSINESS WITH A WRETCH LIKE YOU.
...
IT SEEMS I OVERESTIMATED YOU.
WHAT ARE YOU DOING? YOU'RE ONLY HUMILIATING YOURSELF.
I WANT TO GET STRONGER!!
THRASHED BY THE MONKEYS AND UNABLE TO GO OUT TO SEA...
I HAVE NOTHING TO TEACH A MAN WHO CAN'T FINISH WHAT HE STARTS.
PLIP...
I BEAT THE MONKEYS!
?!
HE DE-FEAT-ED THEM?!
DOOM!!
YOU'RE THE ONLY ONE LEFT TO TAKE DOWN.

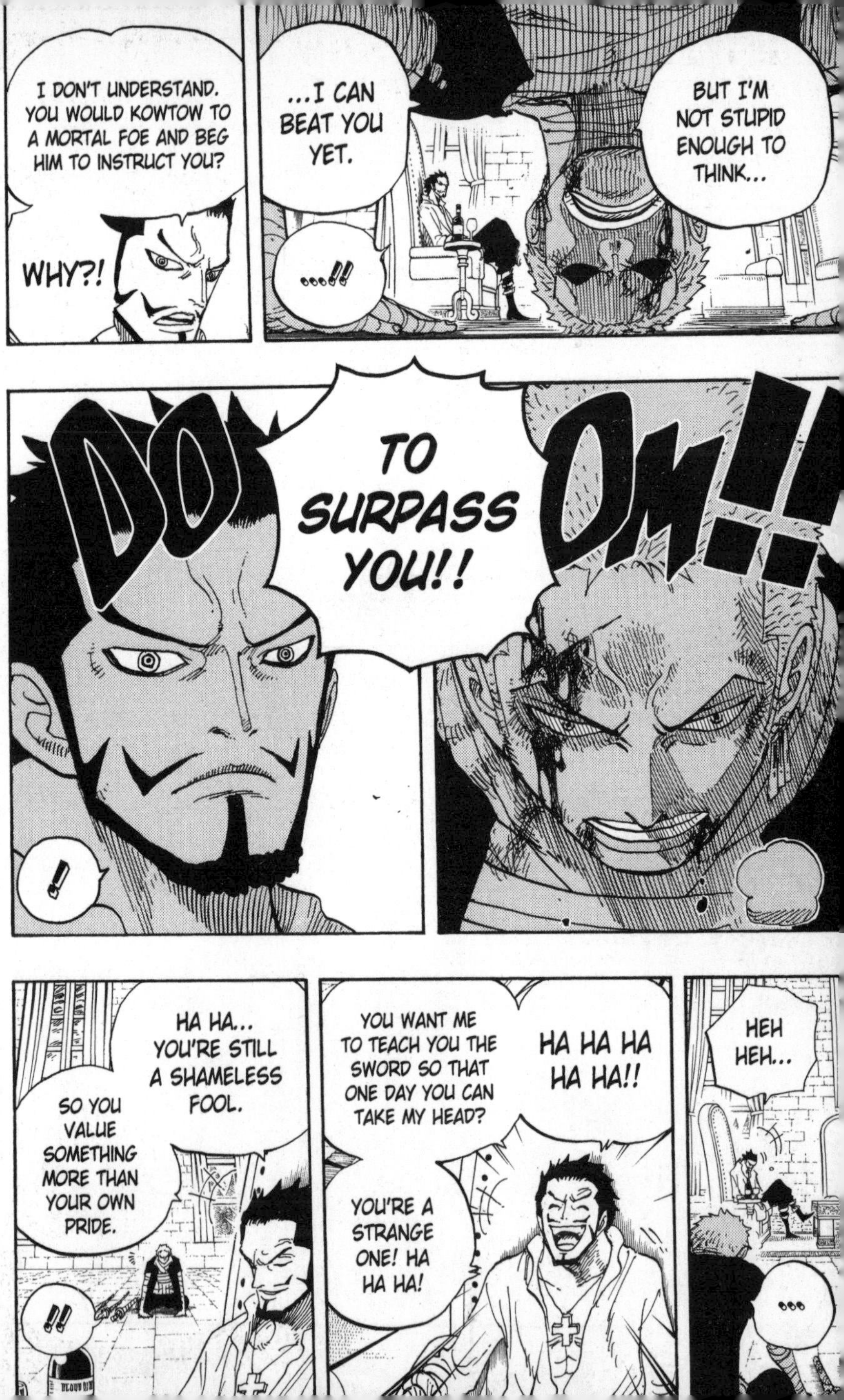

BUT I'M NOT STUPID ENOUGH TO THINK...
...I CAN BEAT YOU YET.
...!!
I DON'T UNDERSTAND. YOU WOULD KOWTOW TO A MORTAL FOE AND BEG HIM TO INSTRUCT YOU?
WHY?!
DOON!!
TO SURPASS YOU!!
!
HEH HEH...
...
HA HA HA HA HA!!
YOU WANT ME TO TEACH YOU THE SWORD SO THAT ONE DAY YOU CAN TAKE MY HEAD?
YOU'RE A STRANGE ONE! HA HA HA!
HA HA... YOU'RE STILL A SHAMELESS FOOL.
SO YOU VALUE SOMETHING MORE THAN YOUR OWN PRIDE.
!!

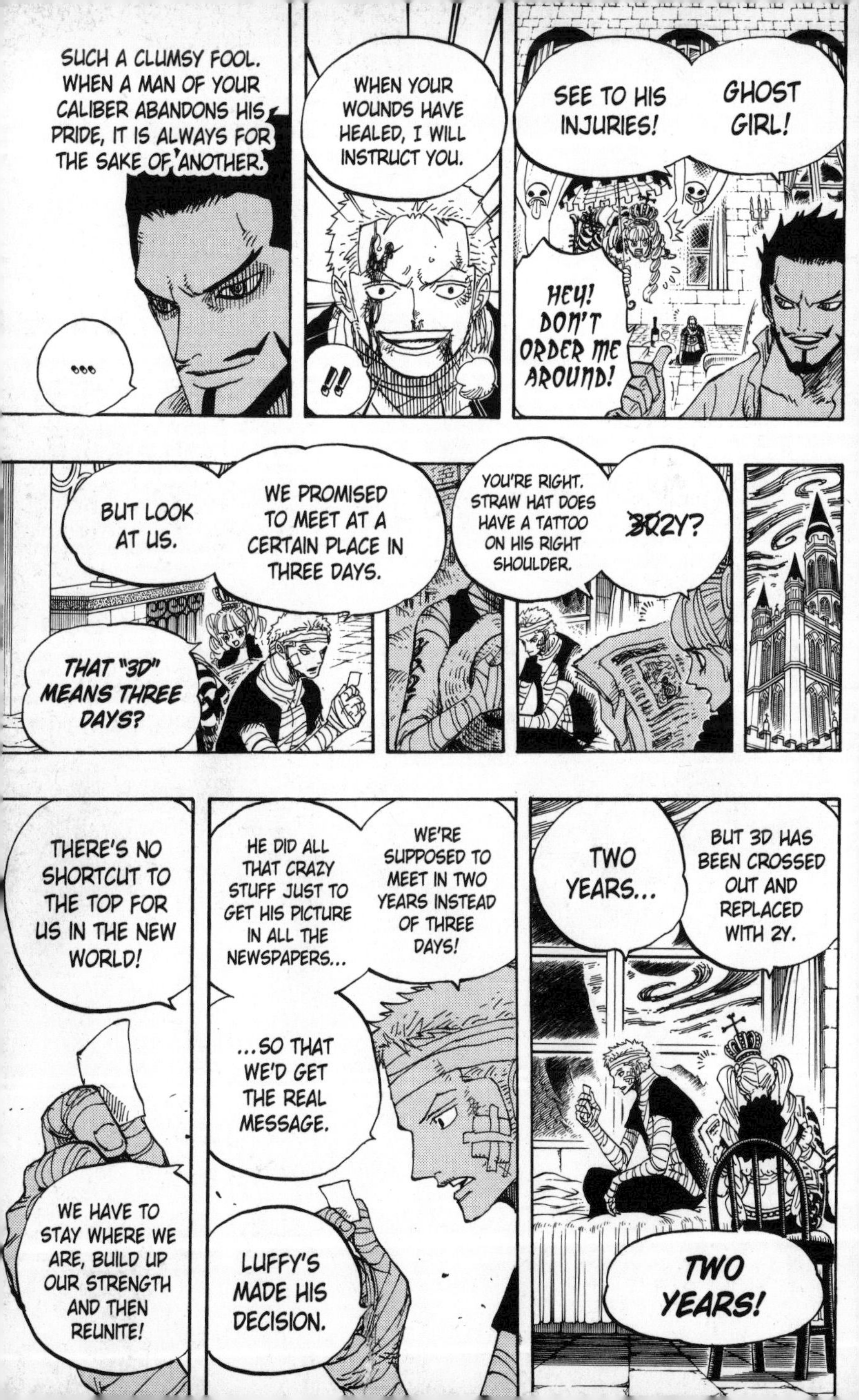
GHOST GIRL!
SEE TO HIS INJURIES!
HEY! DON'T ORDER ME AROUND!
WHEN YOUR WOUNDS HAVE HEALED, I WILL INSTRUCT YOU.
!!
SUCH A CLUMSY FOOL. WHEN A MAN OF YOUR CALIBER ABANDONS HIS PRIDE, IT IS ALWAYS FOR THE SAKE OF ANOTHER.
...
3D2Y?
YOU'RE RIGHT. STRAW HAT DOES HAVE A TATTOO ON HIS RIGHT SHOULDER.
WE PROMISED TO MEET AT A CERTAIN PLACE IN THREE DAYS.
BUT LOOK AT US.
THAT "3D" MEANS THREE DAYS?
BUT 3D HAS BEEN CROSSED OUT AND REPLACED WITH 2Y.
TWO YEARS...
TWO YEARS!
WE'RE SUPPOSED TO MEET IN TWO YEARS INSTEAD OF THREE DAYS!
HE DID ALL THAT CRAZY STUFF JUST TO GET HIS PICTURE IN ALL THE NEWSPAPERS...
...SO THAT WE'D GET THE REAL MESSAGE.
LUFFY'S MADE HIS DECISION.
THERE'S NO SHORTCUT TO THE TOP FOR US IN THE NEW WORLD!
WE HAVE TO STAY WHERE WE ARE, BUILD UP OUR STRENGTH AND THEN REUNITE!

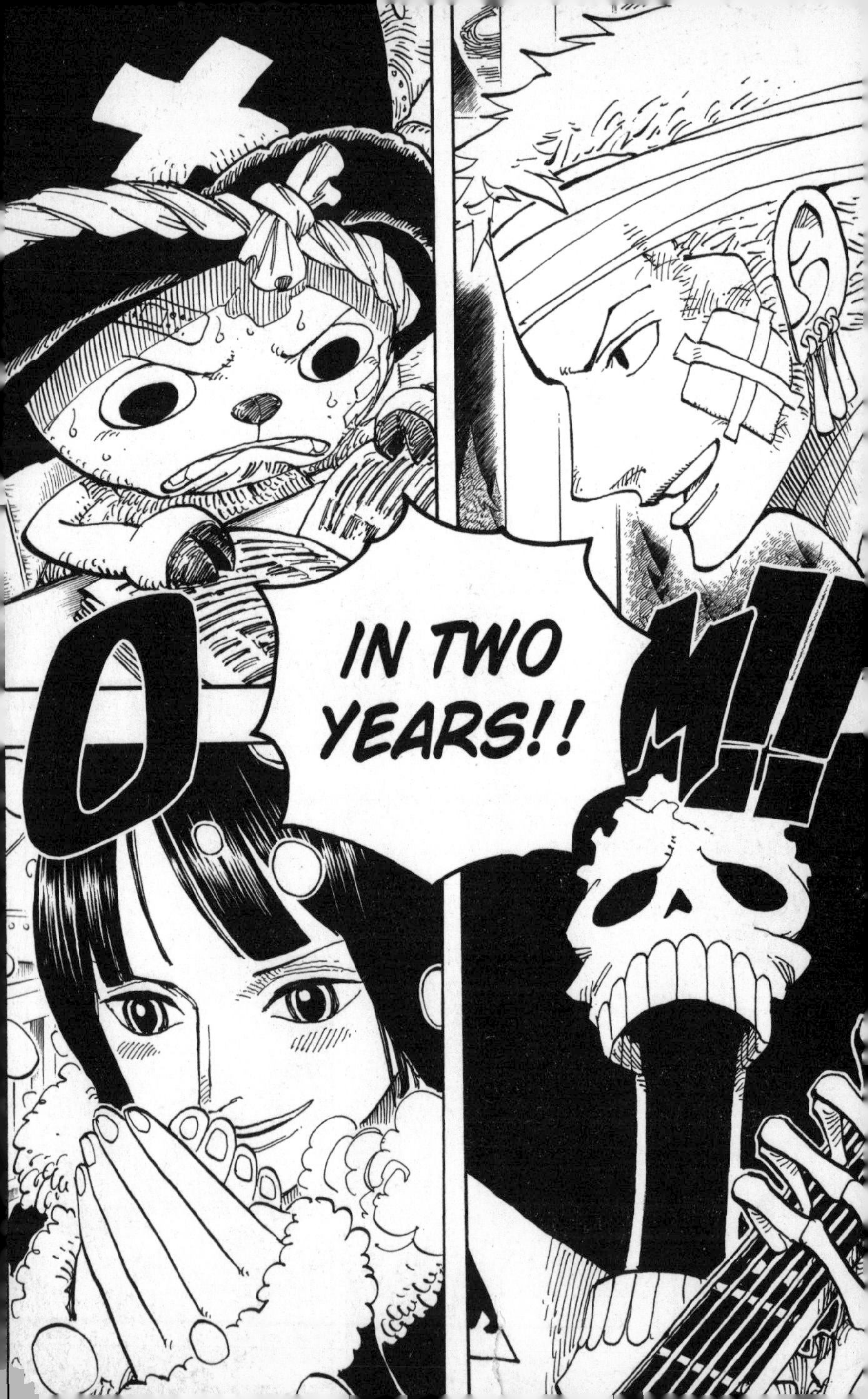
IN TWO YEARS!!

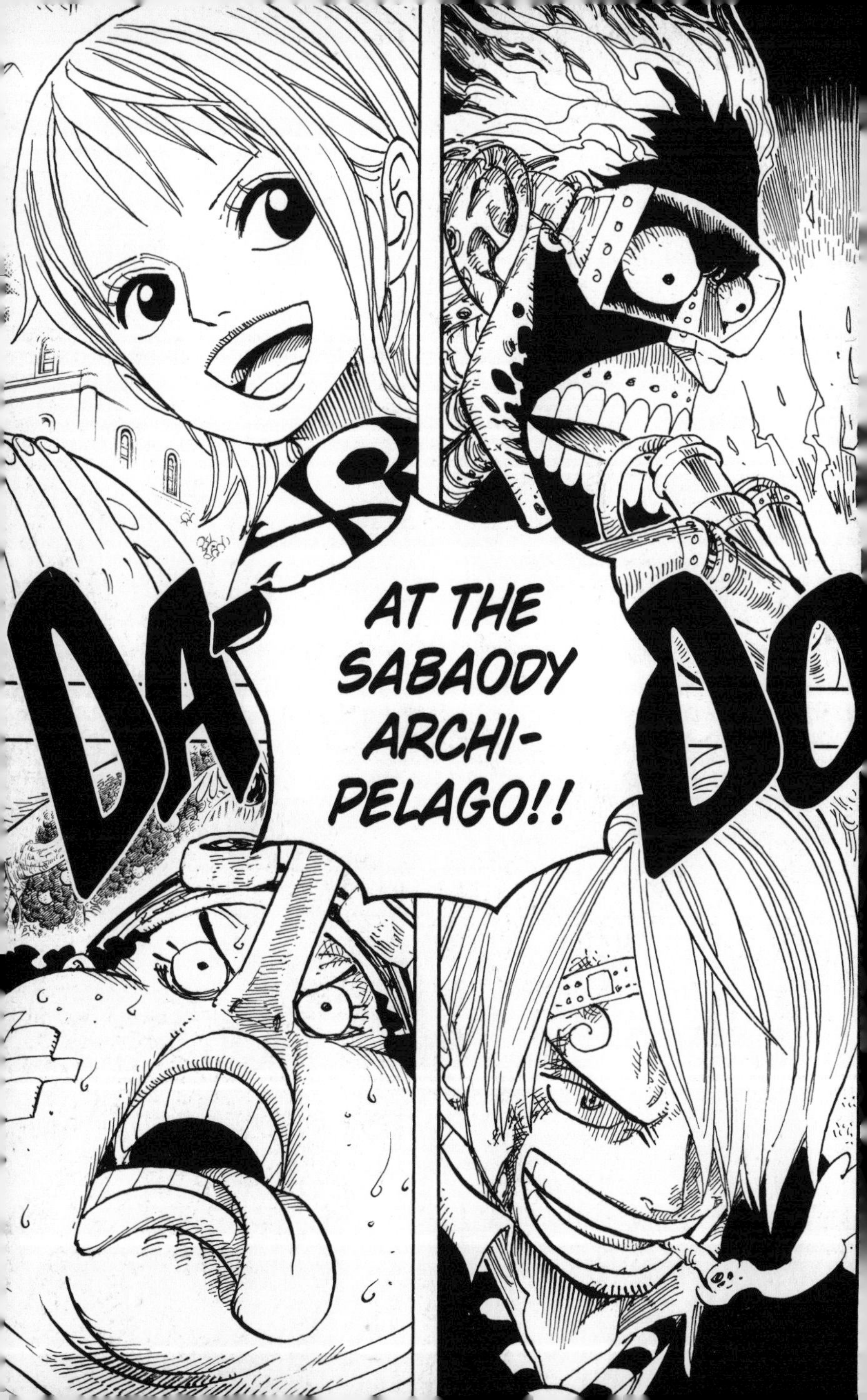

AT THE SABAODY ARCHI-PELAGO!!
DA-
DO

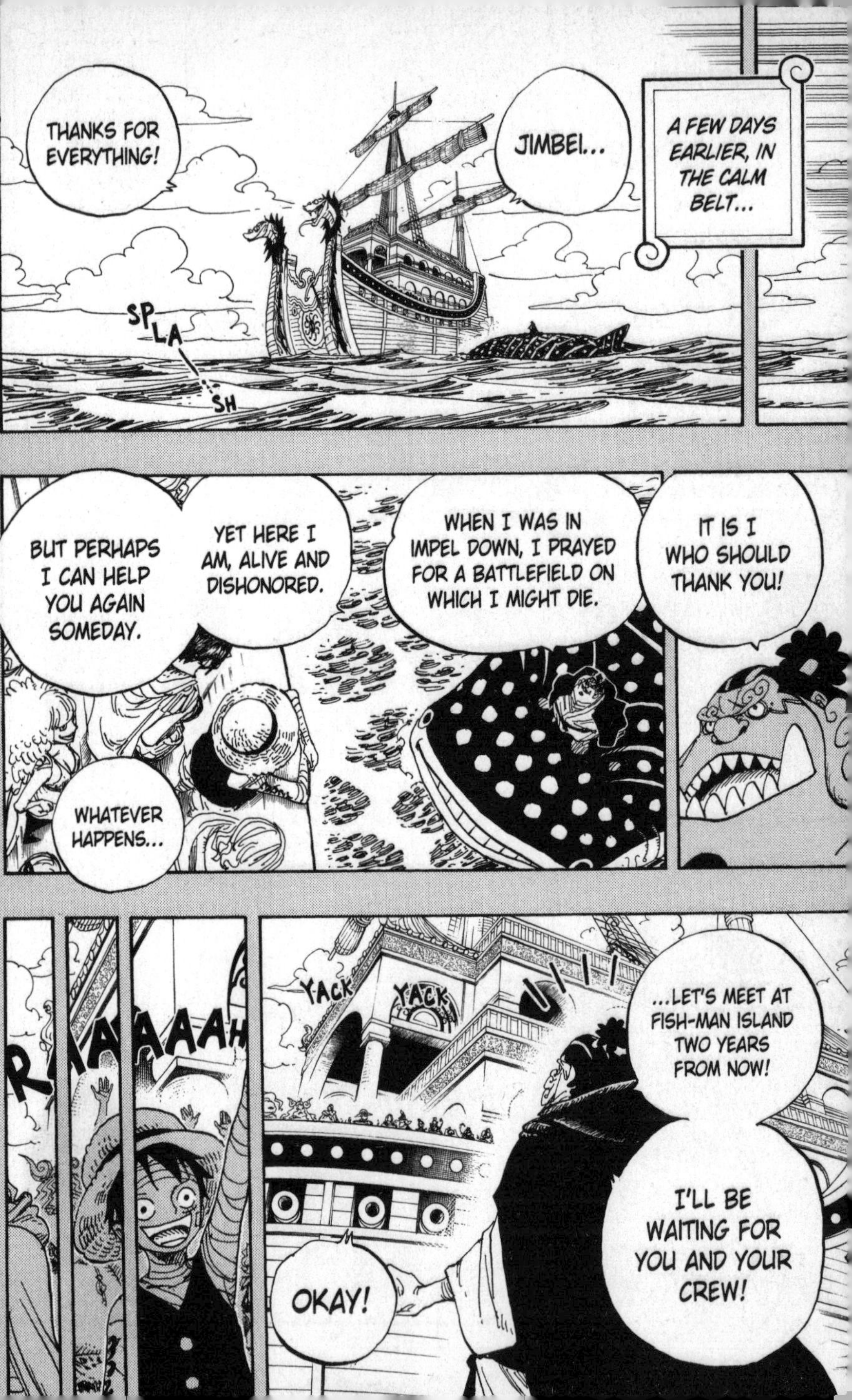
A FEW DAYS EARLIER, IN THE CALM BELT...
JIMBEI...
THANKS FOR EVERYTHING!
SPLA...SH
IT IS I WHO SHOULD THANK YOU!
WHEN I WAS IN IMPEL DOWN, I PRAYED FOR A BATTLEFIELD ON WHICH I MIGHT DIE.
YET HERE I AM, ALIVE AND DISHONORED.
BUT PERHAPS I CAN HELP YOU AGAIN SOMEDAY.
WHATEVER HAPPENS...
...LET'S MEET AT FISH-MAN ISLAND TWO YEARS FROM NOW!
I'LL BE WAITING FOR YOU AND YOUR CREW!
YACK
YACK
OKAY!
RAAAAAH

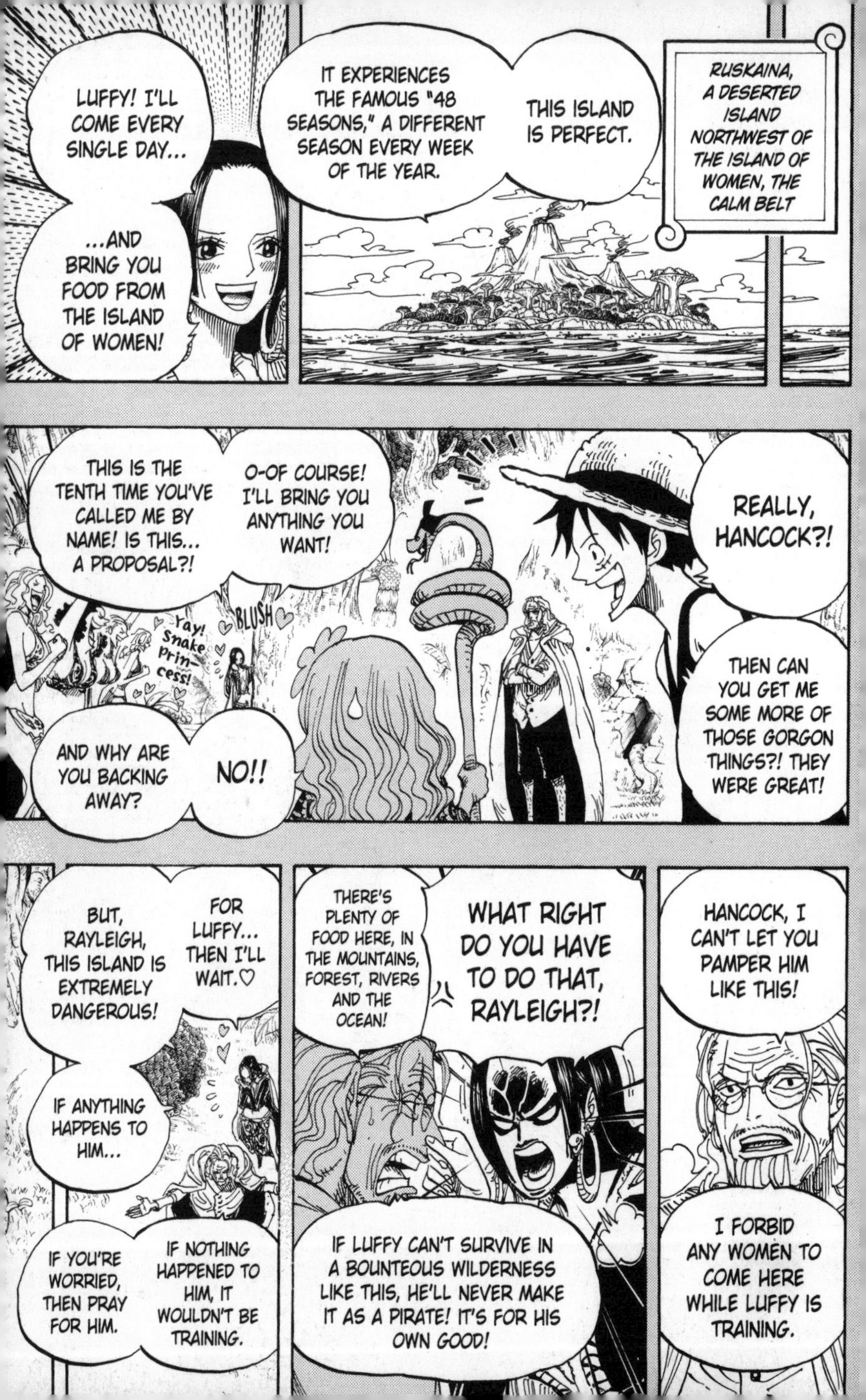
RUSKAINA, A DESERTED ISLAND NORTHWEST OF THE ISLAND OF WOMEN, THE CALM BELT
THIS ISLAND IS PERFECT.
IT EXPERIENCES THE FAMOUS "48 SEASONS," A DIFFERENT SEASON EVERY WEEK OF THE YEAR.
LUFFY! I'LL COME EVERY SINGLE DAY...
...AND BRING YOU FOOD FROM THE ISLAND OF WOMEN!
REALLY, HANCOCK?!
THEN CAN YOU GET ME SOME MORE OF THOSE GORGON THINGS?! THEY WERE GREAT!
O-OF COURSE! I'LL BRING YOU ANYTHING YOU WANT!
THIS IS THE TENTH TIME YOU'VE CALLED ME BY NAME! IS THIS... A PROPOSAL?!
BLUSH
Yay! Snake Princess!
NO!!
AND WHY ARE YOU BACKING AWAY?
HANCOCK, I CAN'T LET YOU PAMPER HIM LIKE THIS!
I FORBID ANY WOMEN TO COME HERE WHILE LUFFY IS TRAINING.
WHAT RIGHT DO YOU HAVE TO DO THAT, RAYLEIGH?!
THERE'S PLENTY OF FOOD HERE, IN THE MOUNTAINS, FOREST, RIVERS AND THE OCEAN!
IF LUFFY CAN'T SURVIVE IN A BOUNTEOUS WILDERNESS LIKE THIS, HE'LL NEVER MAKE IT AS A PIRATE! IT'S FOR HIS OWN GOOD!
FOR LUFFY... THEN I'LL WAIT.♡
BUT, RAYLEIGH, THIS ISLAND IS EXTREMELY DANGEROUS!
IF ANYTHING HAPPENS TO HIM...
IF NOTHING HAPPENED TO HIM, IT WOULDN'T BE TRAINING.
IF YOU'RE WORRIED, THEN PRAY FOR HIM.

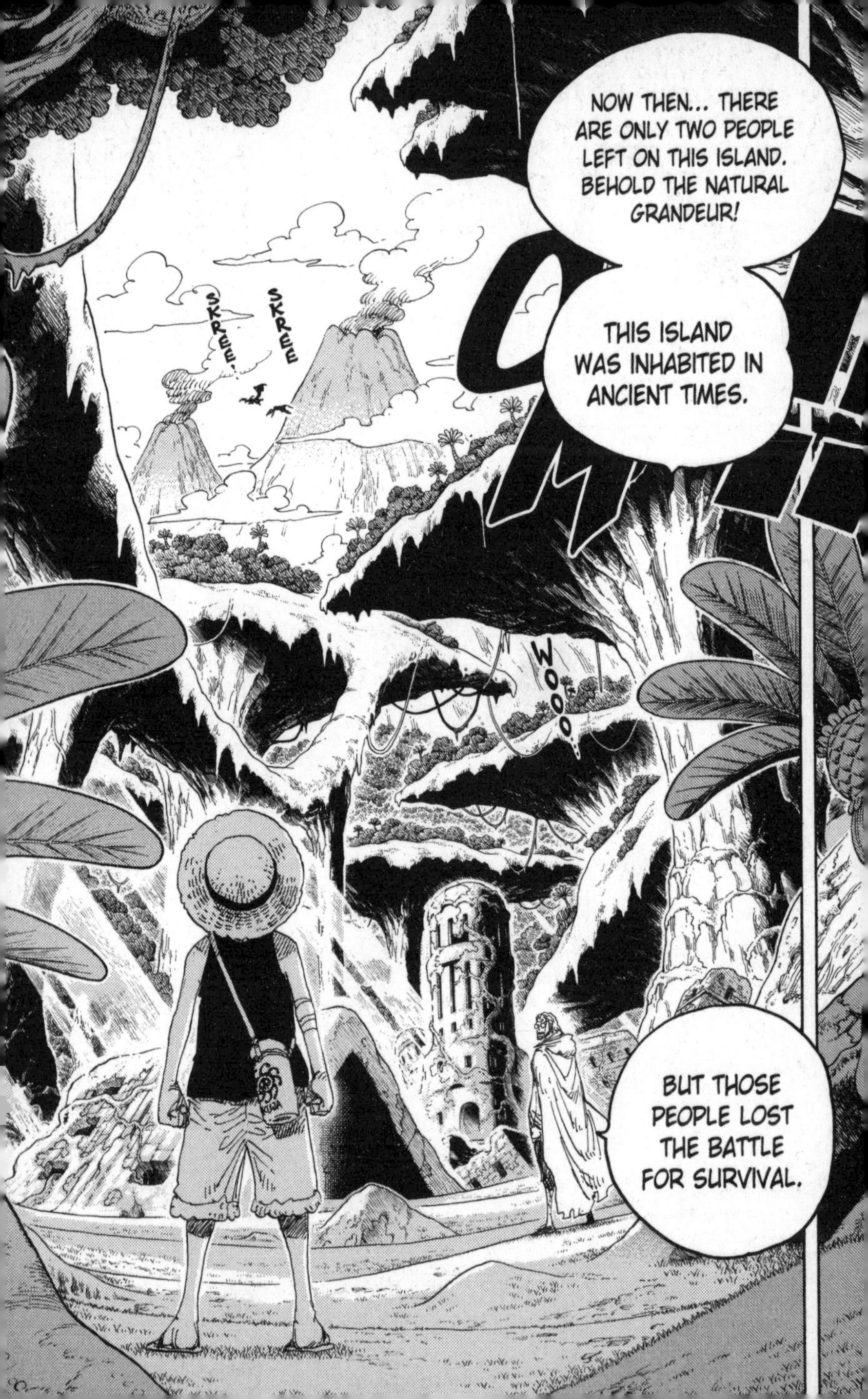
NOW THEN... THERE ARE ONLY TWO PEOPLE LEFT ON THIS ISLAND. BEHOLD THE NATURAL GRANDEUR!
THIS ISLAND WAS INHABITED IN ANCIENT TIMES.
SKREE
SKREE!
WOOO...
BUT THOSE PEOPLE LOST THE BATTLE FOR SURVIVAL.

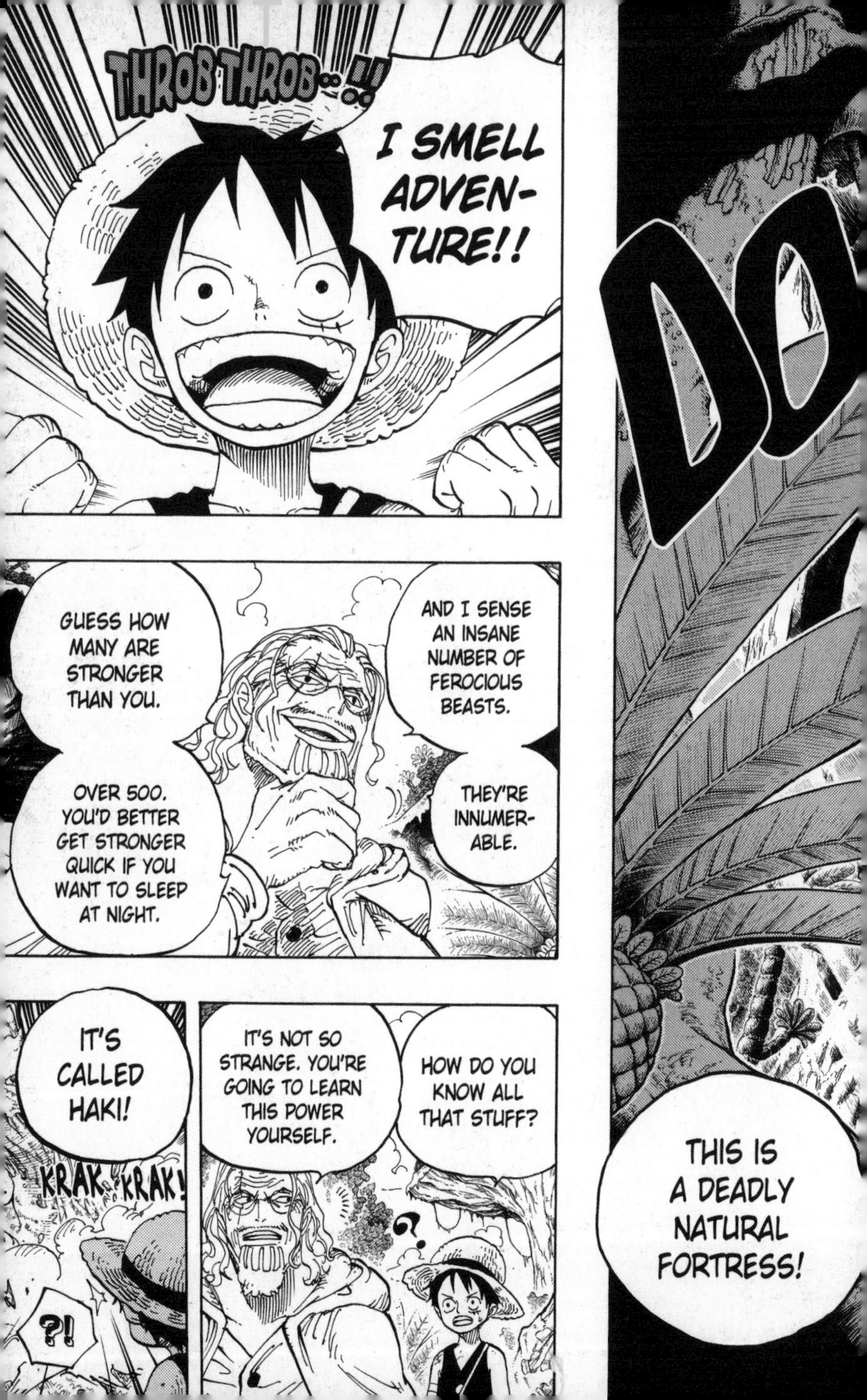

DO
THIS IS A DEADLY NATURAL FORTRESS!
THROB THROB..!!
I SMELL ADVENTURE!!
AND I SENSE AN INSANE NUMBER OF FEROCIOUS BEASTS.
THEY'RE INNUMERABLE.
GUESS HOW MANY ARE STRONGER THAN YOU.
OVER 500. YOU'D BETTER GET STRONGER QUICK IF YOU WANT TO SLEEP AT NIGHT.
HOW DO YOU KNOW ALL THAT STUFF?
IT'S NOT SO STRANGE. YOU'RE GOING TO LEARN THIS POWER YOURSELF.
?
IT'S CALLED HAKI!
KRAK! KRAK!
?!

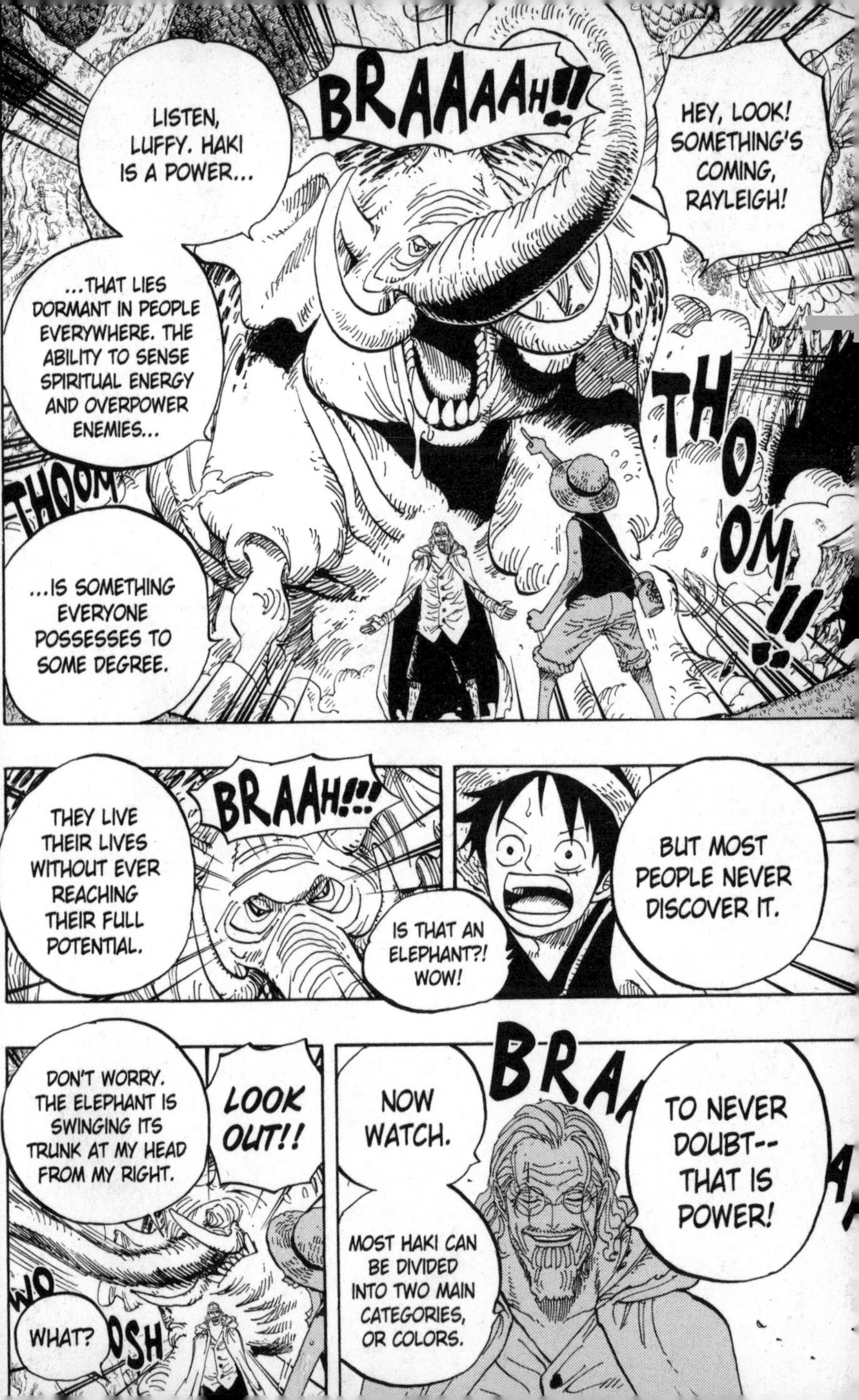
HEY, LOOK! SOMETHING'S COMING, RAYLEIGH!
BRAAAAAH!!
LISTEN, LUFFY. HAKI IS A POWER...
THOOOM!!
...THAT LIES DORMANT IN PEOPLE EVERYWHERE. THE ABILITY TO SENSE SPIRITUAL ENERGY AND OVERPOWER ENEMIES...
THOOM
...IS SOMETHING EVERYONE POSSESSES TO SOME DEGREE.
BUT MOST PEOPLE NEVER DISCOVER IT.
IS THAT AN ELEPHANT?! WOW!
BRAAH!!!
THEY LIVE THEIR LIVES WITHOUT EVER REACHING THEIR FULL POTENTIAL.
TO NEVER DOUBT-- THAT IS POWER!
BRAA
NOW WATCH.
MOST HAKI CAN BE DIVIDED INTO TWO MAIN CATEGORIES, OR COLORS.
LOOK OUT!!
DON'T WORRY. THE ELEPHANT IS SWINGING ITS TRUNK AT MY HEAD FROM MY RIGHT.
WO
WHAT?
OSH

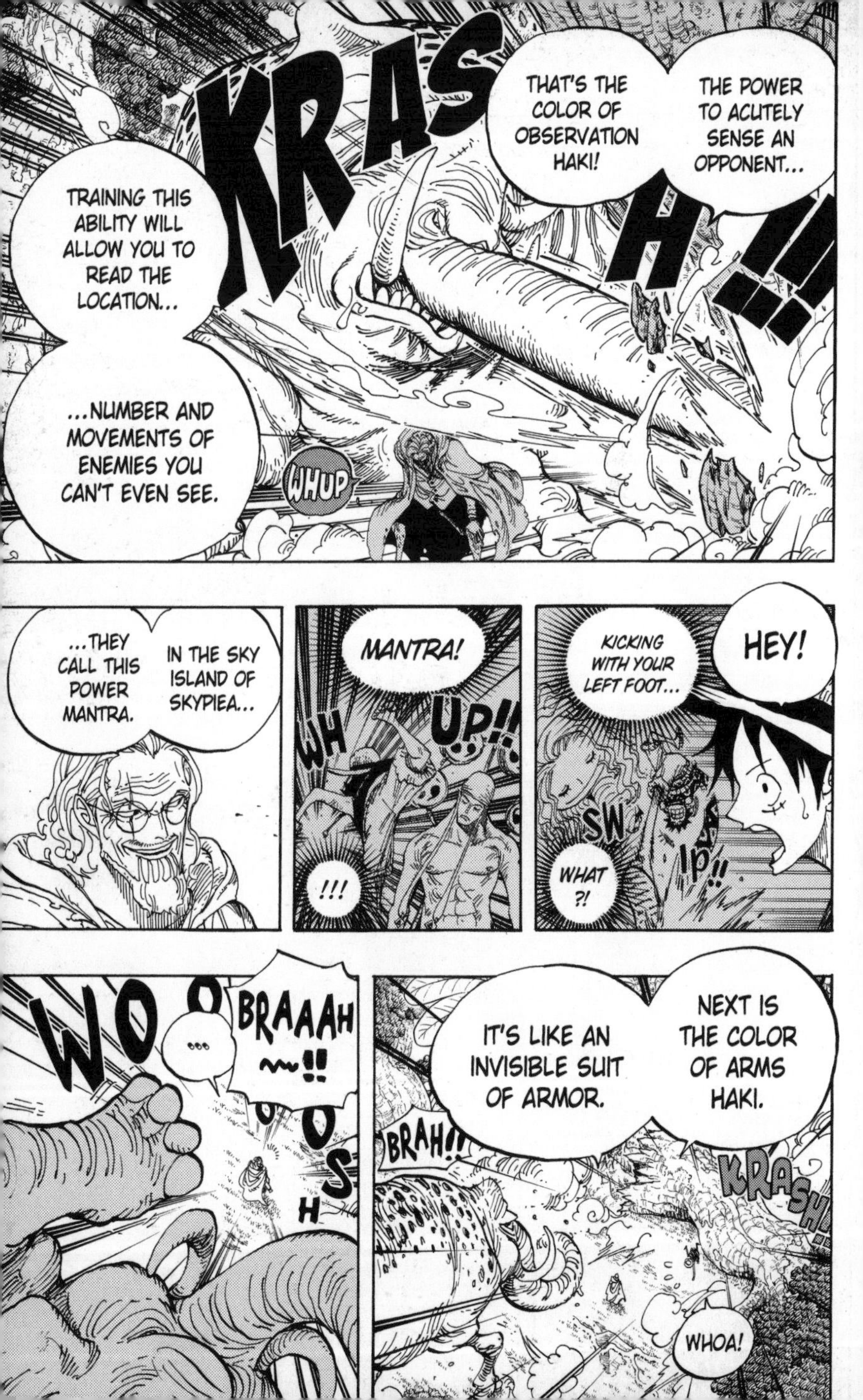
THE POWER TO ACUTELY SENSE AN OPPONENT...
THAT'S THE COLOR OF OBSERVATION HAKI!
KRASH!!!
TRAINING THIS ABILITY WILL ALLOW YOU TO READ THE LOCATION...
...NUMBER AND MOVEMENTS OF ENEMIES YOU CAN'T EVEN SEE.
WHUP
HEY!
KICKING WITH YOUR LEFT FOOT...
SWIP!!
WHAT?!
MANTRA!
WHUP!!
!!!
IN THE SKY ISLAND OF SKYPIEA...
...THEY CALL THIS POWER MANTRA.
NEXT IS THE COLOR OF ARMS HAKI.
IT'S LIKE AN INVISIBLE SUIT OF ARMOR.
KRASH!!
BRAH!!
WHOA!
BRAAAH~!!
...
WOOOSH

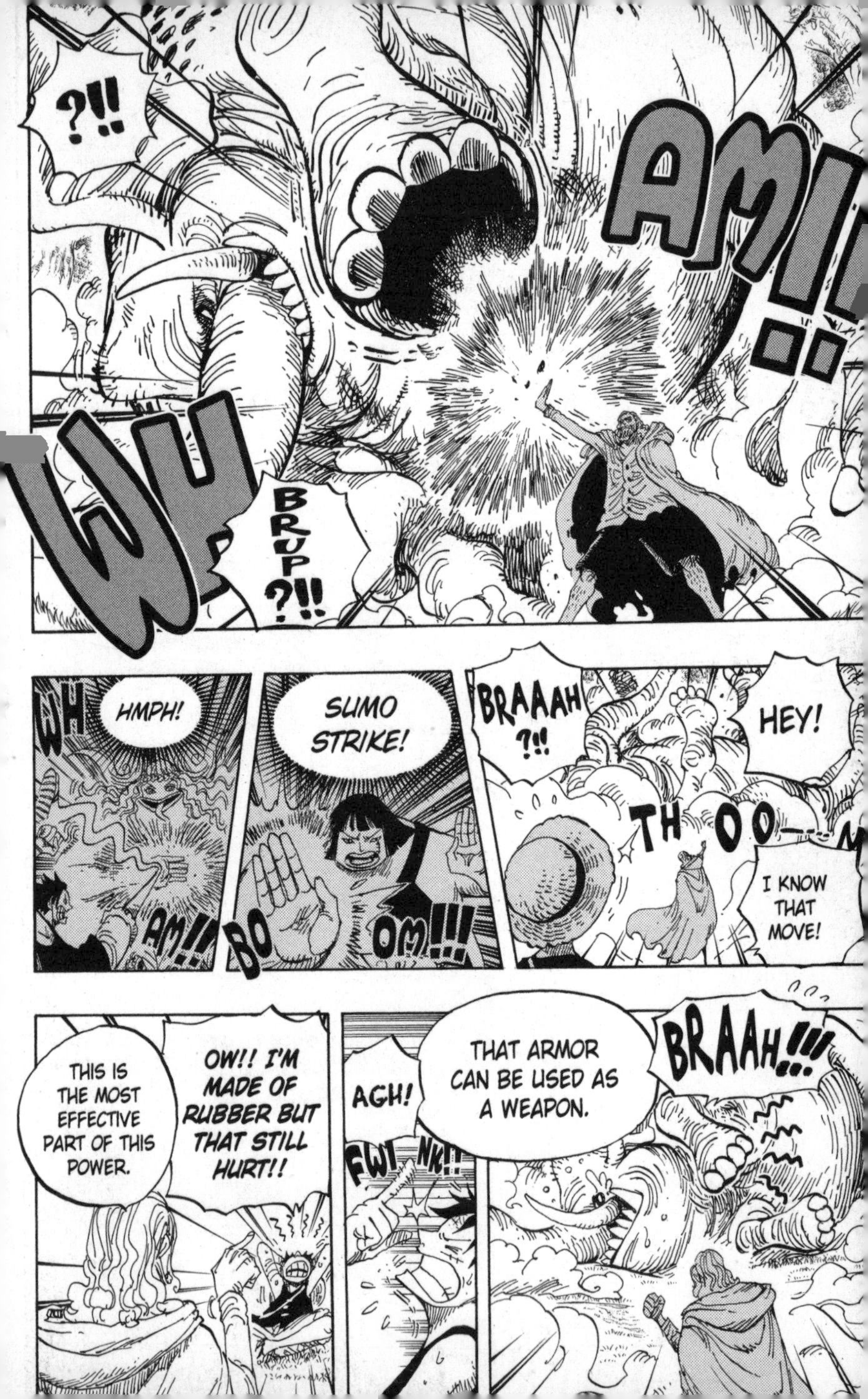
AM!!
?!!
BRUP ?!!
WH
BRAAAH ?!!
HEY!
TH OO—M
I KNOW THAT MOVE!
SUMO STRIKE!
BO OM!!!
HMPH!
WH AM!!
BRAAH!!!
THAT ARMOR CAN BE USED AS A WEAPON.
AGH!
FWI NK!!
OW!! I'M MADE OF RUBBER BUT THAT STILL HURT!!
THIS IS THE MOST EFFECTIVE PART OF THIS POWER.

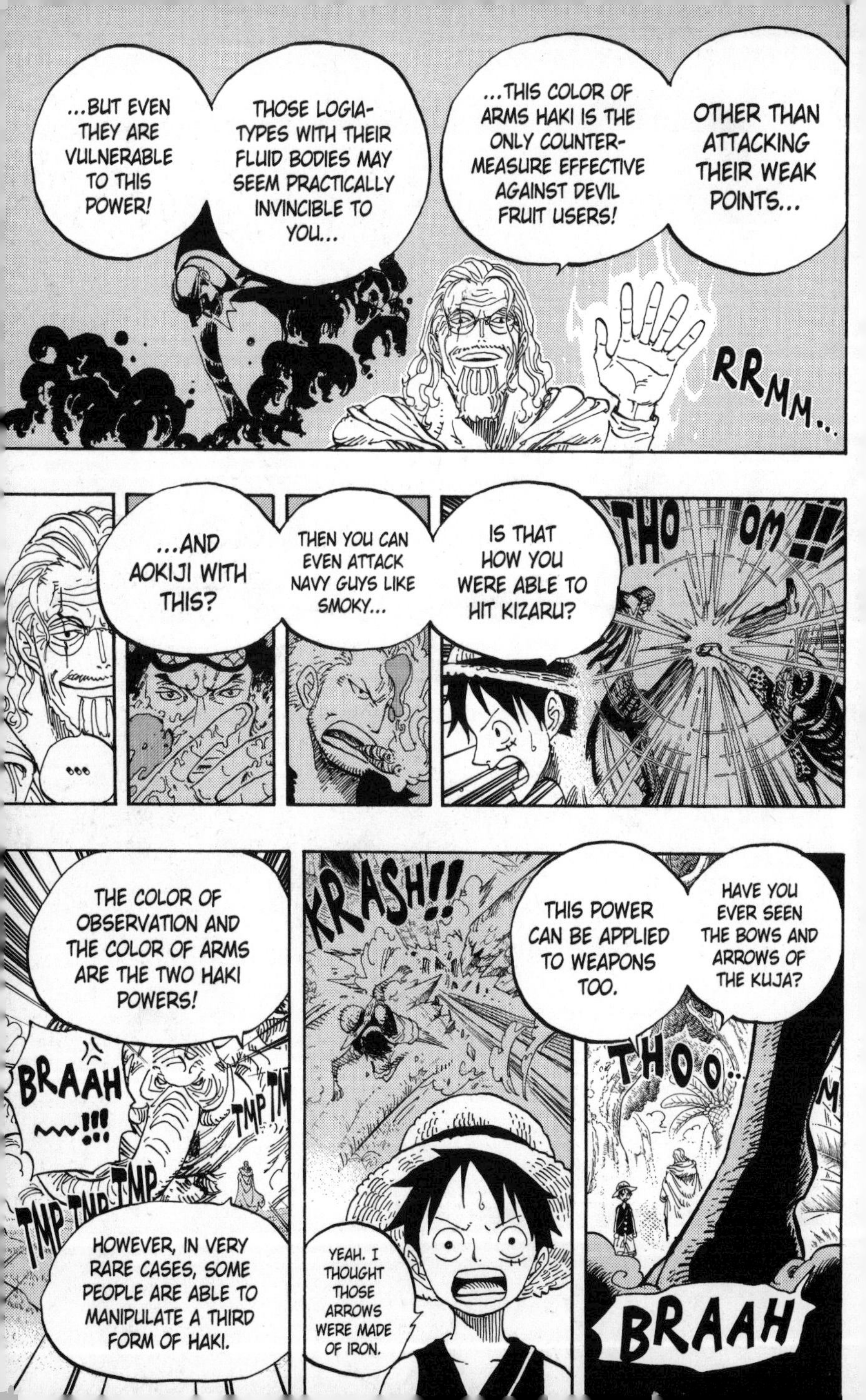

OTHER THAN ATTACKING THEIR WEAK POINTS...
...THIS COLOR OF ARMS HAKI IS THE ONLY COUNTER-MEASURE EFFECTIVE AGAINST DEVIL FRUIT USERS!
THOSE LOGIA-TYPES WITH THEIR FLUID BODIES MAY SEEM PRACTICALLY INVINCIBLE TO YOU...
...BUT EVEN THEY ARE VULNERABLE TO THIS POWER!
RRMM...
THO OM!!
IS THAT HOW YOU WERE ABLE TO HIT KIZARU?
THEN YOU CAN EVEN ATTACK NAVY GUYS LIKE SMOKY...
...AND AOKIJI WITH THIS?
...
HAVE YOU EVER SEEN THE BOWS AND ARROWS OF THE KUJA?
THIS POWER CAN BE APPLIED TO WEAPONS TOO.
THOO...
BRAAH
KRASH!!
YEAH. I THOUGHT THOSE ARROWS WERE MADE OF IRON.
THE COLOR OF OBSERVATION AND THE COLOR OF ARMS ARE THE TWO HAKI POWERS!
BRAAH~~!!!
TMP
TMP TMP TMP
HOWEVER, IN VERY RARE CASES, SOME PEOPLE ARE ABLE TO MANIPULATE A THIRD FORM OF HAKI.

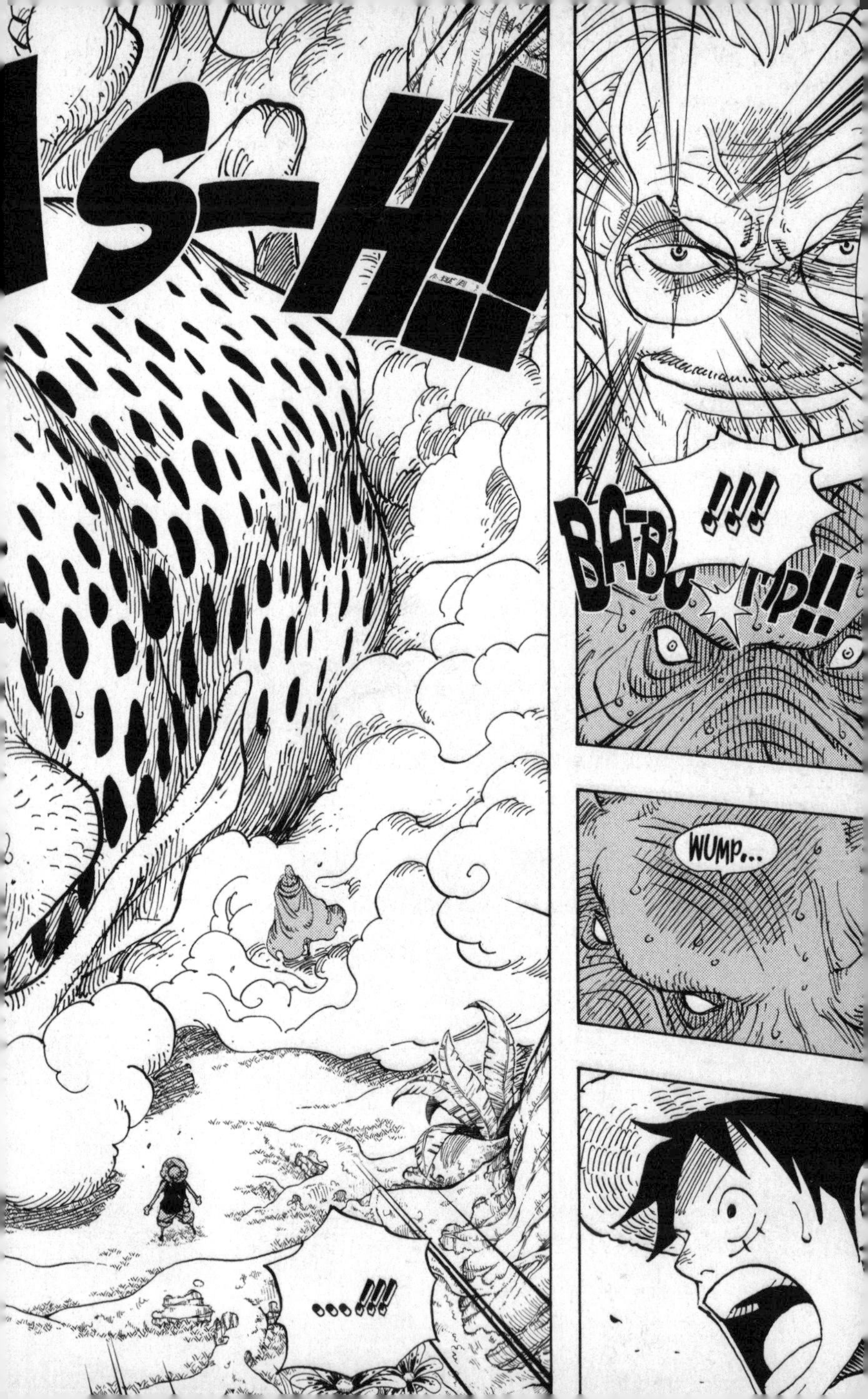
!!!
BA-BUMP!!
WUMP...
S-H!!
...!!!

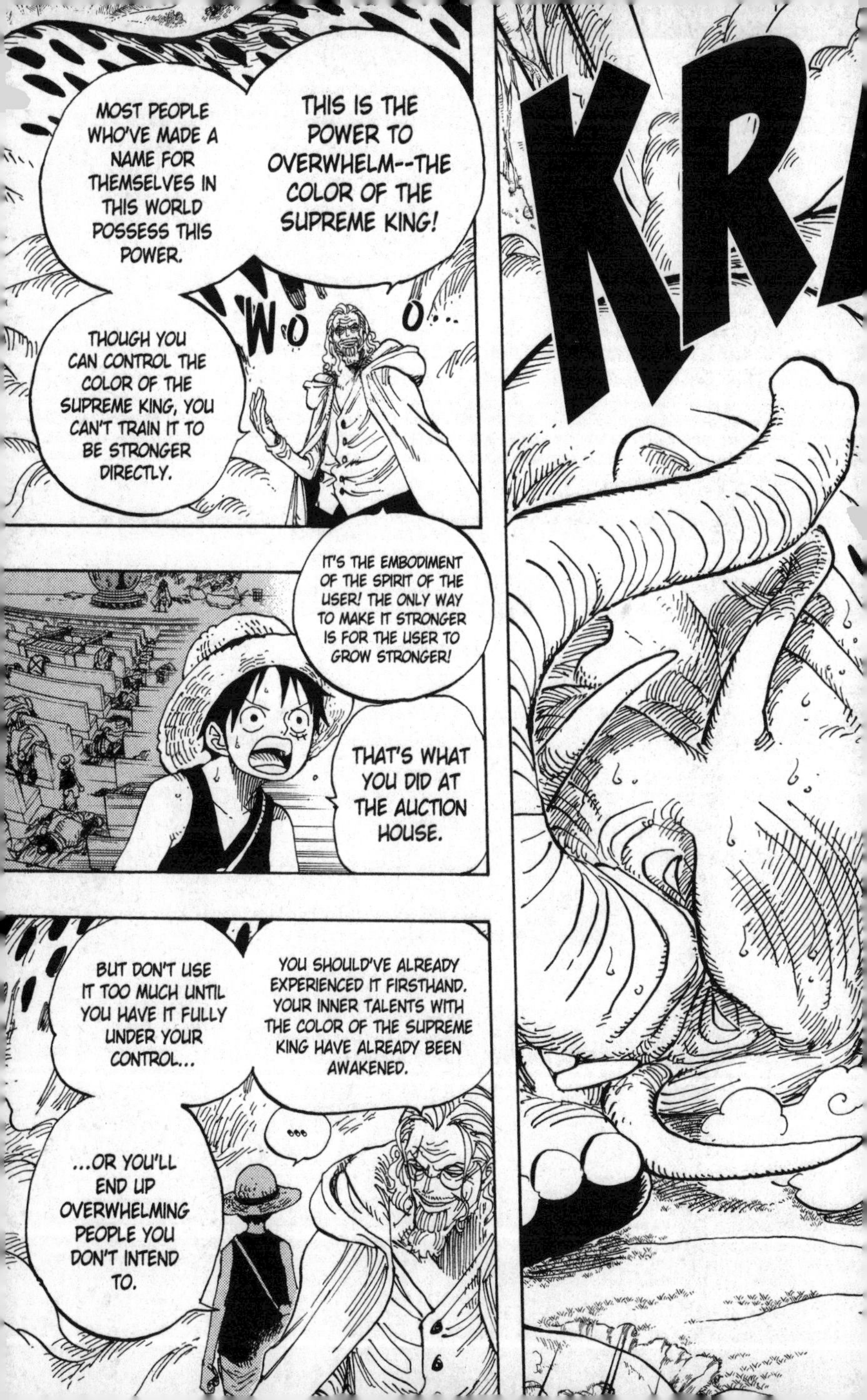
KR
THIS IS THE POWER TO OVERWHELM--THE COLOR OF THE SUPREME KING!
MOST PEOPLE WHO'VE MADE A NAME FOR THEMSELVES IN THIS WORLD POSSESS THIS POWER.
WOO...
THOUGH YOU CAN CONTROL THE COLOR OF THE SUPREME KING, YOU CAN'T TRAIN IT TO BE STRONGER DIRECTLY.
IT'S THE EMBODIMENT OF THE SPIRIT OF THE USER! THE ONLY WAY TO MAKE IT STRONGER IS FOR THE USER TO GROW STRONGER!
THAT'S WHAT YOU DID AT THE AUCTION HOUSE.
YOU SHOULD'VE ALREADY EXPERIENCED IT FIRSTHAND. YOUR INNER TALENTS WITH THE COLOR OF THE SUPREME KING HAVE ALREADY BEEN AWAKENED.
BUT DON'T USE IT TOO MUCH UNTIL YOU HAVE IT FULLY UNDER YOUR CONTROL...
...
...OR YOU'LL END UP OVERWHELMING PEOPLE YOU DON'T INTEND TO.

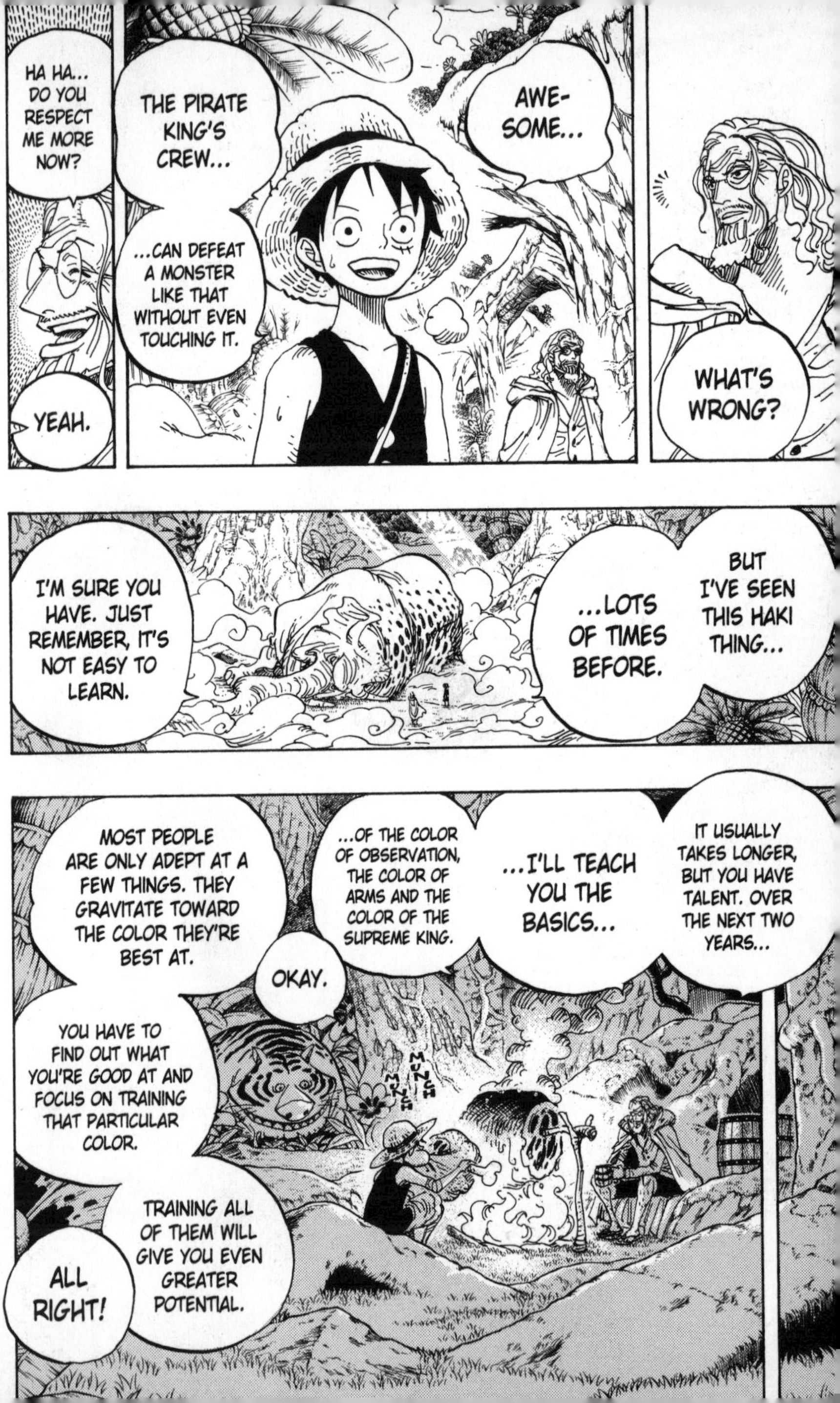
WHAT'S WRONG?
AWE-SOME...
THE PIRATE KING'S CREW...
...CAN DEFEAT A MONSTER LIKE THAT WITHOUT EVEN TOUCHING IT.
HA HA... DO YOU RESPECT ME MORE NOW?
YEAH.
BUT I'VE SEEN THIS HAKI THING...
...LOTS OF TIMES BEFORE.
I'M SURE YOU HAVE. JUST REMEMBER, IT'S NOT EASY TO LEARN.
IT USUALLY TAKES LONGER, BUT YOU HAVE TALENT. OVER THE NEXT TWO YEARS...
...I'LL TEACH YOU THE BASICS...
...OF THE COLOR OF OBSERVATION, THE COLOR OF ARMS AND THE COLOR OF THE SUPREME KING.
MOST PEOPLE ARE ONLY ADEPT AT A FEW THINGS. THEY GRAVITATE TOWARD THE COLOR THEY'RE BEST AT.
OKAY.
MUNCH
MUNCH
YOU HAVE TO FIND OUT WHAT YOU'RE GOOD AT AND FOCUS ON TRAINING THAT PARTICULAR COLOR.
TRAINING ALL OF THEM WILL GIVE YOU EVEN GREATER POTENTIAL.
ALL RIGHT!

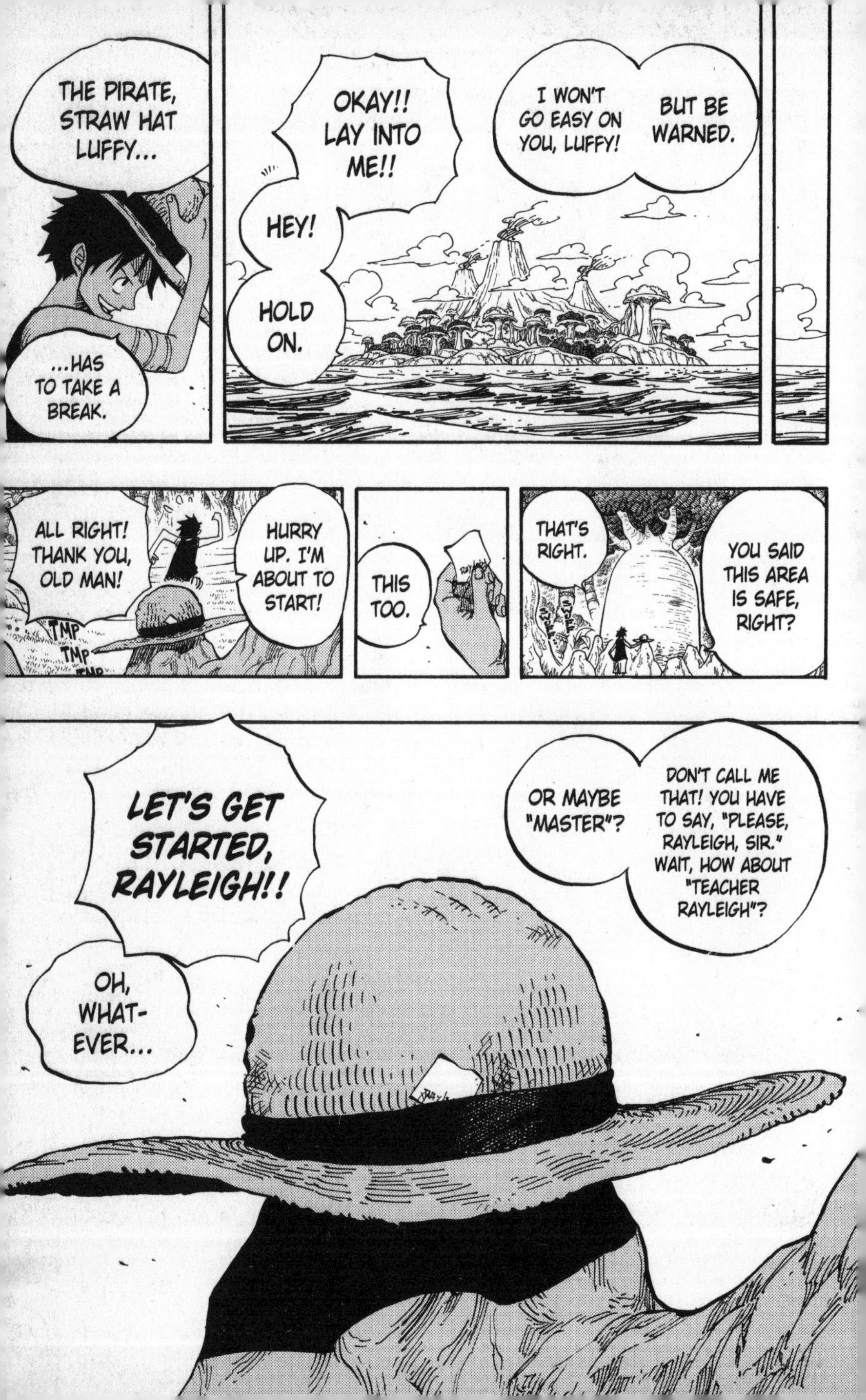
BUT BE WARNED.
I WON'T GO EASY ON YOU, LUFFY!
OKAY!! LAY INTO ME!!
HEY!
HOLD ON.
THE PIRATE, STRAW HAT LUFFY...
...HAS TO TAKE A BREAK.
YOU SAID THIS AREA IS SAFE, RIGHT?
THAT'S RIGHT.
THIS TOO.
HURRY UP. I'M ABOUT TO START!
ALL RIGHT! THANK YOU, OLD MAN!
TMP
TMP
DON'T CALL ME THAT! YOU HAVE TO SAY, "PLEASE, RAYLEIGH, SIR." WAIT, HOW ABOUT "TEACHER RAYLEIGH"?
OR MAYBE "MASTER"?
LET'S GET STARTED, RAYLEIGH!!
OH, WHAT-EVER...

HDYD! How do you do?! Section!!

◉ Now then, has everyone read the first three chapters?
"Look at that! What's going to happen next?"
I can hear everyone saying that!
Let's listen for... ...? ...?
(I actually don't hear it at all. ↘)

◉ As you all know, One Piece is serialized weekly in a
magazine called Jump. I've continued this series for 14
years and now there's been a major development.
Yeah.
So this was my opportunity to ask the editor-in-
chief: "I want to take a break. I want to play... I mean, I
want some time to think of the new story arc,
Editor-in-Chief. Can I have three weeks off?"
After asking that, he said: "All right. If you do extra
color pages on the week you come back, I'll give you a
month."
I responded with: "Really?! That's so generous of you!"
So under the condition that I work, I got a full
month! My readers in Jump had to wait one month
because of this break. I can't express enough grati-
tude to you. I'm so sorry. I really am. Thank you for
your letters.
"Please take care of yourself and enjoy your break."
You're too kind.
"Did you really have a fight with the editing depart-
ment?" Hey, no!
"Are you sick?" Of course not...

It seems like I caused a lot of people to worry, but I'm fine.

I was **actually having fun in Hawaii!**

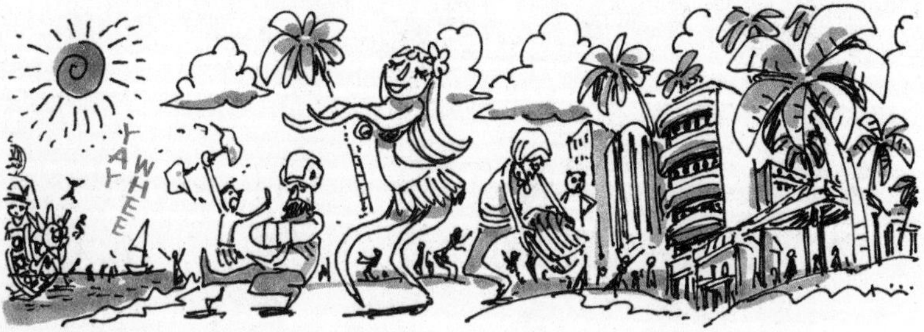
YAY
WHEE

- Well anyway, people heard many rumors, but I thank you all for your concern. I was

ENJOYING MY VACATION!

You got that?
I do what I love for my job, so I never mind being really busy, but I know how much it hurts my family. I'm just glad I was able to spend some time with my family. I have so many people to thank for this.

- Setting aside my private reasons, the One Piece story was able to reach a landmark. But the author hasn't changed and neither will the manga. There are still lots of islands I want to draw. I want to see how Luffy and his crew will continue to grow and mature, meet new people, and continue their adventures. I hope you will enjoy the new arc, New World!

2011 Eiichiro Oda.

How will the crew look in two years?! How will they meet each other again?!

3D2Y SECTION!!

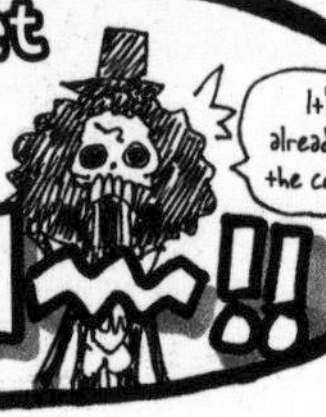
It's already on the cover!

Part 1

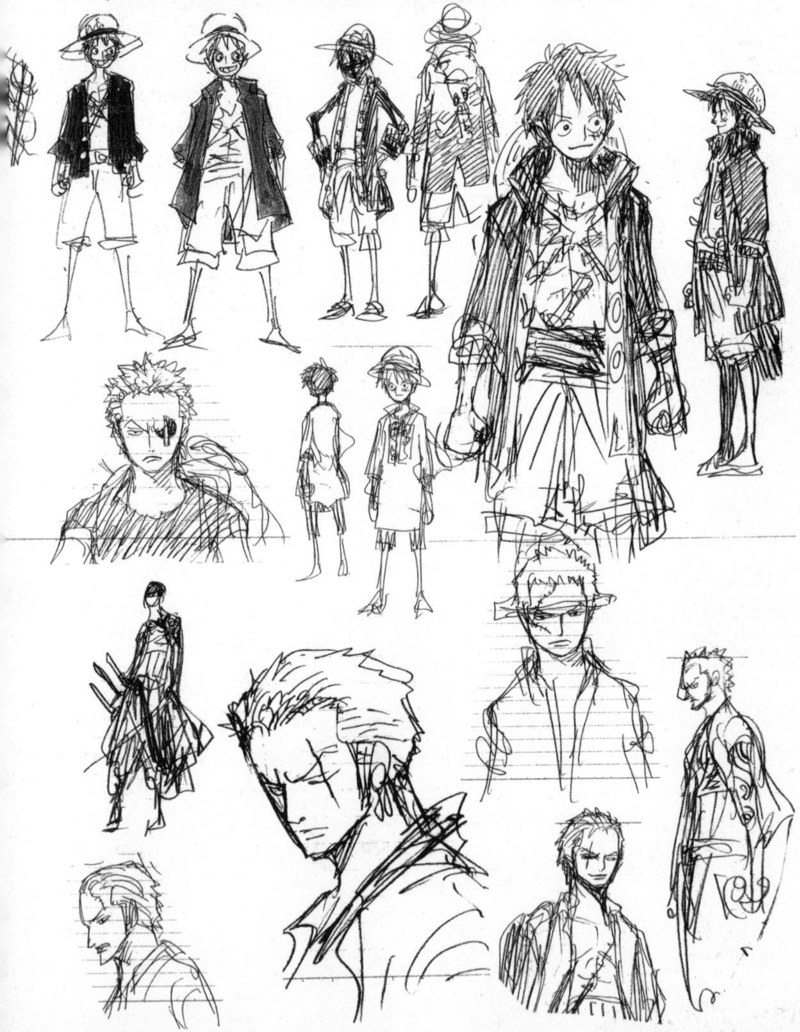

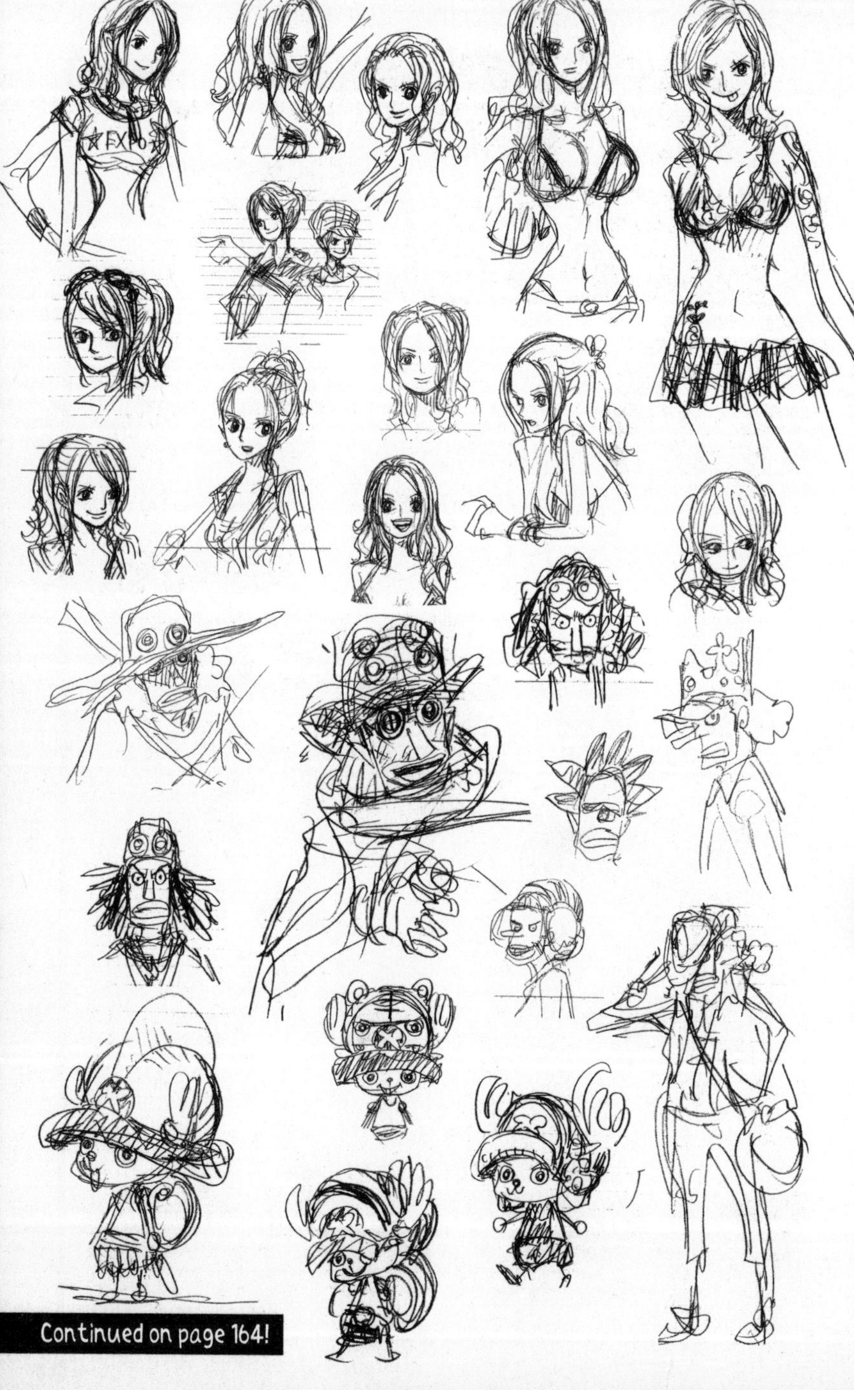

Continued on page 164!

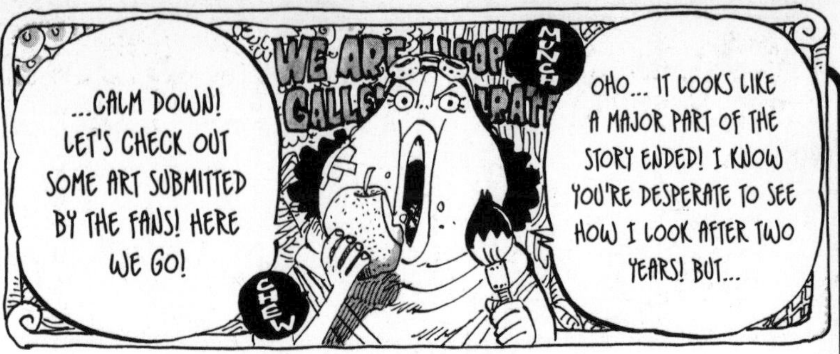

OHO... IT LOOKS LIKE A MAJOR PART OF THE STORY ENDED! I KNOW YOU'RE DESPERATE TO SEE HOW I LOOK AFTER TWO YEARS! BUT...
MUNCH
...CALM DOWN! LET'S CHECK OUT SOME ART SUBMITTED BY THE FANS! HERE WE GO!
CHEW

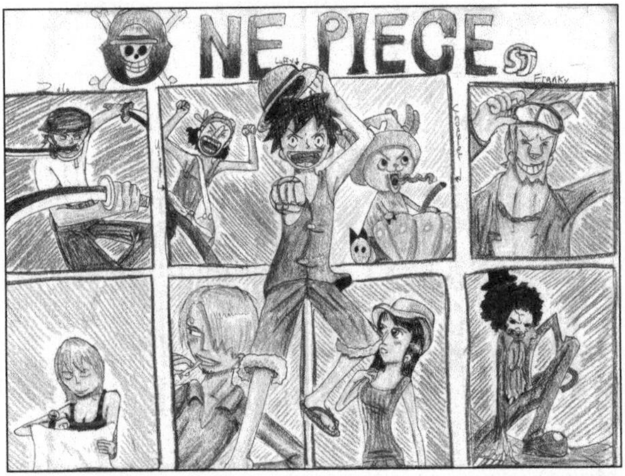

ONE PIECE

(Olivia D.)

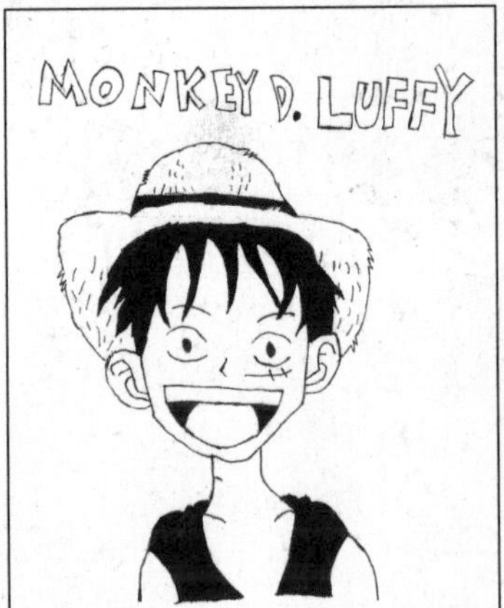

MONKEY D. LUFFY

(John B.)

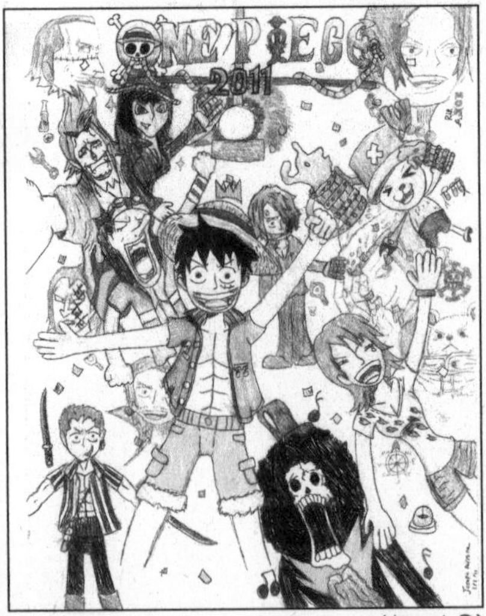

ONE PIECE
2011

(Joseph P.)

ONE PIECE

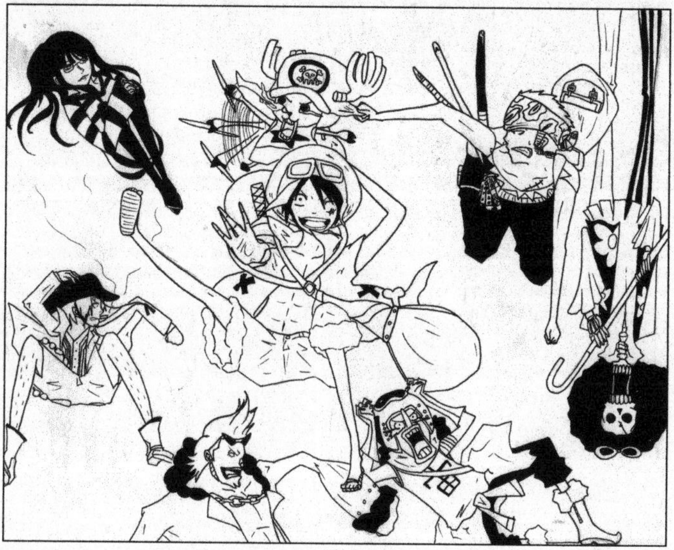

(Erika D.)

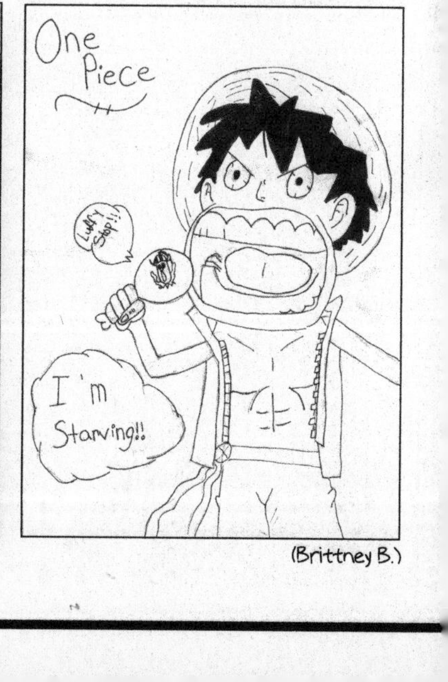
One Piece
Luffy Stop!!
I'm Starving!!

(Brittney B.)

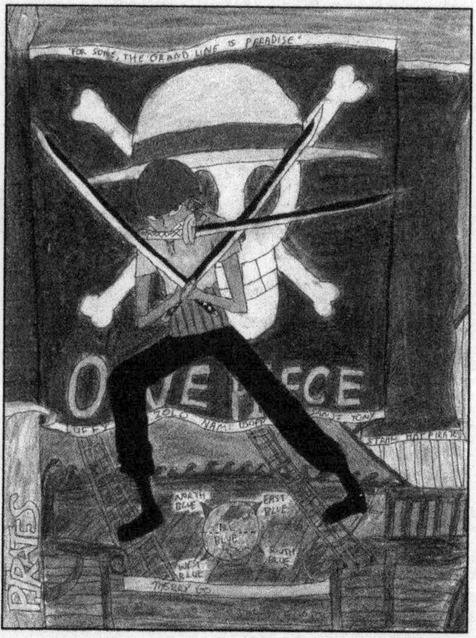
"FOR SOME, THE GRAND LINE IS PARADISE"

(Ami L.)

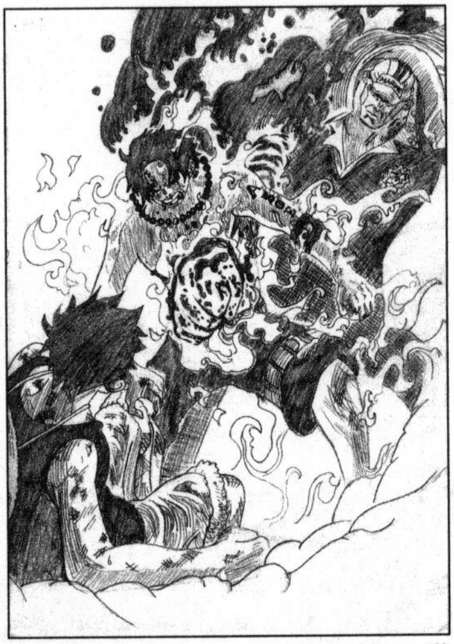

(Jose C.)

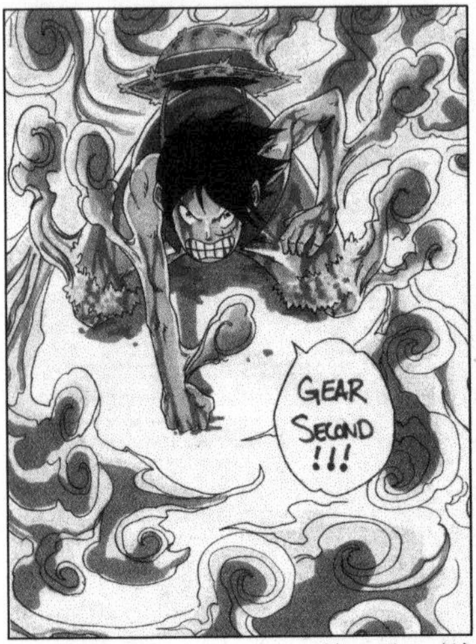
GEAR SECOND !!!

(Jonathan M.)

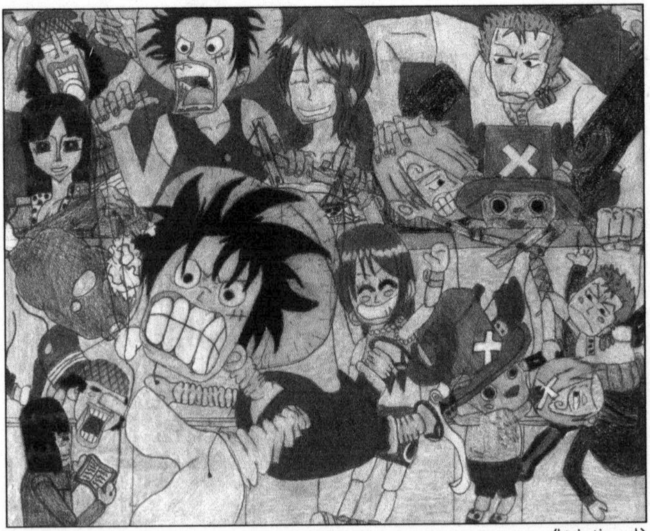

(Kristina J.)

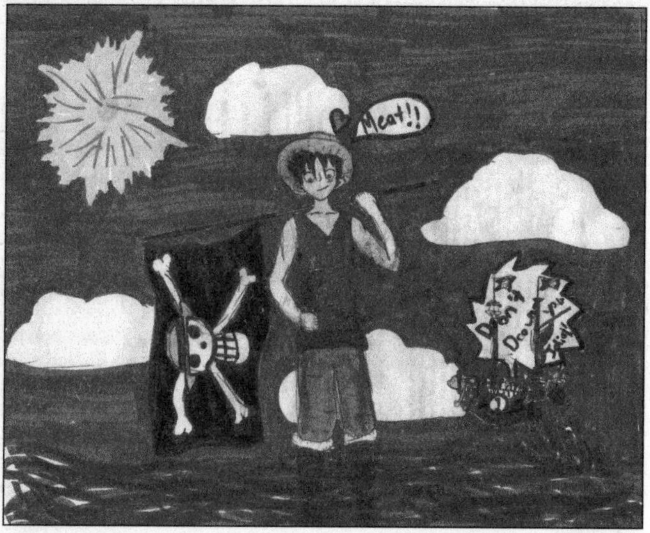
Meat!!

(Kavell M.)

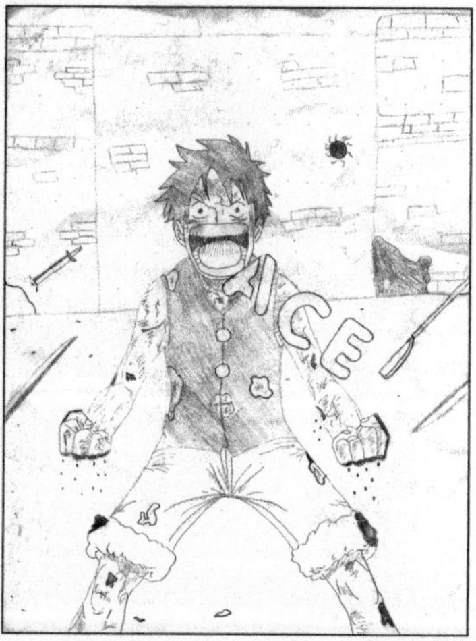

(Brian C.)

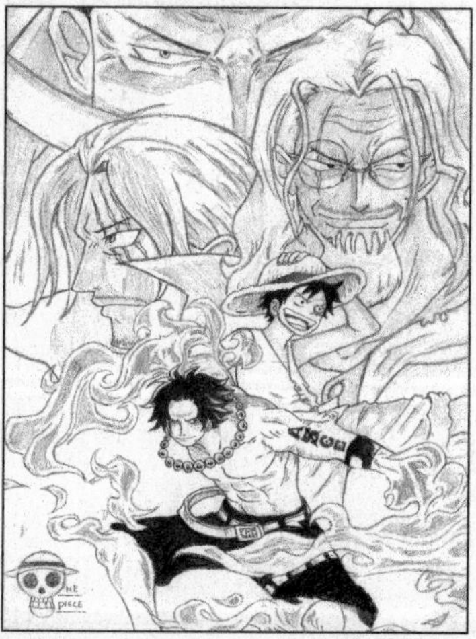

(Wenu M.)

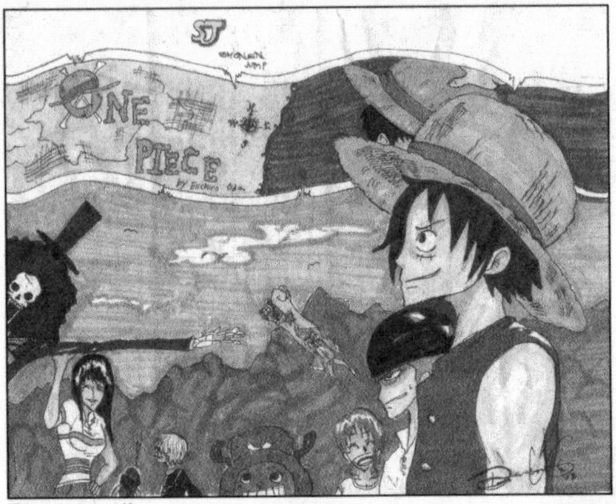
SJ
ONE PIECE
(Patrique V.)

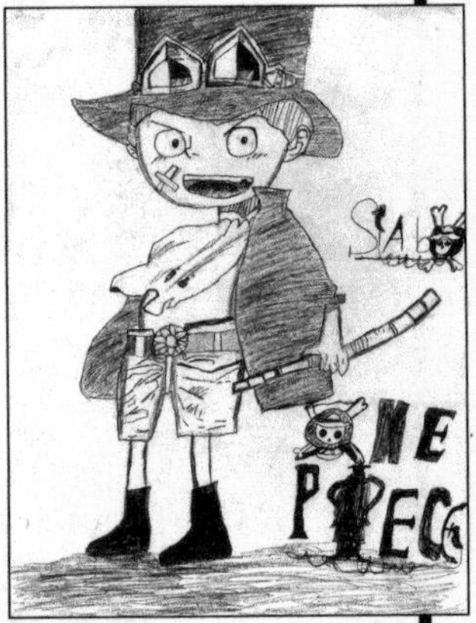
(Dilruk D.)

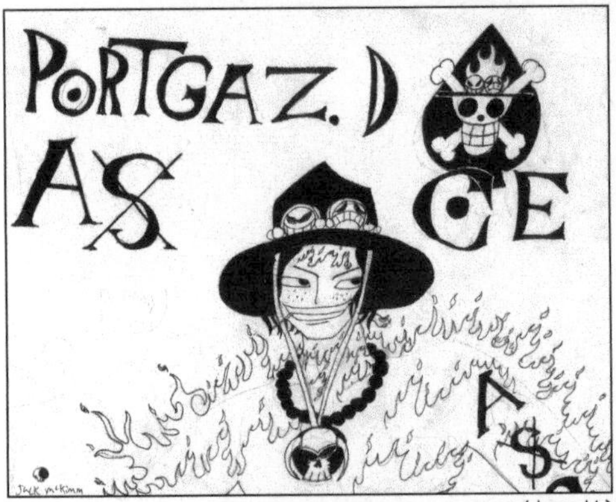
PORTGAZ. D
ASCE
(Jack M.)

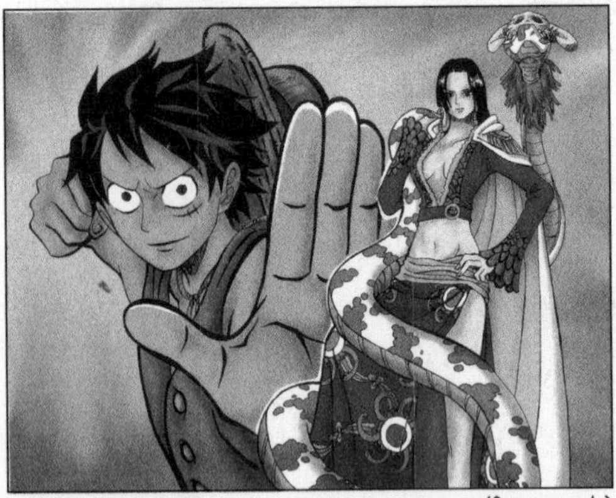
(Roxanna L.)

ONE PIECE

QUESTION CORNER

(REM)

(Sandra E.)

QUESTION CORNER

(Marcella M.)

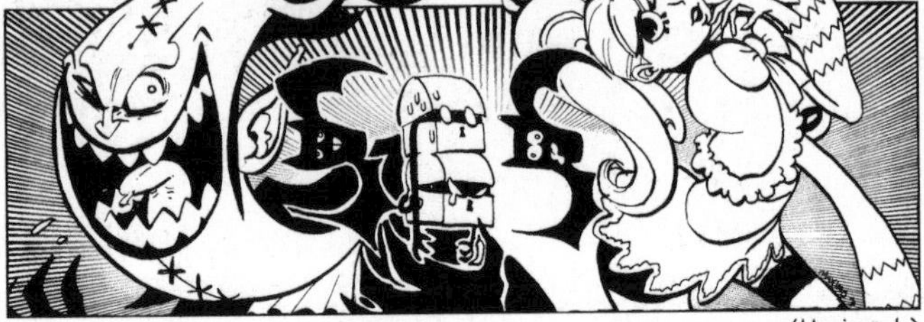
(Maximo L.)

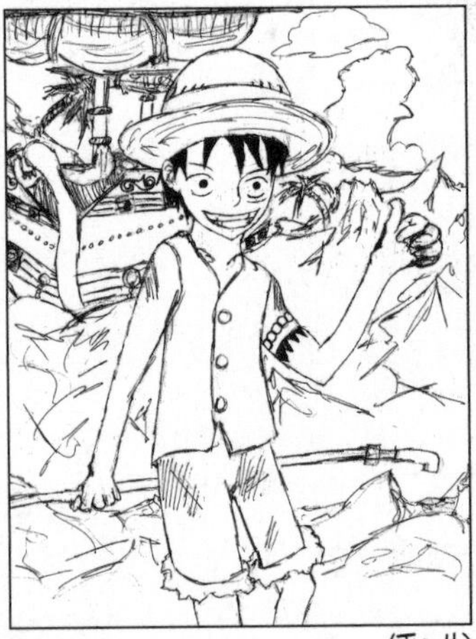
(Tia H.)

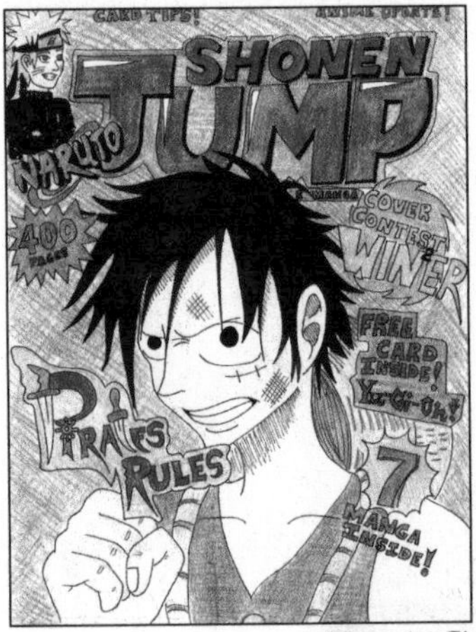
CARD TIPS!
ANIME UPDATE!
SHONEN JUMP
NARUTO
400 PAGES
COVER CONTEST
FREE CARD INSIDE!
Yu-Gi-Oh!
PIRATES RULES
7 MANGA INSIDE!
(Veronica F.)

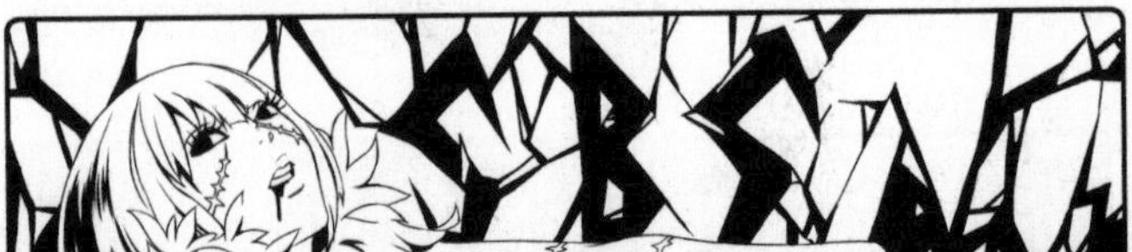
(REM)

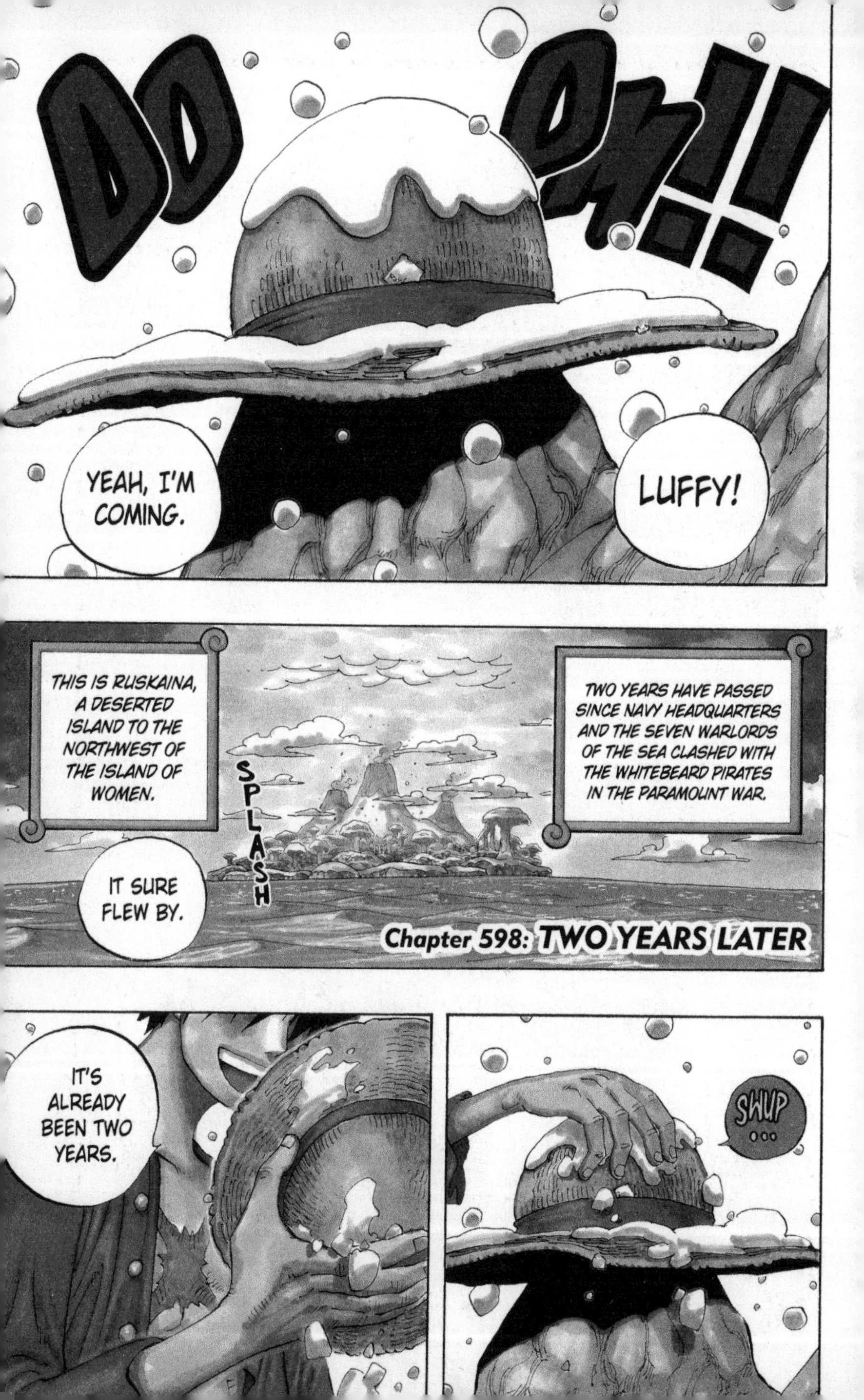
DOOM!!
LUFFY!
YEAH, I'M COMING.
TWO YEARS HAVE PASSED SINCE NAVY HEADQUARTERS AND THE SEVEN WARLORDS OF THE SEA CLASHED WITH THE WHITEBEARD PIRATES IN THE PARAMOUNT WAR.
THIS IS RUSKAINA, A DESERTED ISLAND TO THE NORTHWEST OF THE ISLAND OF WOMEN.
SPLASH
IT SURE FLEW BY.
Chapter 598: TWO YEARS LATER
SHUP ...
IT'S ALREADY BEEN TWO YEARS.

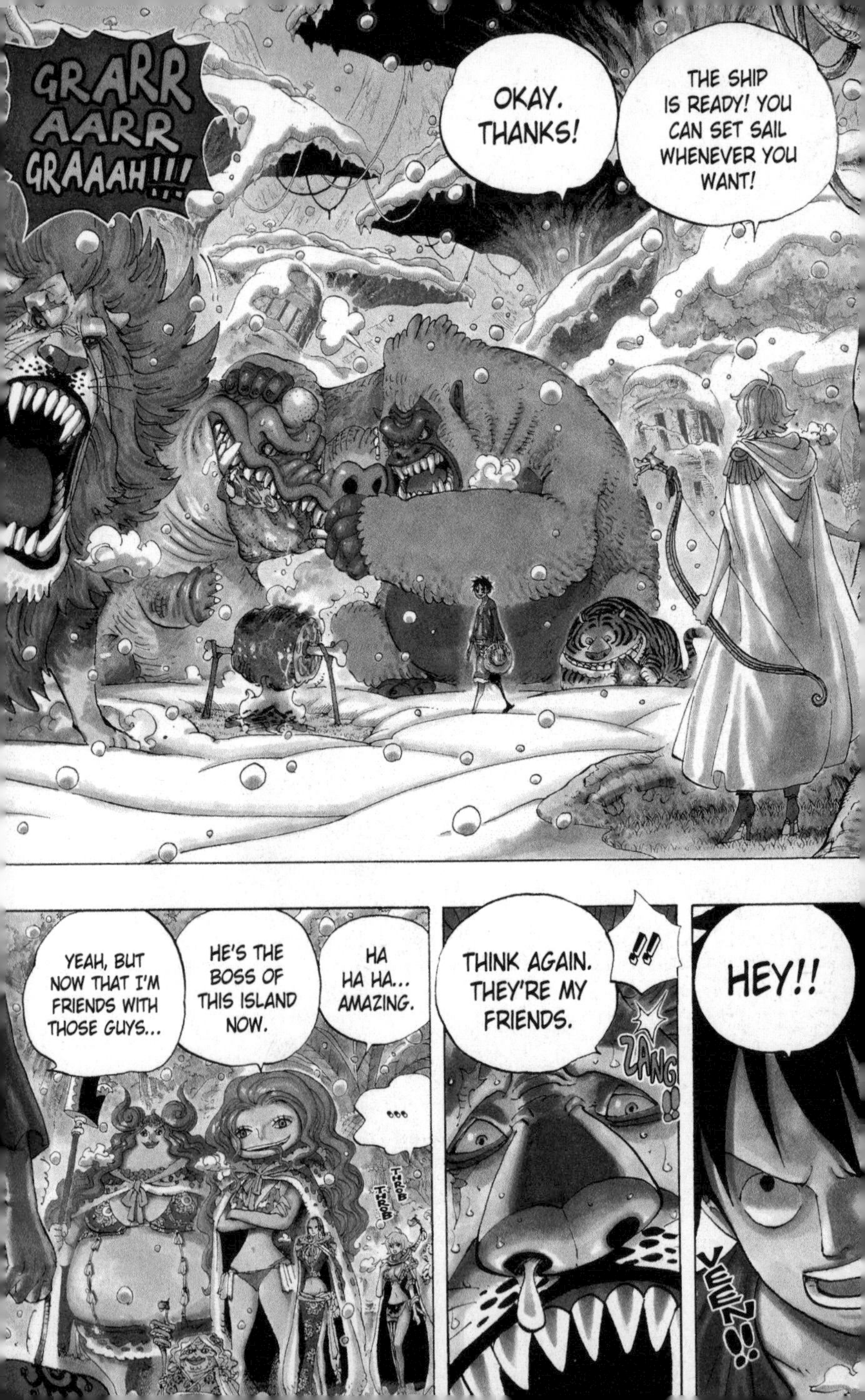
THE SHIP IS READY! YOU CAN SET SAIL WHENEVER YOU WANT!
OKAY. THANKS!
GRARR AARR GRAAAH!!!!
HEY!!
VEEN!!
!!
THINK AGAIN. THEY'RE MY FRIENDS.
ZANG!!
HA HA HA... AMAZING.
HE'S THE BOSS OF THIS ISLAND NOW.
YEAH, BUT NOW THAT I'M FRIENDS WITH THOSE GUYS...
...
THROB THROB

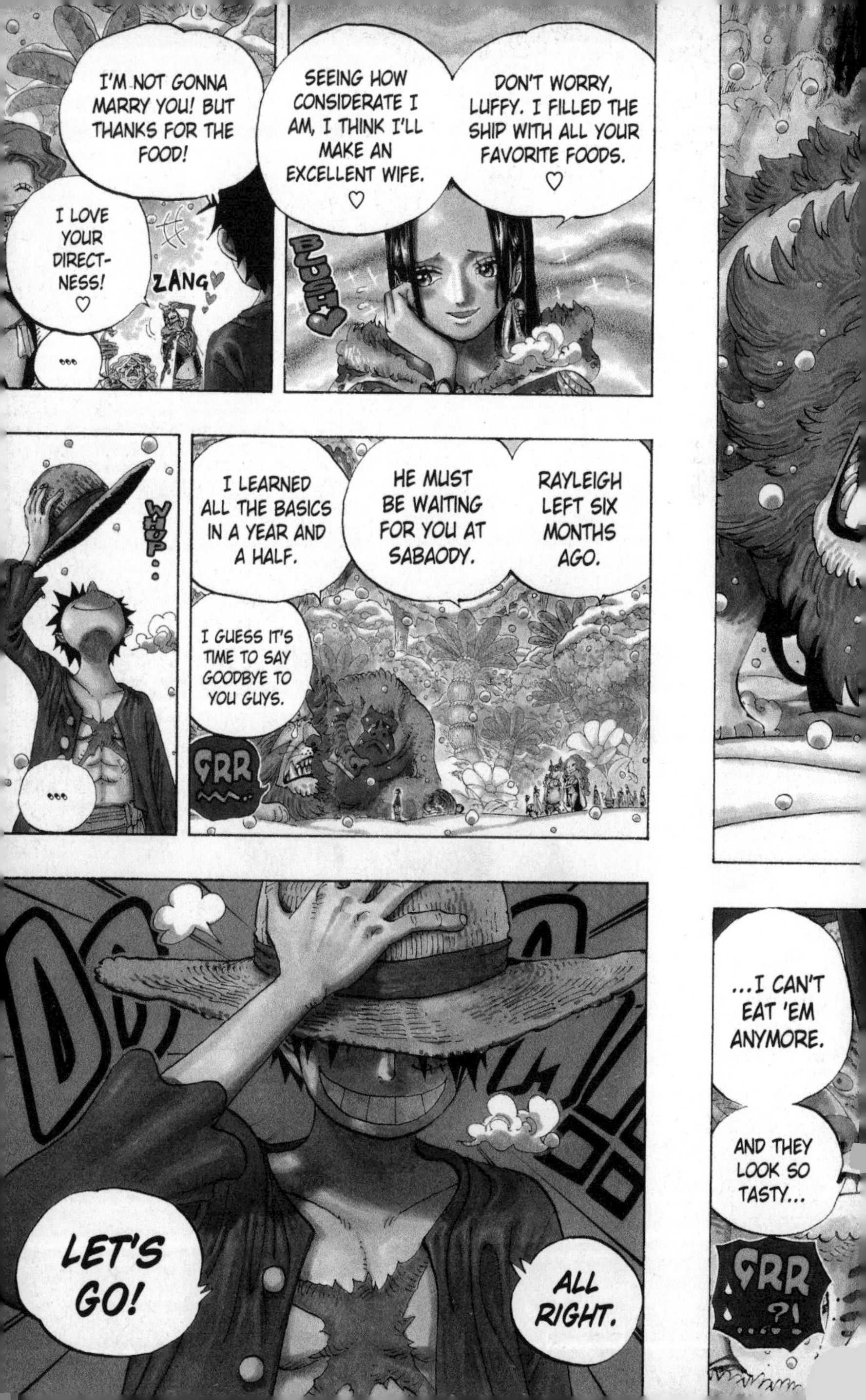
DON'T WORRY, LUFFY. I FILLED THE SHIP WITH ALL YOUR FAVORITE FOODS. ♡
SEEING HOW CONSIDERATE I AM, I THINK I'LL MAKE AN EXCELLENT WIFE. ♡
BLUSH
I'M NOT GONNA MARRY YOU! BUT THANKS FOR THE FOOD!
I LOVE YOUR DIRECT-NESS! ♡
ZANG
...
RAYLEIGH LEFT SIX MONTHS AGO.
HE MUST BE WAITING FOR YOU AT SABAODY.
I LEARNED ALL THE BASICS IN A YEAR AND A HALF.
I GUESS IT'S TIME TO SAY GOODBYE TO YOU GUYS.
GRR
WHUP
...
...I CAN'T EAT 'EM ANYMORE.
AND THEY LOOK SO TASTY...
GRR
?!
ALL RIGHT.
LET'S GO!

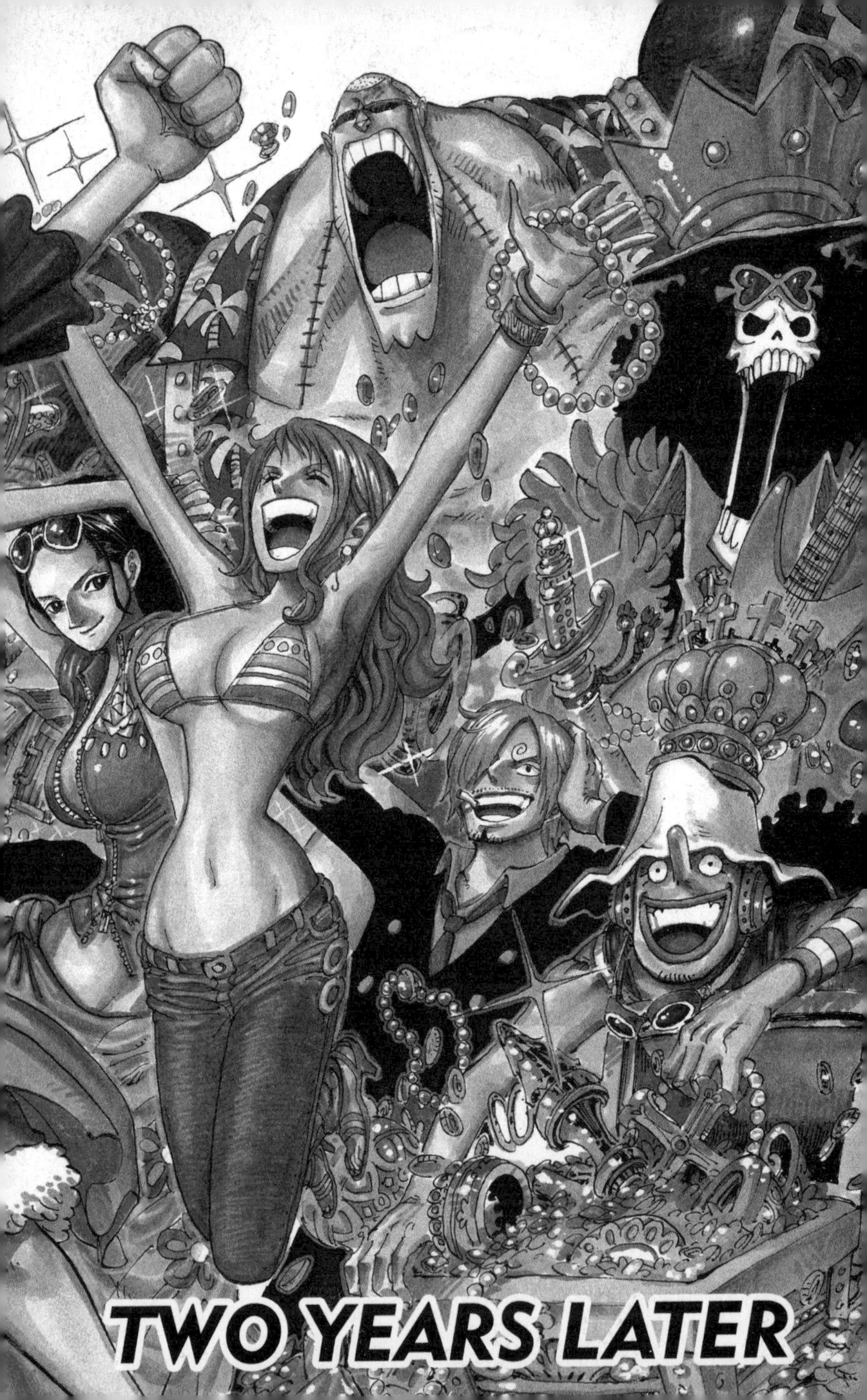
TWO YEARS LATER

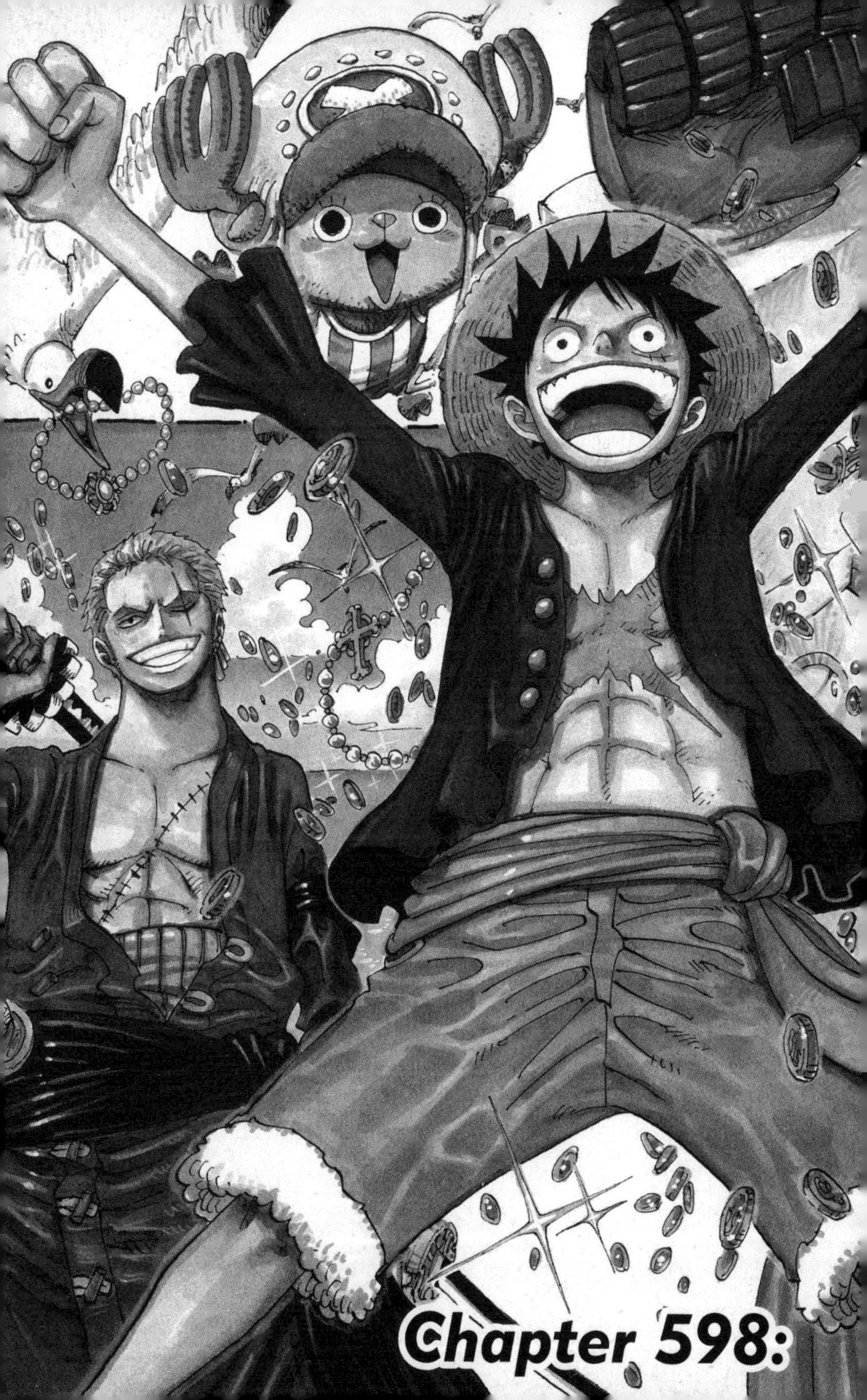
Chapter 598:

vol.61

ONE PIECE

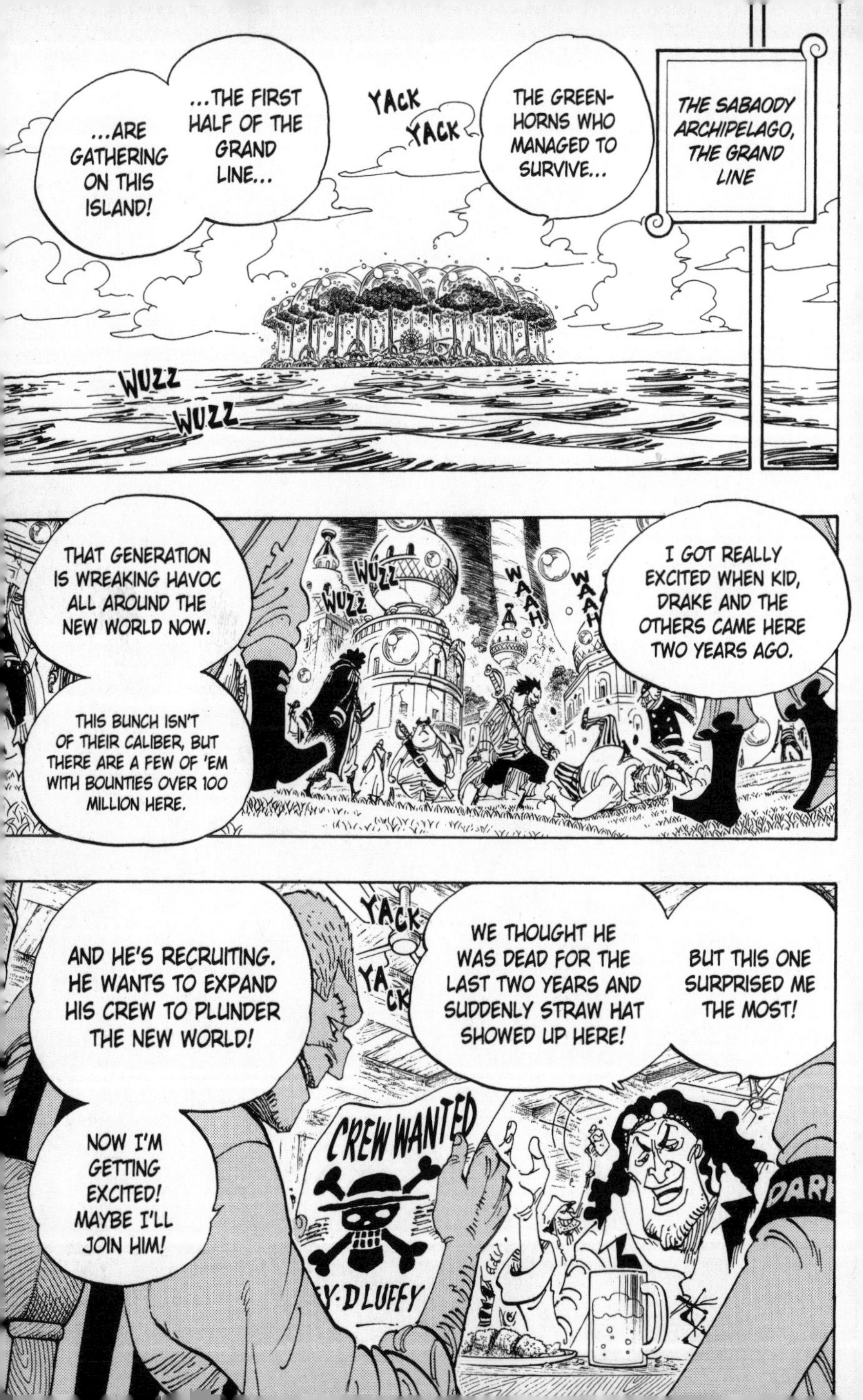
THE SABAODY ARCHIPELAGO, THE GRAND LINE
THE GREENHORNS WHO MANAGED TO SURVIVE...
YACK YACK
...THE FIRST HALF OF THE GRAND LINE...
...ARE GATHERING ON THIS ISLAND!
WUZZ WUZZ
I GOT REALLY EXCITED WHEN KID, DRAKE AND THE OTHERS CAME HERE TWO YEARS AGO.
WAAH WAAH
WUZZ WUZZ
THAT GENERATION IS WREAKING HAVOC ALL AROUND THE NEW WORLD NOW.
THIS BUNCH ISN'T OF THEIR CALIBER, BUT THERE ARE A FEW OF 'EM WITH BOUNTIES OVER 100 MILLION HERE.
BUT THIS ONE SURPRISED ME THE MOST!
WE THOUGHT HE WAS DEAD FOR THE LAST TWO YEARS AND SUDDENLY STRAW HAT SHOWED UP HERE!
YACK YACK
AND HE'S RECRUITING. HE WANTS TO EXPAND HIS CREW TO PLUNDER THE NEW WORLD!
NOW I'M GETTING EXCITED! MAYBE I'LL JOIN HIM!
CREW WANTED

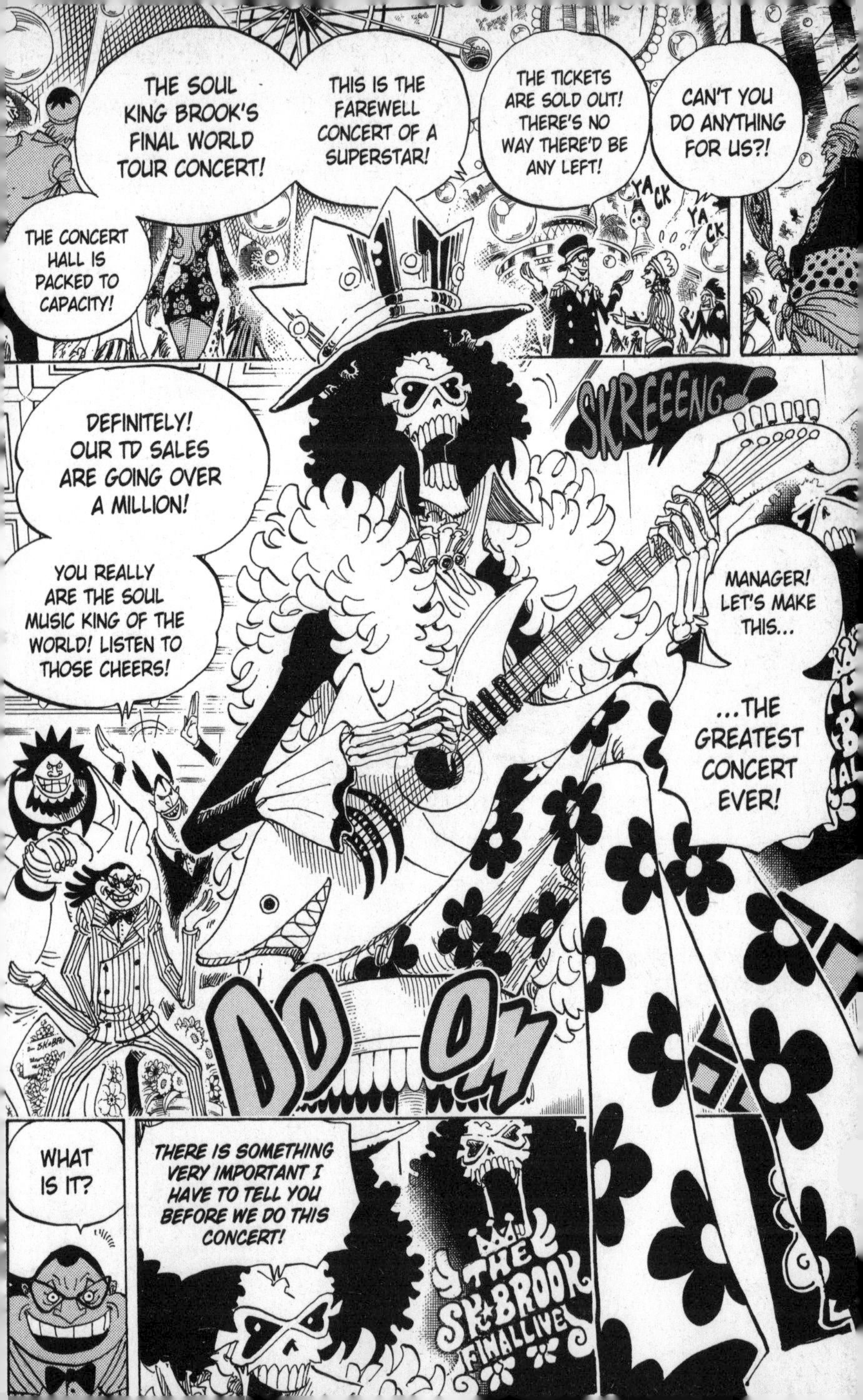
CAN'T YOU DO ANYTHING FOR US?!
THE TICKETS ARE SOLD OUT! THERE'S NO WAY THERE'D BE ANY LEFT!
YACK
YACK
THIS IS THE FAREWELL CONCERT OF A SUPERSTAR!
THE SOUL KING BROOK'S FINAL WORLD TOUR CONCERT!
THE CONCERT HALL IS PACKED TO CAPACITY!
SKREEENG
MANAGER! LET'S MAKE THIS...
...THE GREATEST CONCERT EVER!
DEFINITELY! OUR TD SALES ARE GOING OVER A MILLION!
YOU REALLY ARE THE SOUL MUSIC KING OF THE WORLD! LISTEN TO THOSE CHEERS!
DOOM
THE SK★BROOK FINAL LIVE
THERE IS SOMETHING VERY IMPORTANT I HAVE TO TELL YOU BEFORE WE DO THIS CONCERT!
WHAT IS IT?

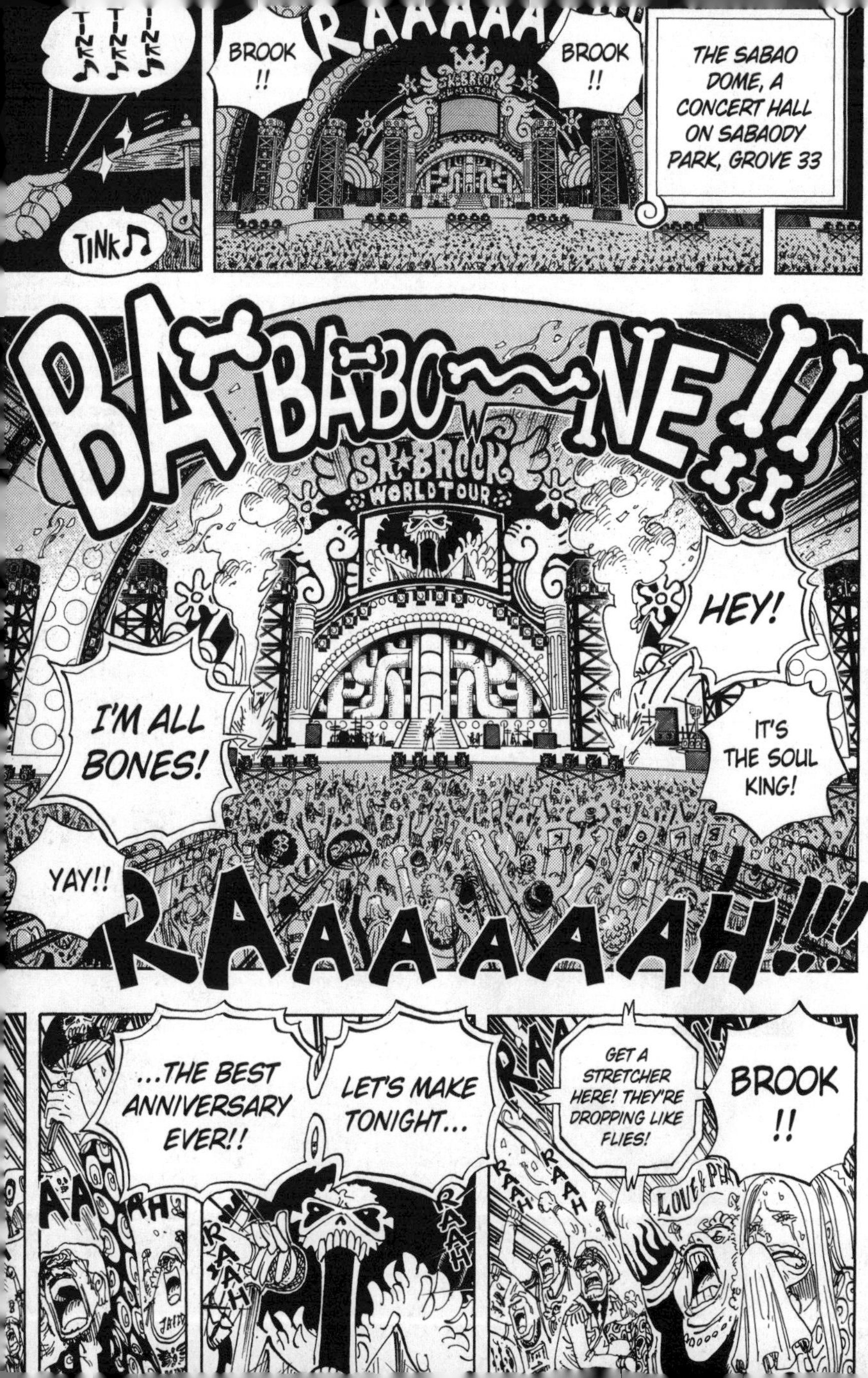
THE SABAO DOME, A CONCERT HALL ON SABAODY PARK, GROVE 33
BROOK !!
RAAAAA
BROOK !!
TINK♪ TINK♪ TINK♪
TINK♫
BA-BABO~~~NE!!
HEY!
IT'S THE SOUL KING!
I'M ALL BONES!
YAY!!
RAAAAAAH!!!
BROOK !!
GET A STRETCHER HERE! THEY'RE DROPPING LIKE FLIES!
LET'S MAKE TONIGHT...
...THE BEST ANNIVERSARY EVER!!

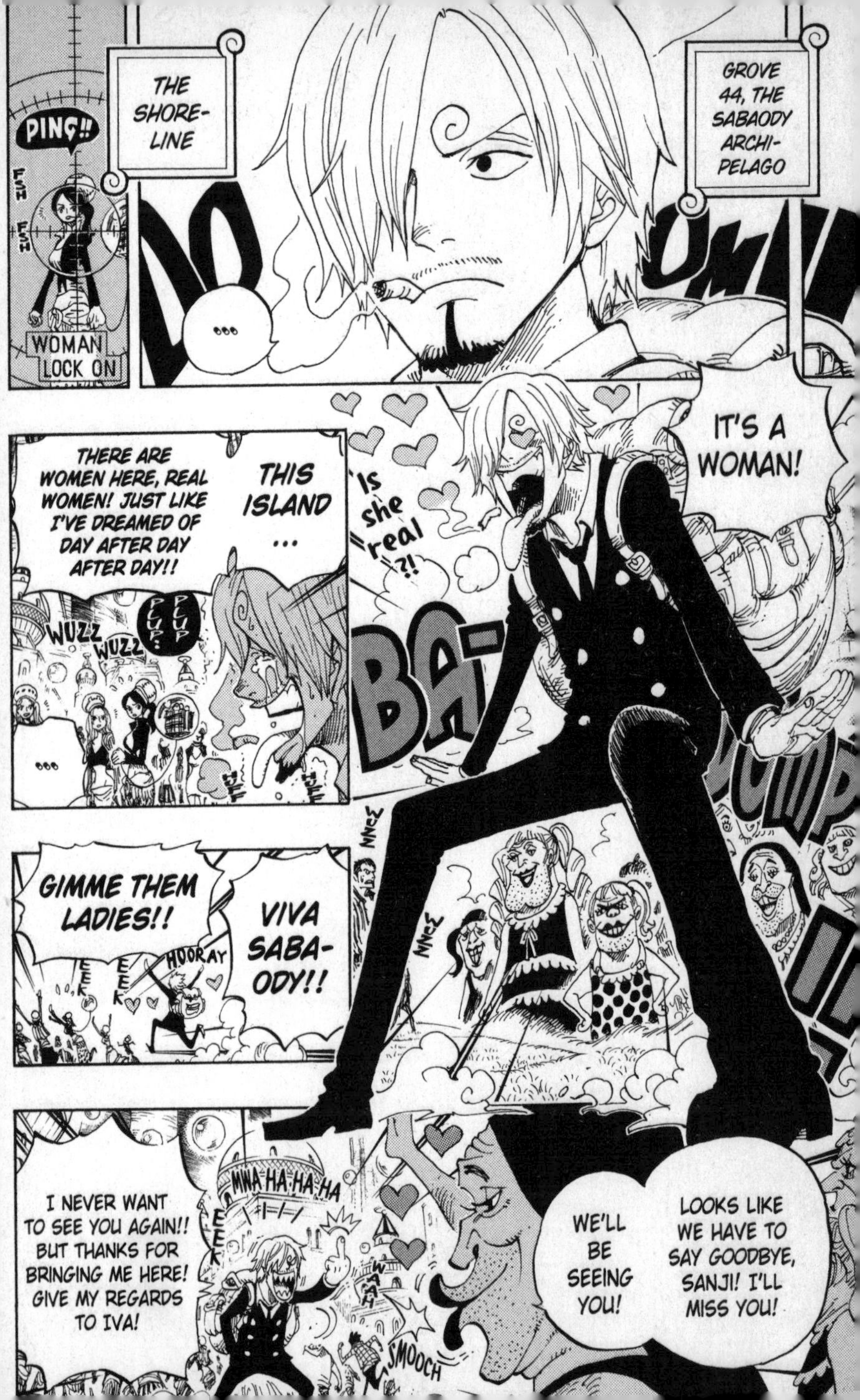
GROVE 44, THE SABAODY ARCHIPELAGO
THE SHORE-LINE
OM
DO
...
PING!!
FSH
FSH
WOMAN LOCK ON
IT'S A WOMAN!
Is she real?!
BA-
THIS ISLAND ...
THERE ARE WOMEN HERE, REAL WOMEN! JUST LIKE I'VE DREAMED OF DAY AFTER DAY AFTER DAY!!
PLUP PLUP
WUZZ WUZZ
...
WNN
WNN
VIVA SABA-ODY!!
GIMME THEM LADIES!!
HOORAY
EEK
EEK
LOOKS LIKE WE HAVE TO SAY GOODBYE, SANJI! I'LL MISS YOU!
WE'LL BE SEEING YOU!
MWA HA HA HA
I NEVER WANT TO SEE YOU AGAIN!! BUT THANKS FOR BRINGING ME HERE! GIVE MY REGARDS TO IVA!
EEK
WAAH
SMOOCH

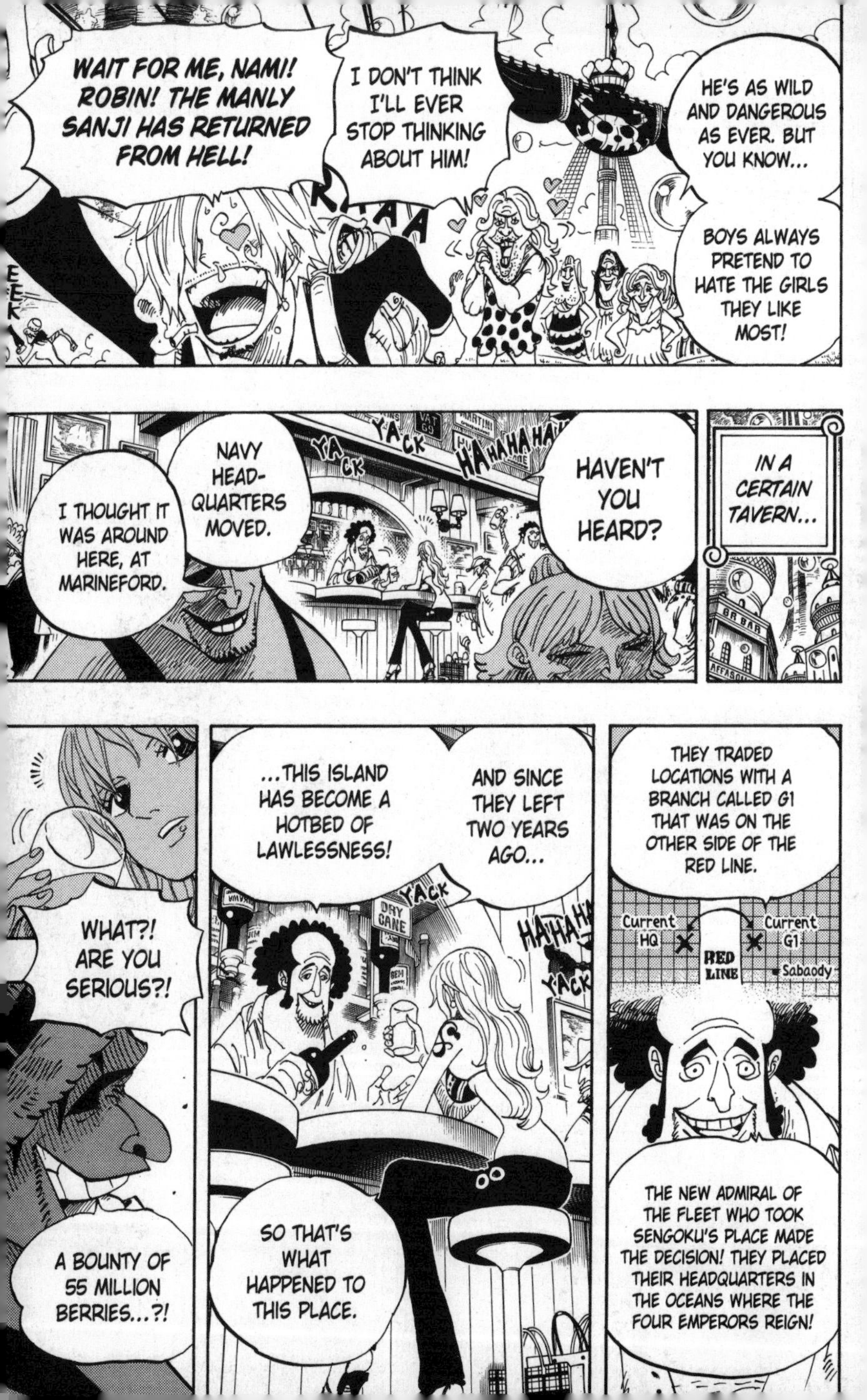
HE'S AS WILD AND DANGEROUS AS EVER. BUT YOU KNOW...
BOYS ALWAYS PRETEND TO HATE THE GIRLS THEY LIKE MOST!
I DON'T THINK I'LL EVER STOP THINKING ABOUT HIM!
WAIT FOR ME, NAMI! ROBIN! THE MANLY SANJI HAS RETURNED FROM HELL!
IN A CERTAIN TAVERN...
GR BAR
HAVEN'T YOU HEARD?
HAHAHA
YACK
MARTINI
YACK
NAVY HEAD-QUARTERS MOVED.
I THOUGHT IT WAS AROUND HERE, AT MARINEFORD.
THEY TRADED LOCATIONS WITH A BRANCH CALLED G1 THAT WAS ON THE OTHER SIDE OF THE RED LINE.
Current G1
Sabaody
RED LINE
Current HQ
THE NEW ADMIRAL OF THE FLEET WHO TOOK SENGOKU'S PLACE MADE THE DECISION! THEY PLACED THEIR HEADQUARTERS IN THE OCEANS WHERE THE FOUR EMPERORS REIGN!
AND SINCE THEY LEFT TWO YEARS AGO...
...THIS ISLAND HAS BECOME A HOTBED OF LAWLESSNESS!
HAHAHA
YACK
YACK
DRY CANE
SO THAT'S WHAT HAPPENED TO THIS PLACE.
WHAT?! ARE YOU SERIOUS?!
A BOUNTY OF 55 MILLION BERRIES...?!

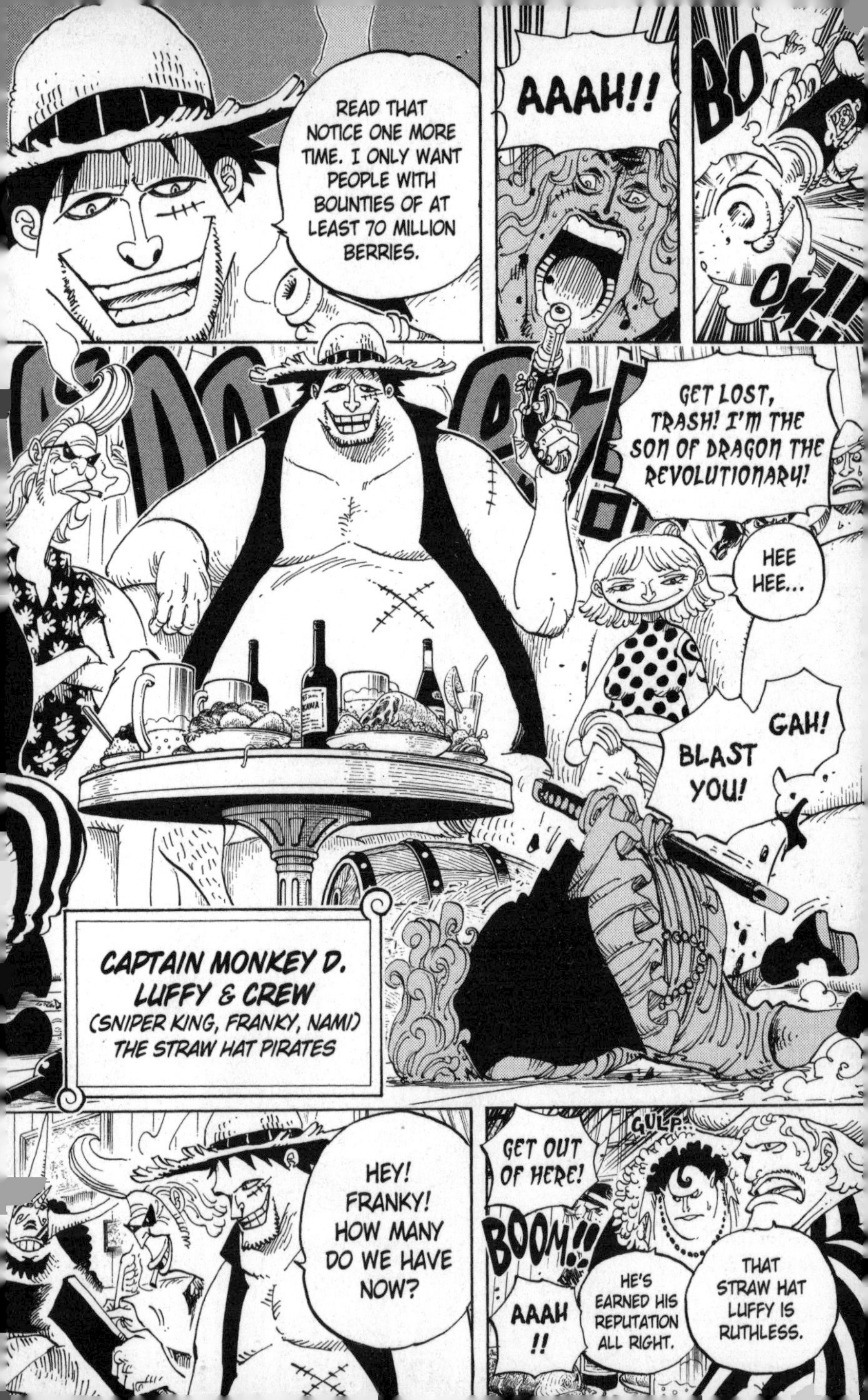
BO
OM!!
AAAH!!
READ THAT NOTICE ONE MORE TIME. I ONLY WANT PEOPLE WITH BOUNTIES OF AT LEAST 70 MILLION BERRIES.
GET LOST, TRASH! I'M THE SON OF DRAGON THE REVOLUTIONARY!
HEE HEE...
GAH!
BLAST YOU!
CAPTAIN MONKEY D. LUFFY & CREW
(SNIPER KING, FRANKY, NAMI)
THE STRAW HAT PIRATES
GULP...
GET OUT OF HERE!
BOOM!!
THAT STRAW HAT LUFFY IS RUTHLESS.
HE'S EARNED HIS REPUTATION ALL RIGHT.
AAAH!!
HEY! FRANKY! HOW MANY DO WE HAVE NOW?

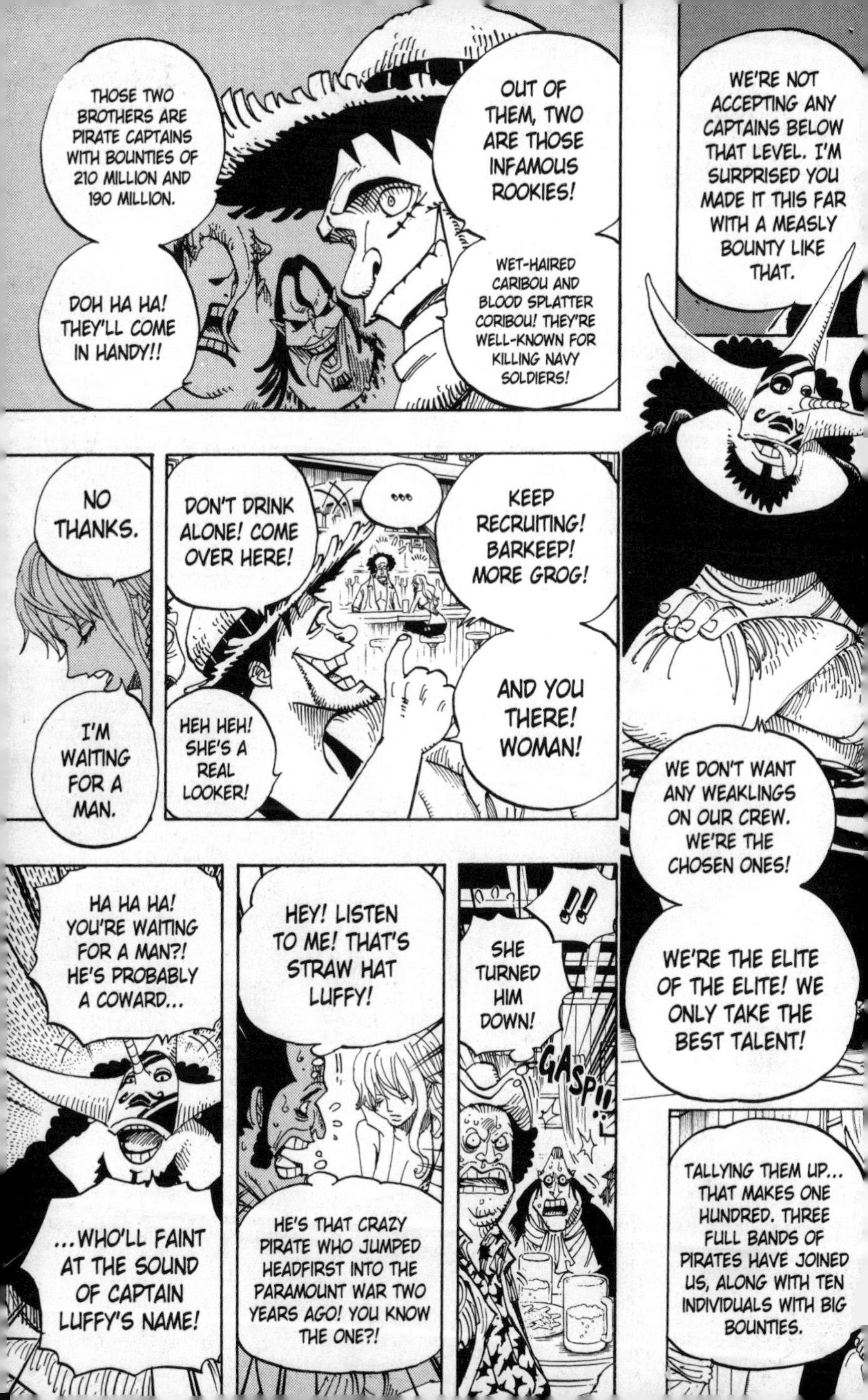
WE'RE NOT ACCEPTING ANY CAPTAINS BELOW THAT LEVEL. I'M SURPRISED YOU MADE IT THIS FAR WITH A MEASLY BOUNTY LIKE THAT.
WE DON'T WANT ANY WEAKLINGS ON OUR CREW. WE'RE THE CHOSEN ONES!
WE'RE THE ELITE OF THE ELITE! WE ONLY TAKE THE BEST TALENT!
OUT OF THEM, TWO ARE THOSE INFAMOUS ROOKIES!
WET-HAIRED CARIBOU AND BLOOD SPLATTER CORIBOU! THEY'RE WELL-KNOWN FOR KILLING NAVY SOLDIERS!
THOSE TWO BROTHERS ARE PIRATE CAPTAINS WITH BOUNTIES OF 210 MILLION AND 190 MILLION.
DOH HA HA! THEY'LL COME IN HANDY!!
KEEP RECRUITING! BARKEEP! MORE GROG!
AND YOU THERE! WOMAN!
...
DON'T DRINK ALONE! COME OVER HERE!
HEH HEH! SHE'S A REAL LOOKER!
NO THANKS.
I'M WAITING FOR A MAN.
TALLYING THEM UP... THAT MAKES ONE HUNDRED. THREE FULL BANDS OF PIRATES HAVE JOINED US, ALONG WITH TEN INDIVIDUALS WITH BIG BOUNTIES.
!!
SHE TURNED HIM DOWN!
GASP!!!
HEY! LISTEN TO ME! THAT'S STRAW HAT LUFFY!
HE'S THAT CRAZY PIRATE WHO JUMPED HEADFIRST INTO THE PARAMOUNT WAR TWO YEARS AGO! YOU KNOW THE ONE?!
HA HA HA! YOU'RE WAITING FOR A MAN?! HE'S PROBABLY A COWARD...
...WHO'LL FAINT AT THE SOUND OF CAPTAIN LUFFY'S NAME!

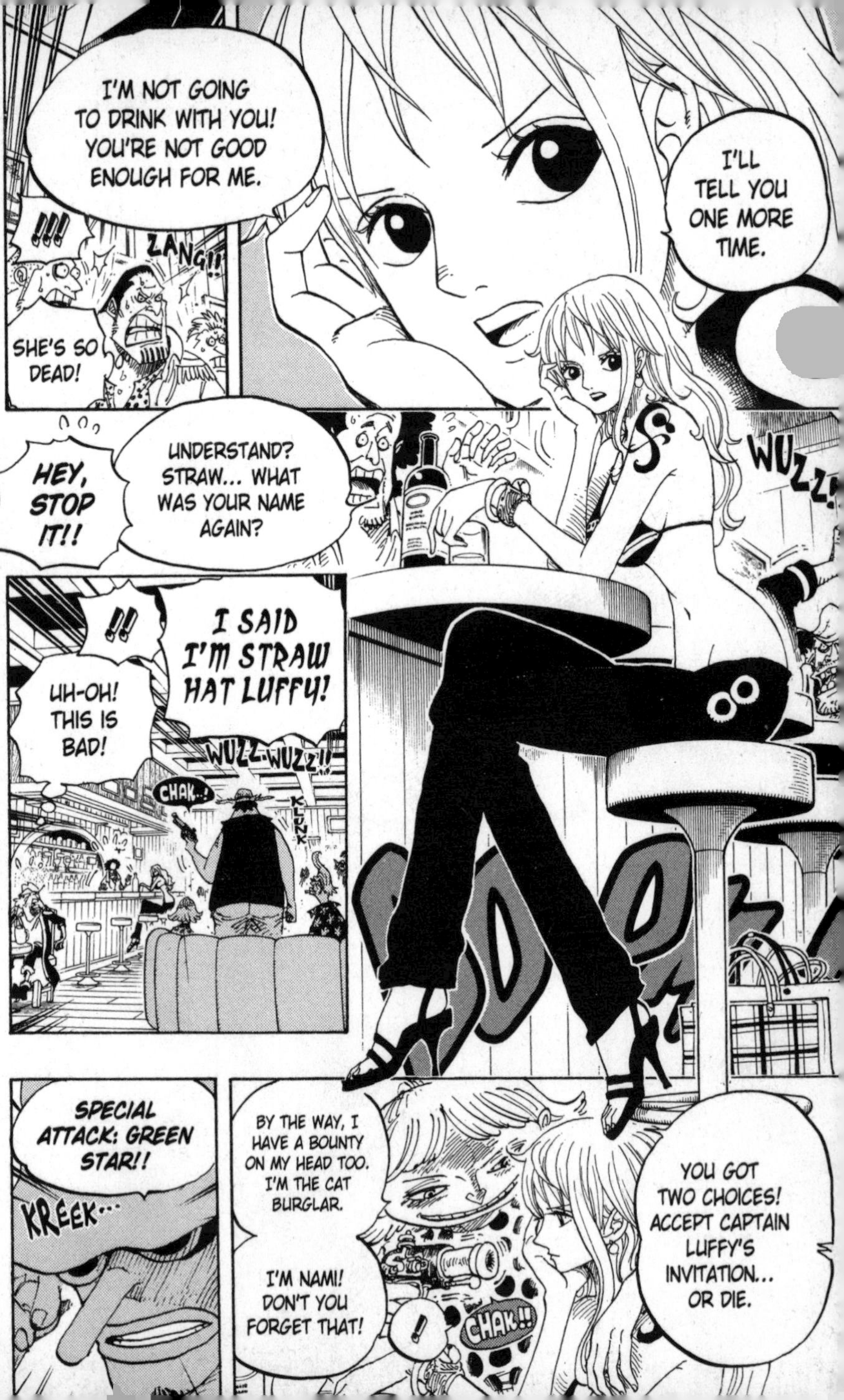
I'LL TELL YOU ONE MORE TIME.
I'M NOT GOING TO DRINK WITH YOU! YOU'RE NOT GOOD ENOUGH FOR ME.
!!!
ZANG!!
SHE'S SO DEAD!
WUZZ!
UNDERSTAND? STRAW... WHAT WAS YOUR NAME AGAIN?
HEY, STOP IT!!
I SAID I'M STRAW HAT LUFFY!
!!
UH-OH! THIS IS BAD!
WUZZ-WUZZ!!
CHAK..!
KLUNK
YOU GOT TWO CHOICES! ACCEPT CAPTAIN LUFFY'S INVITATION... OR DIE.
BY THE WAY, I HAVE A BOUNTY ON MY HEAD TOO. I'M THE CAT BURGLAR.
CHAK!!
!
I'M NAMI! DON'T YOU FORGET THAT!
SPECIAL ATTACK: GREEN STAR!!
KREEK...

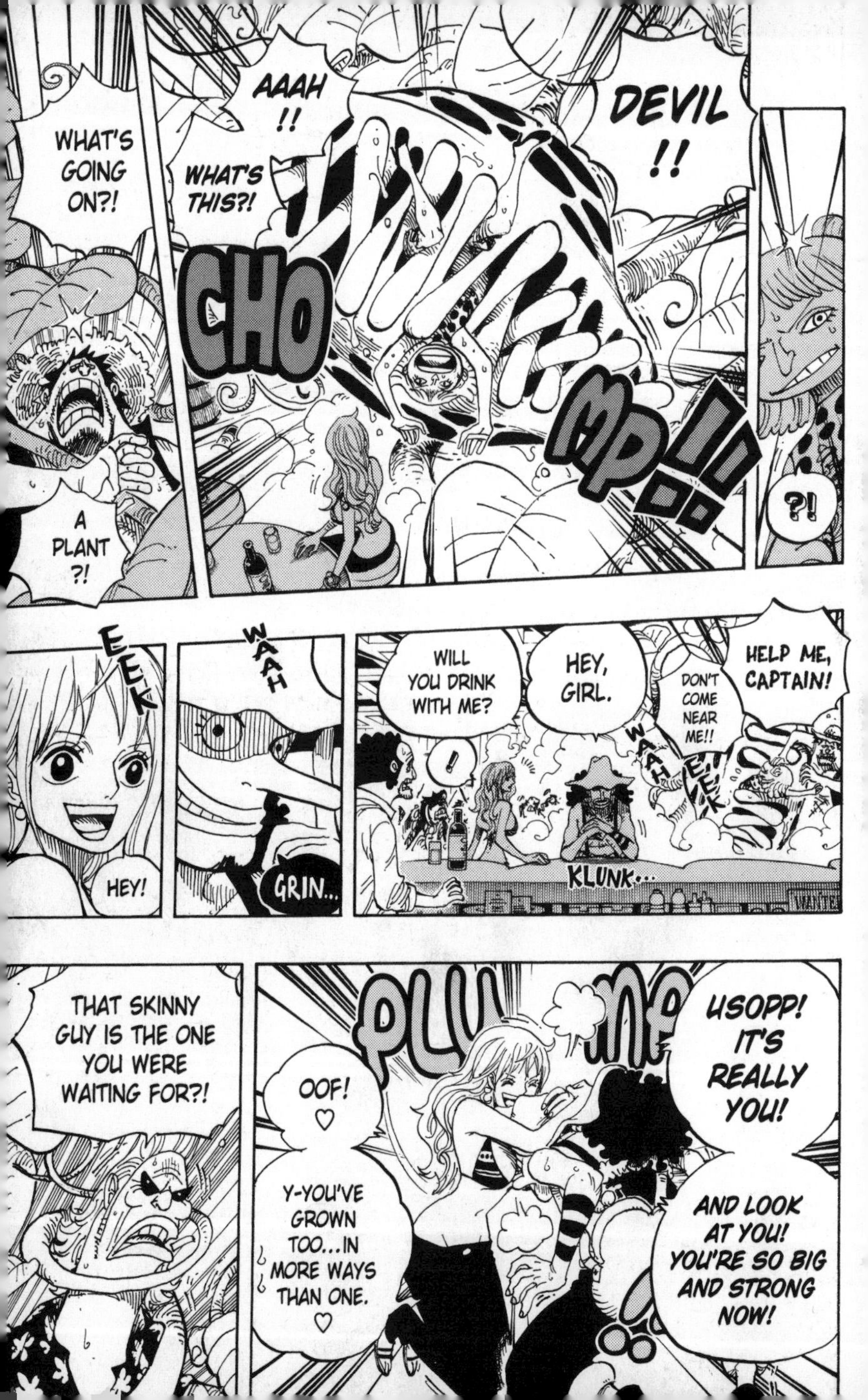
?!
DEVIL!!
AAAH!!
WHAT'S THIS?!
CHOMP!!
WHAT'S GOING ON?!
A PLANT?!
HELP ME, CAPTAIN!
DON'T COME NEAR ME!!
WAAAH
EEEK
HEY, GIRL.
WILL YOU DRINK WITH ME?
!
KLUNK...
WAAAH
GRIN...
EEEK
HEY!
USOPP! IT'S REALLY YOU!
AND LOOK AT YOU! YOU'RE SO BIG AND STRONG NOW!
OOF! ♡
Y-YOU'VE GROWN TOO...IN MORE WAYS THAN ONE. ♡
THAT SKINNY GUY IS THE ONE YOU WERE WAITING FOR?!

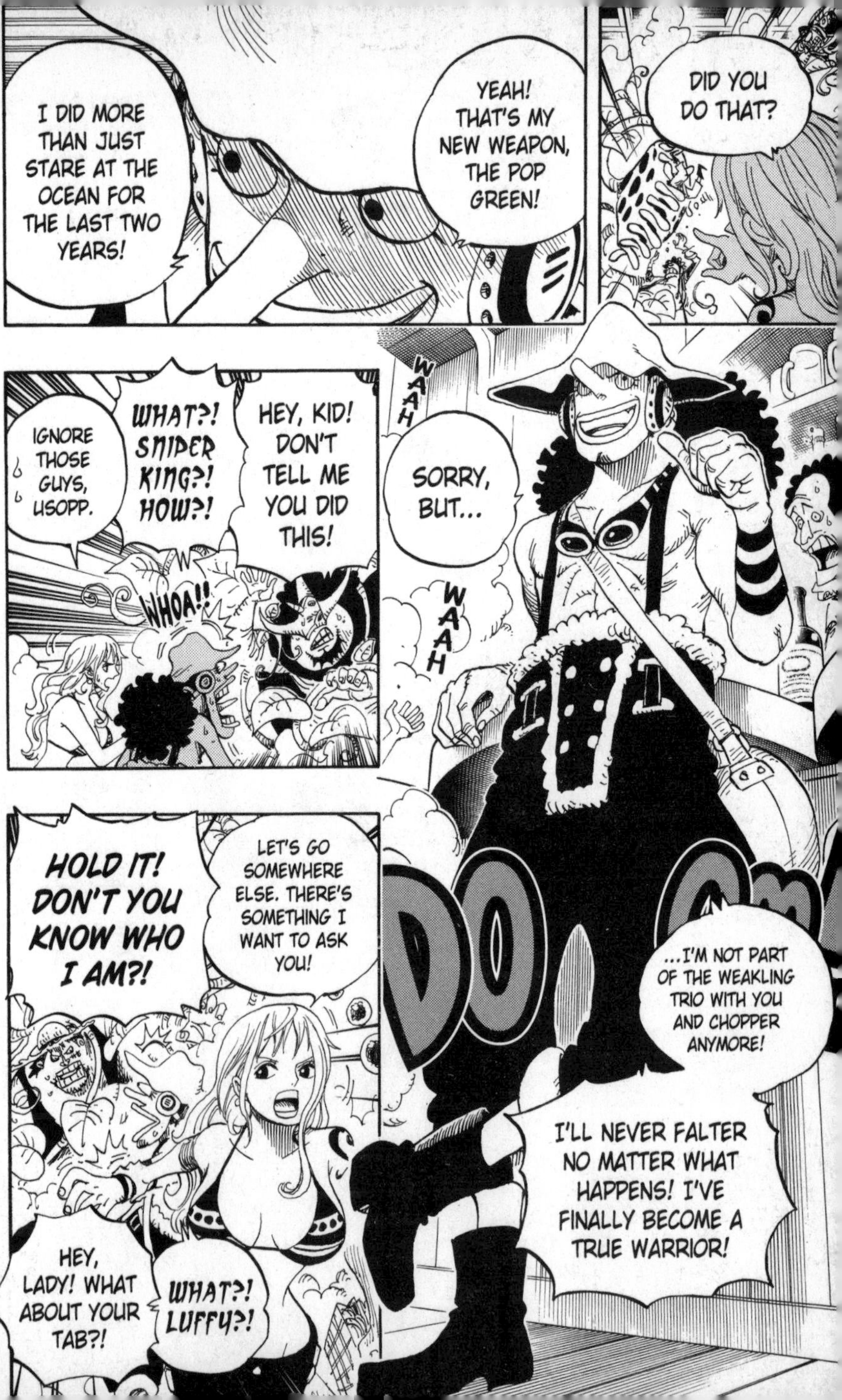

DID YOU DO THAT?
YEAH! THAT'S MY NEW WEAPON, THE POP GREEN!
I DID MORE THAN JUST STARE AT THE OCEAN FOR THE LAST TWO YEARS!
WAAH
SORRY, BUT...
WAAH
DOOM
...I'M NOT PART OF THE WEAKLING TRIO WITH YOU AND CHOPPER ANYMORE!
I'LL NEVER FALTER NO MATTER WHAT HAPPENS! I'VE FINALLY BECOME A TRUE WARRIOR!
HEY, KID! DON'T TELL ME YOU DID THIS!
WHAT?! SNIPER KING?! HOW?!
IGNORE THOSE GUYS, USOPP.
WHOA!!
LET'S GO SOMEWHERE ELSE. THERE'S SOMETHING I WANT TO ASK YOU!
HOLD IT! DON'T YOU KNOW WHO I AM?!
WHAT?! LUFFY?!
HEY, LADY! WHAT ABOUT YOUR TAB?!

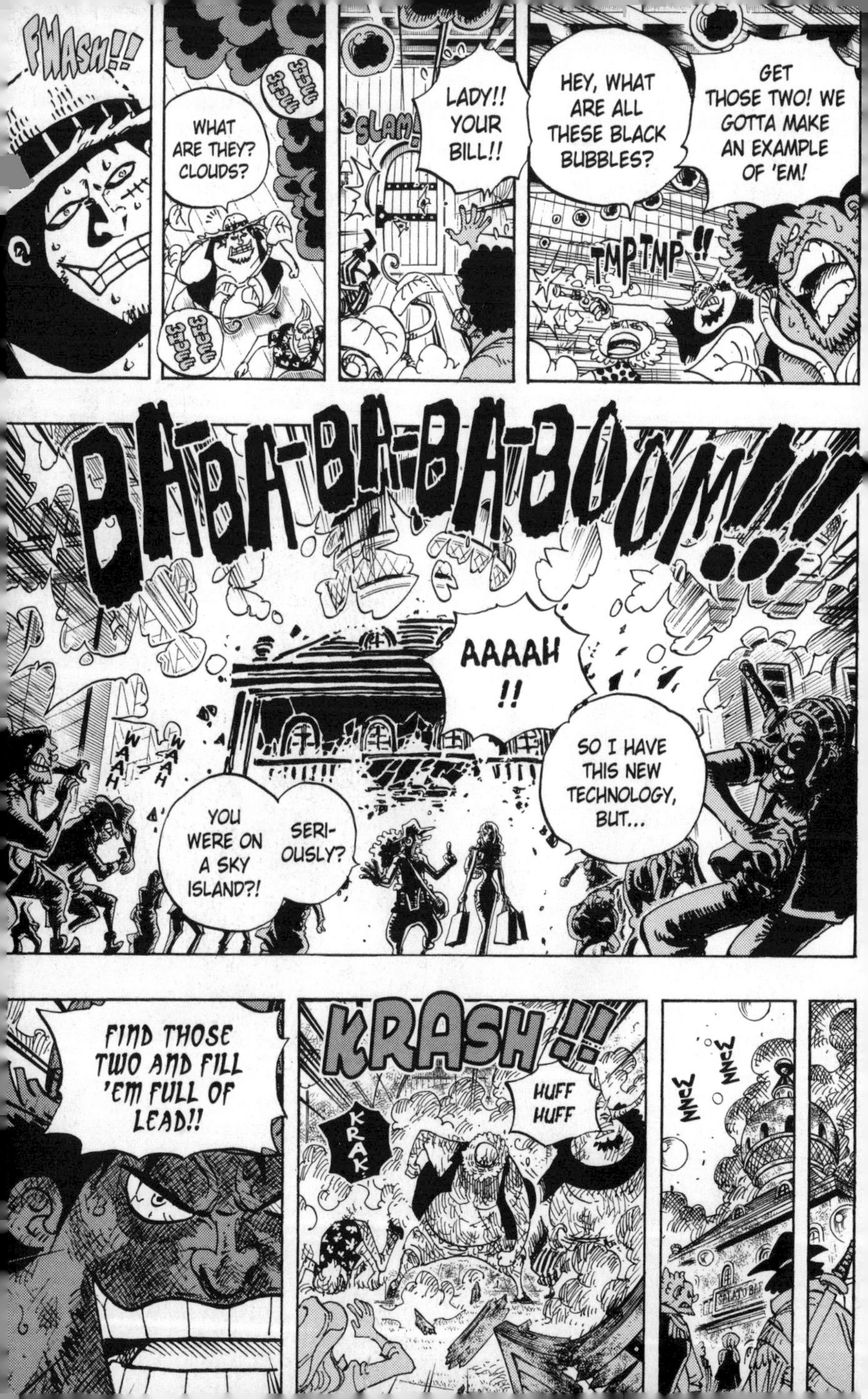
GET THOSE TWO! WE GOTTA MAKE AN EXAMPLE OF 'EM!
HEY, WHAT ARE ALL THESE BLACK BUBBLES?
TMP TMP!!
LADY!! YOUR BILL!!
SLAM
WHAT ARE THEY? CLOUDS?
FWASH!!
BA-BA-BA-BA-BA-BOOM!!
AAAAH!!
SO I HAVE THIS NEW TECHNOLOGY, BUT...
SERI-OUSLY?
YOU WERE ON A SKY ISLAND?!
WAAH WAAH
WUNN WUNN
KRASH!!
HUFF HUFF
KRAK
FIND THOSE TWO AND FILL 'EM FULL OF LEAD!!

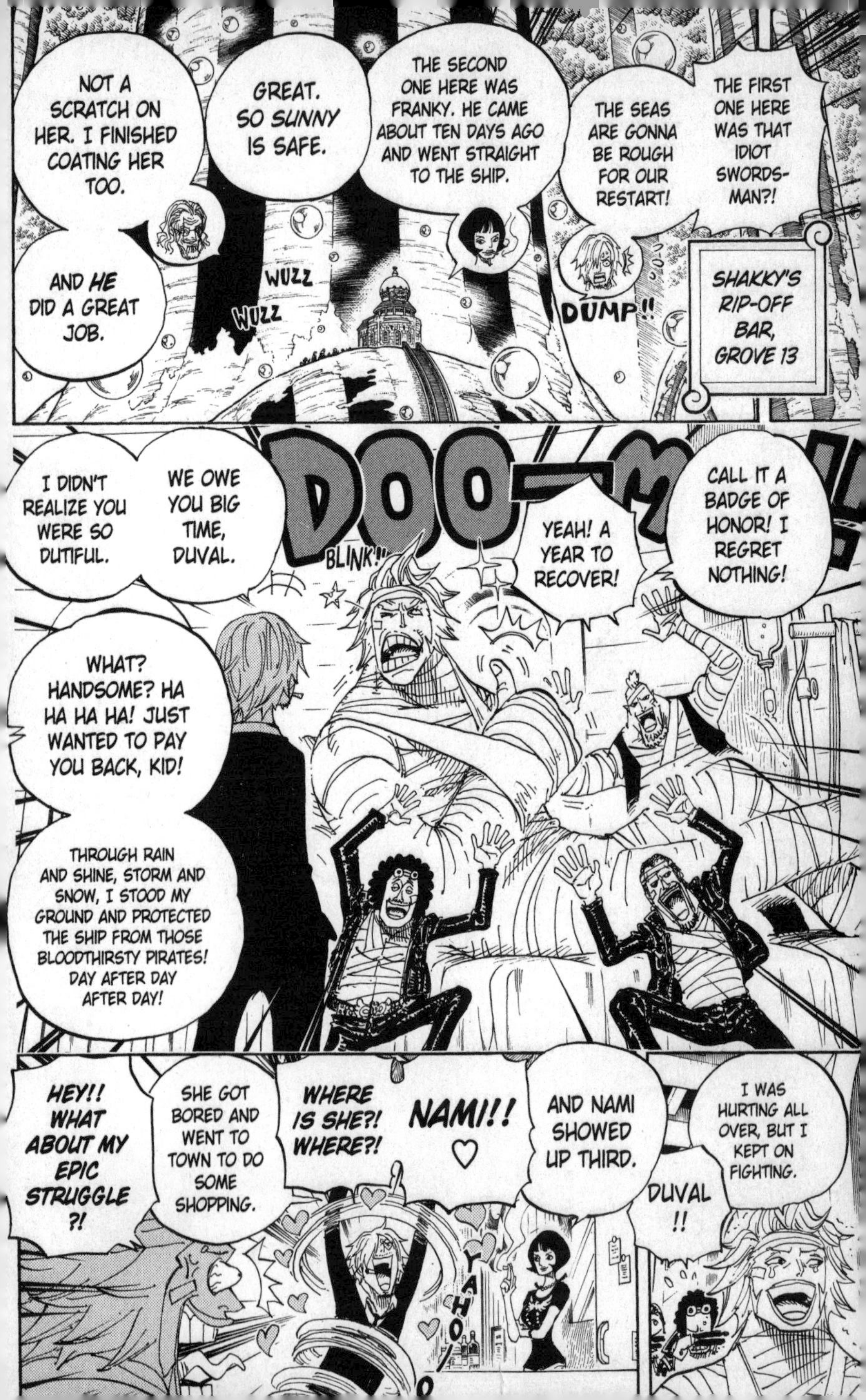
SHAKKY'S RIP-OFF BAR, GROVE 13
THE FIRST ONE HERE WAS THAT IDIOT SWORDS-MAN?!
THE SEAS ARE GONNA BE ROUGH FOR OUR RESTART!
DUMP!!
THE SECOND ONE HERE WAS FRANKY. HE CAME ABOUT TEN DAYS AGO AND WENT STRAIGHT TO THE SHIP.
GREAT. SO SUNNY IS SAFE.
NOT A SCRATCH ON HER. I FINISHED COATING HER TOO.
AND HE DID A GREAT JOB.
WUZZ
WUZZ
DOO-M!!
CALL IT A BADGE OF HONOR! I REGRET NOTHING!
YEAH! A YEAR TO RECOVER!
BLINK!!
WE OWE YOU BIG TIME, DUVAL.
I DIDN'T REALIZE YOU WERE SO DUTIFUL.
WHAT? HANDSOME? HA HA HA HA! JUST WANTED TO PAY YOU BACK, KID!
THROUGH RAIN AND SHINE, STORM AND SNOW, I STOOD MY GROUND AND PROTECTED THE SHIP FROM THOSE BLOODTHIRSTY PIRATES! DAY AFTER DAY AFTER DAY!
I WAS HURTING ALL OVER, BUT I KEPT ON FIGHTING.
DUVAL!!
AND NAMI SHOWED UP THIRD.
NAMI!! ♡
WHERE IS SHE?! WHERE?!
YAHOO
SHE GOT BORED AND WENT TO TOWN TO DO SOME SHOPPING.
HEY!! WHAT ABOUT MY EPIC STRUGGLE?!

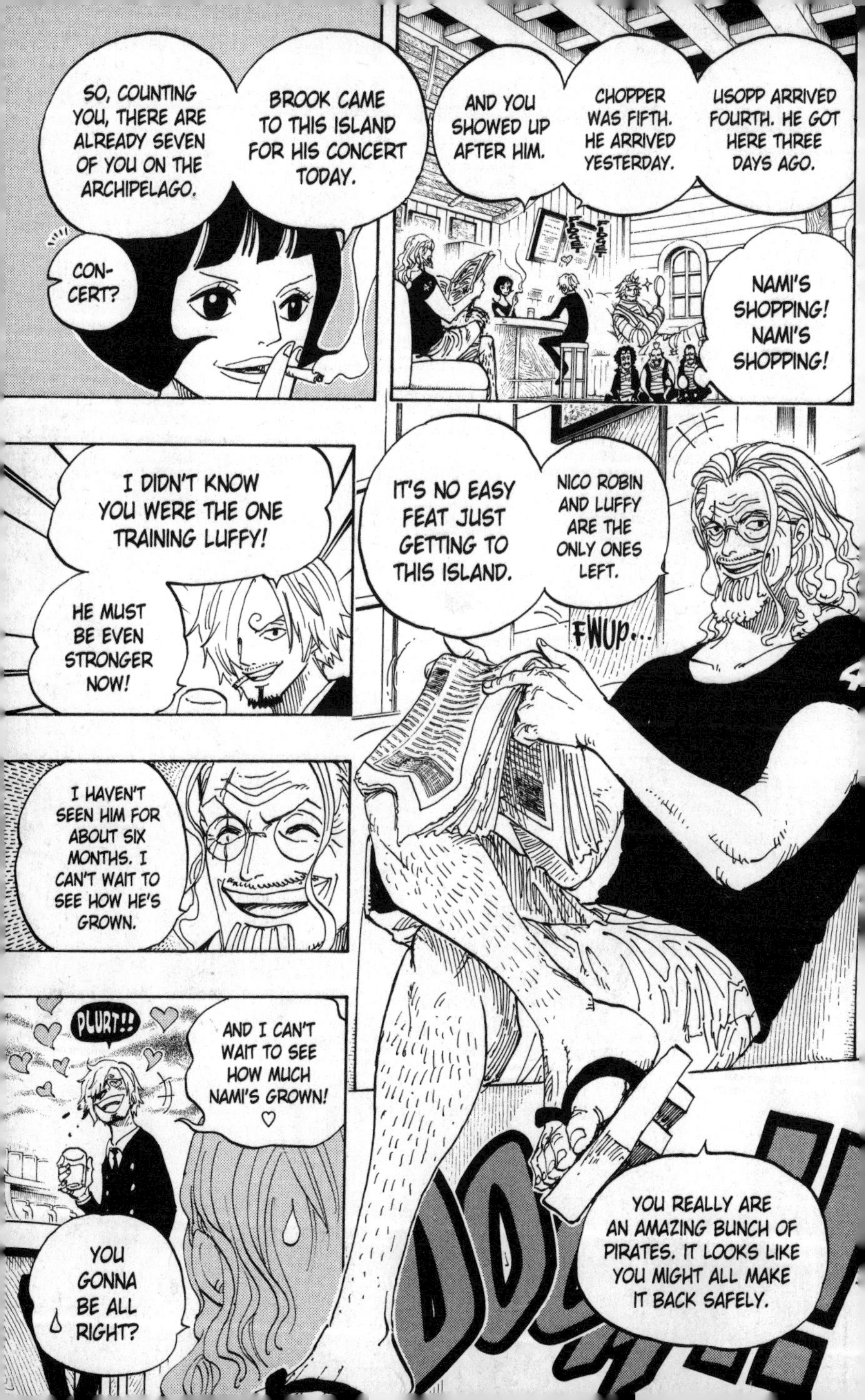
USOPP ARRIVED FOURTH. HE GOT HERE THREE DAYS AGO.
CHOPPER WAS FIFTH. HE ARRIVED YESTERDAY.
AND YOU SHOWED UP AFTER HIM.
NAMI'S SHOPPING! NAMI'S SHOPPING!
BROOK CAME TO THIS ISLAND FOR HIS CONCERT TODAY.
SO, COUNTING YOU, THERE ARE ALREADY SEVEN OF YOU ON THE ARCHIPELAGO.
CON-CERT?
NICO ROBIN AND LUFFY ARE THE ONLY ONES LEFT.
IT'S NO EASY FEAT JUST GETTING TO THIS ISLAND.
FWUP...
YOU REALLY ARE AN AMAZING BUNCH OF PIRATES. IT LOOKS LIKE YOU MIGHT ALL MAKE IT BACK SAFELY.
I DIDN'T KNOW YOU WERE THE ONE TRAINING LUFFY!
HE MUST BE EVEN STRONGER NOW!
I HAVEN'T SEEN HIM FOR ABOUT SIX MONTHS. I CAN'T WAIT TO SEE HOW HE'S GROWN.
AND I CAN'T WAIT TO SEE HOW MUCH NAMI'S GROWN! ♡
PLURT!!
YOU GONNA BE ALL RIGHT?

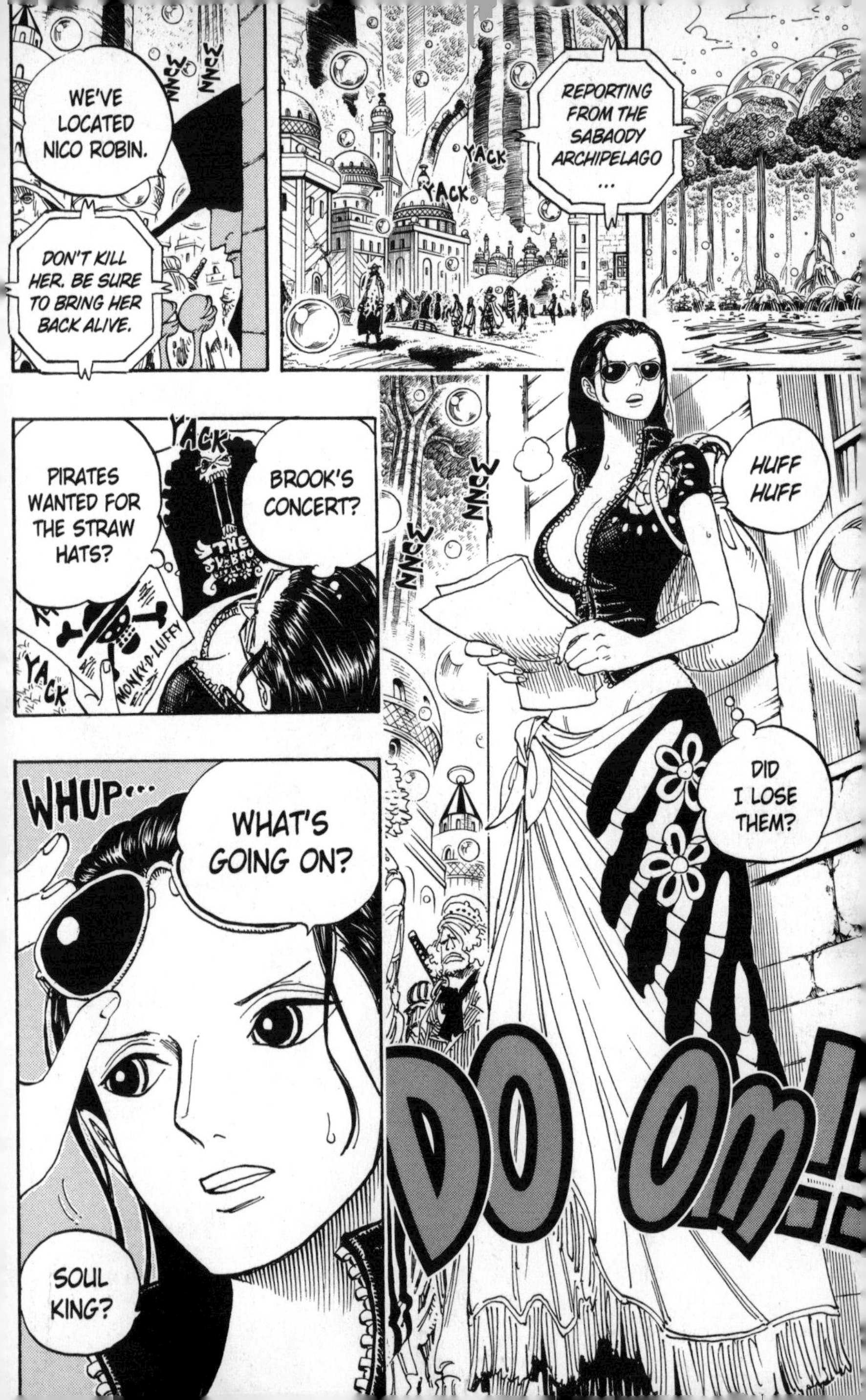
YACK
YACK
REPORTING FROM THE SABAODY ARCHIPELAGO ...
WUNN
WUNN
WE'VE LOCATED NICO ROBIN.
DON'T KILL HER. BE SURE TO BRING HER BACK ALIVE.
HUFF HUFF
WUNN
WUNN
DID I LOSE THEM?
DOOM!!
YACK
BROOK'S CONCERT?
PIRATES WANTED FOR THE STRAW HATS?
YACK
WHUP...
WHAT'S GOING ON?
SOUL KING?

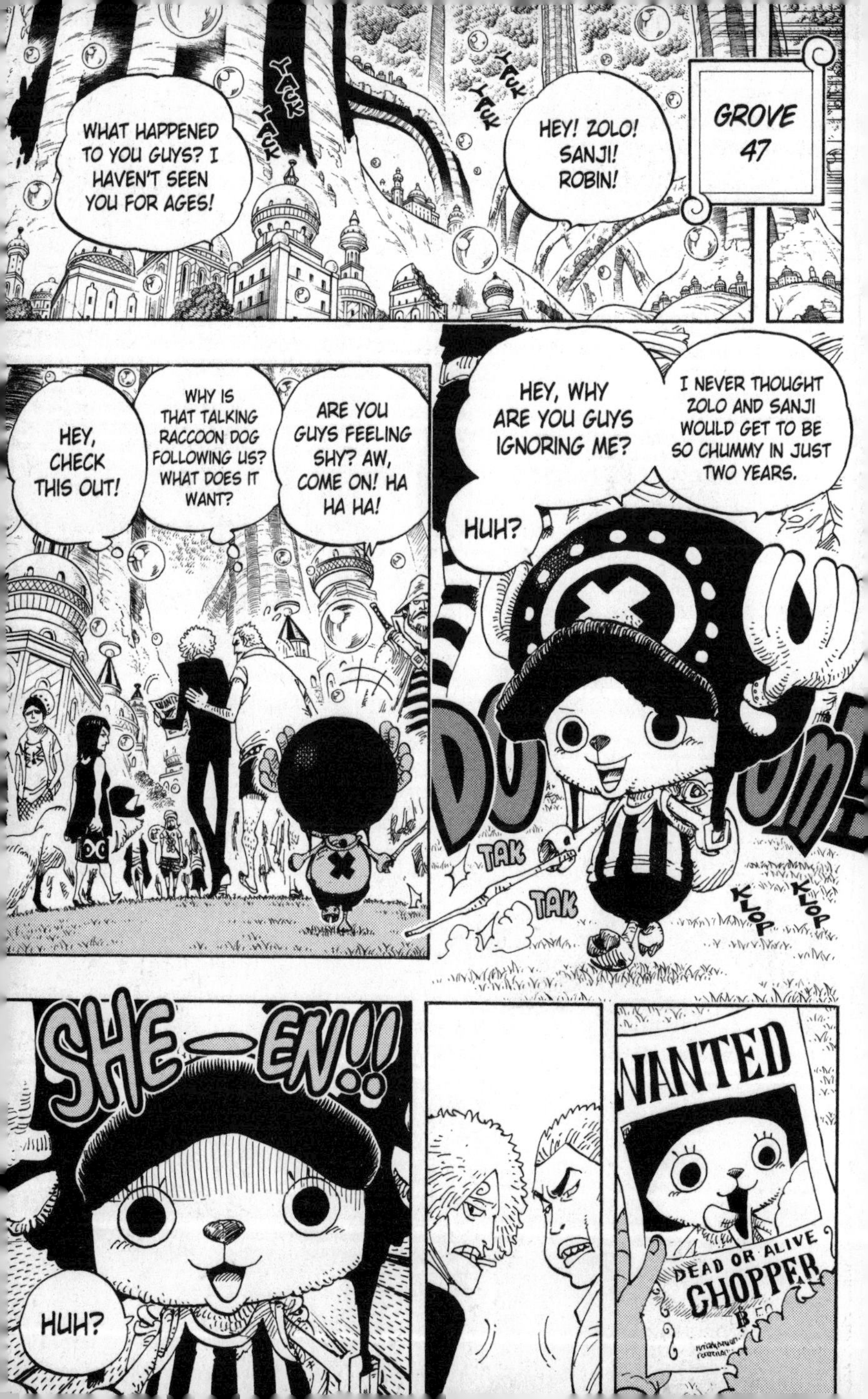
GROVE 47
YACK YACK
HEY! ZOLO! SANJI! ROBIN!
WHAT HAPPENED TO YOU GUYS? I HAVEN'T SEEN YOU FOR AGES!
YACK
I NEVER THOUGHT ZOLO AND SANJI WOULD GET TO BE SO CHUMMY IN JUST TWO YEARS.
HEY, WHY ARE YOU GUYS IGNORING ME?
HUH?
TAK
TAK
KLOP KLOP
ARE YOU GUYS FEELING SHY? AW, COME ON! HA HA HA!
WHY IS THAT TALKING RACCOON DOG FOLLOWING US? WHAT DOES IT WANT?
HEY, CHECK THIS OUT!
WANTED
DEAD OR ALIVE
CHOPPER
SHE—EN!!
HUH?

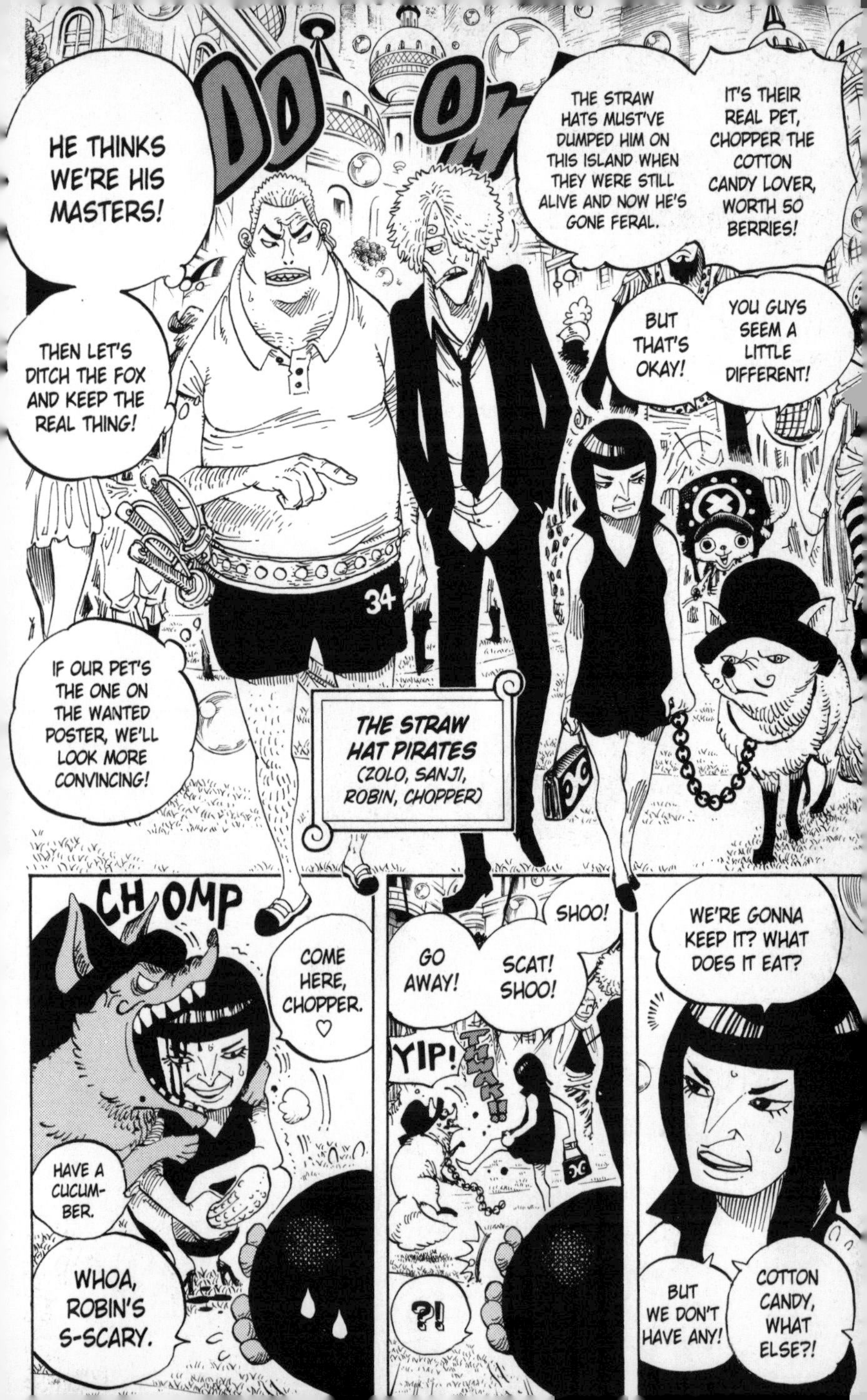
DOOOM
IT'S THEIR REAL PET, CHOPPER THE COTTON CANDY LOVER, WORTH 50 BERRIES!
THE STRAW HATS MUST'VE DUMPED HIM ON THIS ISLAND WHEN THEY WERE STILL ALIVE AND NOW HE'S GONE FERAL.
YOU GUYS SEEM A LITTLE DIFFERENT!
BUT THAT'S OKAY!
HE THINKS WE'RE HIS MASTERS!
THEN LET'S DITCH THE FOX AND KEEP THE REAL THING!
IF OUR PET'S THE ONE ON THE WANTED POSTER, WE'LL LOOK MORE CONVINCING!
THE STRAW HAT PIRATES (ZOLO, SANJI, ROBIN, CHOPPER)
WE'RE GONNA KEEP IT? WHAT DOES IT EAT?
COTTON CANDY, WHAT ELSE?!
BUT WE DON'T HAVE ANY!
SHOO!
SCAT! SHOO!
GO AWAY!
YIP!
?!
CHOMP
COME HERE, CHOPPER. ♡
HAVE A CUCUMBER.
WHOA, ROBIN'S S-SCARY.

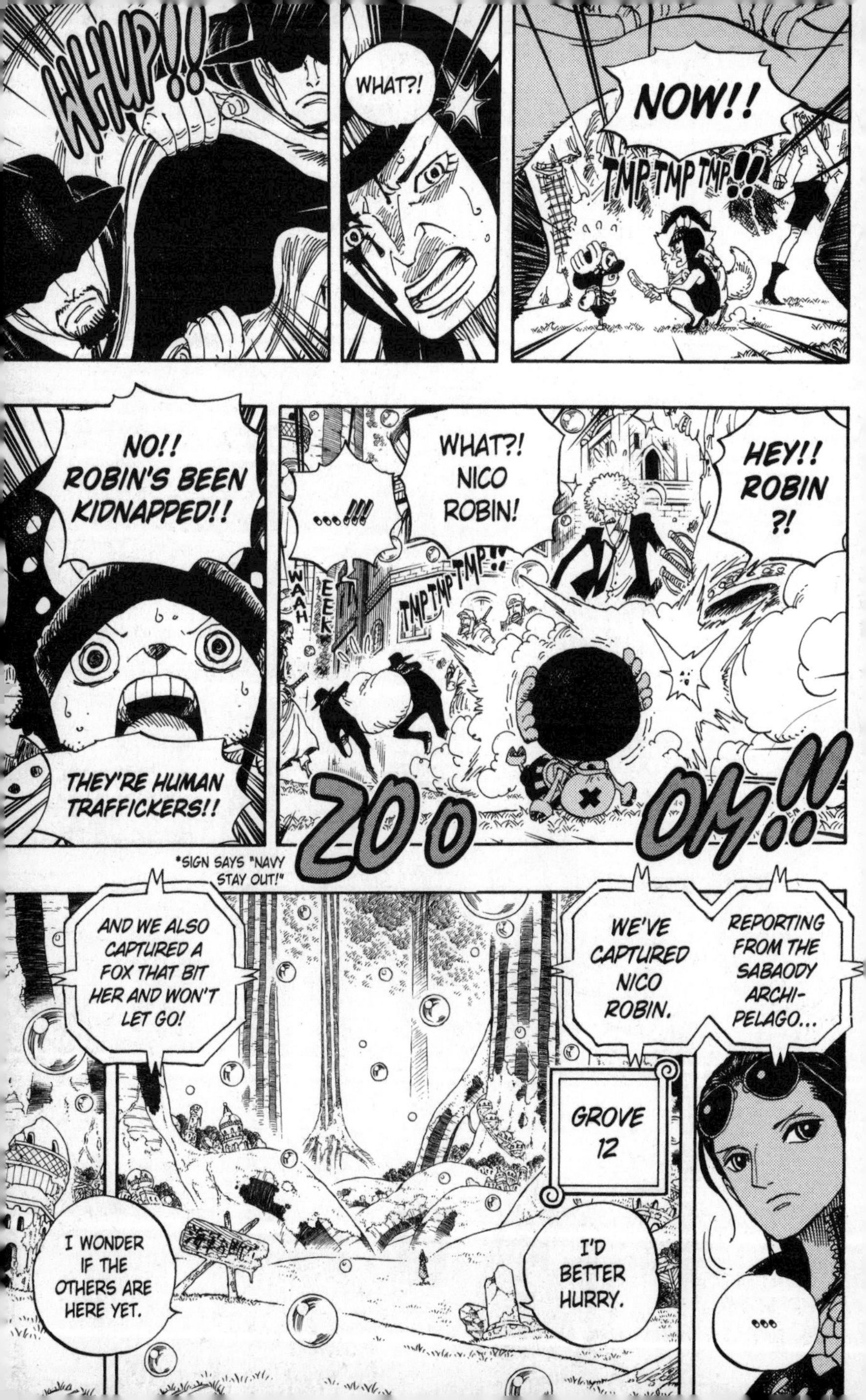
NOW!!
TMP TMP TMP!!
WHAT?!
WHUP!!
HEY!! ROBIN ?!
WHAT?! NICO ROBIN!
...!!!
TMP TMP TMP!!
TMP TMP
EEK
WAAH
ZOOOM!!
NO!! ROBIN'S BEEN KIDNAPPED!!
THEY'RE HUMAN TRAFFICKERS!!
*SIGN SAYS "NAVY STAY OUT!"
REPORTING FROM THE SABAODY ARCHI-PELAGO...
WE'VE CAPTURED NICO ROBIN.
AND WE ALSO CAPTURED A FOX THAT BIT HER AND WON'T LET GO!
GROVE 12
...
I'D BETTER HURRY.
I WONDER IF THE OTHERS ARE HERE YET.

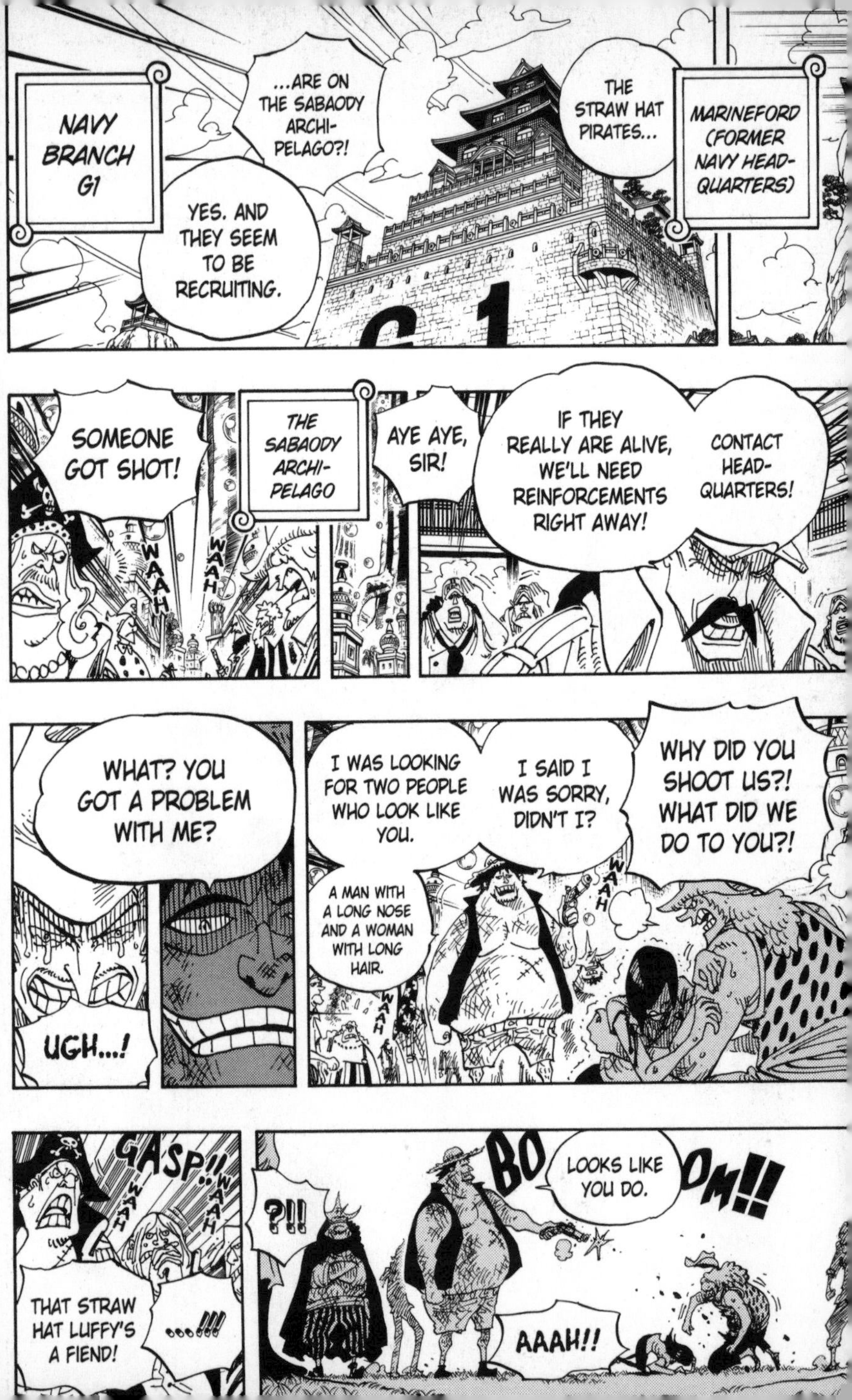
MARINEFORD (FORMER NAVY HEADQUARTERS)
THE STRAW HAT PIRATES...
...ARE ON THE SABAODY ARCHIPELAGO?!
NAVY BRANCH G1
YES. AND THEY SEEM TO BE RECRUITING.
CONTACT HEADQUARTERS!
IF THEY REALLY ARE ALIVE, WE'LL NEED REINFORCEMENTS RIGHT AWAY!
AYE AYE, SIR!
THE SABAODY ARCHIPELAGO
WAAH
WAAH
SOMEONE GOT SHOT!
WHY DID YOU SHOOT US?! WHAT DID WE DO TO YOU?!
I SAID I WAS SORRY, DIDN'T I?
WAAH
I WAS LOOKING FOR TWO PEOPLE WHO LOOK LIKE YOU.
A MAN WITH A LONG NOSE AND A WOMAN WITH LONG HAIR.
WAAH
WHAT? YOU GOT A PROBLEM WITH ME?
UGH...!
BOOM!!
LOOKS LIKE YOU DO.
?!!
AAAH!!
GASP!!
WAAH
WAAH
...!!!
THAT STRAW HAT LUFFY'S A FIEND!

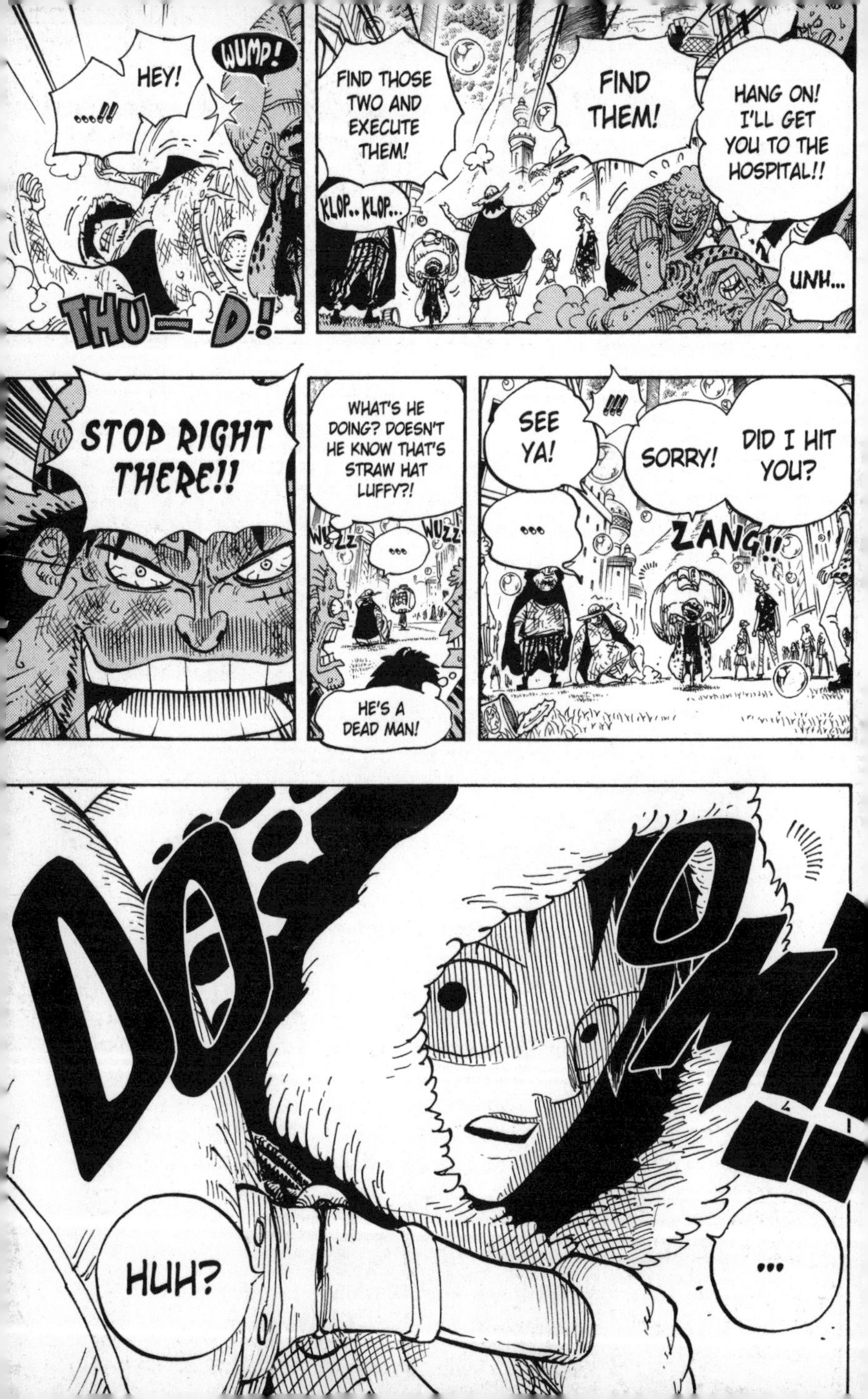
HANG ON! I'LL GET YOU TO THE HOSPITAL!!
FIND THEM!
FIND THOSE TWO AND EXECUTE THEM!
UNH...
KLOP.. KLOP...
WUMP!
HEY!
....!!
THU—D!
!!!
DID I HIT YOU?
SORRY!
SEE YA!
ZANG!!
...
WHAT'S HE DOING? DOESN'T HE KNOW THAT'S STRAW HAT LUFFY?!
WUZZ
...
WUZZ
HE'S A DEAD MAN!
STOP RIGHT THERE!!
DOOM!!
...
HUH?

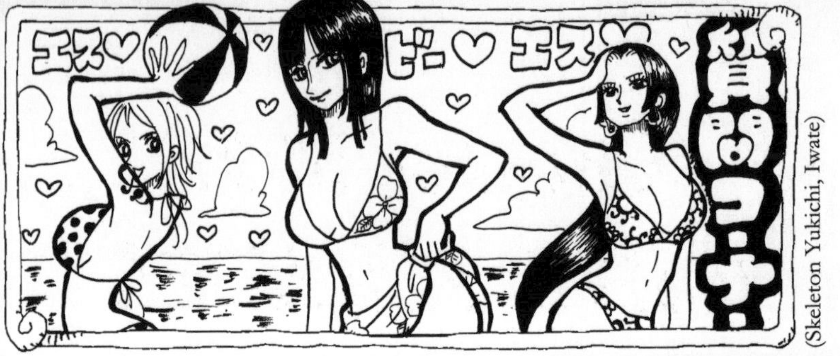
エスビーエス質問コーナー

(Skeleton Yukichi, Iwate)

Q: Hello Mr. Odacchi. Good evening. I have a question about the badges on Ace's hat.

Should I have ever been born?

After meeting Pops and Luffy, I'm so glad I was born. Thank you for loving me.

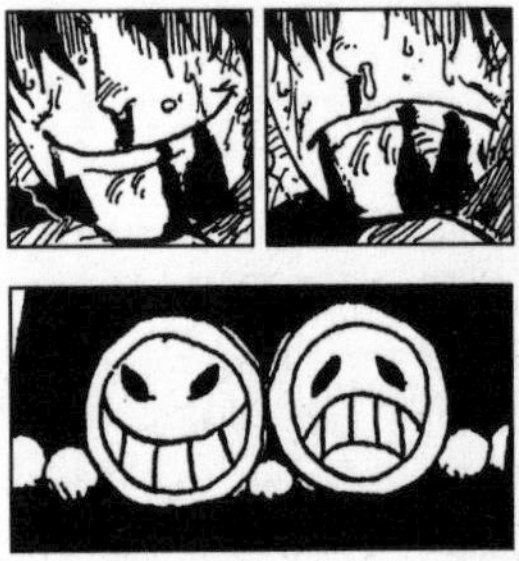

Did those badges symbolize the "answer" Ace found in his journey? No, I'm sure of it! When Ace said his last words, the expressions he showed were exactly like the badges on his hat.

--KY(Considerate Guy) of Nara

A: Hmm, I see. I actually received a lot of letters about this. You're right. The badges are exactly the same as his last expressions. I was so surprised when people pointed it out. That means that it was a complete coincidence. When Ace first appeared, I'd already planned out his fate in the story, but I only meant for those badges to be a fashion statement. As for the last expressions Ace made, I presented it that way because I thought that would be how Ace would feel. He's in pain. He's burning inside and out. He feels sorry and doesn't want to die. But at the same time, he doesn't regret anything in his life. I think he wanted to tell that to Luffy. That's why he also smiled. When trying to cheer up a baby, everyone smiles, right? It's the same as that. He's smiling because he wants others to smile. That last expression is a parting gift to the ones he will leave behind. That's why I put those two panels together. Well, I guess this is getting a bit longwinded. Anyway, I'm surprised how many people noticed.

Q: Why do the dishes on the conveyor belt at sushi restaurants spin?

-- Phoenix Maruko

A: Probably the same reason why the world goes round.

Chapter 599:
NINE PIRATES

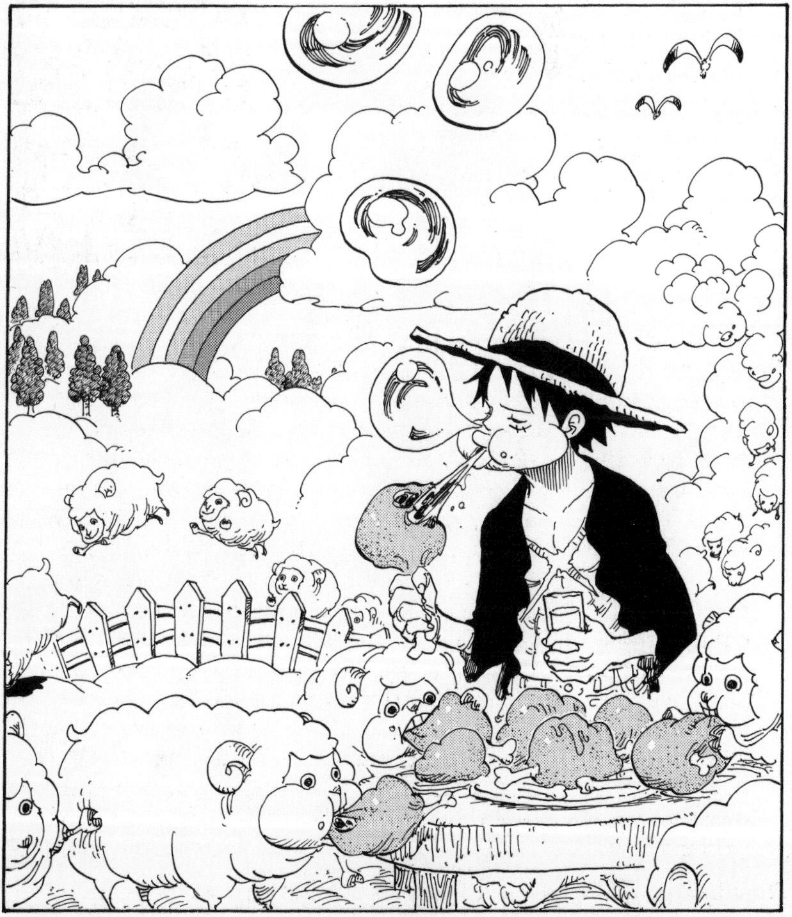

REQUEST: "LUFFY COUNTS SHEEP TO FALL ASLEEP AND THEY TAKE HIS FOOD" BY TWINS MOTHER FROM HYOGO

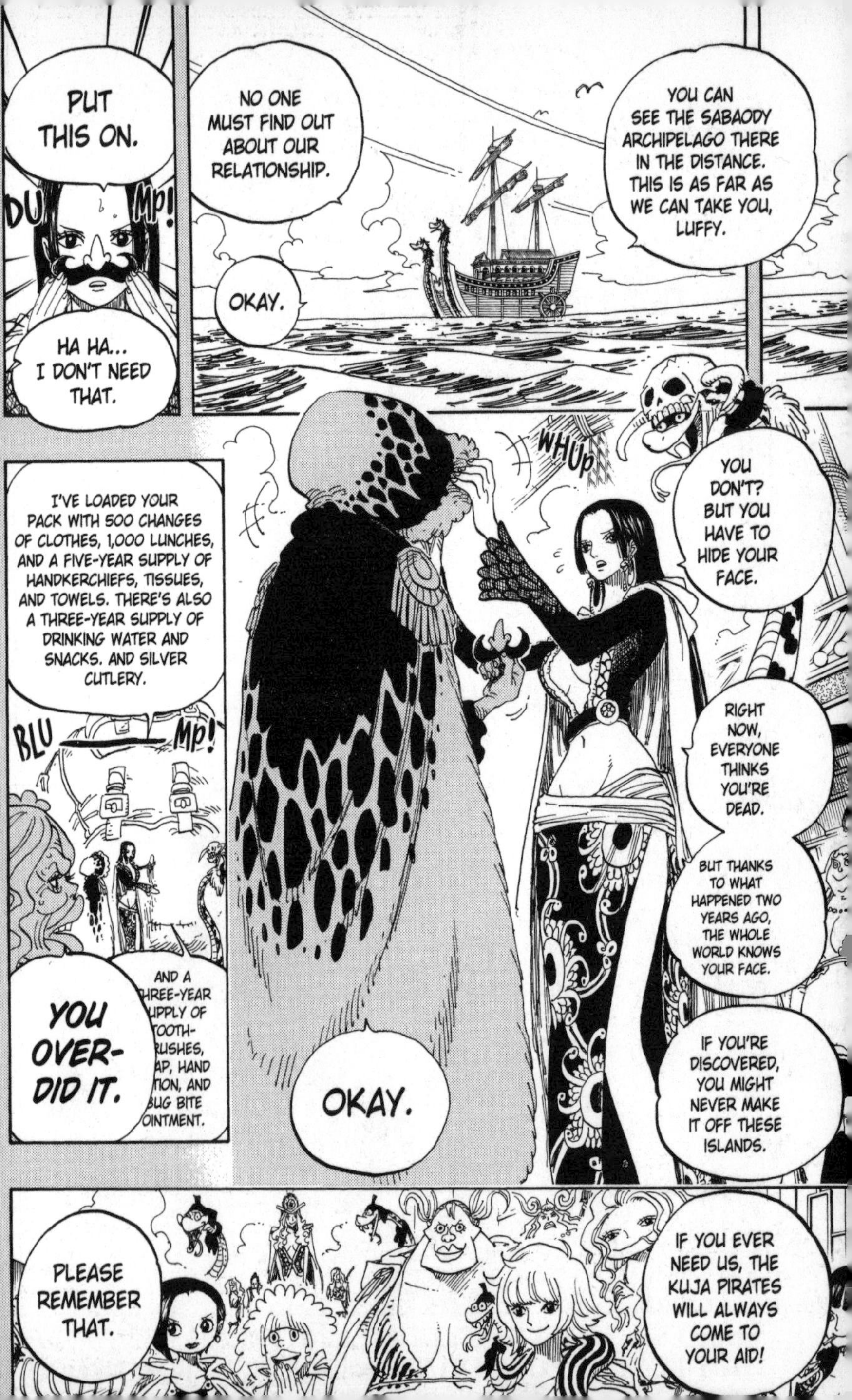
YOU CAN SEE THE SABAODY ARCHIPELAGO THERE IN THE DISTANCE. THIS IS AS FAR AS WE CAN TAKE YOU, LUFFY.
NO ONE MUST FIND OUT ABOUT OUR RELATIONSHIP.
OKAY.
PUT THIS ON.
DUMP!
HA HA... I DON'T NEED THAT.
WHUP
YOU DON'T? BUT YOU HAVE TO HIDE YOUR FACE.
RIGHT NOW, EVERYONE THINKS YOU'RE DEAD.
BUT THANKS TO WHAT HAPPENED TWO YEARS AGO, THE WHOLE WORLD KNOWS YOUR FACE.
IF YOU'RE DISCOVERED, YOU MIGHT NEVER MAKE IT OFF THESE ISLANDS.
OKAY.
I'VE LOADED YOUR PACK WITH 500 CHANGES OF CLOTHES, 1,000 LUNCHES, AND A FIVE-YEAR SUPPLY OF HANDKERCHIEFS, TISSUES, AND TOWELS. THERE'S ALSO A THREE-YEAR SUPPLY OF DRINKING WATER AND SNACKS. AND SILVER CUTLERY.
BLUMP!
AND A THREE-YEAR UPPLY OF TOOTH- RUSHES, AP, HAND TION, AND BUG BITE OINTMENT.
YOU OVER-DID IT.
IF YOU EVER NEED US, THE KUJA PIRATES WILL ALWAYS COME TO YOUR AID!
PLEASE REMEMBER THAT.

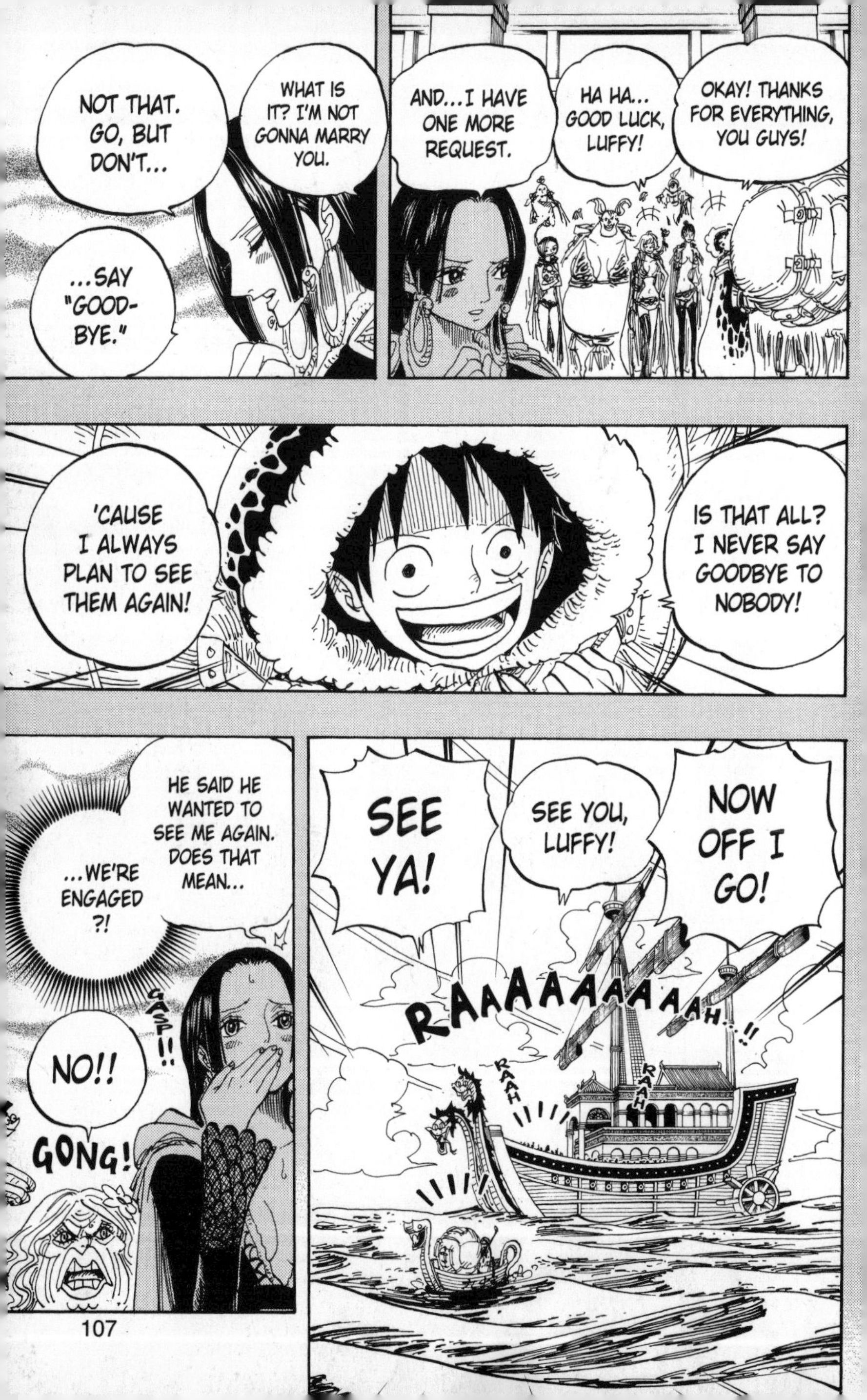
OKAY! THANKS FOR EVERYTHING, YOU GUYS!
HA HA... GOOD LUCK, LUFFY!
AND...I HAVE ONE MORE REQUEST.
WHAT IS IT? I'M NOT GONNA MARRY YOU.
NOT THAT. GO, BUT DON'T...
...SAY "GOOD-BYE."
IS THAT ALL? I NEVER SAY GOODBYE TO NOBODY!
'CAUSE I ALWAYS PLAN TO SEE THEM AGAIN!
NOW OFF I GO!
SEE YOU, LUFFY!
SEE YA!
RAAAAAAAAAAH..!!
RAAH
RAAH
HE SAID HE WANTED TO SEE ME AGAIN. DOES THAT MEAN...
...WE'RE ENGAGED?!
GASP!!
NO!!
GONG!

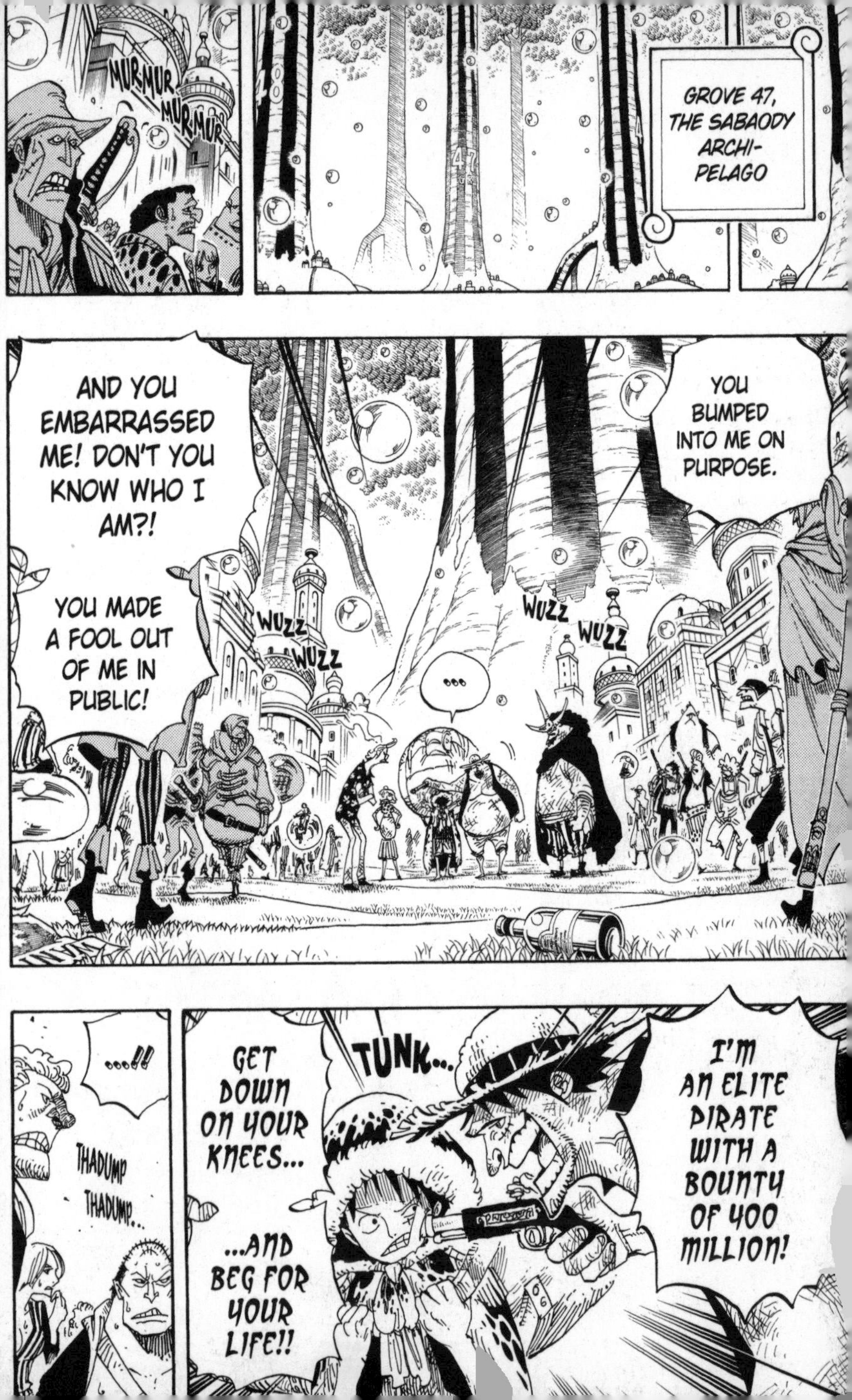
GROVE 47, THE SABAODY ARCHI-PELAGO
MUR-MUR MUR-MUR
YOU BUMPED INTO ME ON PURPOSE.
AND YOU EMBARRASSED ME! DON'T YOU KNOW WHO I AM?!
YOU MADE A FOOL OUT OF ME IN PUBLIC!
WUZZ WUZZ
WUZZ WUZZ
...
I'M AN ELITE PIRATE WITH A BOUNTY OF 400 MILLION!
TUNK...
GET DOWN ON YOUR KNEES...
...AND BEG FOR YOUR LIFE!!
...!!
THADUMP THADUMP...

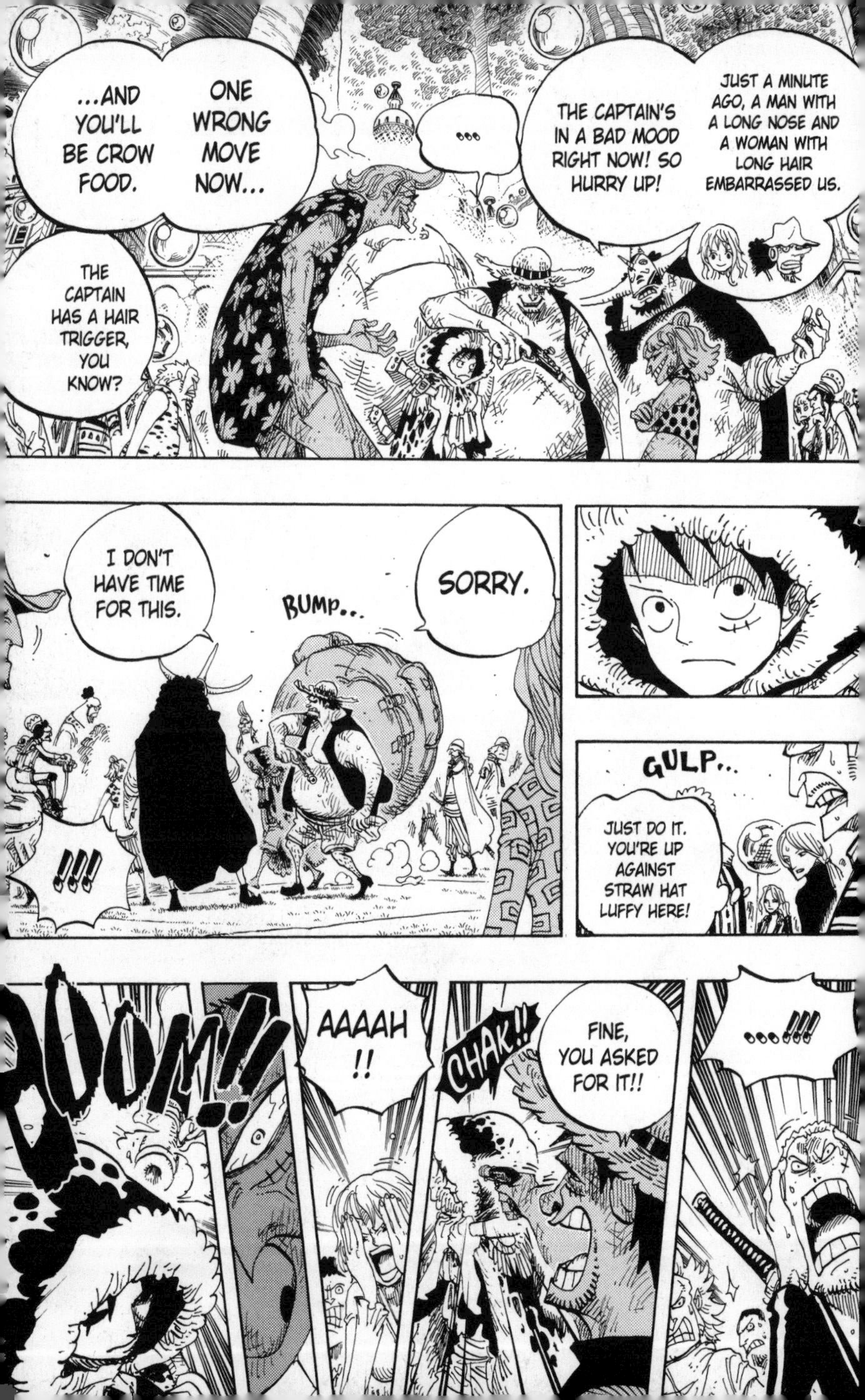
JUST A MINUTE AGO, A MAN WITH A LONG NOSE AND A WOMAN WITH LONG HAIR EMBARRASSED US.
THE CAPTAIN'S IN A BAD MOOD RIGHT NOW! SO HURRY UP!
...
ONE WRONG MOVE NOW...
...AND YOU'LL BE CROW FOOD.
THE CAPTAIN HAS A HAIR TRIGGER, YOU KNOW?
GULP...
JUST DO IT. YOU'RE UP AGAINST STRAW HAT LUFFY HERE!
SORRY.
BUMP...
I DON'T HAVE TIME FOR THIS.
!!!
...!!!
FINE, YOU ASKED FOR IT!!
CHAK!!
AAAAH!!
OOM!!

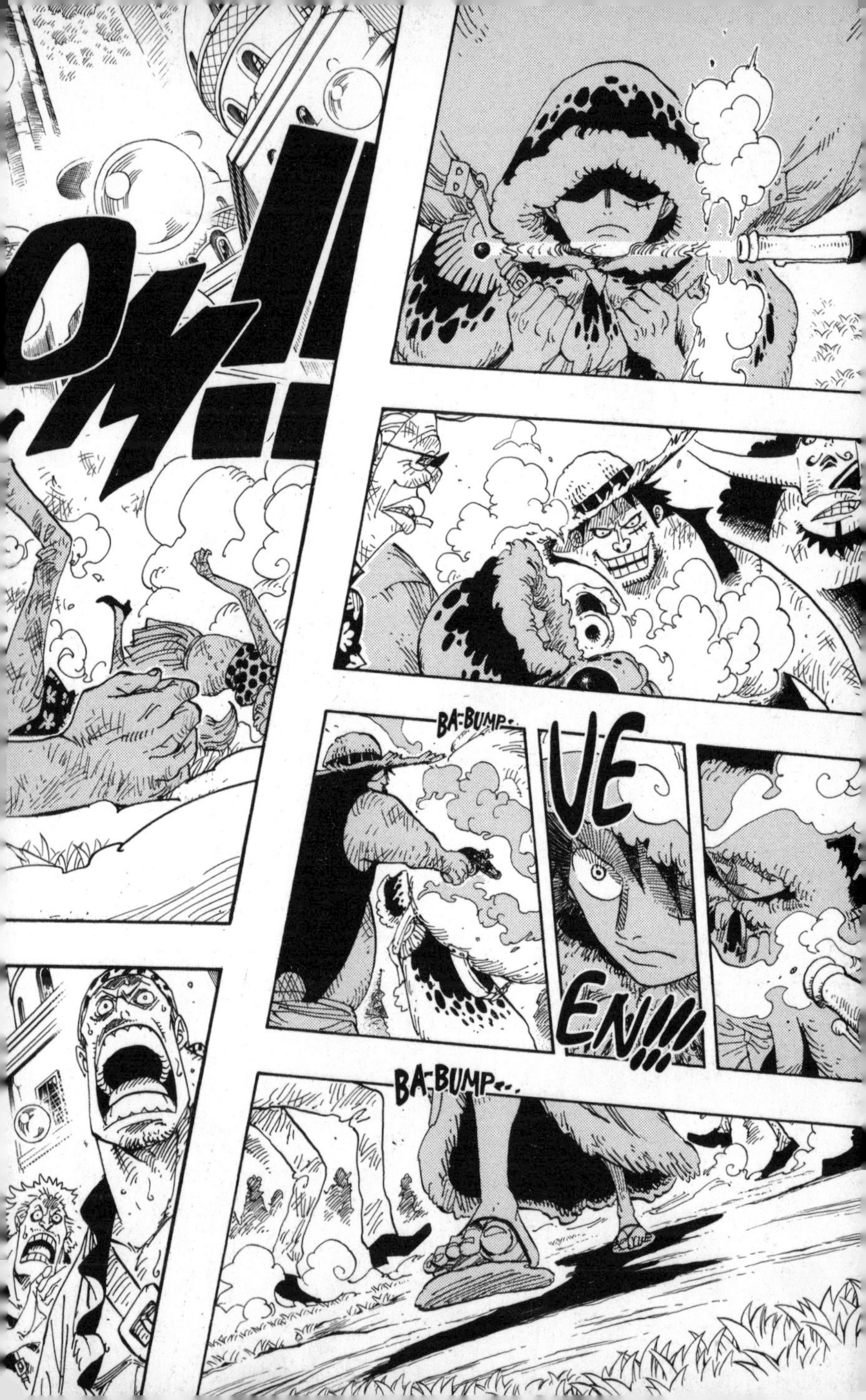
VE
EN!!!
BA-BUMP..
BA-BUMP...
OW..!!

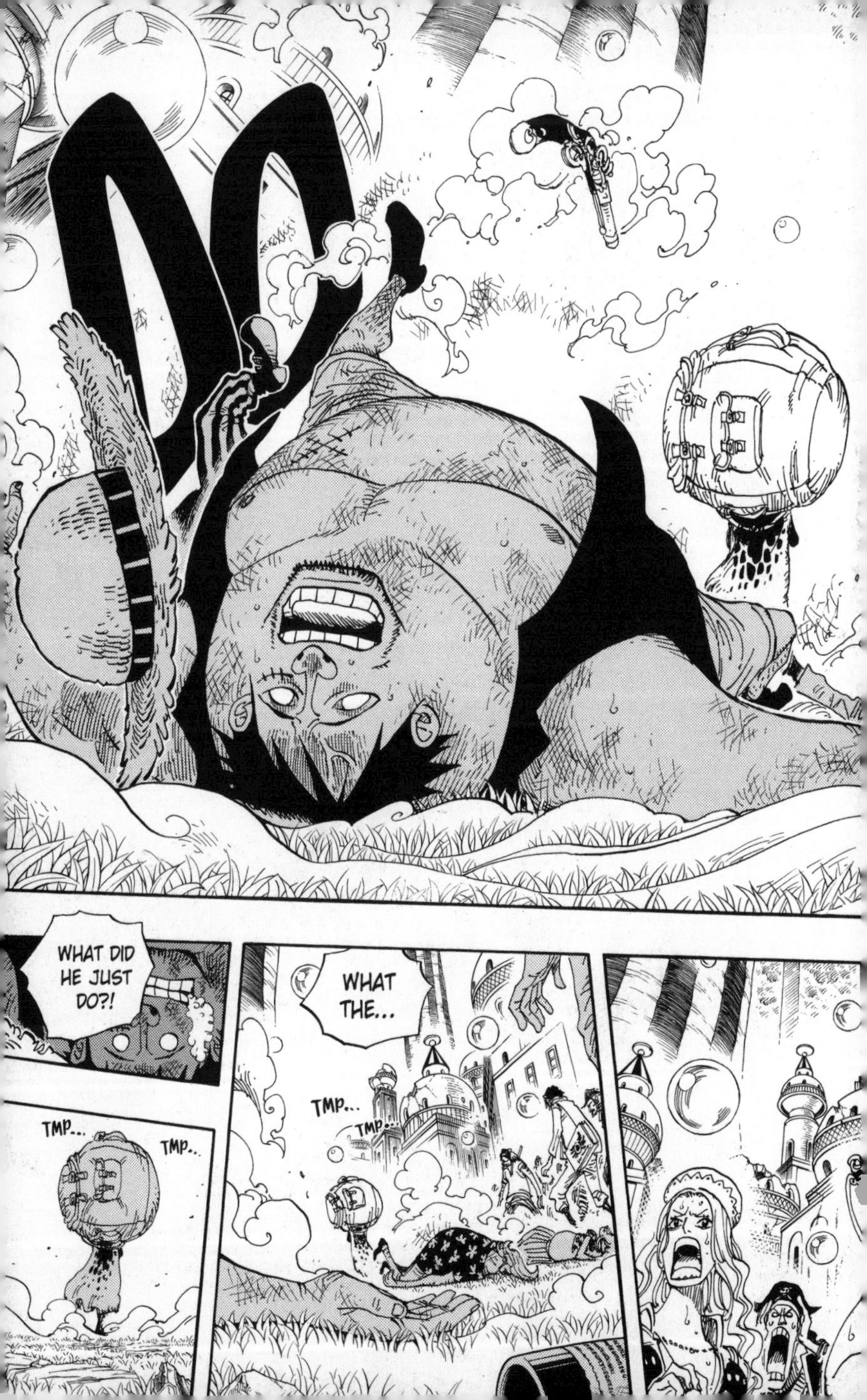
WHAT THE...
TMP...
TMP...
WHAT DID HE JUST DO?!
TMP...
TMP...

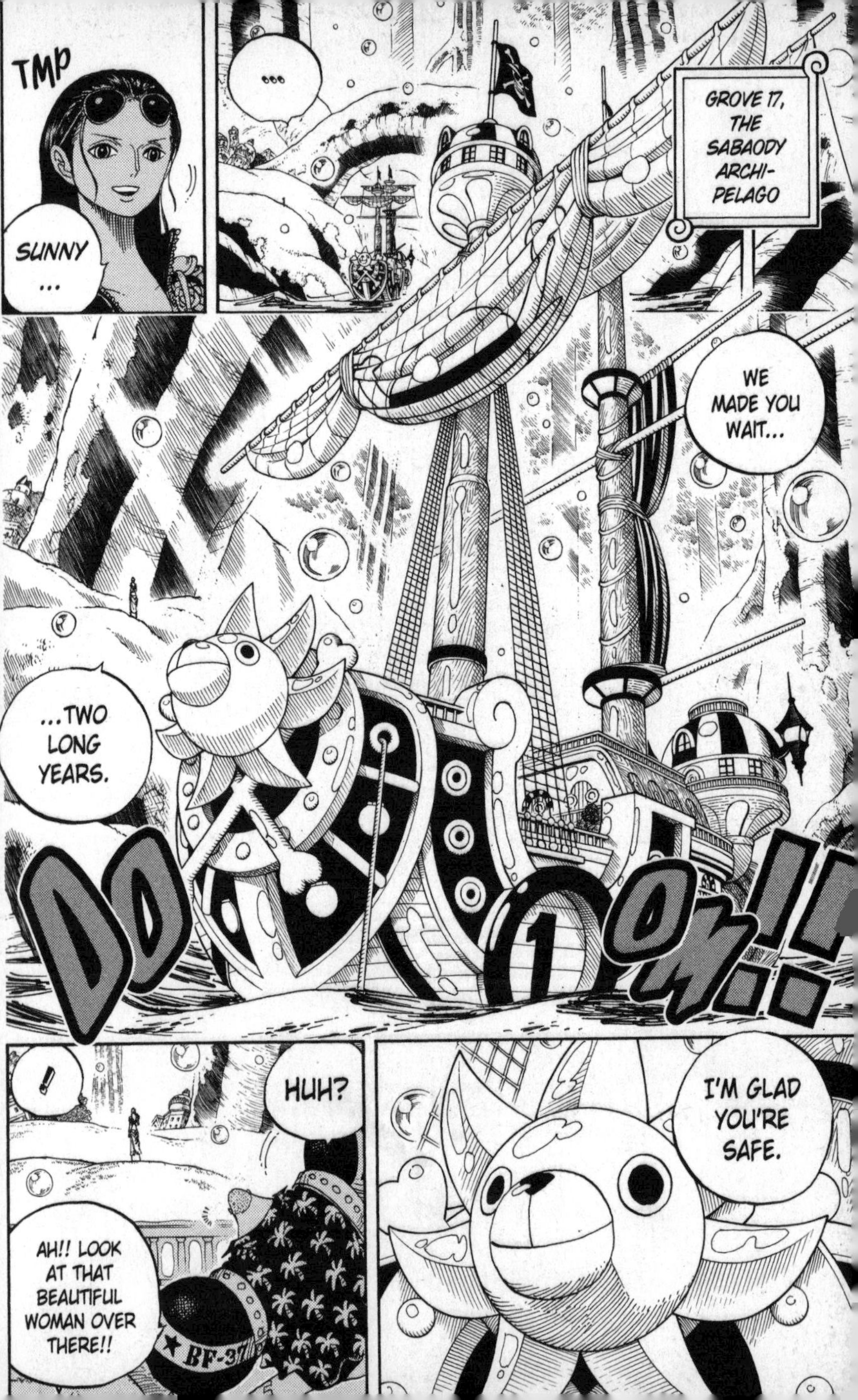
GROVE 17, THE SABAODY ARCHI-PELAGO
WE MADE YOU WAIT...
...TWO LONG YEARS.
DOOON!!
...
TMP
SUNNY ...
I'M GLAD YOU'RE SAFE.
HUH?
!
AH!! LOOK AT THAT BEAUTIFUL WOMAN OVER THERE!!
BF-37

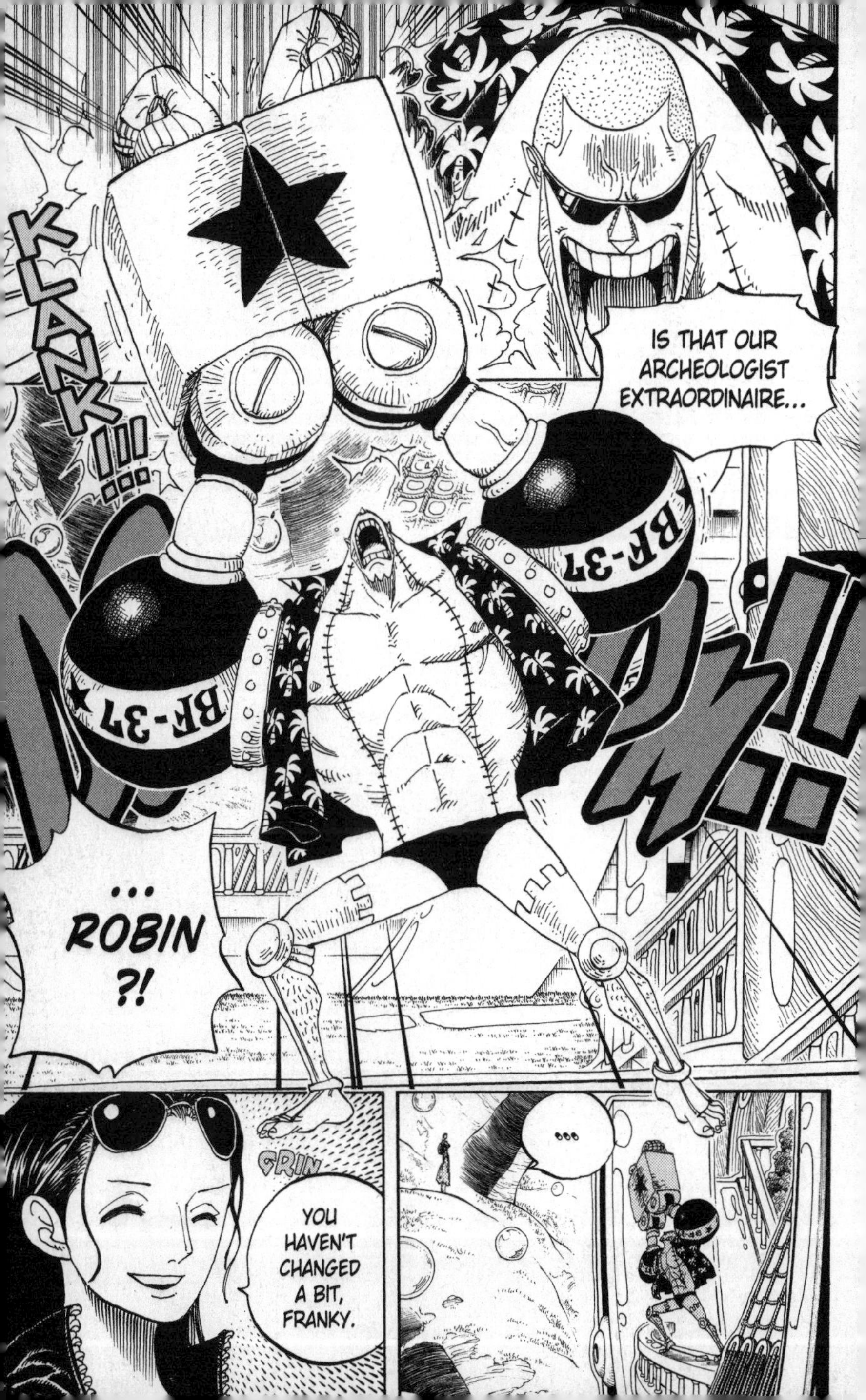
IS THAT OUR ARCHEOLOGIST EXTRAORDINAIRE...
KLANK!!!
BF-37
BF-37
... ROBIN ?!
...
GRIN
YOU HAVEN'T CHANGED A BIT, FRANKY.

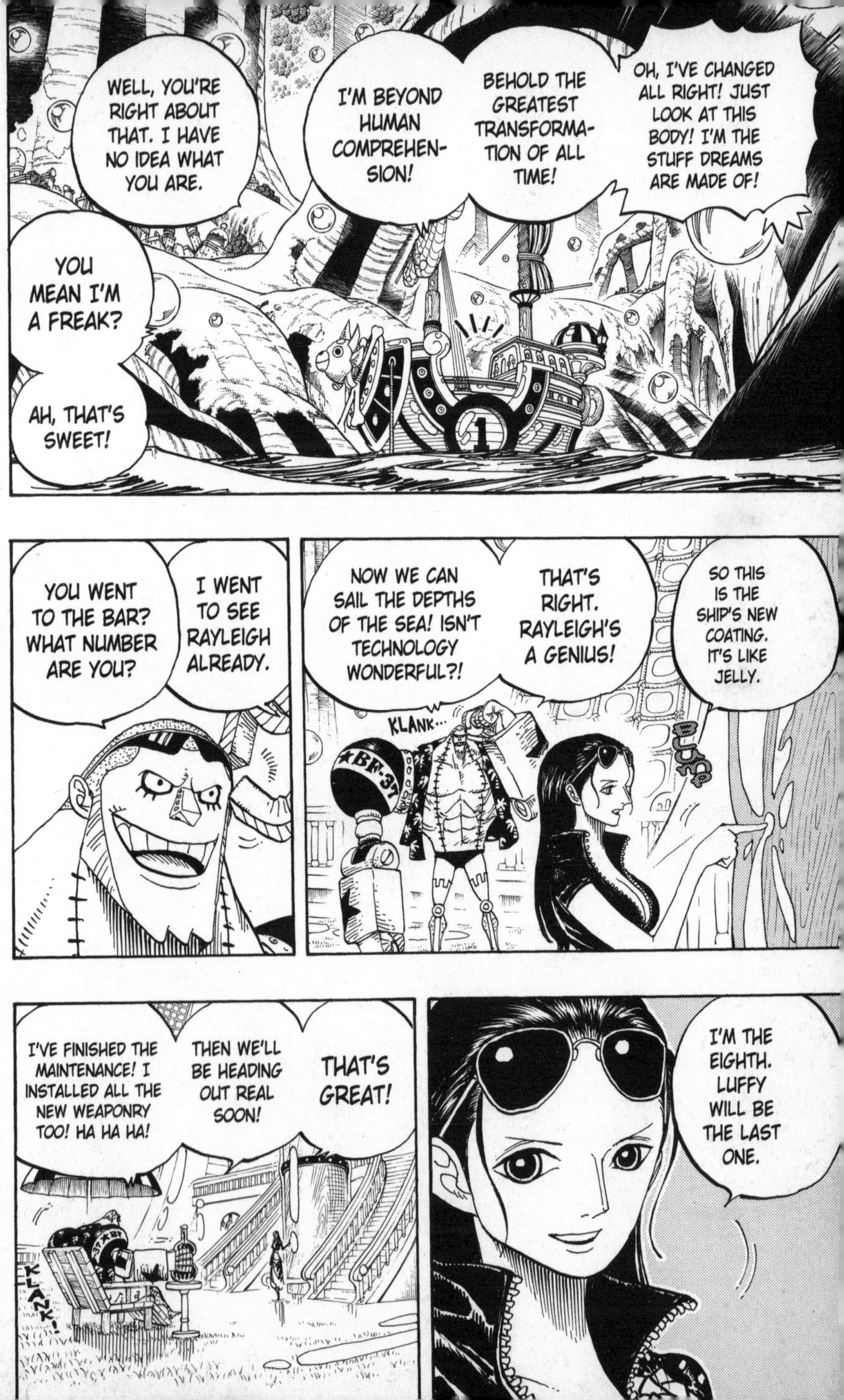
OH, I'VE CHANGED ALL RIGHT! JUST LOOK AT THIS BODY! I'M THE STUFF DREAMS ARE MADE OF!
BEHOLD THE GREATEST TRANSFORMATION OF ALL TIME!
I'M BEYOND HUMAN COMPREHENSION!
WELL, YOU'RE RIGHT ABOUT THAT. I HAVE NO IDEA WHAT YOU ARE.
YOU MEAN I'M A FREAK?
AH, THAT'S SWEET!
SO THIS IS THE SHIP'S NEW COATING. IT'S LIKE JELLY.
THAT'S RIGHT. RAYLEIGH'S A GENIUS!
NOW WE CAN SAIL THE DEPTHS OF THE SEA! ISN'T TECHNOLOGY WONDERFUL?!
KLANK...
I WENT TO SEE RAYLEIGH ALREADY.
YOU WENT TO THE BAR? WHAT NUMBER ARE YOU?
I'M THE EIGHTH. LUFFY WILL BE THE LAST ONE.
THAT'S GREAT!
THEN WE'LL BE HEADING OUT REAL SOON!
I'VE FINISHED THE MAINTENANCE! I INSTALLED ALL THE NEW WEAPONRY TOO! HA HA HA!
KLANK!

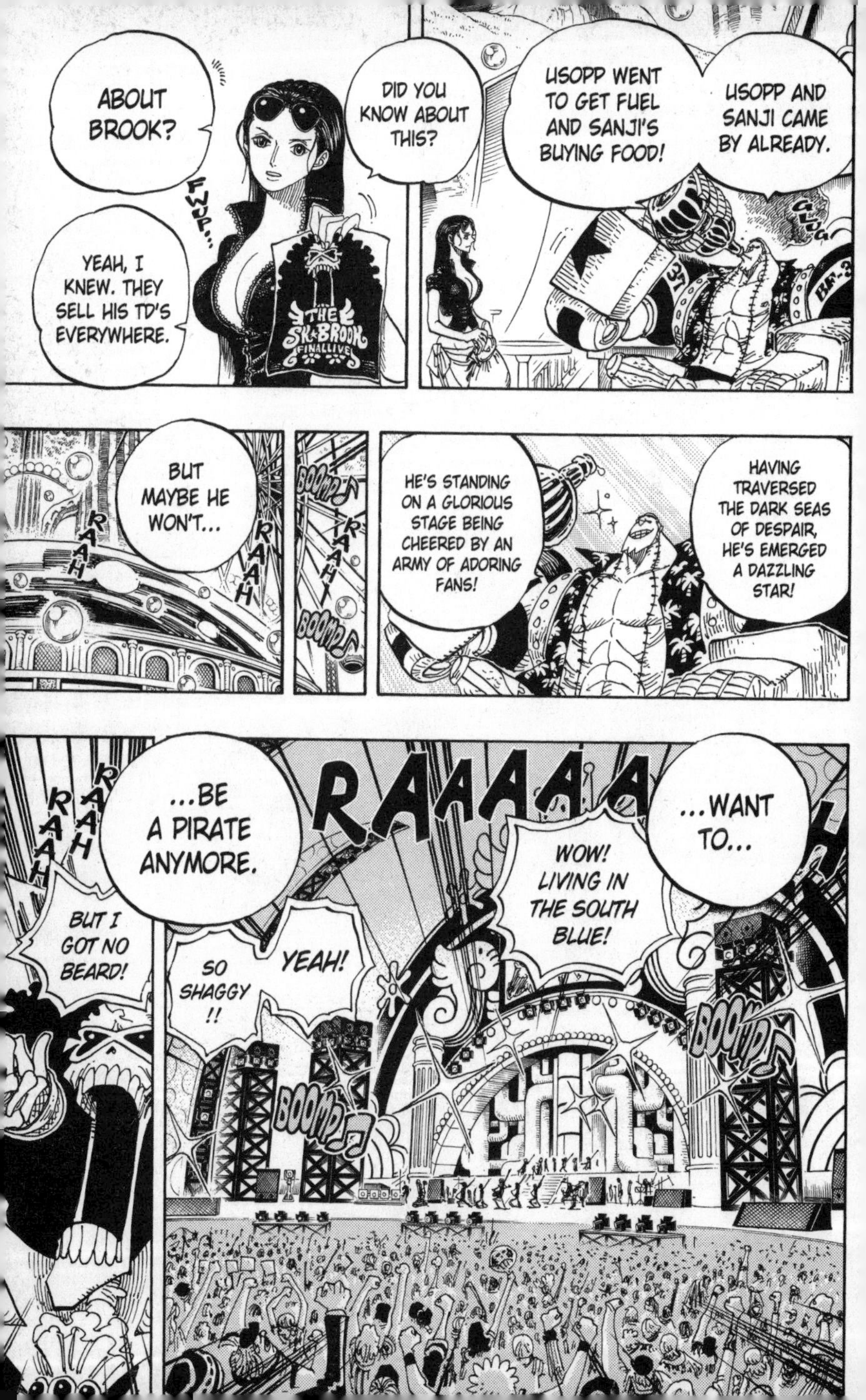
USOPP AND SANJI CAME BY ALREADY.
USOPP WENT TO GET FUEL AND SANJI'S BUYING FOOD!
GLUG
DID YOU KNOW ABOUT THIS?
ABOUT BROOK?
FWUP...
THE SK★BROOK FINAL LIVE
YEAH, I KNEW. THEY SELL HIS TD'S EVERYWHERE.
HAVING TRAVERSED THE DARK SEAS OF DESPAIR, HE'S EMERGED A DAZZLING STAR!
HE'S STANDING ON A GLORIOUS STAGE BEING CHEERED BY AN ARMY OF ADORING FANS!
BOOMP
RAAH
BOOMP
BUT MAYBE HE WON'T...
RAAH
RAAH
...WANT TO...
RAAAAAH
WOW! LIVING IN THE SOUTH BLUE!
BOOMP
YEAH!
SO SHAGGY!!
BOOMP
...BE A PIRATE ANYMORE.
RAAH
RAAH
BUT I GOT NO BEARD!

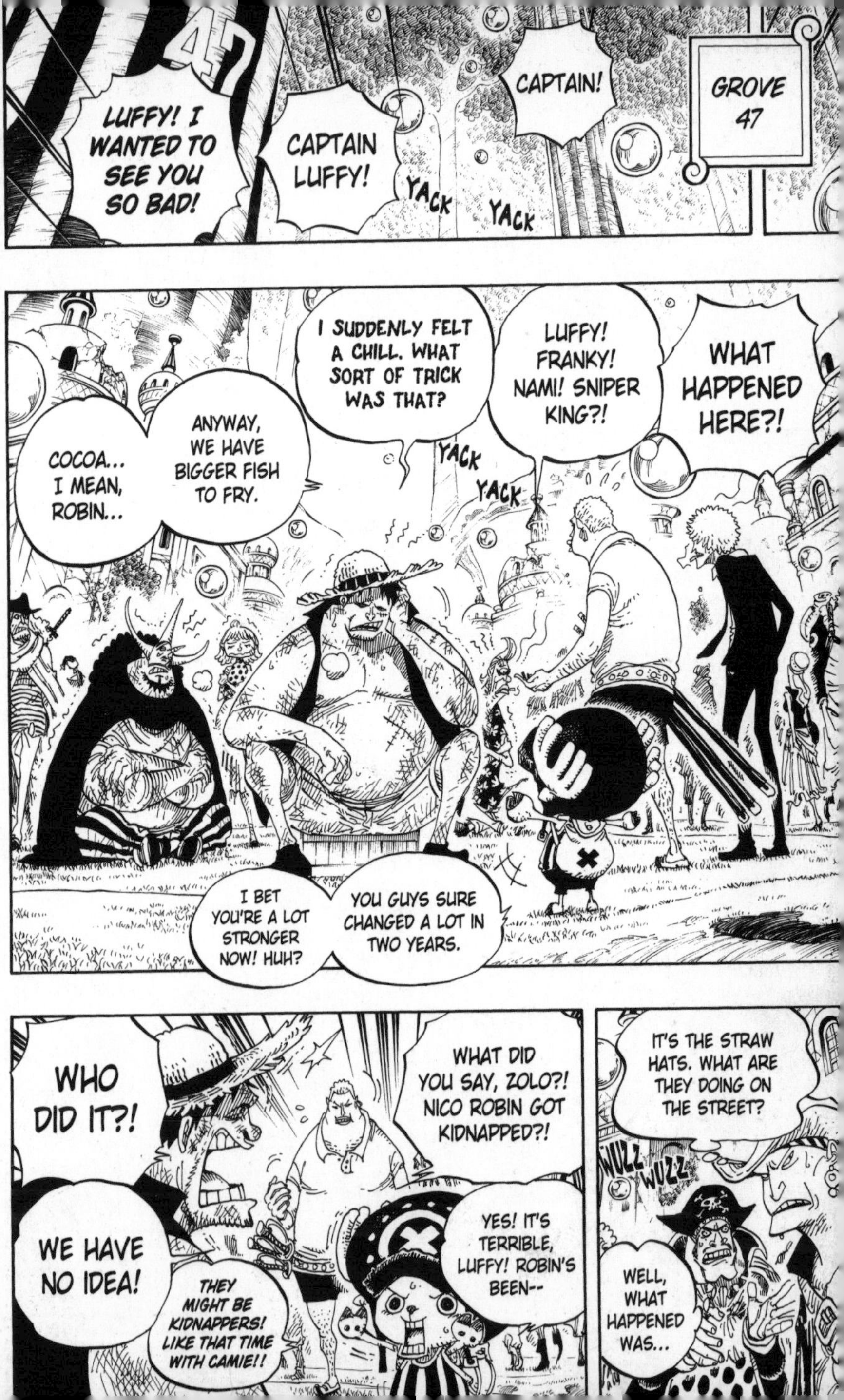
GROVE 47
CAPTAIN!
CAPTAIN LUFFY!
YACK
YACK
LUFFY! I WANTED TO SEE YOU SO BAD!
WHAT HAPPENED HERE?!
LUFFY! FRANKY! NAMI! SNIPER KING?!
YACK
YACK
I SUDDENLY FELT A CHILL. WHAT SORT OF TRICK WAS THAT?
ANYWAY, WE HAVE BIGGER FISH TO FRY.
COCOA... I MEAN, ROBIN...
YOU GUYS SURE CHANGED A LOT IN TWO YEARS.
I BET YOU'RE A LOT STRONGER NOW! HUH?
IT'S THE STRAW HATS. WHAT ARE THEY DOING ON THE STREET?
WUZZ
WUZZ
WELL, WHAT HAPPENED WAS...
WHAT DID YOU SAY, ZOLO?! NICO ROBIN GOT KIDNAPPED?!
WHO DID IT?!
YES! IT'S TERRIBLE, LUFFY! ROBIN'S BEEN--
WE HAVE NO IDEA!
THEY MIGHT BE KIDNAPPERS! LIKE THAT TIME WITH CAMIE!!

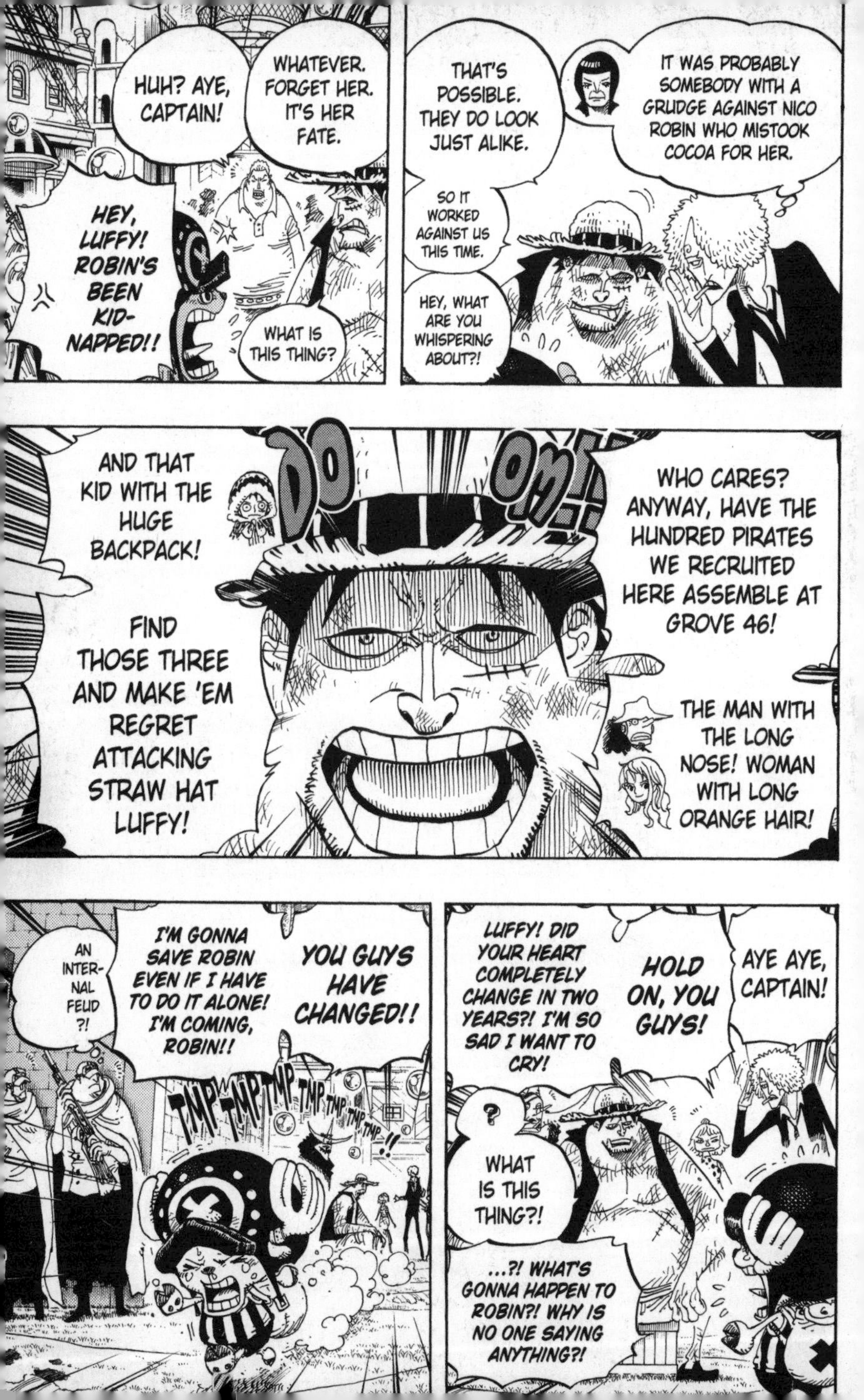
IT WAS PROBABLY SOMEBODY WITH A GRUDGE AGAINST NICO ROBIN WHO MISTOOK COCOA FOR HER.
THAT'S POSSIBLE. THEY DO LOOK JUST ALIKE.
SO IT WORKED AGAINST US THIS TIME.
HEY, WHAT ARE YOU WHISPERING ABOUT?!
WHATEVER. FORGET HER. IT'S HER FATE.
HUH? AYE, CAPTAIN!
HEY, LUFFY! ROBIN'S BEEN KID-NAPPED!!
WHAT IS THIS THING?
DOOM
WHO CARES? ANYWAY, HAVE THE HUNDRED PIRATES WE RECRUITED HERE ASSEMBLE AT GROVE 46!
THE MAN WITH THE LONG NOSE! WOMAN WITH LONG ORANGE HAIR!
AND THAT KID WITH THE HUGE BACKPACK!
FIND THOSE THREE AND MAKE 'EM REGRET ATTACKING STRAW HAT LUFFY!
AYE AYE, CAPTAIN!
HOLD ON, YOU GUYS!
LUFFY! DID YOUR HEART COMPLETELY CHANGE IN TWO YEARS?! I'M SO SAD I WANT TO CRY!
?
WHAT IS THIS THING?!
...?! WHAT'S GONNA HAPPEN TO ROBIN?! WHY IS NO ONE SAYING ANYTHING?!
YOU GUYS HAVE CHANGED!!
I'M GONNA SAVE ROBIN EVEN IF I HAVE TO DO IT ALONE! I'M COMING, ROBIN!!
AN INTER-NAL FEUD?!
TMP TMP TMP TMP TMP TMP TMP TMP !!

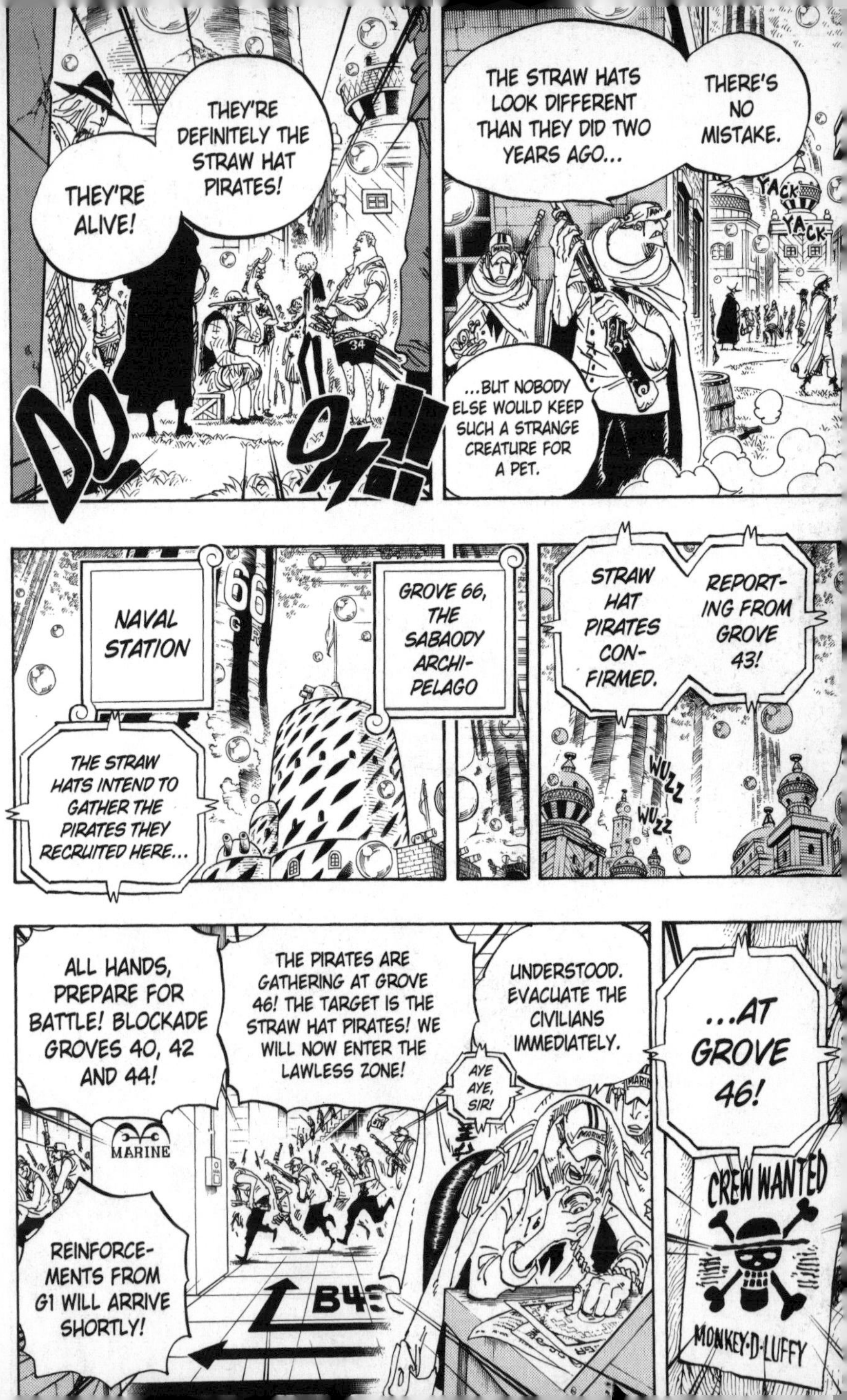
THERE'S NO MISTAKE.
THE STRAW HATS LOOK DIFFERENT THAN THEY DID TWO YEARS AGO...
YACK YACK
...BUT NOBODY ELSE WOULD KEEP SUCH A STRANGE CREATURE FOR A PET.
THEY'RE DEFINITELY THE STRAW HAT PIRATES!
THEY'RE ALIVE!
34
DOOM!!
REPORTING FROM GROVE 43!
STRAW HAT PIRATES CONFIRMED.
WUZZ WUZZ
GROVE 66, THE SABAODY ARCHIPELAGO
66
NAVAL STATION
THE STRAW HATS INTEND TO GATHER THE PIRATES THEY RECRUITED HERE...
...AT GROVE 46!
CREW WANTED
MONKEY·D·LUFFY
UNDERSTOOD. EVACUATE THE CIVILIANS IMMEDIATELY.
AYE AYE, SIR!
THE PIRATES ARE GATHERING AT GROVE 46! THE TARGET IS THE STRAW HAT PIRATES! WE WILL NOW ENTER THE LAWLESS ZONE!
ALL HANDS, PREPARE FOR BATTLE! BLOCKADE GROVES 40, 42 AND 44!
MARINE
REINFORCEMENTS FROM G1 WILL ARRIVE SHORTLY!
B43

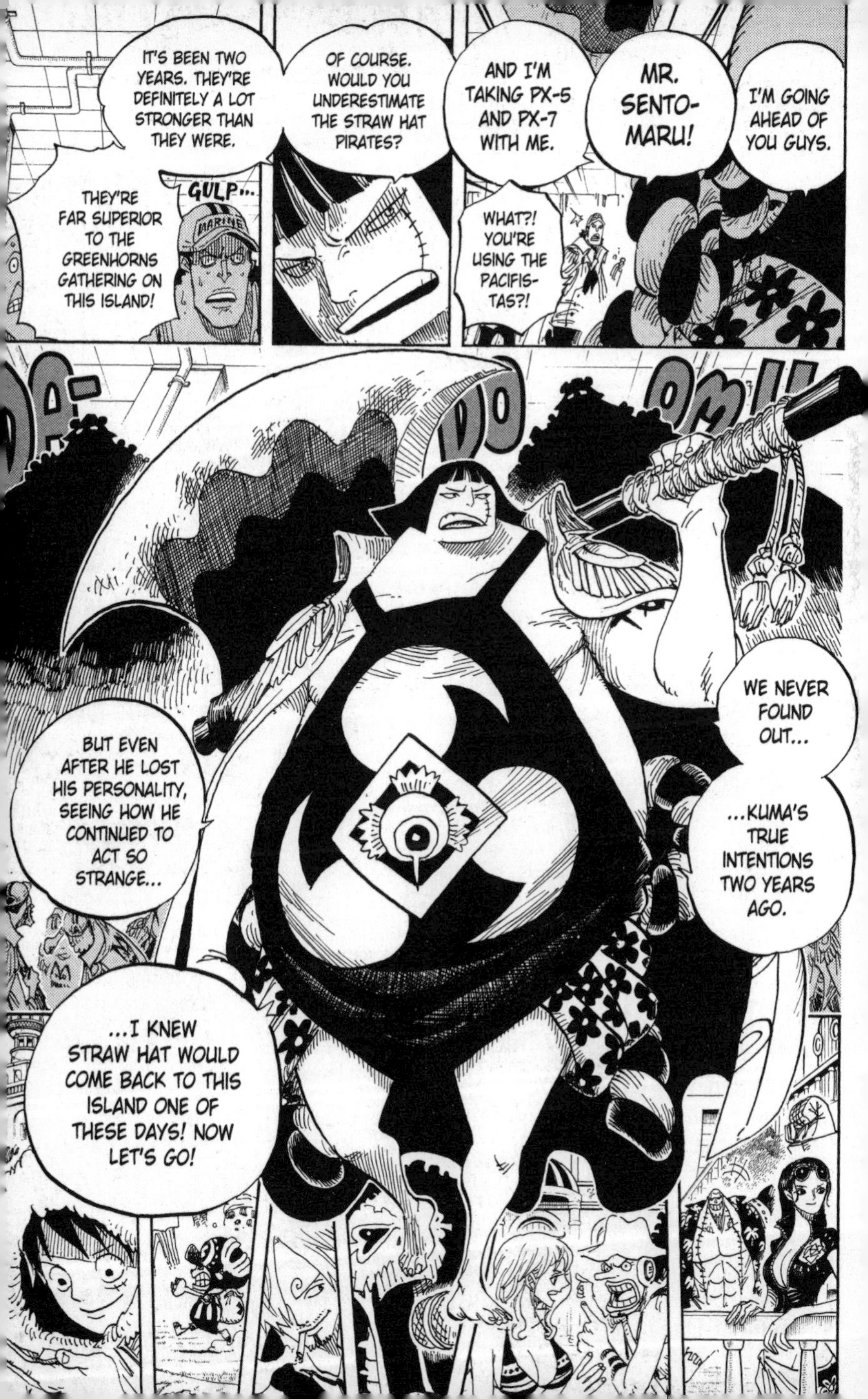
I'M GOING AHEAD OF YOU GUYS.
MR. SENTO-MARU!
AND I'M TAKING PX-5 AND PX-7 WITH ME.
WHAT?! YOU'RE USING THE PACIFIS-TAS?!
OF COURSE. WOULD YOU UNDERESTIMATE THE STRAW HAT PIRATES?
IT'S BEEN TWO YEARS. THEY'RE DEFINITELY A LOT STRONGER THAN THEY WERE.
GULP...
THEY'RE FAR SUPERIOR TO THE GREENHORNS GATHERING ON THIS ISLAND!
DO- DO OM!!
WE NEVER FOUND OUT...
...KUMA'S TRUE INTENTIONS TWO YEARS AGO.
BUT EVEN AFTER HE LOST HIS PERSONALITY, SEEING HOW HE CONTINUED TO ACT SO STRANGE...
...I KNEW STRAW HAT WOULD COME BACK TO THIS ISLAND ONE OF THESE DAYS! NOW LET'S GO!

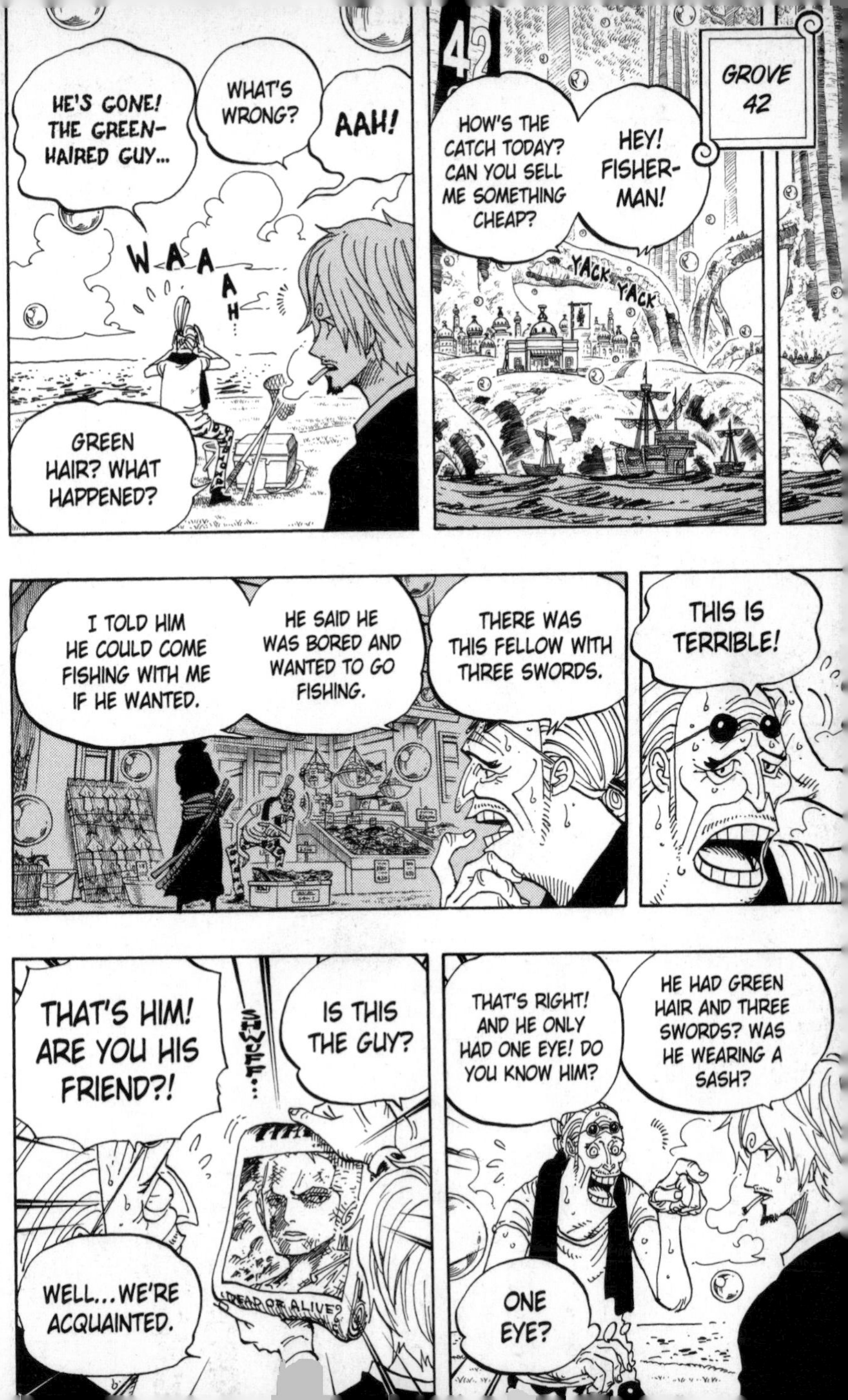
GROVE 42
42
HEY! FISHERMAN!
HOW'S THE CATCH TODAY? CAN YOU SELL ME SOMETHING CHEAP?
YACK YACK
AAH!
WHAT'S WRONG?
HE'S GONE! THE GREEN-HAIRED GUY...
WAAAAH...
GREEN HAIR? WHAT HAPPENED?
THIS IS TERRIBLE!
THERE WAS THIS FELLOW WITH THREE SWORDS.
HE SAID HE WAS BORED AND WANTED TO GO FISHING.
I TOLD HIM HE COULD COME FISHING WITH ME IF HE WANTED.
HE HAD GREEN HAIR AND THREE SWORDS? WAS HE WEARING A SASH?
THAT'S RIGHT! AND HE ONLY HAD ONE EYE! DO YOU KNOW HIM?
ONE EYE?
IS THIS THE GUY?
SHWUFF...
THAT'S HIM! ARE YOU HIS FRIEND?!
DEAD OR ALIVE
WELL...WE'RE ACQUAINTED.

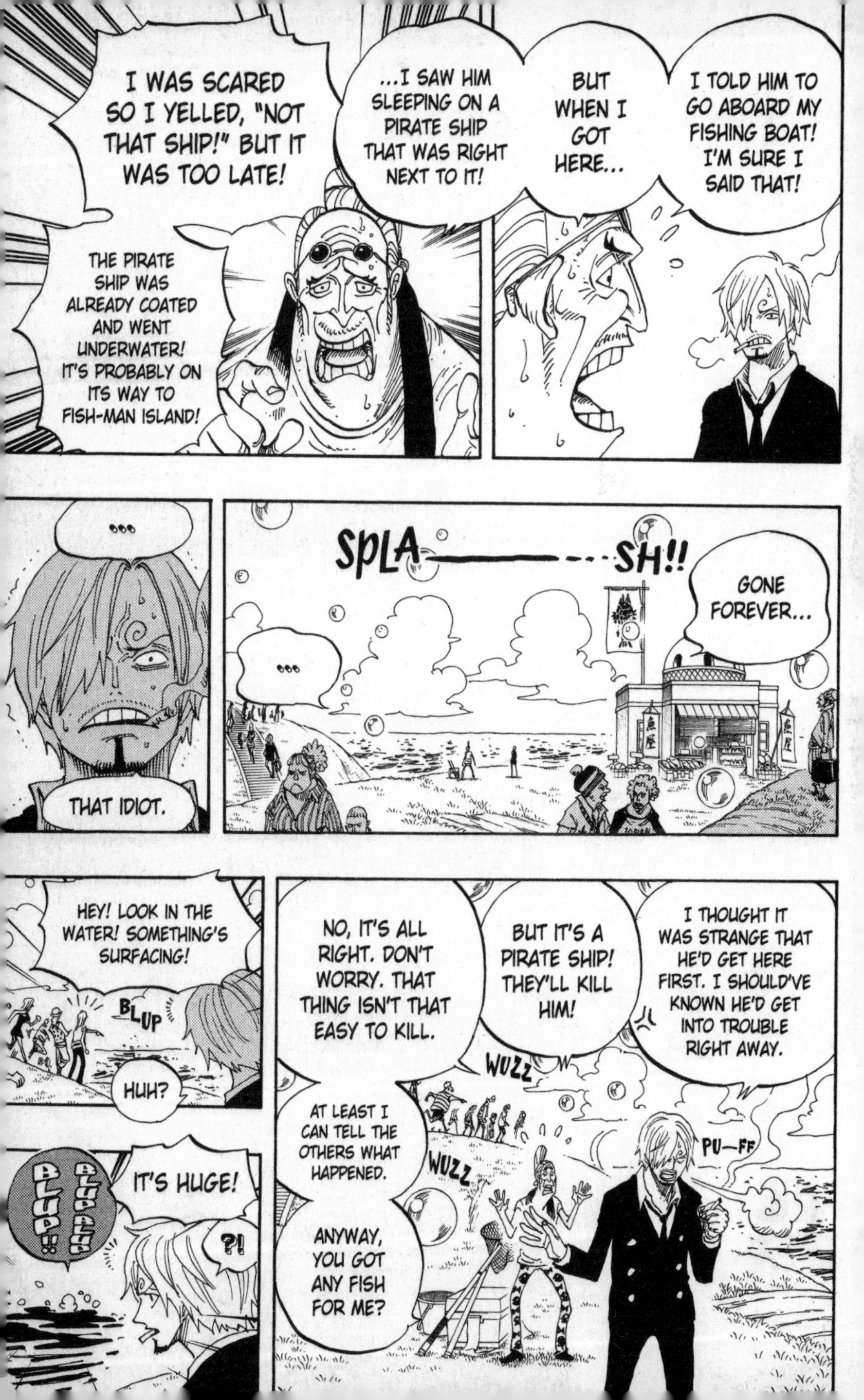
I TOLD HIM TO GO ABOARD MY FISHING BOAT! I'M SURE I SAID THAT!
BUT WHEN I GOT HERE...
...I SAW HIM SLEEPING ON A PIRATE SHIP THAT WAS RIGHT NEXT TO IT!
I WAS SCARED SO I YELLED, "NOT THAT SHIP!" BUT IT WAS TOO LATE!
THE PIRATE SHIP WAS ALREADY COATED AND WENT UNDERWATER! IT'S PROBABLY ON ITS WAY TO FISH-MAN ISLAND!
SPLA———SH!!
GONE FOREVER...
...
...
THAT IDIOT.
I THOUGHT IT WAS STRANGE THAT HE'D GET HERE FIRST. I SHOULD'VE KNOWN HE'D GET INTO TROUBLE RIGHT AWAY.
BUT IT'S A PIRATE SHIP! THEY'LL KILL HIM!
NO, IT'S ALL RIGHT. DON'T WORRY. THAT THING ISN'T THAT EASY TO KILL.
WUZZ
PU—FF
AT LEAST I CAN TELL THE OTHERS WHAT HAPPENED.
WUZZ
ANYWAY, YOU GOT ANY FISH FOR ME?
HEY! LOOK IN THE WATER! SOMETHING'S SURFACING!
BLUP
HUH?
BLUP BLUP BLUP
BLUP!!
IT'S HUGE!
?!

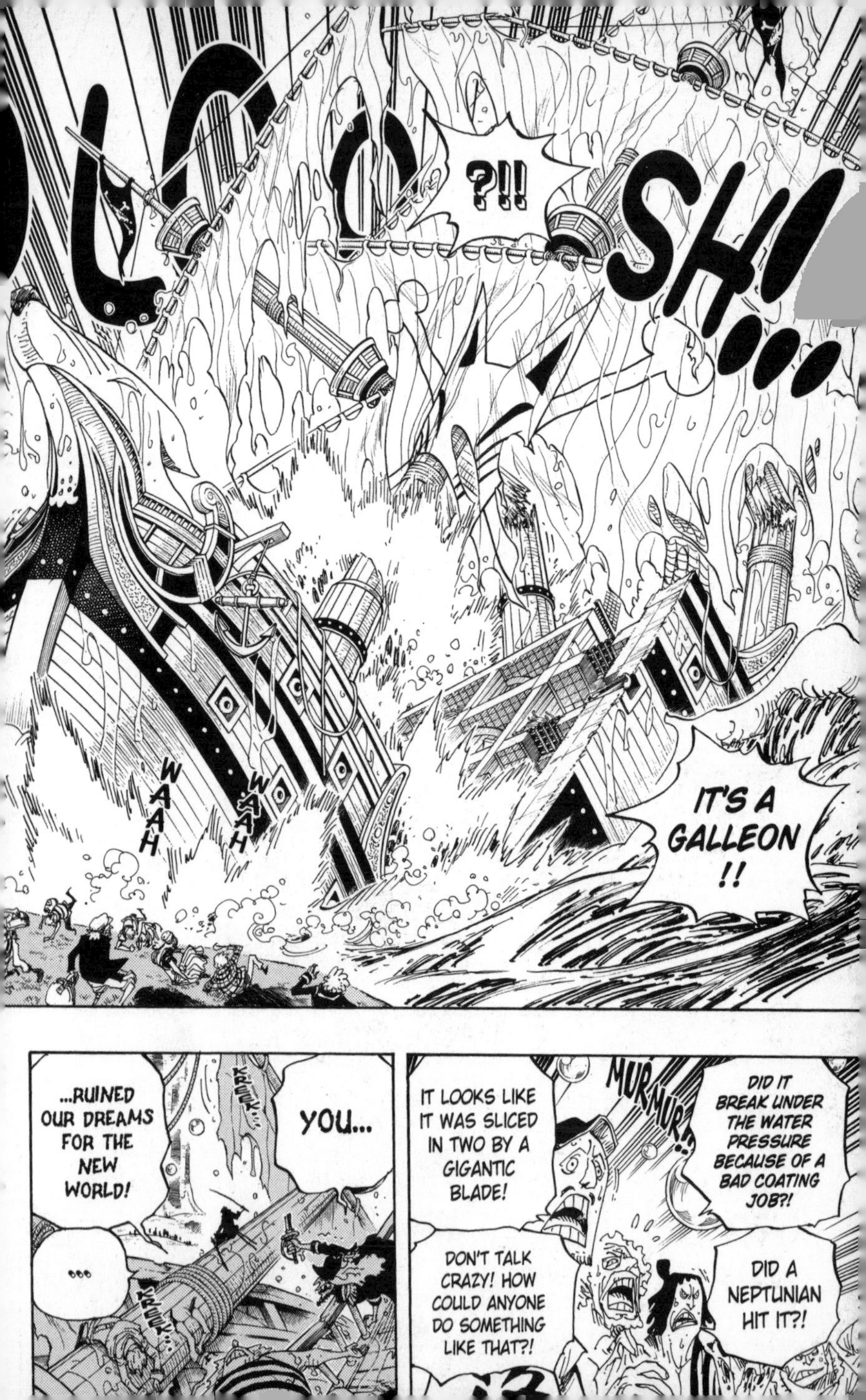
?!!
SH!...
WAAH
WAAH
IT'S A GALLEON !!
DID IT BREAK UNDER THE WATER PRESSURE BECAUSE OF A BAD COATING JOB?!
MURMUR..
IT LOOKS LIKE IT WAS SLICED IN TWO BY A GIGANTIC BLADE!
DID A NEPTUNIAN HIT IT?!
DON'T TALK CRAZY! HOW COULD ANYONE DO SOMETHING LIKE THAT?!
YOU...
KREEK...
...RUINED OUR DREAMS FOR THE NEW WORLD!
...
KREEK...

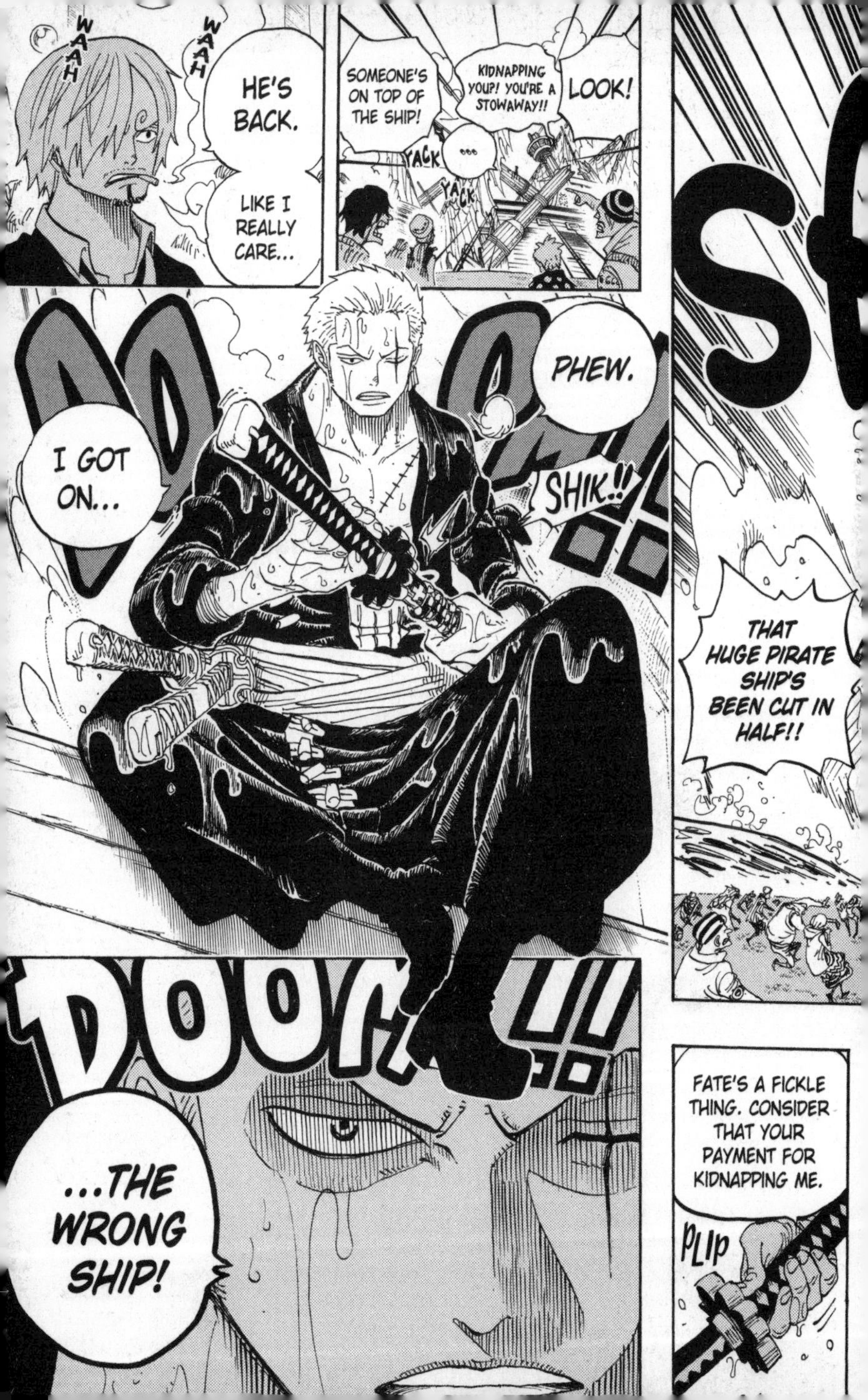

SF
THAT HUGE PIRATE SHIP'S BEEN CUT IN HALF!!
LOOK!
KIDNAPPING YOU?! YOU'RE A STOWAWAY!!
SOMEONE'S ON TOP OF THE SHIP!
...
YACK
YACK
WAAH
WAAH
HE'S BACK.
LIKE I REALLY CARE...
PHEW.
SHIK!!
I GOT ON...
DOOM
FATE'S A FICKLE THING. CONSIDER THAT YOUR PAYMENT FOR KIDNAPPING ME.
PLIP
...THE WRONG SHIP!

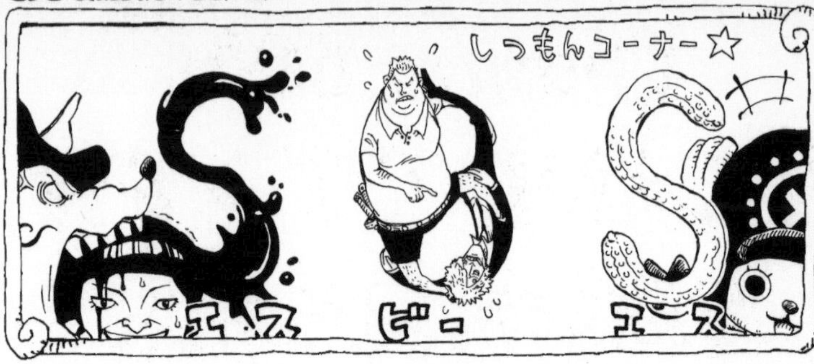
しつもんコーナー☆

(Cute Yacht, Tokyo)

Q: "Dear Odacchi!" Oh, just because I wrote that first part in English doesn't mean I'm a foreigner. I was watching TV the other day and they were talking about the Bermuda Triangle. Is this where your Florian Triangle comes from?

--Michishita

A: Yes, of course. Didn't I talk about it before? The Bermuda Triangle is a section of the North Atlantic Ocean people call the Devil's Triangle. I don't know about now, but originally, about 100 ships and airplanes disappeared there annually. Since they haven't figured it out completely, I think some planes and ships are still disappearing. Some say that it has to do with electromagnetic waves or methane gas. If you're interested, I suggest you go research it on your own.

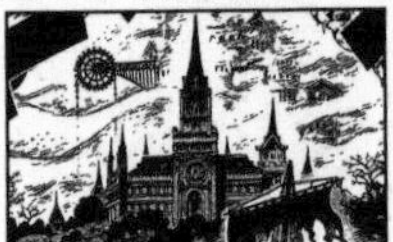

Q: I noticed this right away in the movie *Strong World.* In the deserted island Ruskaina, why is that section the only place that's safe? It must have something to do with that tree. Does it have the same effect as the tree called Daft Green in the movie? Go ahead and explain yourself if you want.

--Takaaki T

A: As you noticed, I didn't have enough pages, so I skipped the explanations. In the movie, I came up with the tree called Daft Green which emits poison and a smell that animals hate. I need something like that in the story so I used it here. But it's not the exact same tree. It's from the same family, but this one is not poisonous.

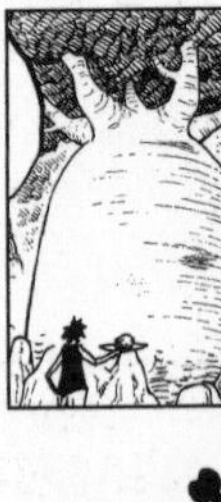

Chapter 600:

ISLAND OF NEW BEGINNINGS

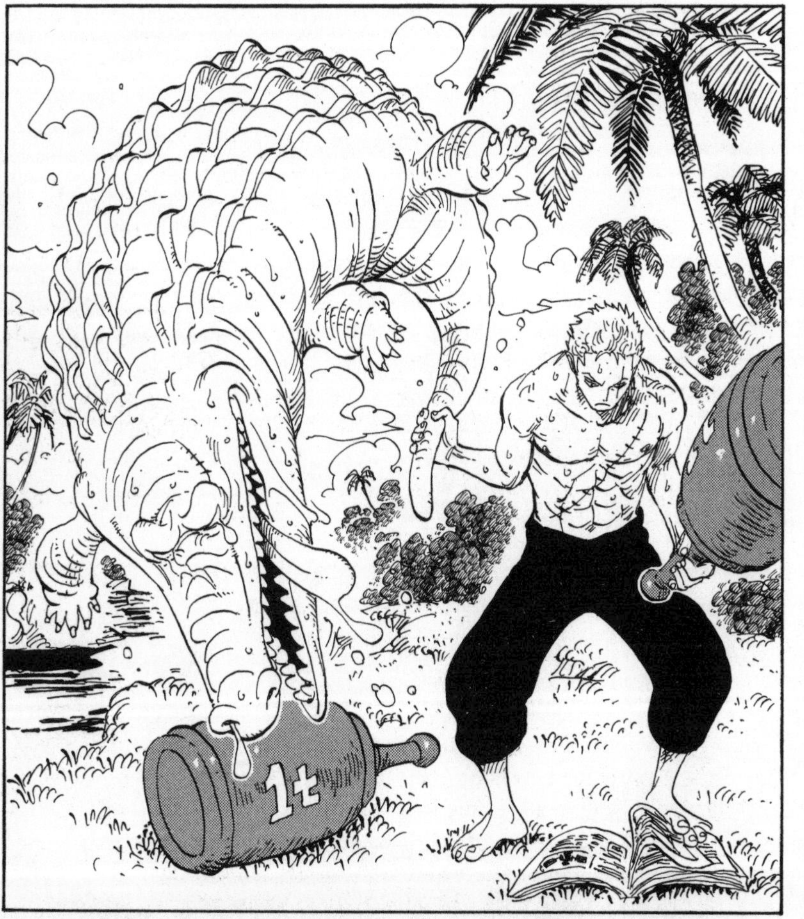
1t

REQUEST: "ZOLO MISTAKES A CROCODILE FOR A WEIGHT DURING TRAINING AND SWINGS IT AROUND" BY KORORU FROM KANAGAWA

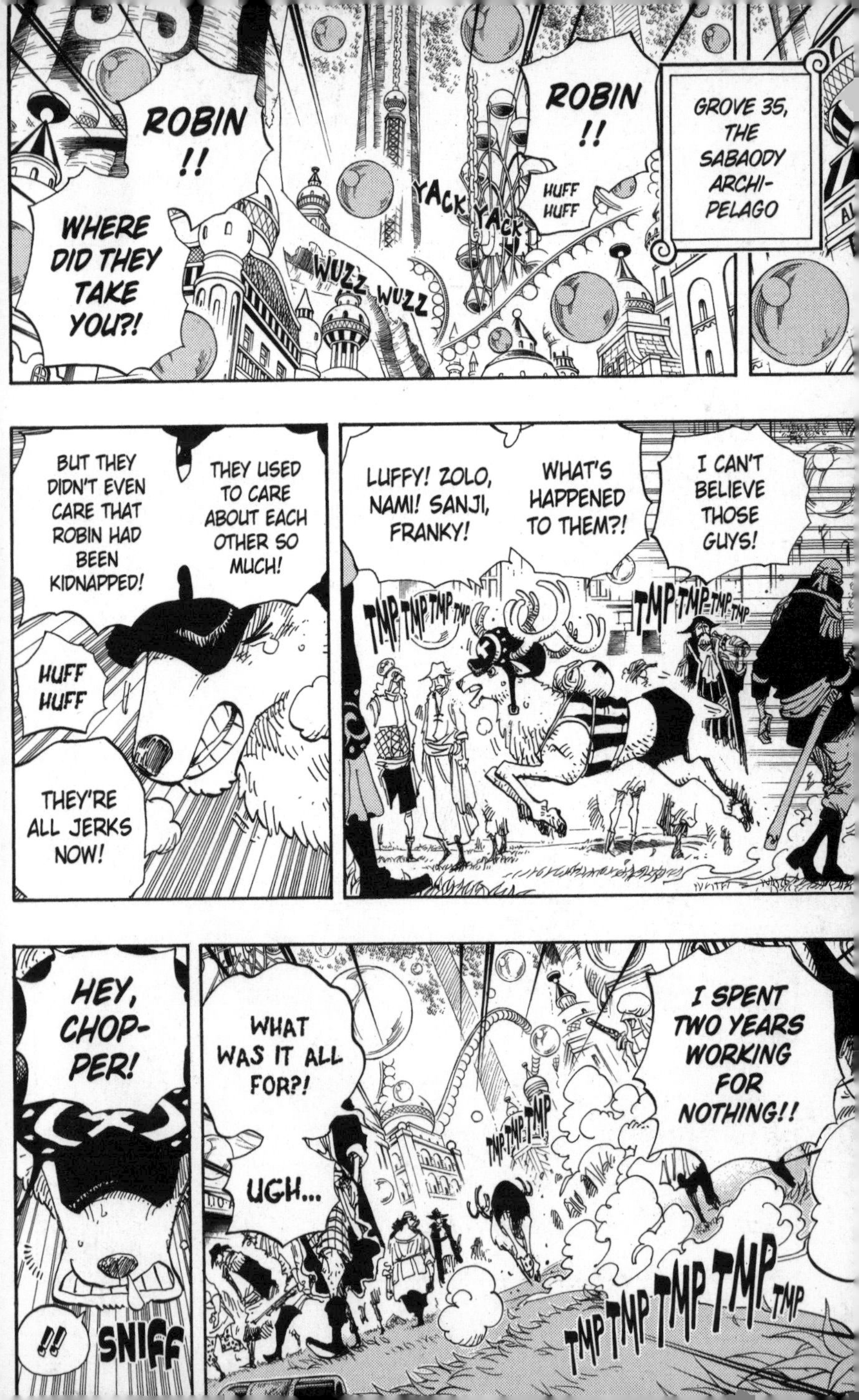
GROVE 35, THE SABAODY ARCHI-PELAGO
ROBIN!!
HUFF HUFF
YACK YACK
WUZZ WUZZ
ROBIN!!
WHERE DID THEY TAKE YOU?!
I CAN'T BELIEVE THOSE GUYS!
WHAT'S HAPPENED TO THEM?!
LUFFY! ZOLO, NAMI! SANJI, FRANKY!
TMP TMP TMP TMP
TMP TMP TMP TMP TMP
THEY USED TO CARE ABOUT EACH OTHER SO MUCH!
BUT THEY DIDN'T EVEN CARE THAT ROBIN HAD BEEN KIDNAPPED!
HUFF HUFF
THEY'RE ALL JERKS NOW!
I SPENT TWO YEARS WORKING FOR NOTHING!!
WHAT WAS IT ALL FOR?!
TMP TMP TMP
UGH...
TMP TMP TMP TMP TMP
HEY, CHOP-PER!
!!
SNIFF

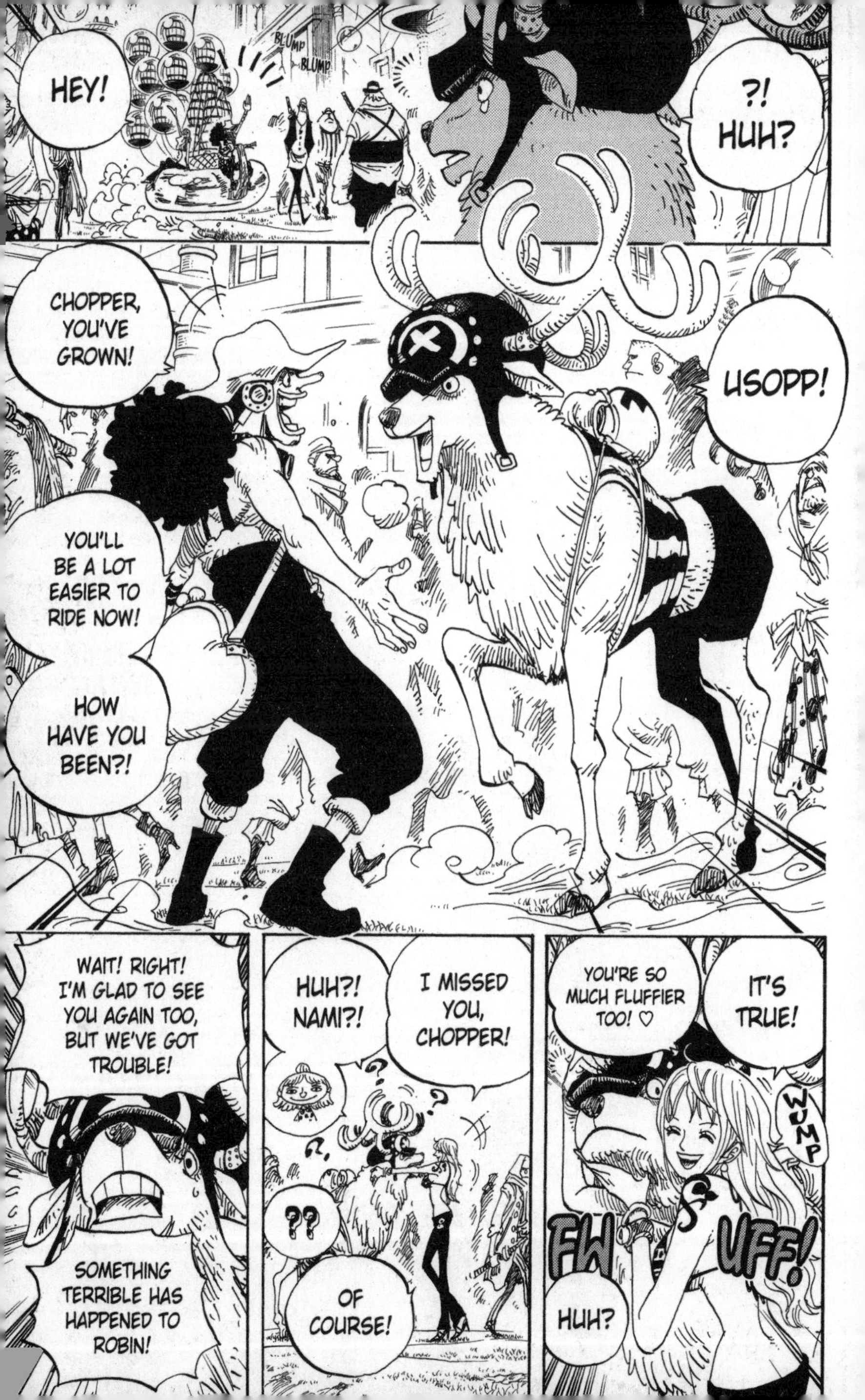
?! HUH?
HEY!
BLUMP BLUMP
USOPP!
CHOPPER, YOU'VE GROWN!
YOU'LL BE A LOT EASIER TO RIDE NOW!
HOW HAVE YOU BEEN?!
IT'S TRUE!
YOU'RE SO MUCH FLUFFIER TOO! ♡
WUMP
FW UFF!
HUH?
I MISSED YOU, CHOPPER!
HUH?! NAMI?!
??
OF COURSE!
WAIT! RIGHT! I'M GLAD TO SEE YOU AGAIN TOO, BUT WE'VE GOT TROUBLE!
SOMETHING TERRIBLE HAS HAPPENED TO ROBIN!

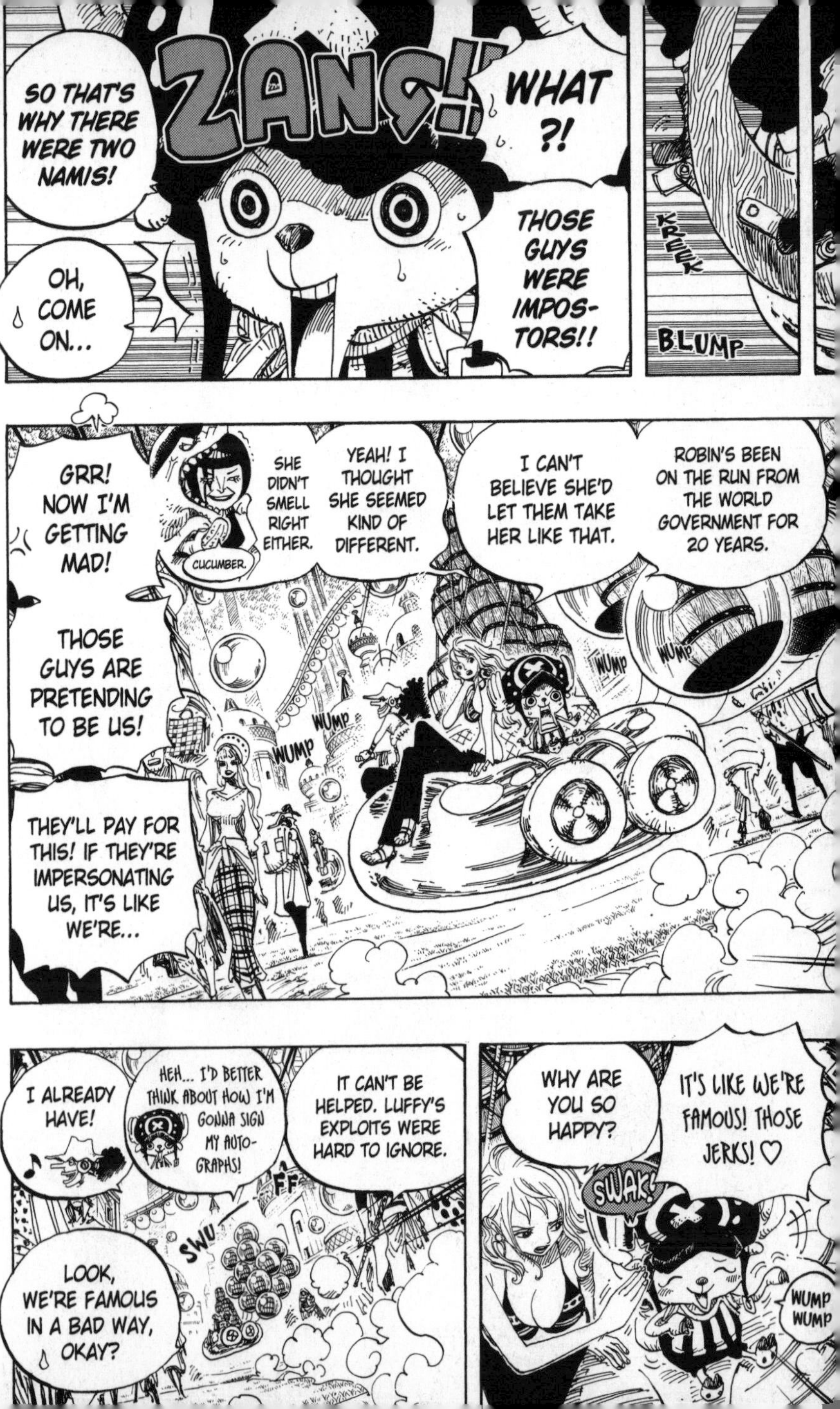
KREEK
BLUMP
ZANG!!
WHAT?!
THOSE GUYS WERE IMPOSTORS!!
SO THAT'S WHY THERE WERE TWO NAMIS!
OH, COME ON...
ROBIN'S BEEN ON THE RUN FROM THE WORLD GOVERNMENT FOR 20 YEARS.
I CAN'T BELIEVE SHE'D LET THEM TAKE HER LIKE THAT.
YEAH! I THOUGHT SHE SEEMED KIND OF DIFFERENT.
SHE DIDN'T SMELL RIGHT EITHER.
CUCUMBER.
GRR! NOW I'M GETTING MAD!
THOSE GUYS ARE PRETENDING TO BE US!
THEY'LL PAY FOR THIS! IF THEY'RE IMPERSONATING US, IT'S LIKE WE'RE...
WUMP
WUMP
WUMP
WUMP
IT'S LIKE WE'RE FAMOUS! THOSE JERKS! ♡
WHY ARE YOU SO HAPPY?
SWAK!
WUMP WUMP
IT CAN'T BE HELPED. LUFFY'S EXPLOITS WERE HARD TO IGNORE.
HEH... I'D BETTER THINK ABOUT HOW I'M GONNA SIGN MY AUTO-GRAPHS!
I ALREADY HAVE!
FF
SWU
LOOK, WE'RE FAMOUS IN A BAD WAY, OKAY?

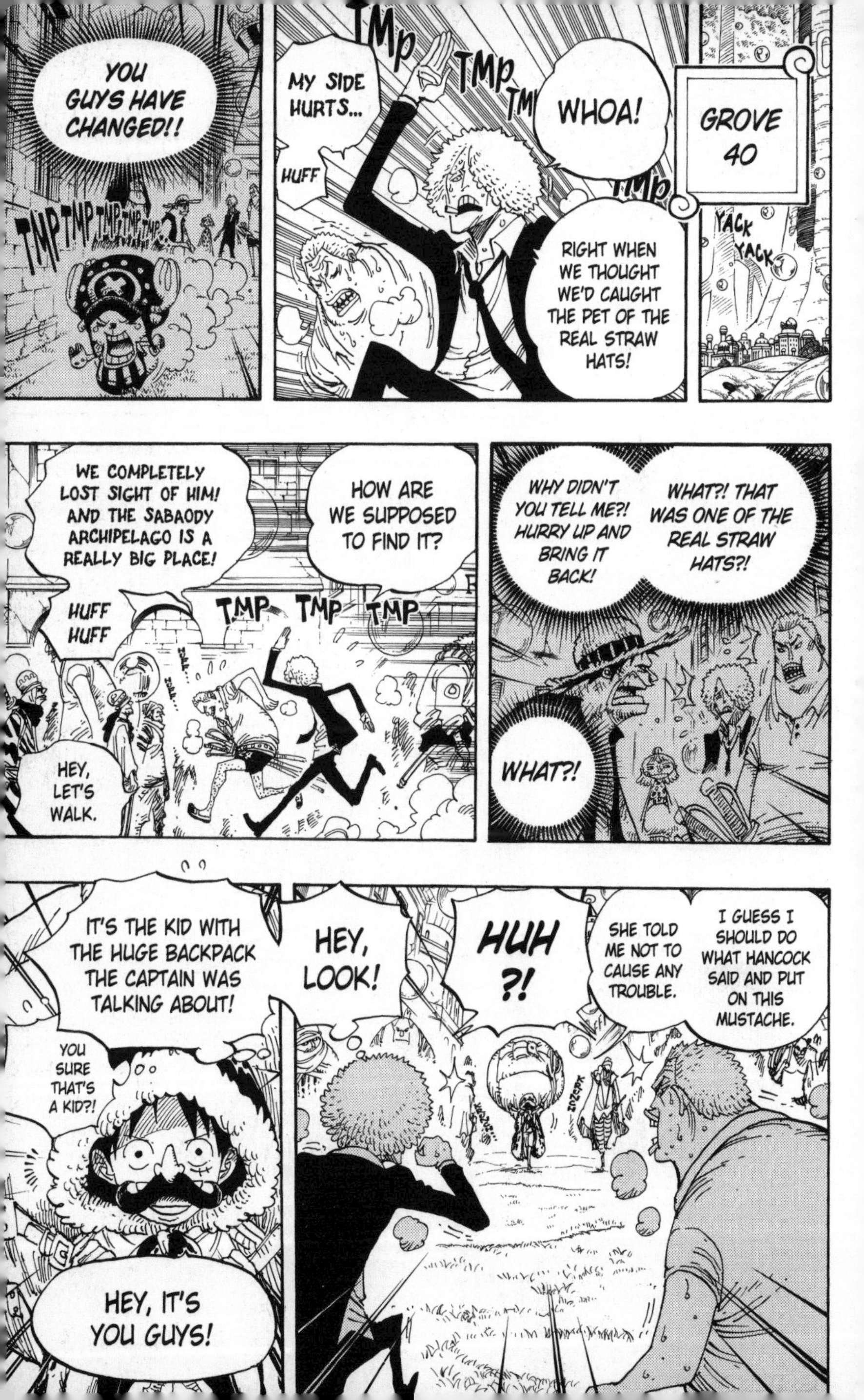

GROVE 40
YACK YACK
WHOA!
TMp TMp TM
MY SIDE HURTS...
RIGHT WHEN WE THOUGHT WE'D CAUGHT THE PET OF THE REAL STRAW HATS!
HUFF
YOU GUYS HAVE CHANGED!!
TMP TMP TMP TMP TMP
WHAT?! THAT WAS ONE OF THE REAL STRAW HATS?!
WHY DIDN'T YOU TELL ME?! HURRY UP AND BRING IT BACK!
WHAT?!
HOW ARE WE SUPPOSED TO FIND IT?
WE COMPLETELY LOST SIGHT OF HIM! AND THE SABAODY ARCHIPELAGO IS A REALLY BIG PLACE!
TMP TMP TMP
HUFF HUFF
HEY, LET'S WALK.
I GUESS I SHOULD DO WHAT HANCOCK SAID AND PUT ON THIS MUSTACHE.
SHE TOLD ME NOT TO CAUSE ANY TROUBLE.
HUH ?!
HEY, LOOK!
IT'S THE KID WITH THE HUGE BACKPACK THE CAPTAIN WAS TALKING ABOUT!
YOU SURE THAT'S A KID?!
HEY, IT'S YOU GUYS!

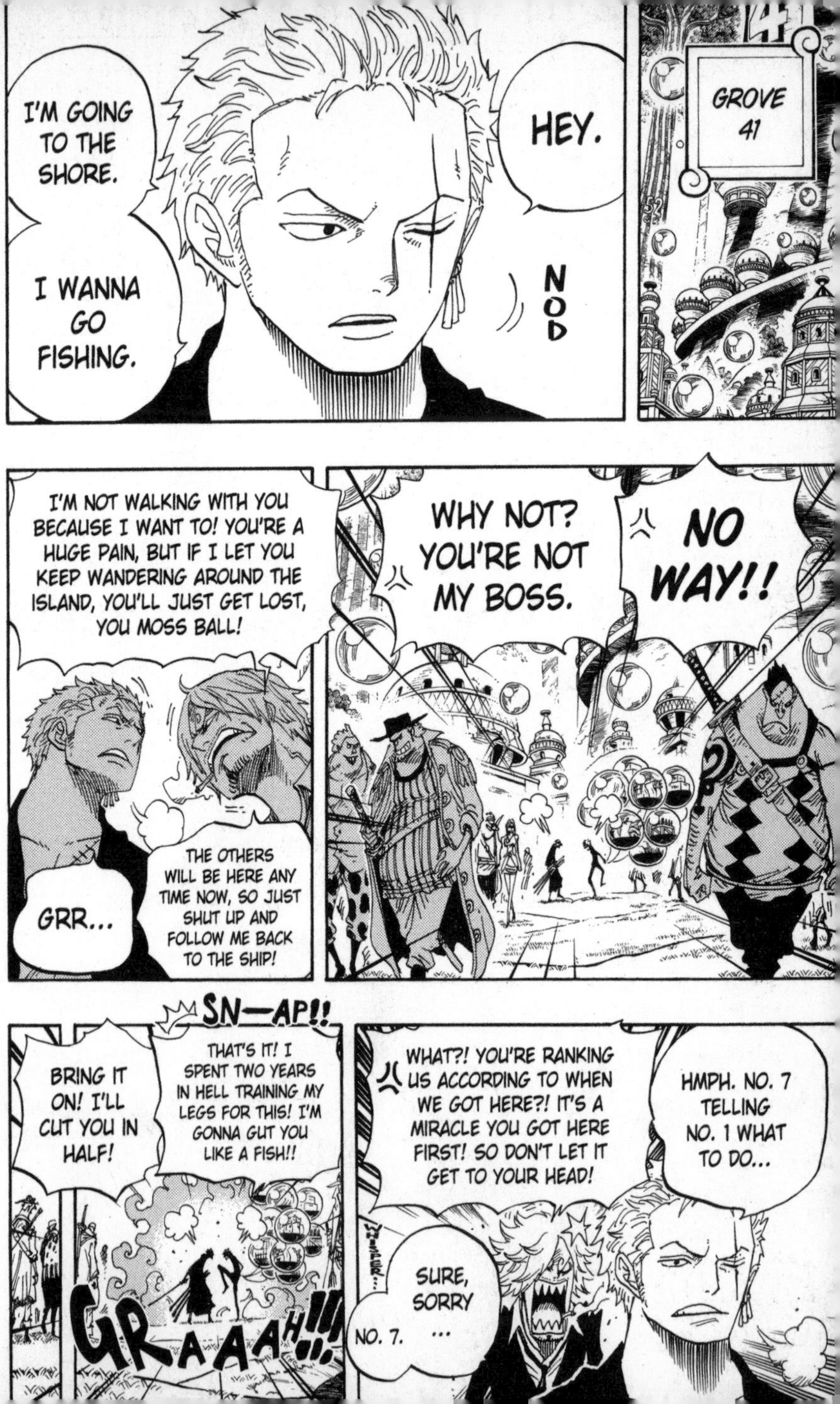
GROVE 41
HEY.
NOD
I'M GOING TO THE SHORE.
I WANNA GO FISHING.
NO WAY!!
WHY NOT? YOU'RE NOT MY BOSS.
I'M NOT WALKING WITH YOU BECAUSE I WANT TO! YOU'RE A HUGE PAIN, BUT IF I LET YOU KEEP WANDERING AROUND THE ISLAND, YOU'LL JUST GET LOST, YOU MOSS BALL!
THE OTHERS WILL BE HERE ANY TIME NOW, SO JUST SHUT UP AND FOLLOW ME BACK TO THE SHIP!
GRR...
HMPH. NO. 7 TELLING NO. 1 WHAT TO DO...
WHAT?! YOU'RE RANKING US ACCORDING TO WHEN WE GOT HERE?! IT'S A MIRACLE YOU GOT HERE FIRST! SO DON'T LET IT GET TO YOUR HEAD!
SURE, SORRY ...
NO. 7.
SN—AP!!
THAT'S IT! I SPENT TWO YEARS IN HELL TRAINING MY LEGS FOR THIS! I'M GONNA GUT YOU LIKE A FISH!!
BRING IT ON! I'LL CUT YOU IN HALF!
GRAAAAH!!!

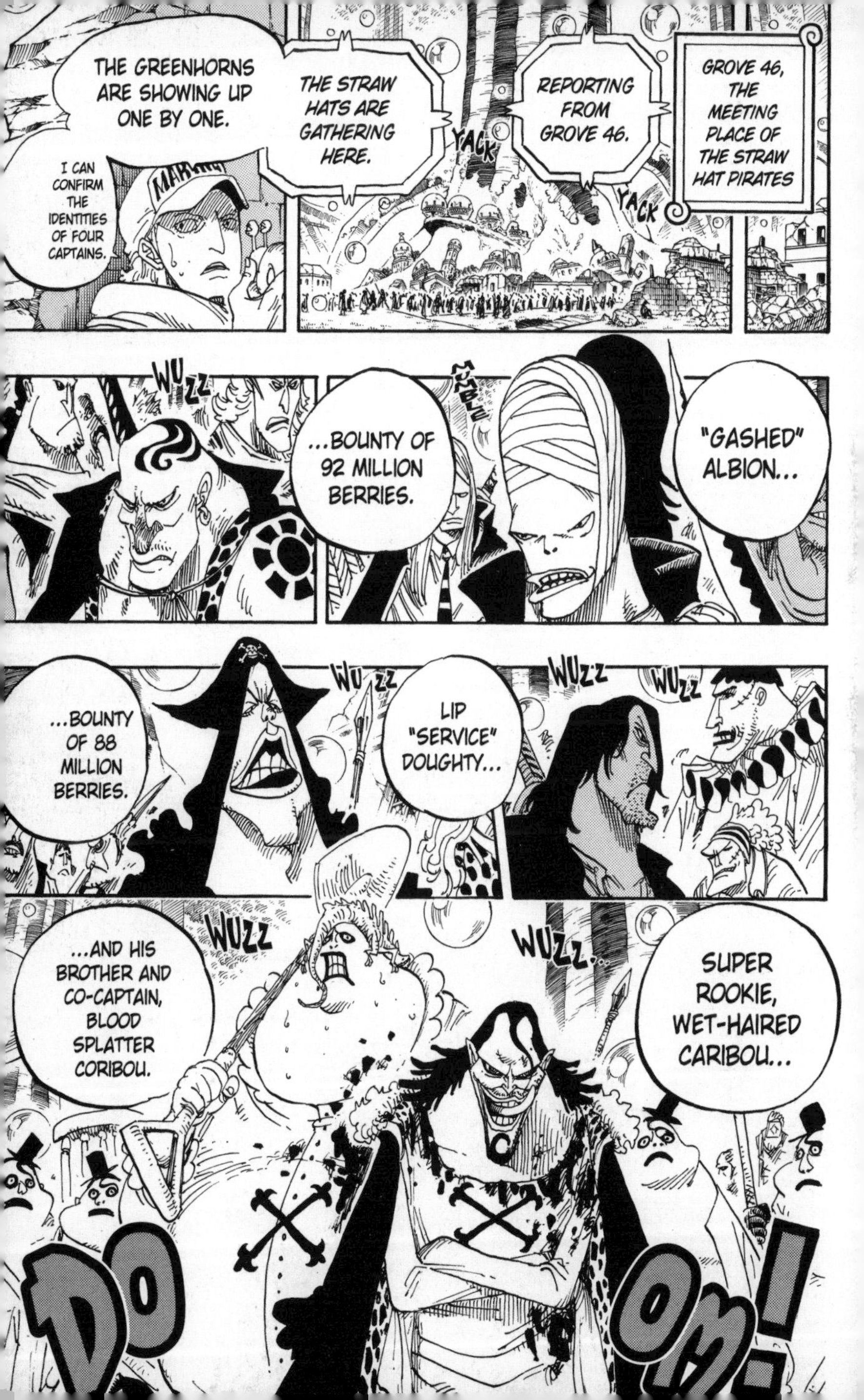
GROVE 46, THE MEETING PLACE OF THE STRAW HAT PIRATES
REPORTING FROM GROVE 46.
YACK
YACK
THE STRAW HATS ARE GATHERING HERE.
THE GREENHORNS ARE SHOWING UP ONE BY ONE.
I CAN CONFIRM THE IDENTITIES OF FOUR CAPTAINS.
"GASHED" ALBION...
MUMBLE
...BOUNTY OF 92 MILLION BERRIES.
WUZZ
WUZZ
WUZZ
LIP "SERVICE" DOUGHTY...
WUZZ
...BOUNTY OF 88 MILLION BERRIES.
SUPER ROOKIE, WET-HAIRED CARIBOU...
WUZZ..
WUZZ
...AND HIS BROTHER AND CO-CAPTAIN, BLOOD SPLATTER CORIBOU.
DOOM!

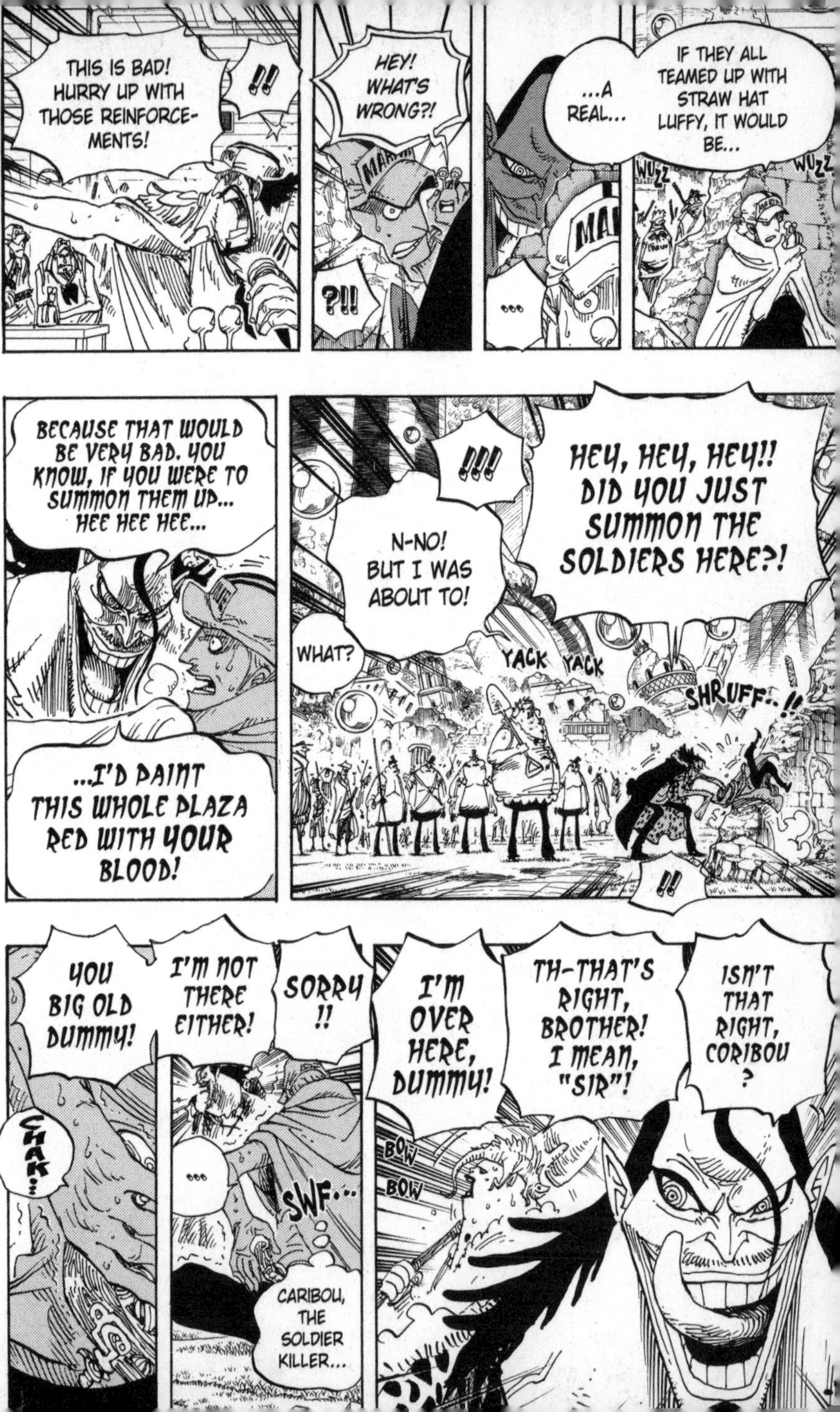

IF THEY ALL TEAMED UP WITH STRAW HAT LUFFY, IT WOULD BE...
WUZZ
WUZZ
...A REAL...
...
HEY! WHAT'S WRONG?!
?!!
!!
THIS IS BAD! HURRY UP WITH THOSE REINFORCE-MENTS!
HEY, HEY, HEY!! DID YOU JUST SUMMON THE SOLDIERS HERE?!
!!!
N-NO! BUT I WAS ABOUT TO!
WHAT?
YACK YACK
SHRUFF..!!
!!
BECAUSE THAT WOULD BE VERY BAD. YOU KNOW, IF YOU WERE TO SUMMON THEM UP... HEE HEE HEE...
...I'D PAINT THIS WHOLE PLAZA RED WITH YOUR BLOOD!
ISN'T THAT RIGHT, CORIBOU?
TH-THAT'S RIGHT, BROTHER! I MEAN, "SIR"!
I'M OVER HERE, DUMMY!
BOW
BOW
SORRY!!
I'M NOT THERE EITHER!
...
SWF...
CARIBOU, THE SOLDIER KILLER...
YOU BIG OLD DUMMY!
CHAK..!

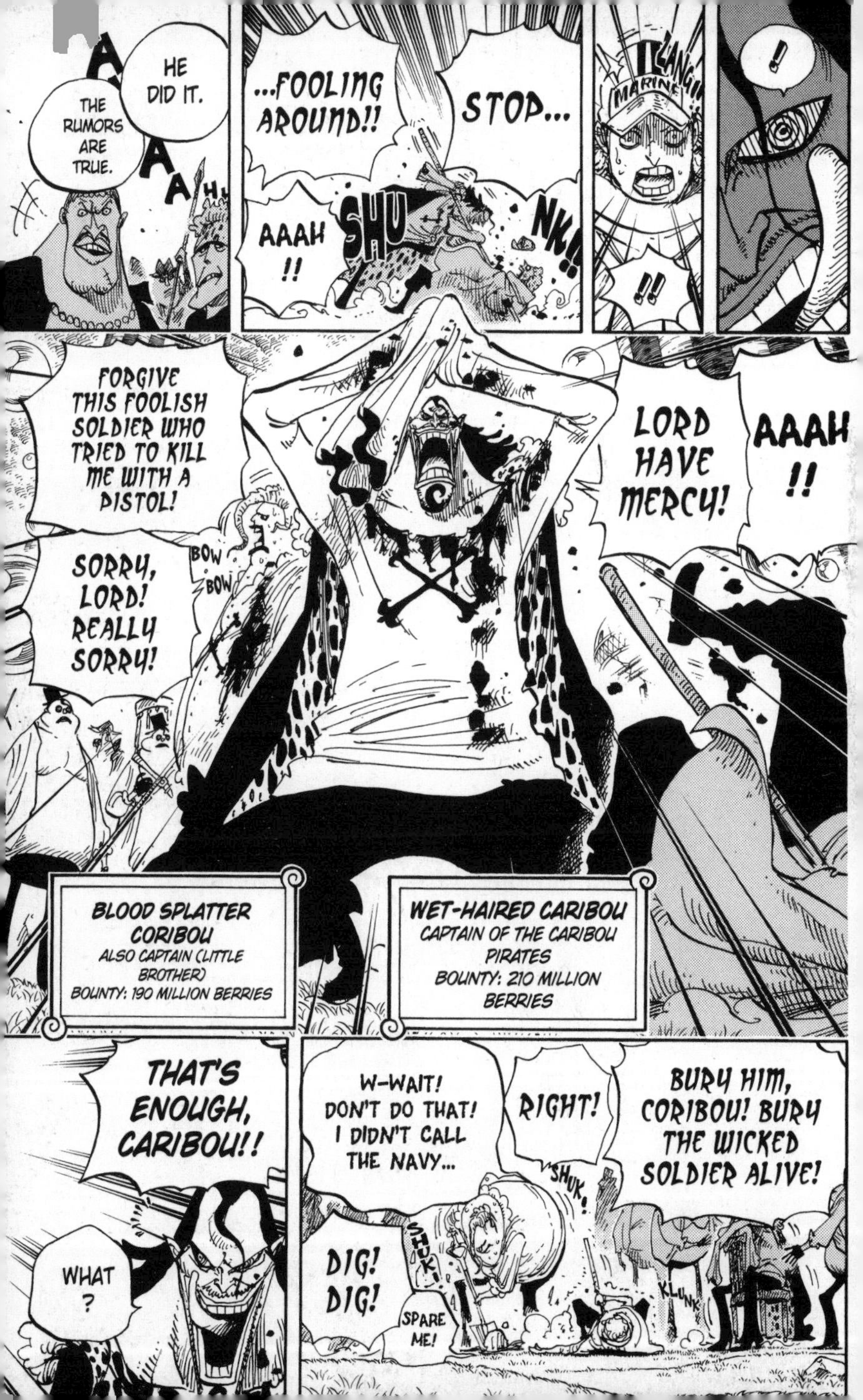
!
CLANG
MARINE
!!
STOP...
...FOOLING AROUND!!
SHUNK!!
AAAH !!
HE DID IT.
THE RUMORS ARE TRUE.
AAA
AAAH !!
LORD HAVE MERCY!
FORGIVE THIS FOOLISH SOLDIER WHO TRIED TO KILL ME WITH A PISTOL!
BOW BOW
SORRY, LORD! REALLY SORRY!
WET-HAIRED CARIBOU
CAPTAIN OF THE CARIBOU PIRATES
BOUNTY: 210 MILLION BERRIES
BLOOD SPLATTER CORIBOU
ALSO CAPTAIN (LITTLE BROTHER)
BOUNTY: 190 MILLION BERRIES
BURY HIM, CORIBOU! BURY THE WICKED SOLDIER ALIVE!
RIGHT!
W-WAIT! DON'T DO THAT! I DIDN'T CALL THE NAVY...
SHUK
SHUK!
KLUNK
DIG! DIG!
SPARE ME!
THAT'S ENOUGH, CARIBOU!!
WHAT ?

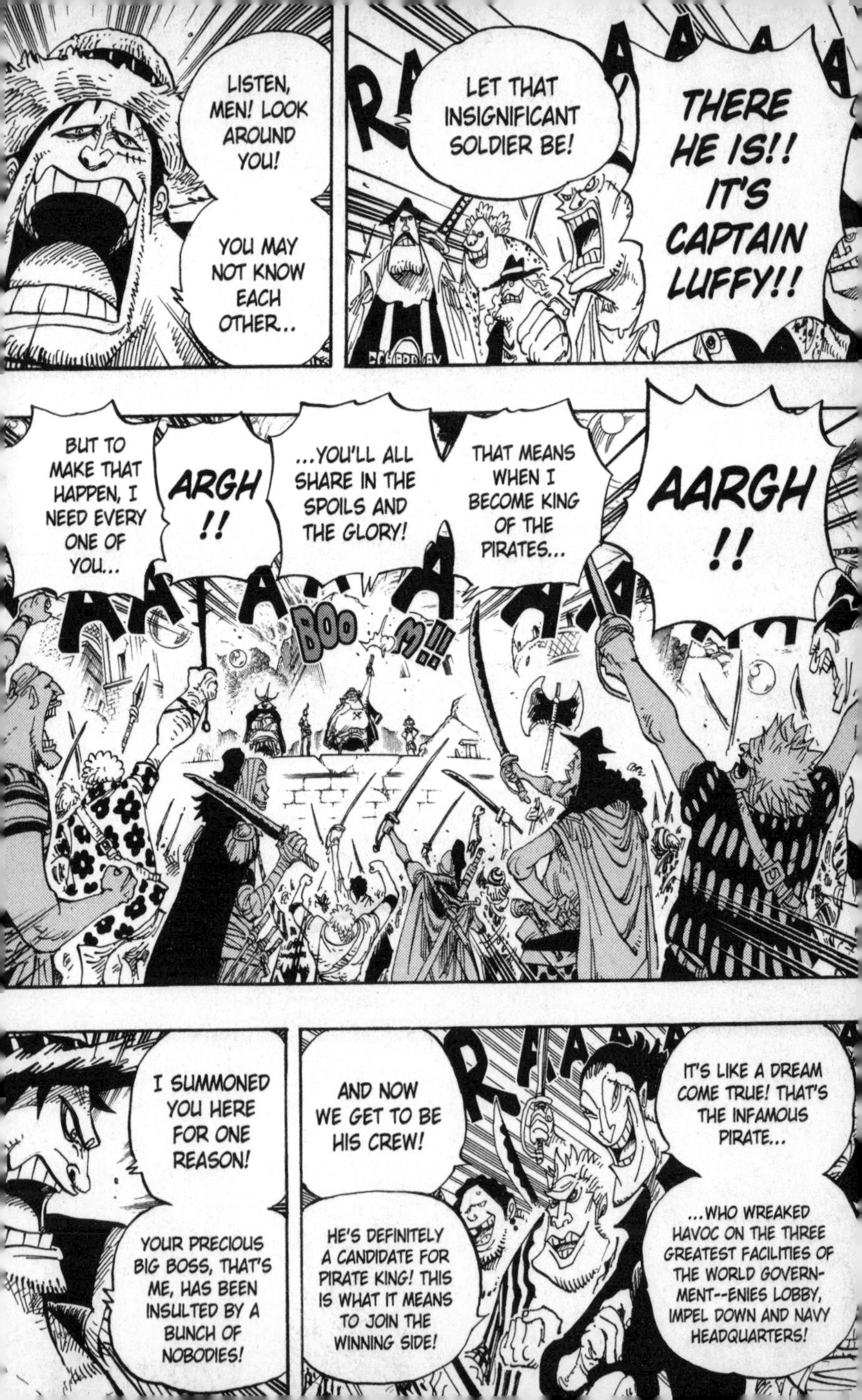
THERE HE IS!! IT'S CAPTAIN LUFFY!!
LET THAT INSIGNIFICANT SOLDIER BE!
LISTEN, MEN! LOOK AROUND YOU!
YOU MAY NOT KNOW EACH OTHER...
AARGH!!
THAT MEANS WHEN I BECOME KING OF THE PIRATES...
...YOU'LL ALL SHARE IN THE SPOILS AND THE GLORY!
ARGH!!
BUT TO MAKE THAT HAPPEN, I NEED EVERY ONE OF YOU...
BOOM!!
IT'S LIKE A DREAM COME TRUE! THAT'S THE INFAMOUS PIRATE...
...WHO WREAKED HAVOC ON THE THREE GREATEST FACILITIES OF THE WORLD GOVERNMENT--ENIES LOBBY, IMPEL DOWN AND NAVY HEADQUARTERS!
AND NOW WE GET TO BE HIS CREW!
HE'S DEFINITELY A CANDIDATE FOR PIRATE KING! THIS IS WHAT IT MEANS TO JOIN THE WINNING SIDE!
I SUMMONED YOU HERE FOR ONE REASON!
YOUR PRECIOUS BIG BOSS, THAT'S ME, HAS BEEN INSULTED BY A BUNCH OF NOBODIES!

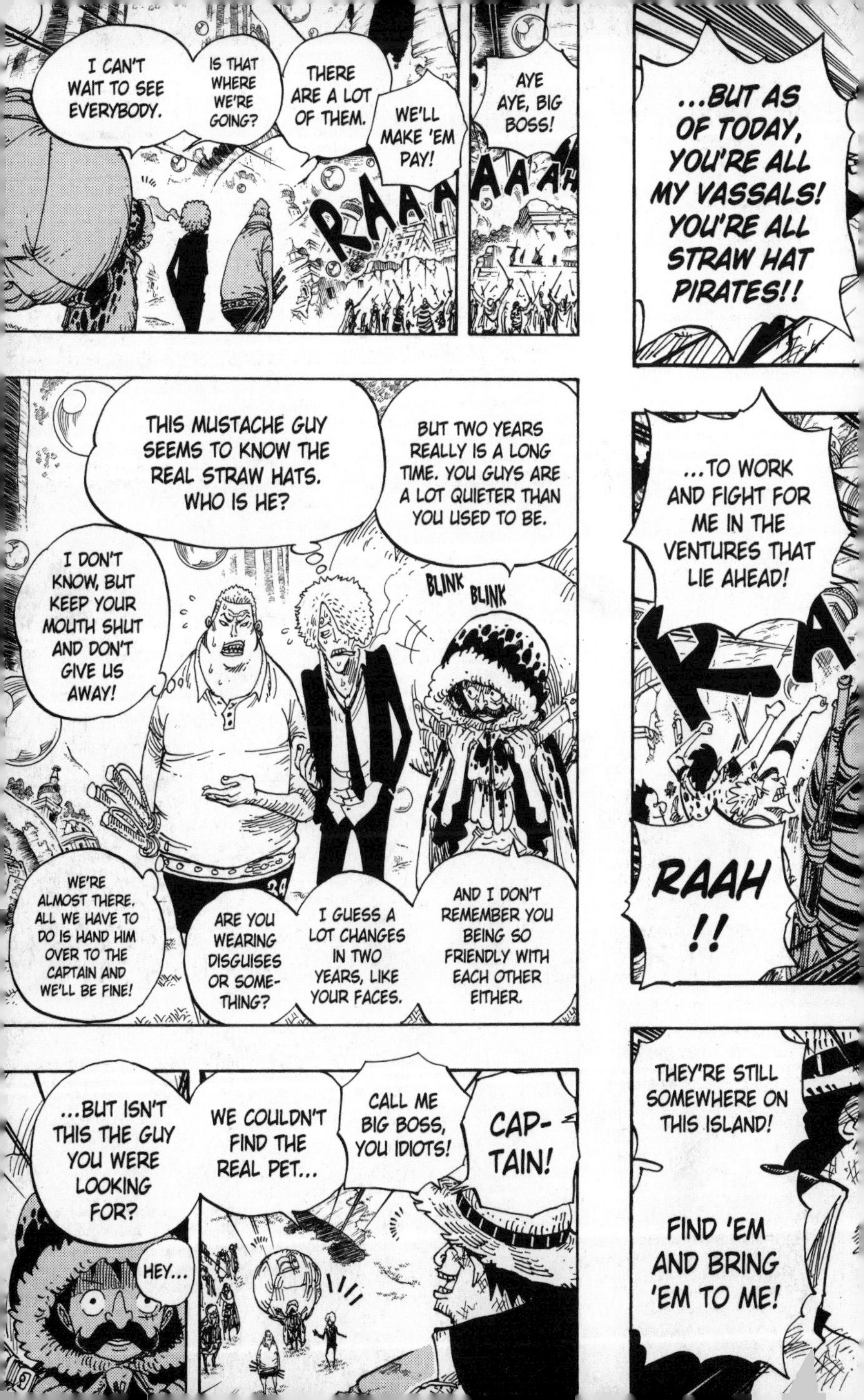
...BUT AS OF TODAY, YOU'RE ALL MY VASSALS! YOU'RE ALL STRAW HAT PIRATES!!
...TO WORK AND FIGHT FOR ME IN THE VENTURES THAT LIE AHEAD!
RAAH!!
THEY'RE STILL SOMEWHERE ON THIS ISLAND!
FIND 'EM AND BRING 'EM TO ME!
AYE AYE, BIG BOSS!
RAAAAAAH
WE'LL MAKE 'EM PAY!
THERE ARE A LOT OF THEM.
IS THAT WHERE WE'RE GOING?
I CAN'T WAIT TO SEE EVERYBODY.
BUT TWO YEARS REALLY IS A LONG TIME. YOU GUYS ARE A LOT QUIETER THAN YOU USED TO BE.
THIS MUSTACHE GUY SEEMS TO KNOW THE REAL STRAW HATS. WHO IS HE?
BLINK BLINK
I DON'T KNOW, BUT KEEP YOUR MOUTH SHUT AND DON'T GIVE US AWAY!
AND I DON'T REMEMBER YOU BEING SO FRIENDLY WITH EACH OTHER EITHER.
I GUESS A LOT CHANGES IN TWO YEARS, LIKE YOUR FACES.
ARE YOU WEARING DISGUISES OR SOMETHING?
WE'RE ALMOST THERE. ALL WE HAVE TO DO IS HAND HIM OVER TO THE CAPTAIN AND WE'LL BE FINE!
CAPTAIN!
CALL ME BIG BOSS, YOU IDIOTS!
WE COULDN'T FIND THE REAL PET...
...BUT ISN'T THIS THE GUY YOU WERE LOOKING FOR?
HEY...

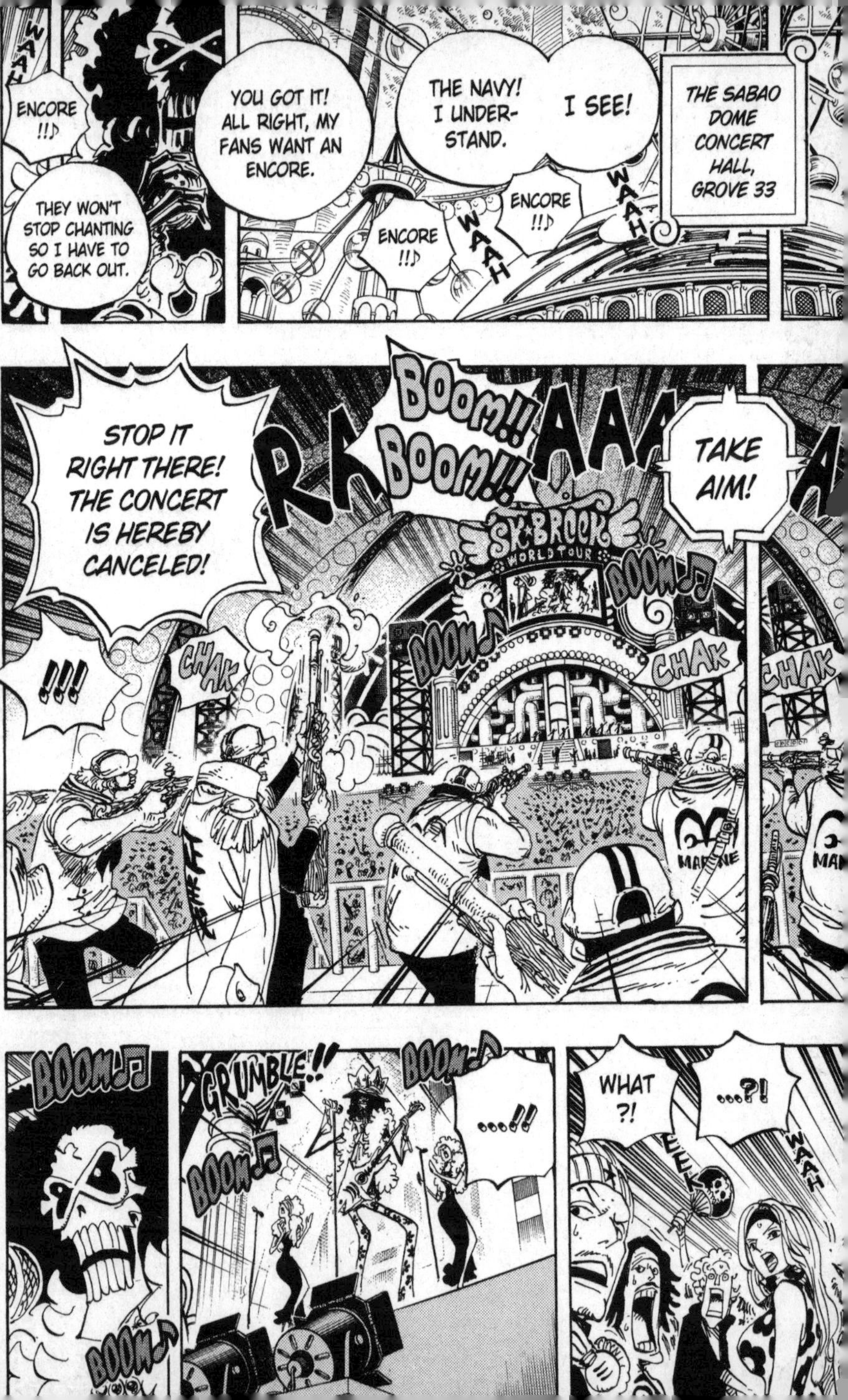
THE SABAO DOME CONCERT HALL, GROVE 33
WAAH
I SEE!
THE NAVY! I UNDER-STAND.
ENCORE !!♪
WAAH
ENCORE !!♪
YOU GOT IT! ALL RIGHT, MY FANS WANT AN ENCORE.
WAAH
ENCORE !!♪
THEY WON'T STOP CHANTING SO I HAVE TO GO BACK OUT.
TAKE AIM!
RAAAA
BOOM!! BOOM!!
STOP IT RIGHT THERE! THE CONCERT IS HEREBY CANCELED!
SK★BROOK WORLD TOUR
BOOM♫
CHAK
CHAK
BOOM♪
CHAK
!!!
MARINE
...?!
WHAT ?!
WAAH
EEEK
BOOM♪
...!!
GRUMBLE!!
BOOM♫
BOOM♫
BOOM♪

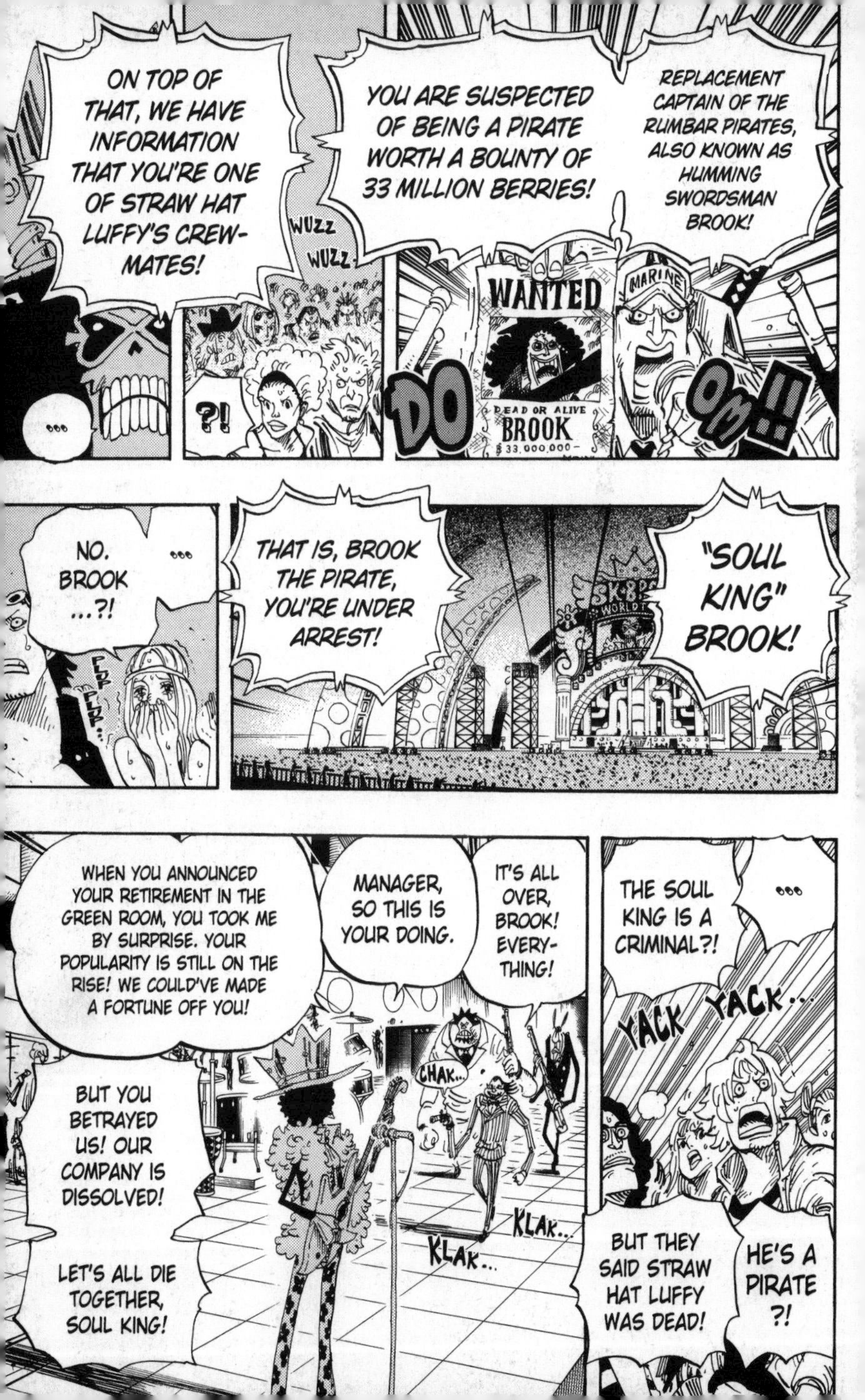
REPLACEMENT CAPTAIN OF THE RUMBAR PIRATES, ALSO KNOWN AS HUMMING SWORDSMAN BROOK!
YOU ARE SUSPECTED OF BEING A PIRATE WORTH A BOUNTY OF 33 MILLION BERRIES!
MARINE
WANTED
DEAD OR ALIVE
BROOK
฿ 33,000,000-
DOOM!!
WUZZ
WUZZ
?!
ON TOP OF THAT, WE HAVE INFORMATION THAT YOU'RE ONE OF STRAW HAT LUFFY'S CREW-MATES!
...
"SOUL KING" BROOK!
THAT IS, BROOK THE PIRATE, YOU'RE UNDER ARREST!
...
NO. BROOK ...?!
PLOP PLOP...
...
THE SOUL KING IS A CRIMINAL?!
YACK YACK...
HE'S A PIRATE ?!
BUT THEY SAID STRAW HAT LUFFY WAS DEAD!
IT'S ALL OVER, BROOK! EVERY-THING!
MANAGER, SO THIS IS YOUR DOING.
WHEN YOU ANNOUNCED YOUR RETIREMENT IN THE GREEN ROOM, YOU TOOK ME BY SURPRISE. YOUR POPULARITY IS STILL ON THE RISE! WE COULD'VE MADE A FORTUNE OFF YOU!
CHAK...
BUT YOU BETRAYED US! OUR COMPANY IS DISSOLVED!
KLAK...
KLAK...
LET'S ALL DIE TOGETHER, SOUL KING!

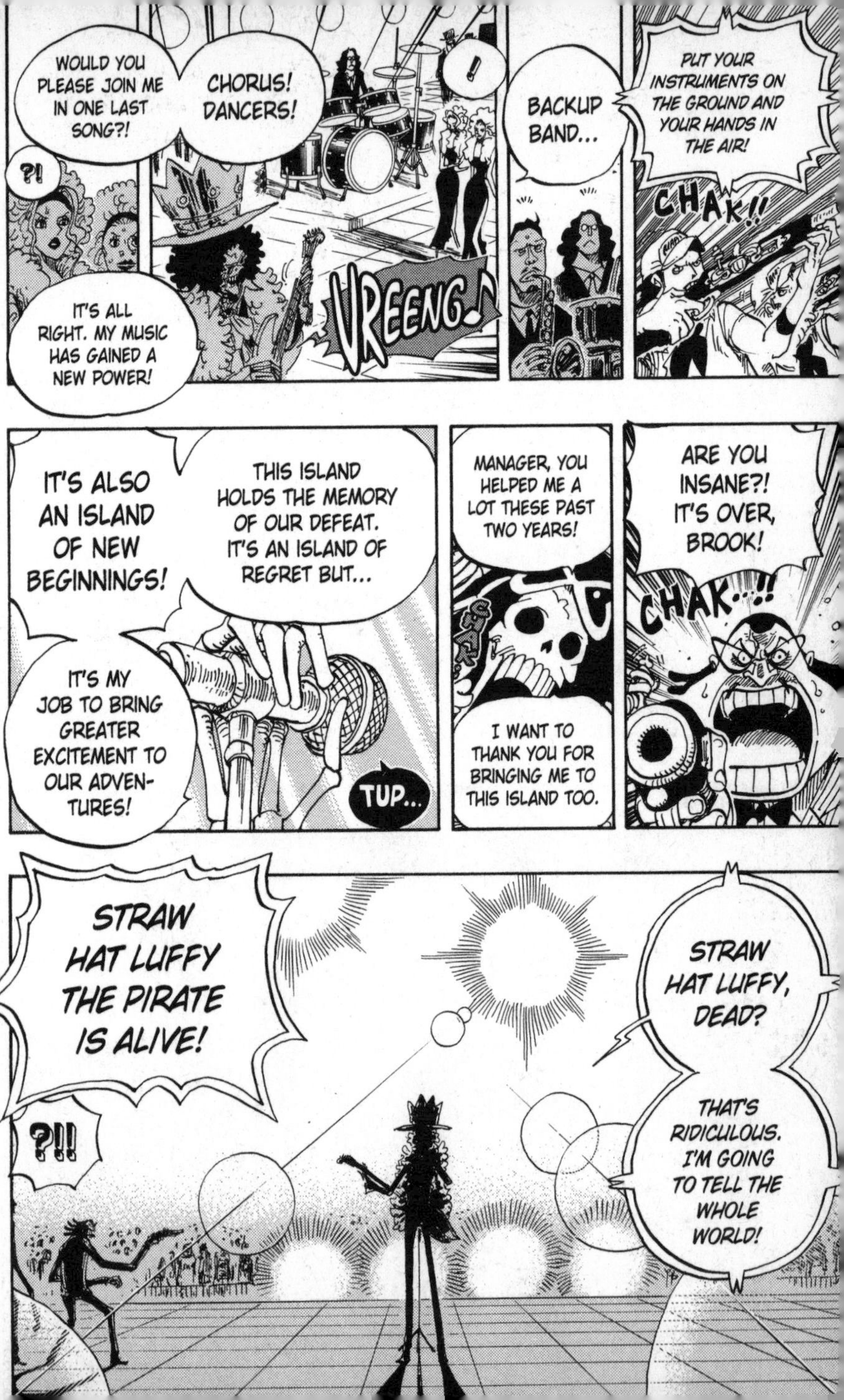
PUT YOUR INSTRUMENTS ON THE GROUND AND YOUR HANDS IN THE AIR!
CHAK!!
BACKUP BAND...
!
CHORUS! DANCERS!
WOULD YOU PLEASE JOIN ME IN ONE LAST SONG?!
?!
VREENG
IT'S ALL RIGHT. MY MUSIC HAS GAINED A NEW POWER!
ARE YOU INSANE?! IT'S OVER, BROOK!
CHAK...!!
MANAGER, YOU HELPED ME A LOT THESE PAST TWO YEARS!
I WANT TO THANK YOU FOR BRINGING ME TO THIS ISLAND TOO.
THIS ISLAND HOLDS THE MEMORY OF OUR DEFEAT. IT'S AN ISLAND OF REGRET BUT...
IT'S ALSO AN ISLAND OF NEW BEGINNINGS!
IT'S MY JOB TO BRING GREATER EXCITEMENT TO OUR ADVEN-TURES!
TUP...
STRAW HAT LUFFY, DEAD?
THAT'S RIDICULOUS. I'M GOING TO TELL THE WHOLE WORLD!
STRAW HAT LUFFY THE PIRATE IS ALIVE!
?!!

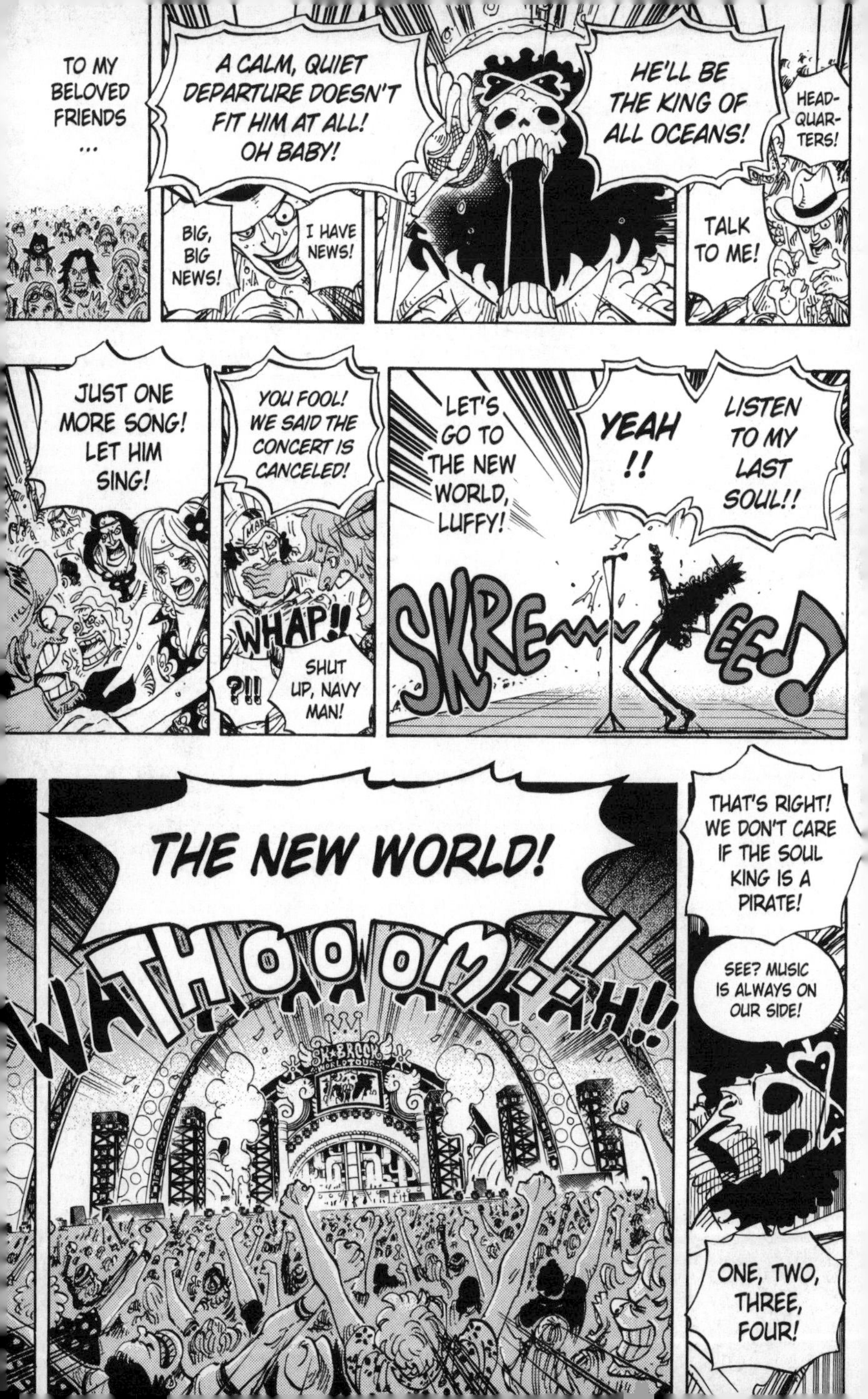
HEAD-QUARTERS!
TALK TO ME!
HE'LL BE THE KING OF ALL OCEANS!
A CALM, QUIET DEPARTURE DOESN'T FIT HIM AT ALL! OH BABY!
I HAVE NEWS!
BIG, BIG NEWS!
TO MY BELOVED FRIENDS ...
LISTEN TO MY LAST SOUL!!
YEAH !!
LET'S GO TO THE NEW WORLD, LUFFY!
SKRE~~EE♪
YOU FOOL! WE SAID THE CONCERT IS CANCELED!
WHAP!!
SHUT UP, NAVY MAN!
?!!
JUST ONE MORE SONG! LET HIM SING!
THAT'S RIGHT! WE DON'T CARE IF THE SOUL KING IS A PIRATE!
SEE? MUSIC IS ALWAYS ON OUR SIDE!
ONE, TWO, THREE, FOUR!
THE NEW WORLD!
WHOOOOAAAAAH!!
SK★BROOK WORLD TOUR

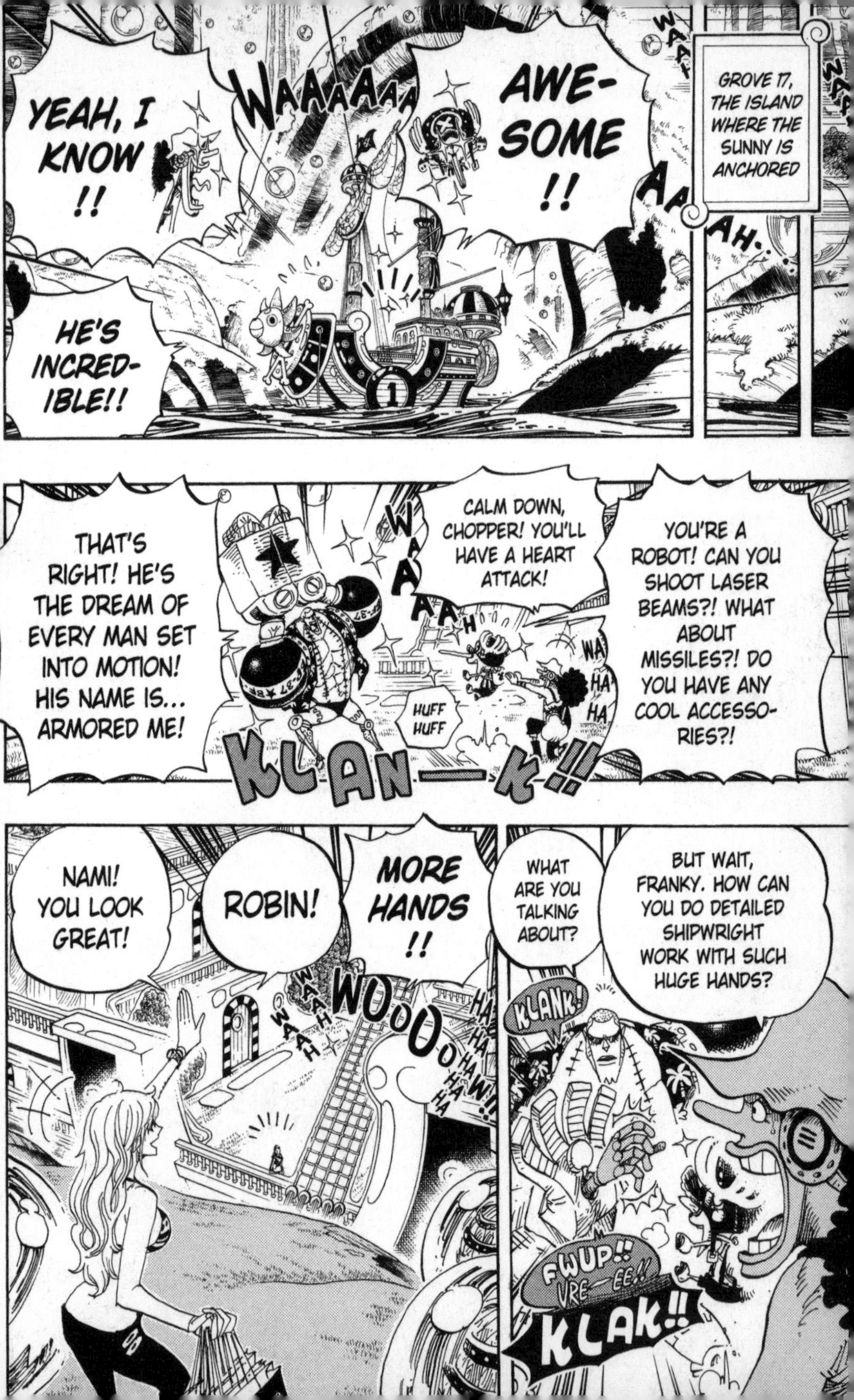
GROVE 17, THE ISLAND WHERE THE SUNNY IS ANCHORED
WAAAAAAH...
AWE-SOME!!
WAAAAAA
YEAH, I KNOW!!
HE'S INCREDIBLE!!
YOU'RE A ROBOT! CAN YOU SHOOT LASER BEAMS?! WHAT ABOUT MISSILES?! DO YOU HAVE ANY COOL ACCESSORIES?!
CALM DOWN, CHOPPER! YOU'LL HAVE A HEART ATTACK!
WAAAAH
WA HA HA HA
HUFF HUFF
THAT'S RIGHT! HE'S THE DREAM OF EVERY MAN SET INTO MOTION! HIS NAME IS... ARMORED ME!
KLAN—K!!
BUT WAIT, FRANKY. HOW CAN YOU DO DETAILED SHIPWRIGHT WORK WITH SUCH HUGE HANDS?
WHAT ARE YOU TALKING ABOUT?
KLANK!
FWUP!! VRE—EE!!
KLAK!!
MORE HANDS!!
ROBIN!
NAMI! YOU LOOK GREAT!
WAAH WAAH
WOOOOO
HA HA HAW!! HA HA

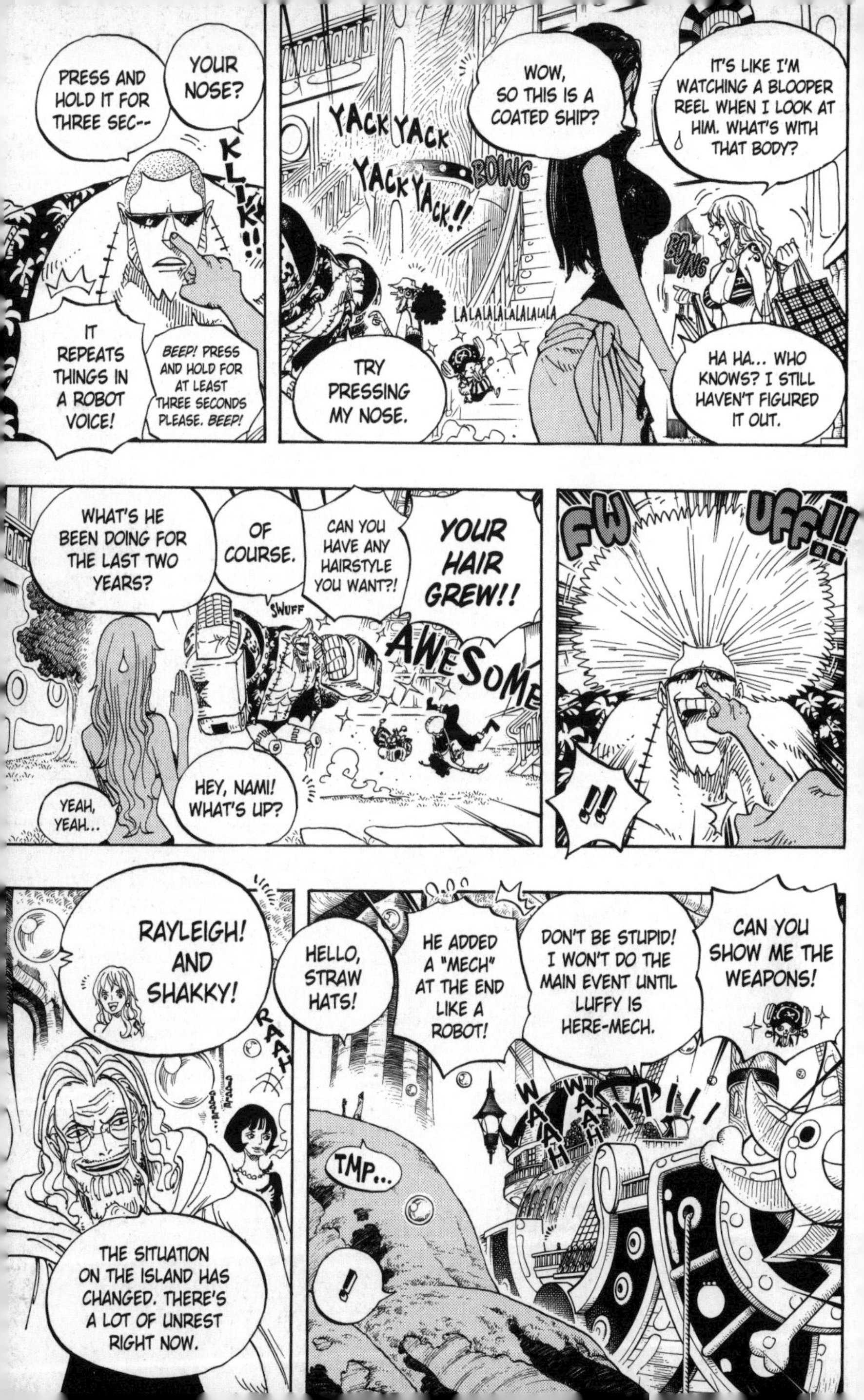
IT'S LIKE I'M WATCHING A BLOOPER REEL WHEN I LOOK AT HIM. WHAT'S WITH THAT BODY?
WOW, SO THIS IS A COATED SHIP?
YACK YACK
YACK YACK!!
BOING
BOING
LALALALALALALALA
HA HA... WHO KNOWS? I STILL HAVEN'T FIGURED IT OUT.
TRY PRESSING MY NOSE.
YOUR NOSE?
PRESS AND HOLD IT FOR THREE SEC--
KLIK!!
BEEP! PRESS AND HOLD FOR AT LEAST THREE SECONDS PLEASE. BEEP!
IT REPEATS THINGS IN A ROBOT VOICE!
FWUFF!!
!!
YOUR HAIR GREW!!
CAN YOU HAVE ANY HAIRSTYLE YOU WANT?!
OF COURSE.
SWUFF
WHAT'S HE BEEN DOING FOR THE LAST TWO YEARS?
AWESOME
HEY, NAMI! WHAT'S UP?
YEAH, YEAH...
CAN YOU SHOW ME THE WEAPONS!
DON'T BE STUPID! I WON'T DO THE MAIN EVENT UNTIL LUFFY IS HERE-MECH.
HE ADDED A "MECH" AT THE END LIKE A ROBOT!
HELLO, STRAW HATS!
WAAAH WAAAH!!!!
TMP...
!
RAYLEIGH! AND SHAKKY!
RAAH
THE SITUATION ON THE ISLAND HAS CHANGED. THERE'S A LOT OF UNREST RIGHT NOW.

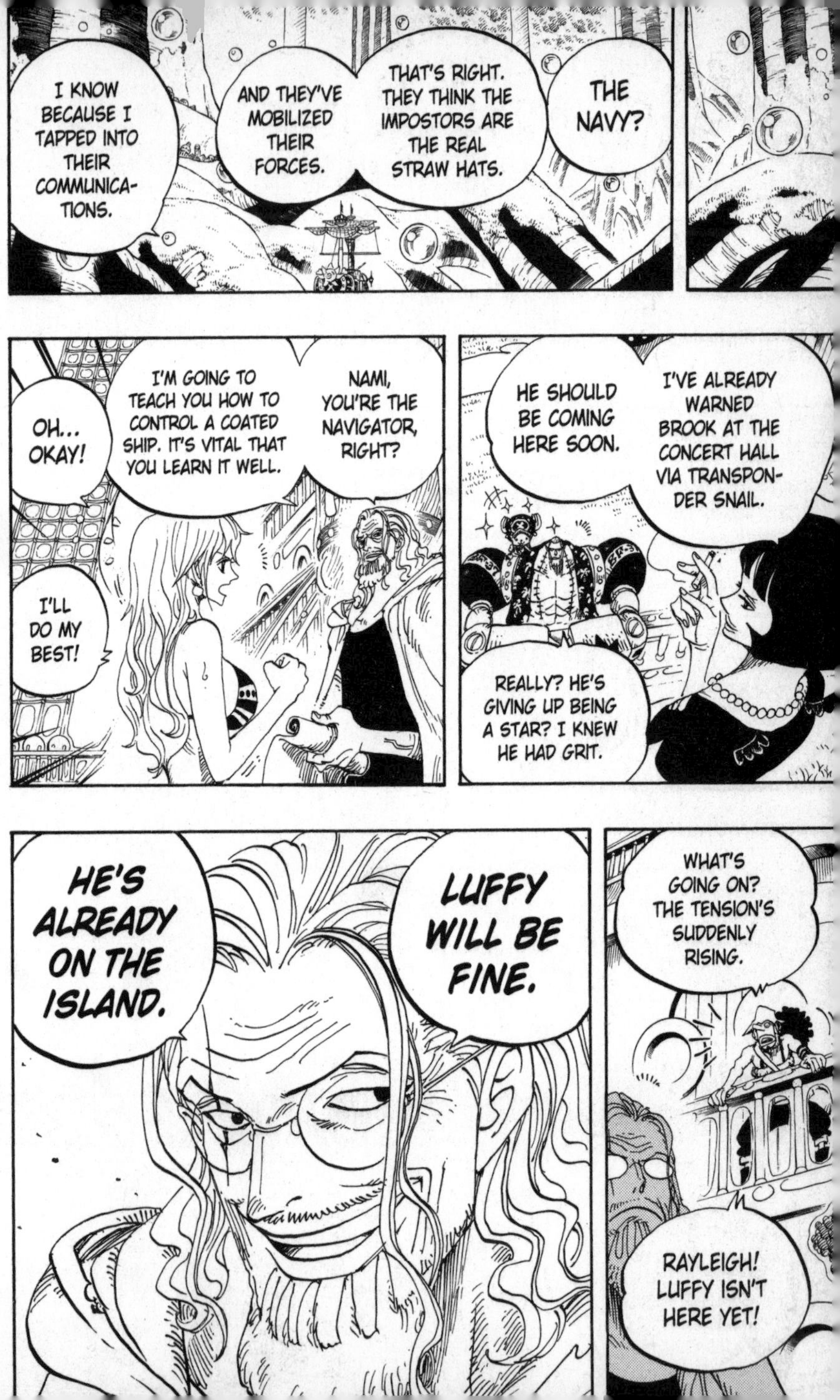
THE NAVY?
THAT'S RIGHT. THEY THINK THE IMPOSTORS ARE THE REAL STRAW HATS.
AND THEY'VE MOBILIZED THEIR FORCES.
I KNOW BECAUSE I TAPPED INTO THEIR COMMUNICATIONS.
I'VE ALREADY WARNED BROOK AT THE CONCERT HALL VIA TRANSPONDER SNAIL.
HE SHOULD BE COMING HERE SOON.
REALLY? HE'S GIVING UP BEING A STAR? I KNEW HE HAD GRIT.
NAMI, YOU'RE THE NAVIGATOR, RIGHT?
I'M GOING TO TEACH YOU HOW TO CONTROL A COATED SHIP. IT'S VITAL THAT YOU LEARN IT WELL.
OH... OKAY!
I'LL DO MY BEST!
WHAT'S GOING ON? THE TENSION'S SUDDENLY RISING.
RAYLEIGH! LUFFY ISN'T HERE YET!
LUFFY WILL BE FINE.
HE'S ALREADY ON THE ISLAND.

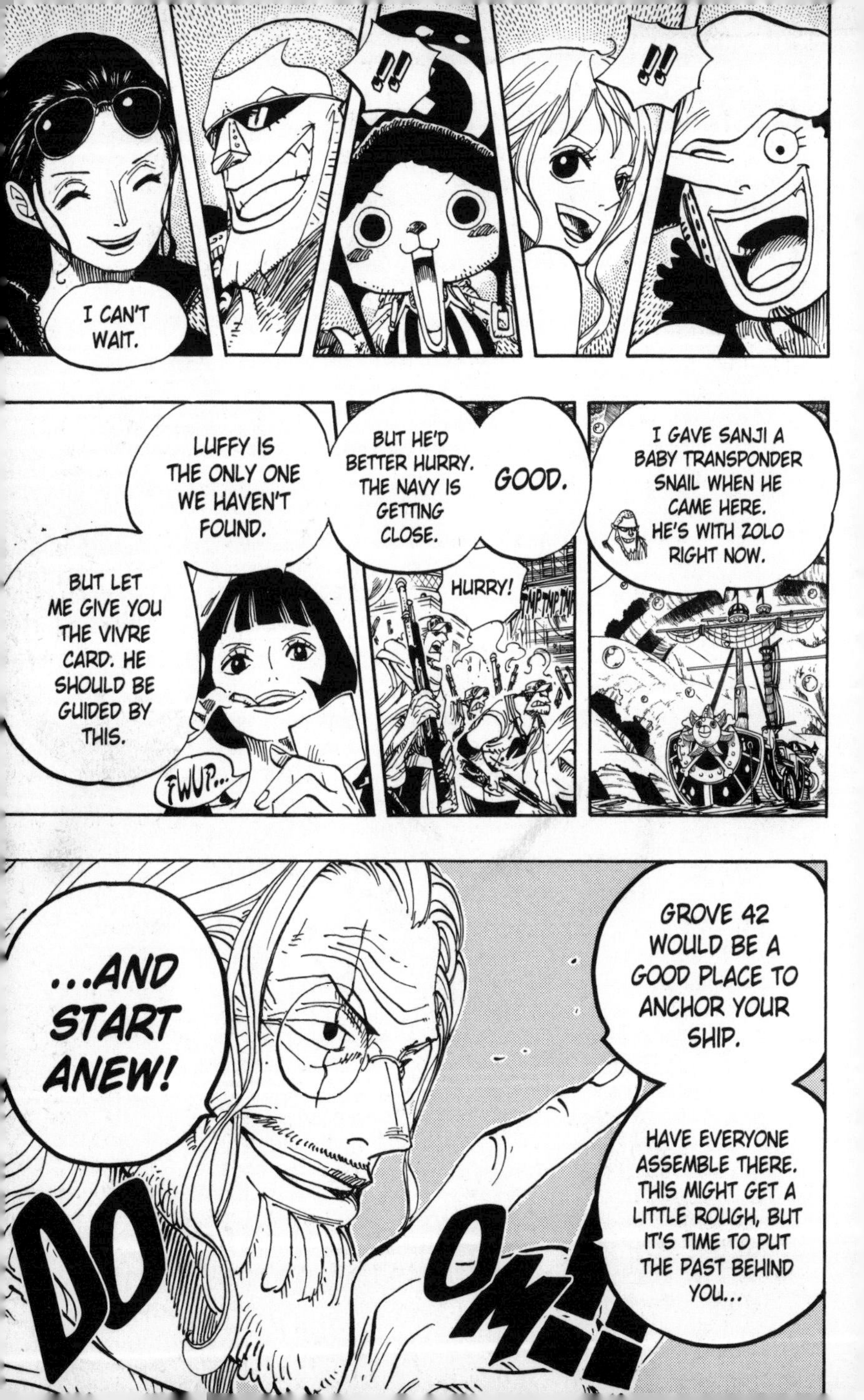
!!
!!
I CAN'T WAIT.
I GAVE SANJI A BABY TRANSPONDER SNAIL WHEN HE CAME HERE. HE'S WITH ZOLO RIGHT NOW.
GOOD.
BUT HE'D BETTER HURRY. THE NAVY IS GETTING CLOSE.
HURRY!
LUFFY IS THE ONLY ONE WE HAVEN'T FOUND.
BUT LET ME GIVE YOU THE VIVRE CARD. HE SHOULD BE GUIDED BY THIS.
FWUP...
GROVE 42 WOULD BE A GOOD PLACE TO ANCHOR YOUR SHIP.
HAVE EVERYONE ASSEMBLE THERE. THIS MIGHT GET A LITTLE ROUGH, BUT IT'S TIME TO PUT THE PAST BEHIND YOU...
...AND START ANEW!
DO
OM!!

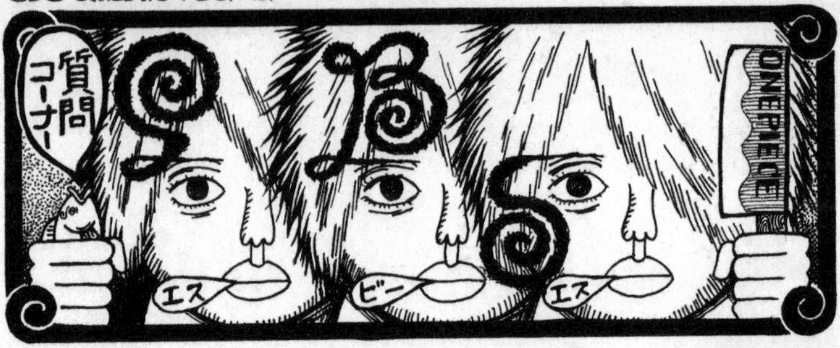
質問コーナー
ONE PIECE
エス
ビー
エス

(Side Job Musician, Tokyo)

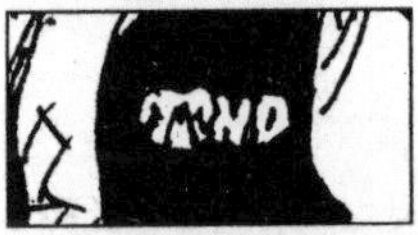
ND

Q: Hello Odacchi. I figured out the meaning of the tank top in chapter 589 you were talking about in volume 60. It's "Bound." Since it's a "dog" and "ND," it's like "Bow(wow)+nd." I love how you completely forgot about that.

--Burdock

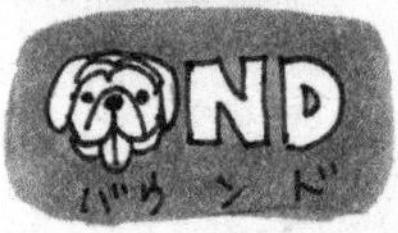
ND
バウンド

A: Oh, yeah! I get it now! You're right! It's definitely that! I'm surprised you found out! I thought about it for a while, but I couldn't figure it out. Thanks!

Q: Odacchi, what is your motivation right now? Say it in three words!

--Monkey D. Emi

A: I don't know.

Q: My chest region feels sick and I want to throw up. Is this the Haki power you were talking about?

--vlue

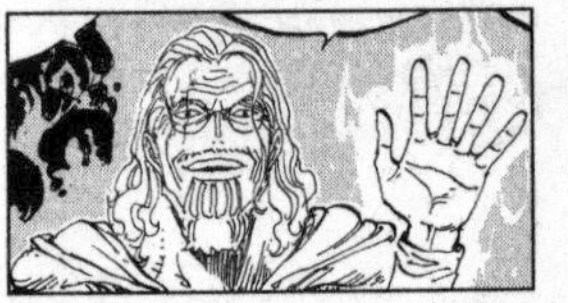

A: Yes. That's the "Color of Nausea."

Q: There's something that's really bothering me so I decided to write to you for the first time! My question is about Sanji's CRASH!! After two years… it's out! Why are you hiding the CRASH this time?! My guesses are the following! Pick one you like!
1) Mistake in drawing, 2) Change in hairstyle 3) It's his twin brother Yonji.

--Aiya

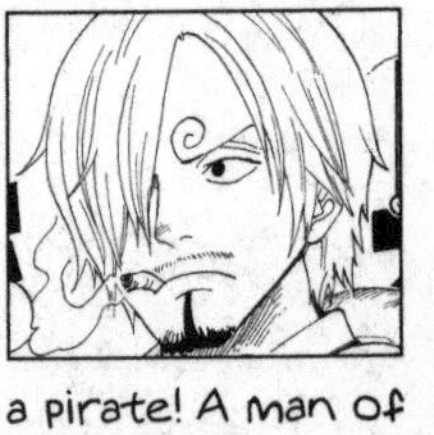

A: Sorry. They're doing construction near where I live, so I couldn't really hear you. But Sanji hasn't changed at all, right? From two years ago... Oh! You mean his mustache?! Yeah, he grew it out! I like how he looks even more like a pirate! A man of the high seas! One of his eyes had always been covered... His eyebrows are still twirly... The rest of the crew didn't say anything when they saw him again... Yup! He hasn't changed at all! But if I had to choose, it would be number one.
Anyway, starting on page 182 will be our voice actor SBS! I'll see you in the next volume!

Chapter 601:
ROMANCE DAWN FOR THE NEW WORLD

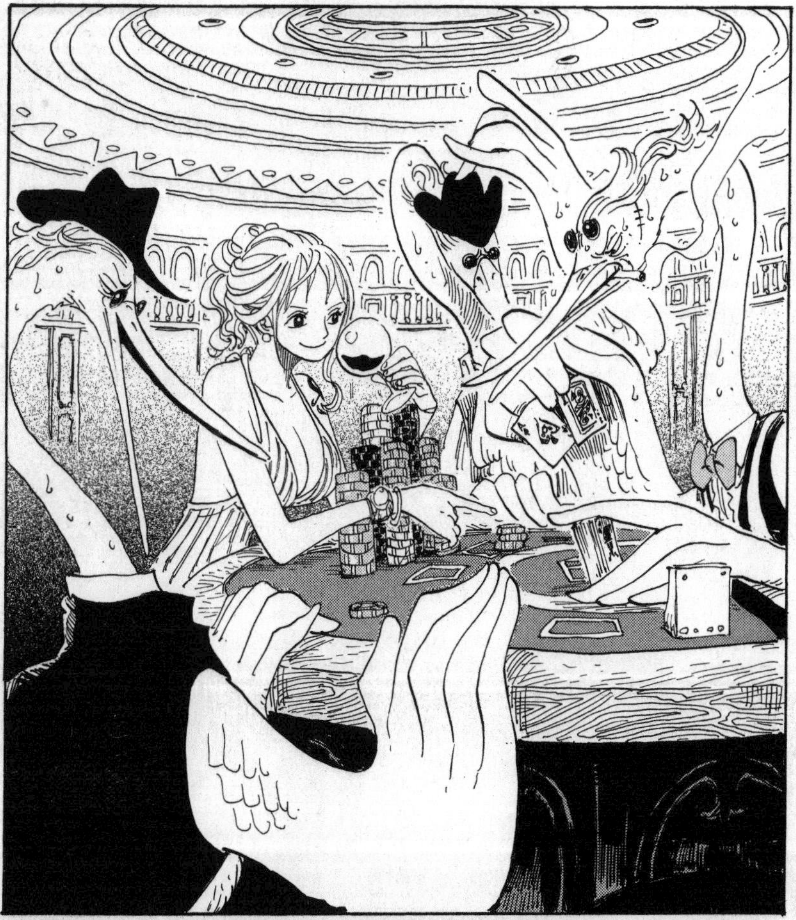

REQUEST: "NAMI PLAYING CARDS IN A CASINO WITH SOME UNSCRUPULOUS HERONS" BY ANONYMOUS

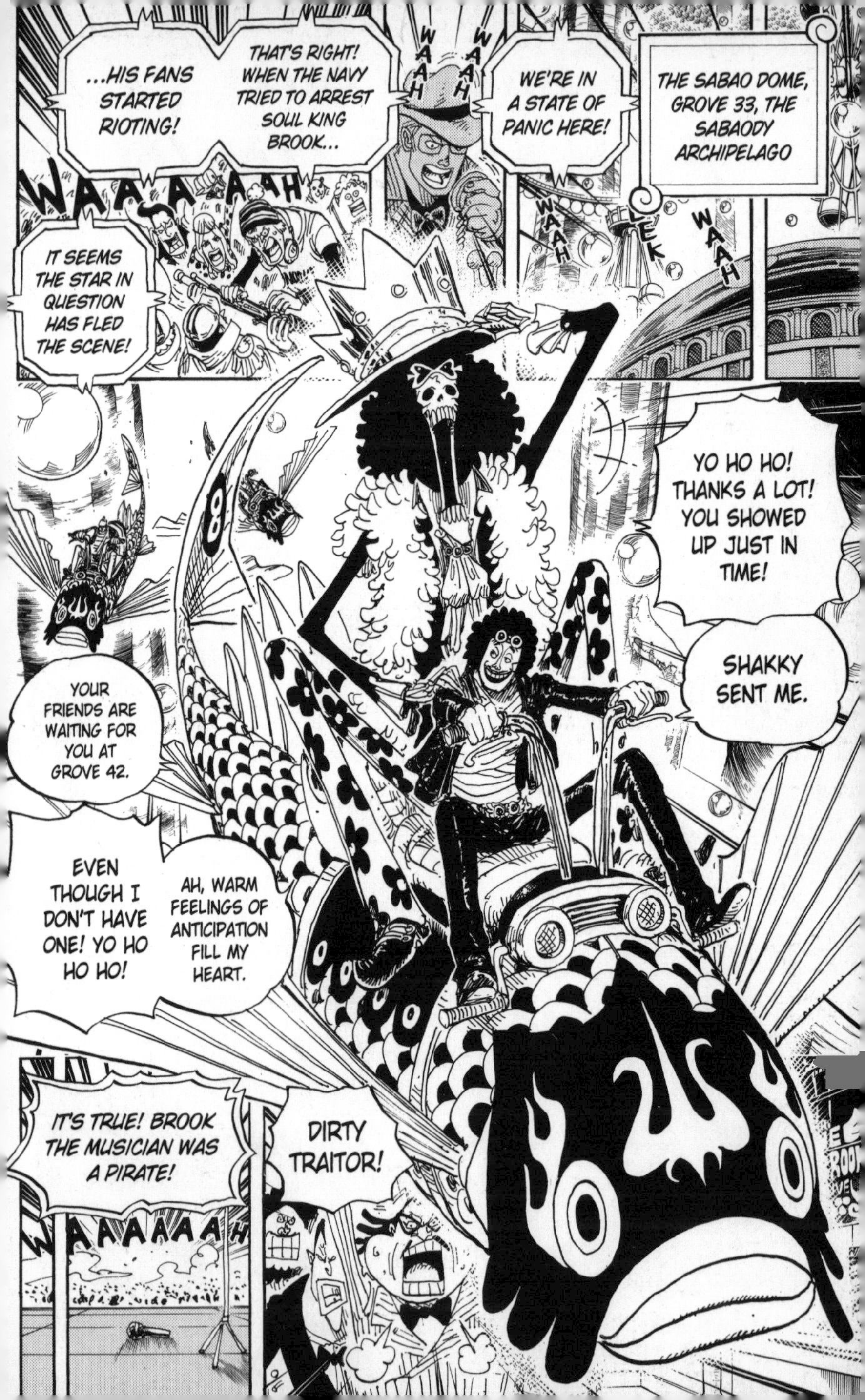

THE SABAO DOME, GROVE 33, THE SABAODY ARCHIPELAGO
WAAH
WAAH
WE'RE IN A STATE OF PANIC HERE!
WAAH
WAAH
THAT'S RIGHT! WHEN THE NAVY TRIED TO ARREST SOUL KING BROOK...
...HIS FANS STARTED RIOTING!
WAAAAAH
IT SEEMS THE STAR IN QUESTION HAS FLED THE SCENE!
YO HO HO! THANKS A LOT! YOU SHOWED UP JUST IN TIME!
SHAKKY SENT ME.
YOUR FRIENDS ARE WAITING FOR YOU AT GROVE 42.
AH, WARM FEELINGS OF ANTICIPATION FILL MY HEART.
EVEN THOUGH I DON'T HAVE ONE! YO HO HO HO!
DIRTY TRAITOR!
IT'S TRUE! BROOK THE MUSICIAN WAS A PIRATE!
WAAAAAAH

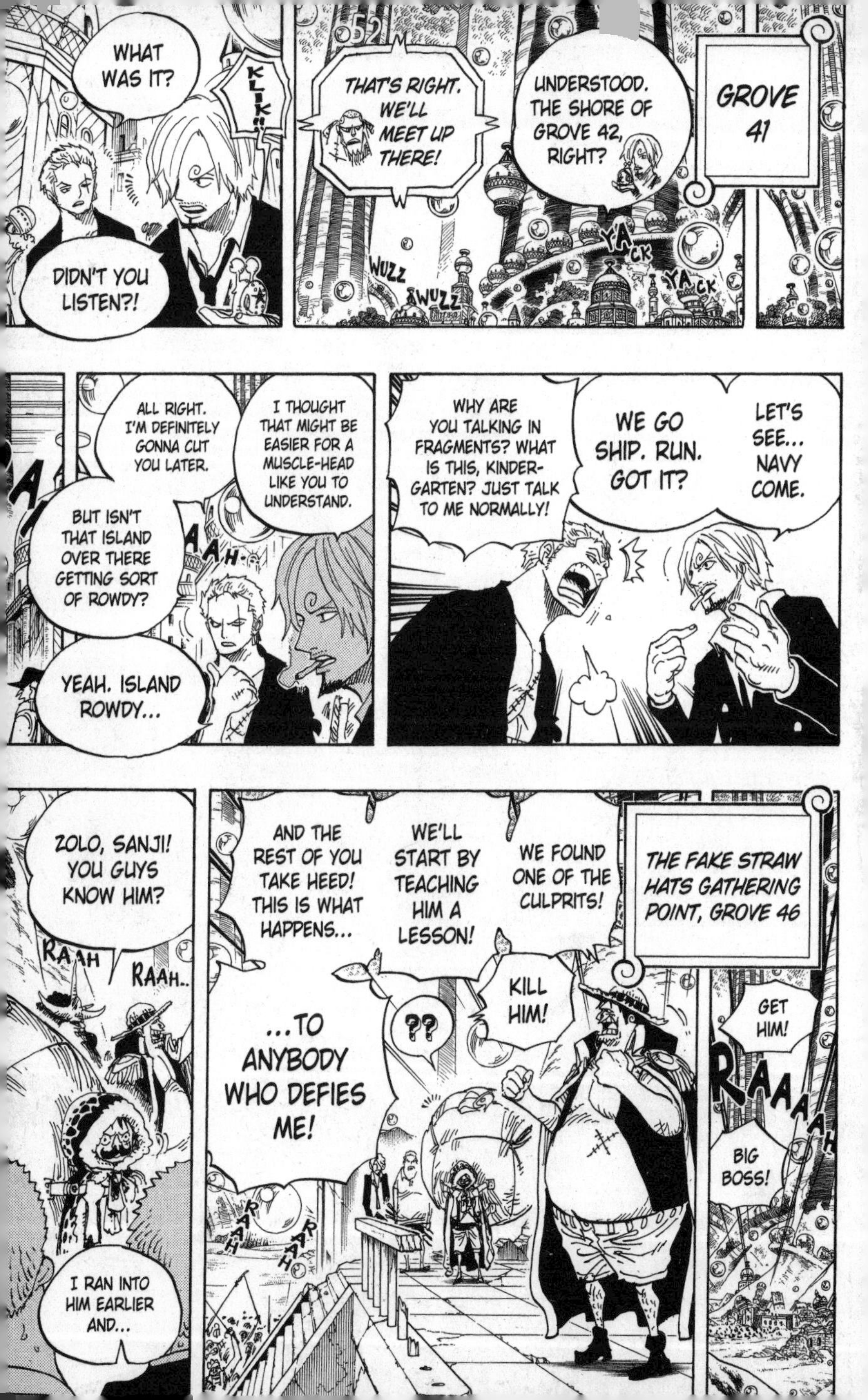
GROVE 41
UNDERSTOOD. THE SHORE OF GROVE 42, RIGHT?
THAT'S RIGHT. WE'LL MEET UP THERE!
YACK
YACK
WUZZ
WUZZ
KLIK!!
WHAT WAS IT?
DIDN'T YOU LISTEN?!
LET'S SEE... NAVY COME.
WE GO SHIP. RUN. GOT IT?
WHY ARE YOU TALKING IN FRAGMENTS? WHAT IS THIS, KINDER-GARTEN? JUST TALK TO ME NORMALLY!
I THOUGHT THAT MIGHT BE EASIER FOR A MUSCLE-HEAD LIKE YOU TO UNDERSTAND.
ALL RIGHT. I'M DEFINITELY GONNA CUT YOU LATER.
AAAH
BUT ISN'T THAT ISLAND OVER THERE GETTING SORT OF ROWDY?
YEAH. ISLAND ROWDY...
GET HIM!
RAAAAH
BIG BOSS!
THE FAKE STRAW HATS GATHERING POINT, GROVE 46
WE FOUND ONE OF THE CULPRITS!
WE'LL START BY TEACHING HIM A LESSON!
AND THE REST OF YOU TAKE HEED! THIS IS WHAT HAPPENS...
KILL HIM!
??
...TO ANYBODY WHO DEFIES ME!
RAAH
RAAH
ZOLO, SANJI! YOU GUYS KNOW HIM?
RAAH
RAAH..
I RAN INTO HIM EARLIER AND...

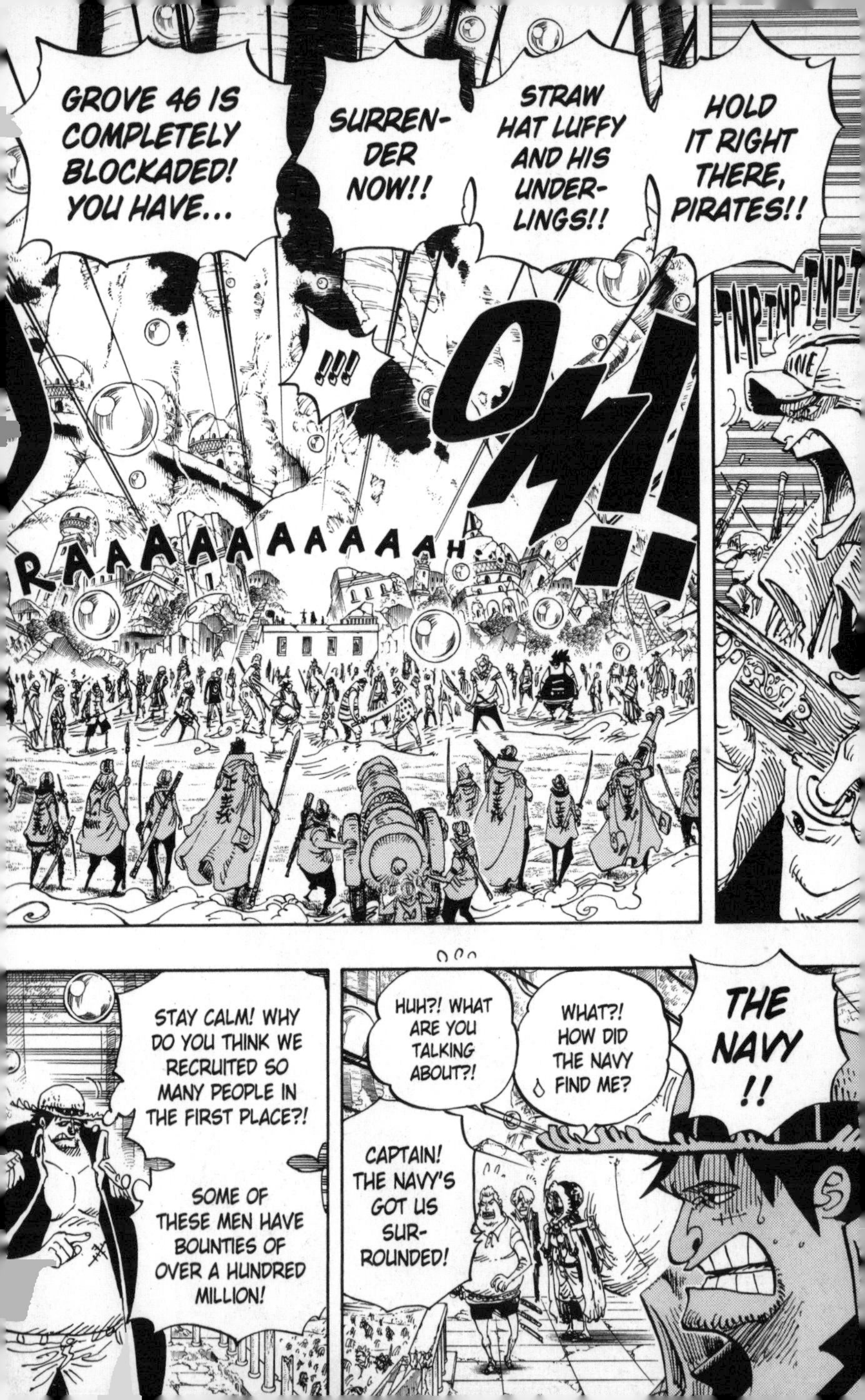
HOLD IT RIGHT THERE, PIRATES!!
STRAW HAT LUFFY AND HIS UNDER-LINGS!!
SURREN-DER NOW!!
GROVE 46 IS COMPLETELY BLOCKADED! YOU HAVE...
TMP TMP TMP
!!!
OH!!
RAAAAAAAAAAAH
THE NAVY !!
WHAT?! HOW DID THE NAVY FIND ME?
HUH?! WHAT ARE YOU TALKING ABOUT?!
CAPTAIN! THE NAVY'S GOT US SUR-ROUNDED!
STAY CALM! WHY DO YOU THINK WE RECRUITED SO MANY PEOPLE IN THE FIRST PLACE?!
SOME OF THESE MEN HAVE BOUNTIES OF OVER A HUNDRED MILLION!

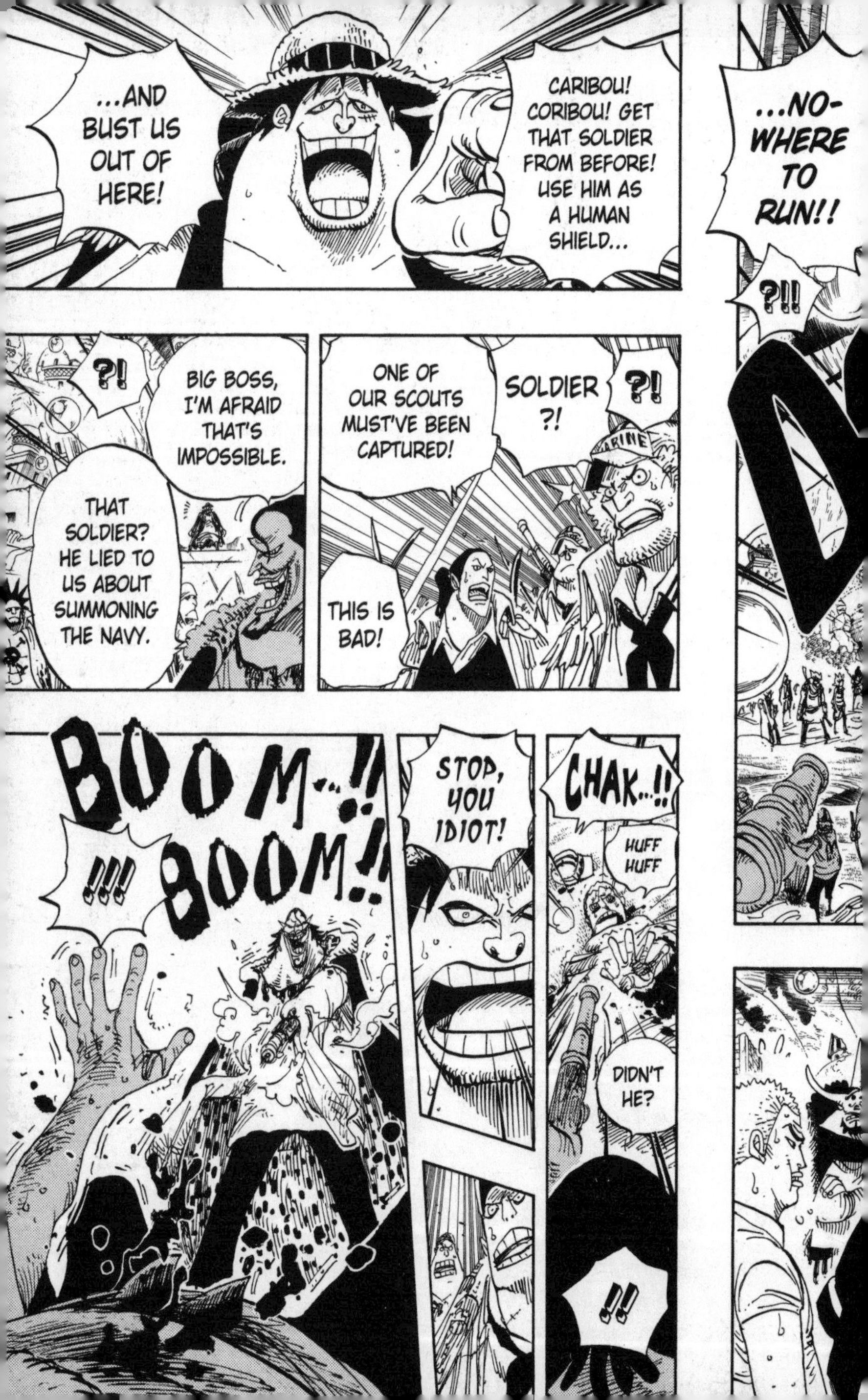

...NO-WHERE TO RUN!!
?!!
CARIBOU! CORIBOU! GET THAT SOLDIER FROM BEFORE! USE HIM AS A HUMAN SHIELD...
...AND BUST US OUT OF HERE!
SOLDIER ?!
?!
ONE OF OUR SCOUTS MUST'VE BEEN CAPTURED!
THIS IS BAD!
?!
BIG BOSS, I'M AFRAID THAT'S IMPOSSIBLE.
THAT SOLDIER? HE LIED TO US ABOUT SUMMONING THE NAVY.
CHAK...!!
HUFF HUFF
DIDN'T HE?
!!
STOP, YOU IDIOT!
BOOM...!!
BOOM!!
!!!

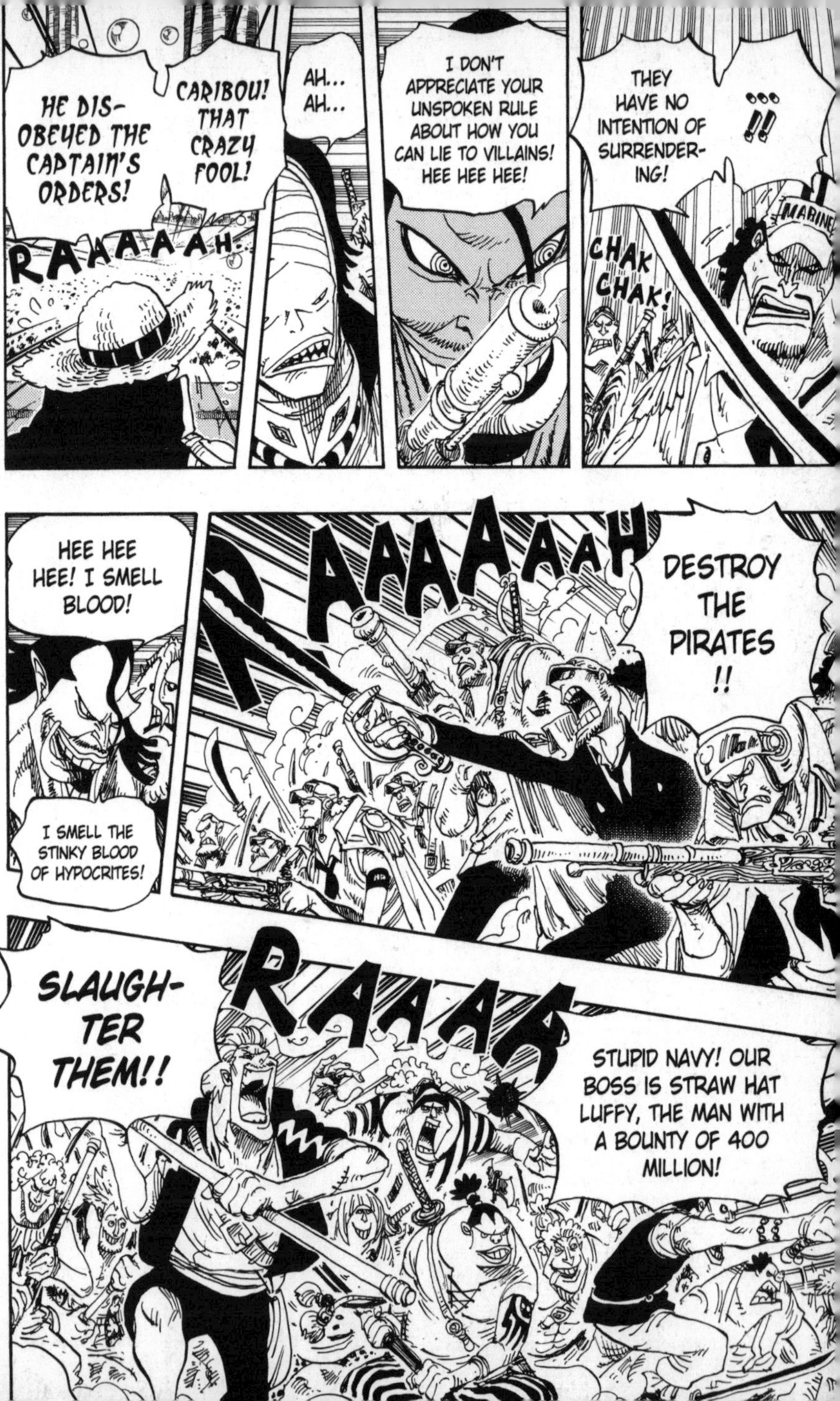
THEY HAVE NO INTENTION OF SURRENDER-ING!
...!!
MARINE
CHAK CHAK!
I DON'T APPRECIATE YOUR UNSPOKEN RULE ABOUT HOW YOU CAN LIE TO VILLAINS! HEE HEE HEE!
AH... AH...
CARIBOU! THAT CRAZY FOOL!
HE DIS-OBEYED THE CAPTAIN'S ORDERS!
RAAAAAAH
RAAAAAAH
DESTROY THE PIRATES!!
HEE HEE HEE! I SMELL BLOOD!
I SMELL THE STINKY BLOOD OF HYPOCRITES!
STUPID NAVY! OUR BOSS IS STRAW HAT LUFFY, THE MAN WITH A BOUNTY OF 400 MILLION!
RAAAR
SLAUGH-TER THEM!!

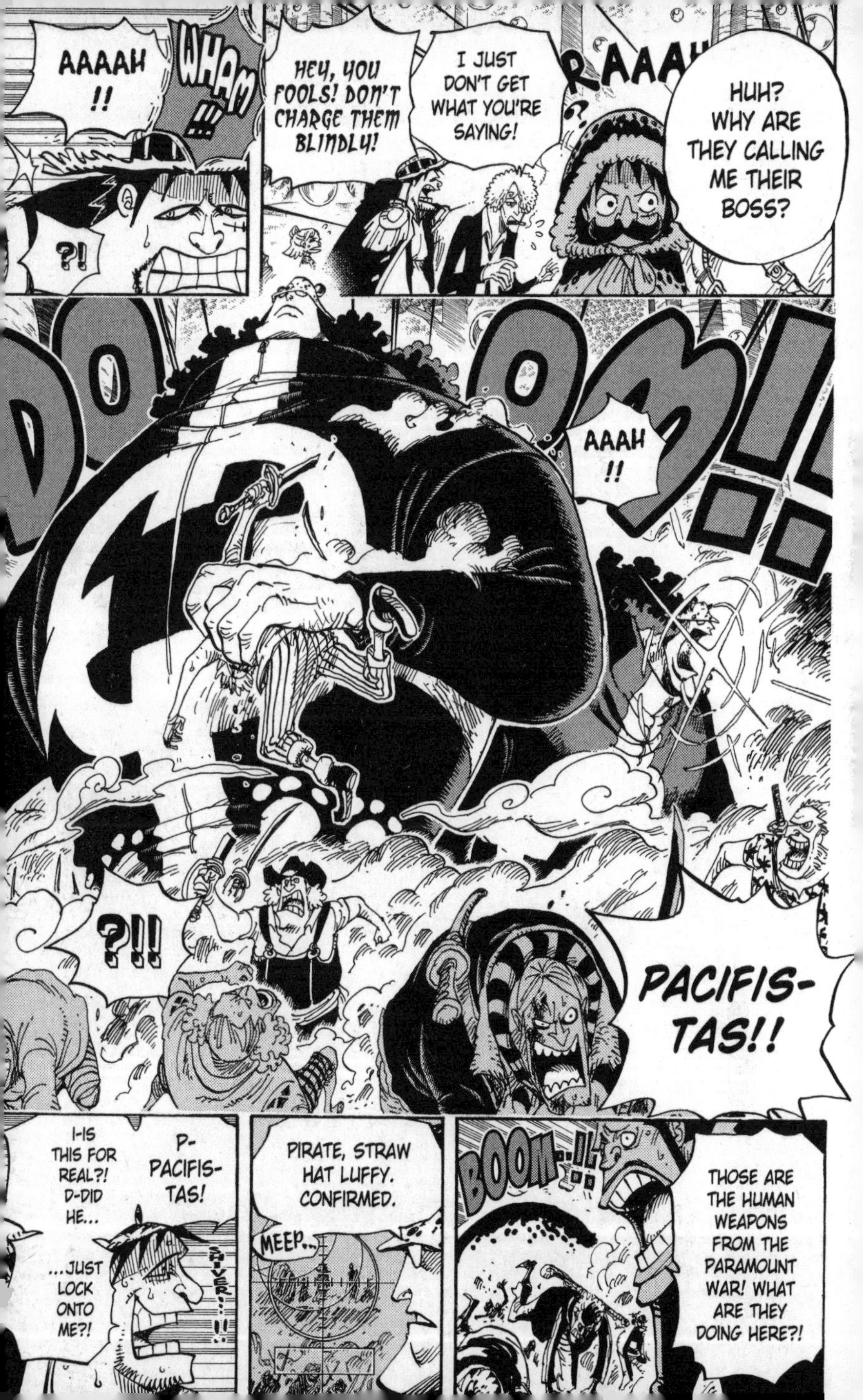
RAAA
HUH? WHY ARE THEY CALLING ME THEIR BOSS?
I JUST DON'T GET WHAT YOU'RE SAYING!
HEY, YOU FOOLS! DON'T CHARGE THEM BLINDLY!
WHAM!!
AAAAH!!
?!
DOOM!!
AAAH!!
PACIFISTAS!!
?!!
THOSE ARE THE HUMAN WEAPONS FROM THE PARAMOUNT WAR! WHAT ARE THEY DOING HERE?!
BOOM!!
PIRATE, STRAW HAT LUFFY. CONFIRMED.
MEEP...
P-PACIFISTAS!
I-IS THIS FOR REAL?! D-DID HE...
...JUST LOCK ONTO ME?!
SHIVER...!!

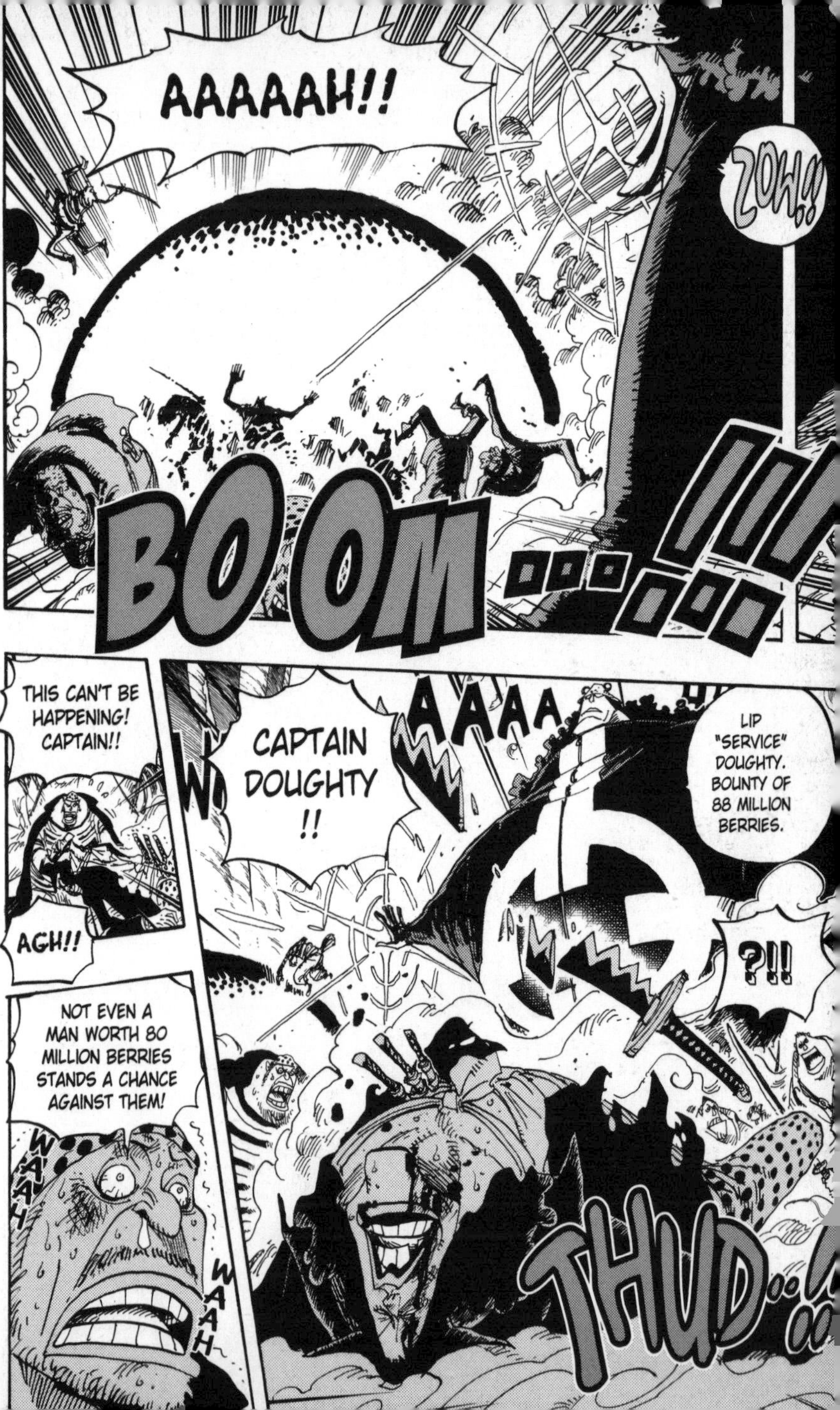
ZOW!!
AAAAAH!!
BOOM...!!
LIP "SERVICE" DOUGHTY. BOUNTY OF 88 MILLION BERRIES.
WAAAA
CAPTAIN DOUGHTY !!
?!!
THUD...!!
THIS CAN'T BE HAPPENING! CAPTAIN!!
AGH!!
NOT EVEN A MAN WORTH 80 MILLION BERRIES STANDS A CHANCE AGAINST THEM!
WAAH
WAAH

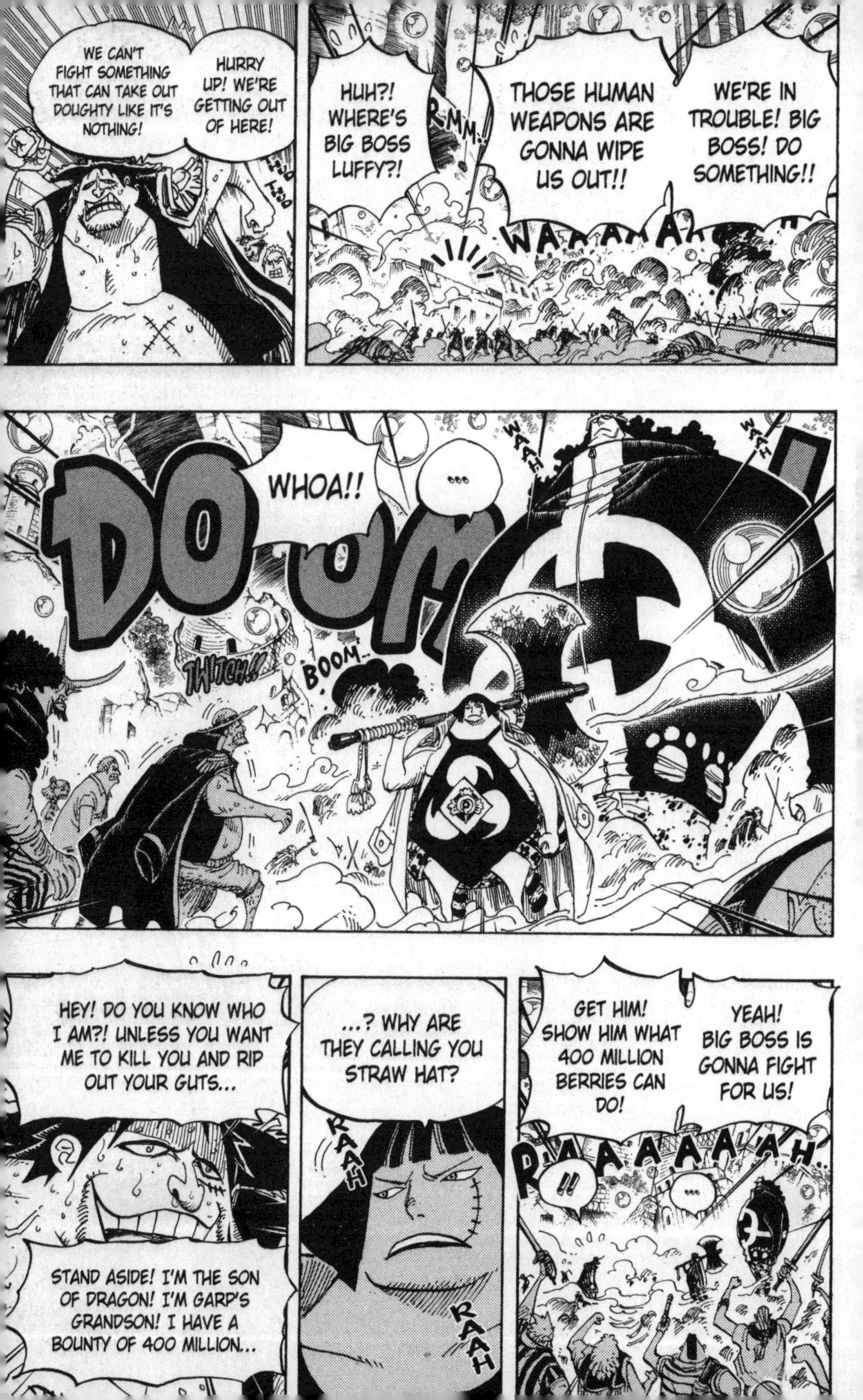
WE'RE IN TROUBLE! BIG BOSS! DO SOMETHING!!
THOSE HUMAN WEAPONS ARE GONNA WIPE US OUT!!
HUH?! WHERE'S BIG BOSS LUFFY?!
RMM..
WAAAAAA
HURRY UP! WE'RE GETTING OUT OF HERE!
WE CAN'T FIGHT SOMETHING THAT CAN TAKE OUT DOUGHTY LIKE IT'S NOTHING!
THUD THUD
WAAH
WAAH
...
WHOA!!
DOOM
BOOM..
TWITCH!!
YEAH! BIG BOSS IS GONNA FIGHT FOR US!
GET HIM! SHOW HIM WHAT 400 MILLION BERRIES CAN DO!
RAAAAAAAH..
!!
...
...? WHY ARE THEY CALLING YOU STRAW HAT?
RAAH
RAAH
HEY! DO YOU KNOW WHO I AM?! UNLESS YOU WANT ME TO KILL YOU AND RIP OUT YOUR GUTS...
STAND ASIDE! I'M THE SON OF DRAGON! I'M GARP'S GRANDSON! I HAVE A BOUNTY OF 400 MILLION...

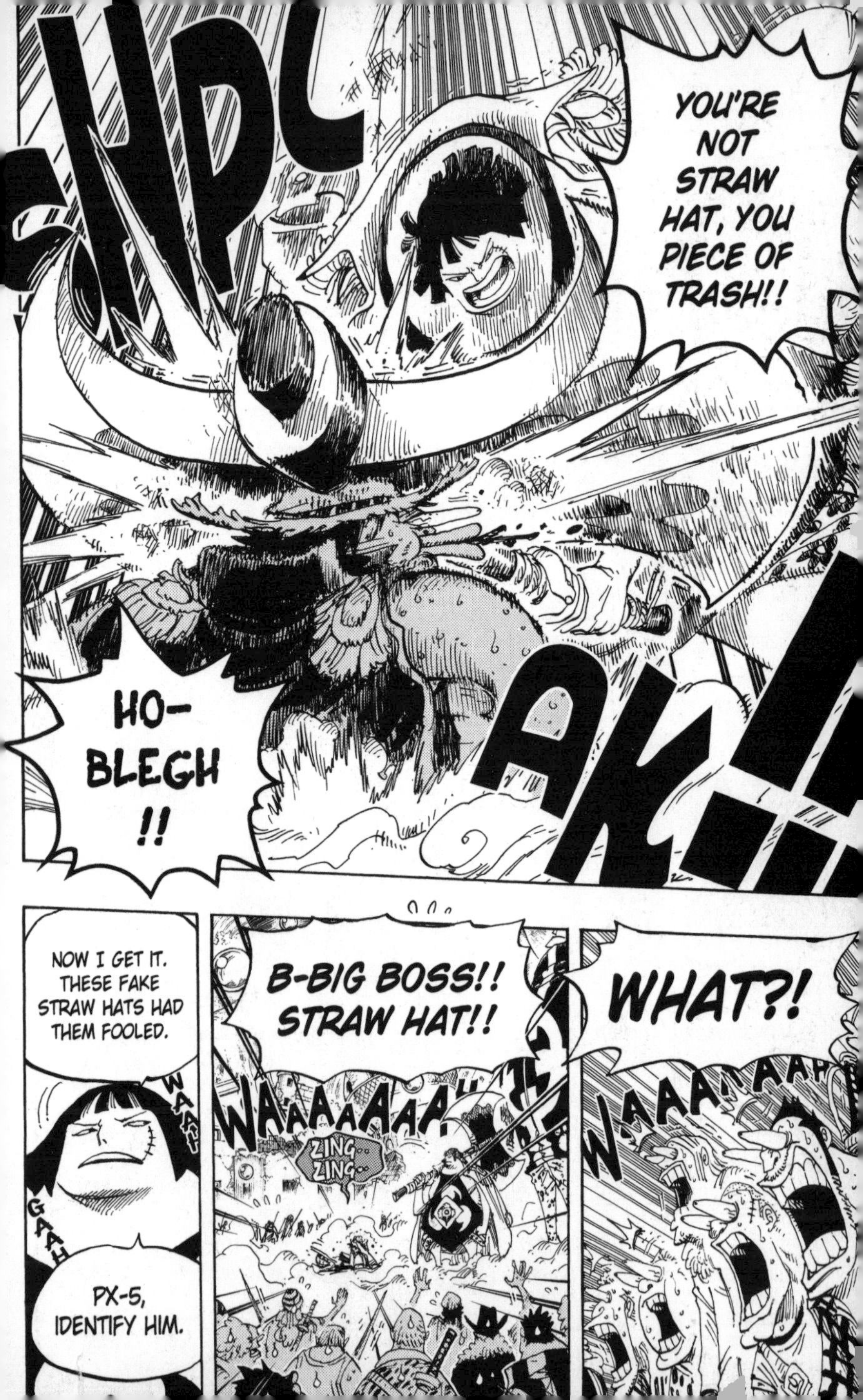
YOU'RE NOT STRAW HAT, YOU PIECE OF TRASH!!
HO-BLEGH!!
WHAT?!
B-BIG BOSS!! STRAW HAT!!
WAAAAAAAA
ZING ZING
NOW I GET IT. THESE FAKE STRAW HATS HAD THEM FOOLED.
GAAH
PX-5, IDENTIFY HIM.

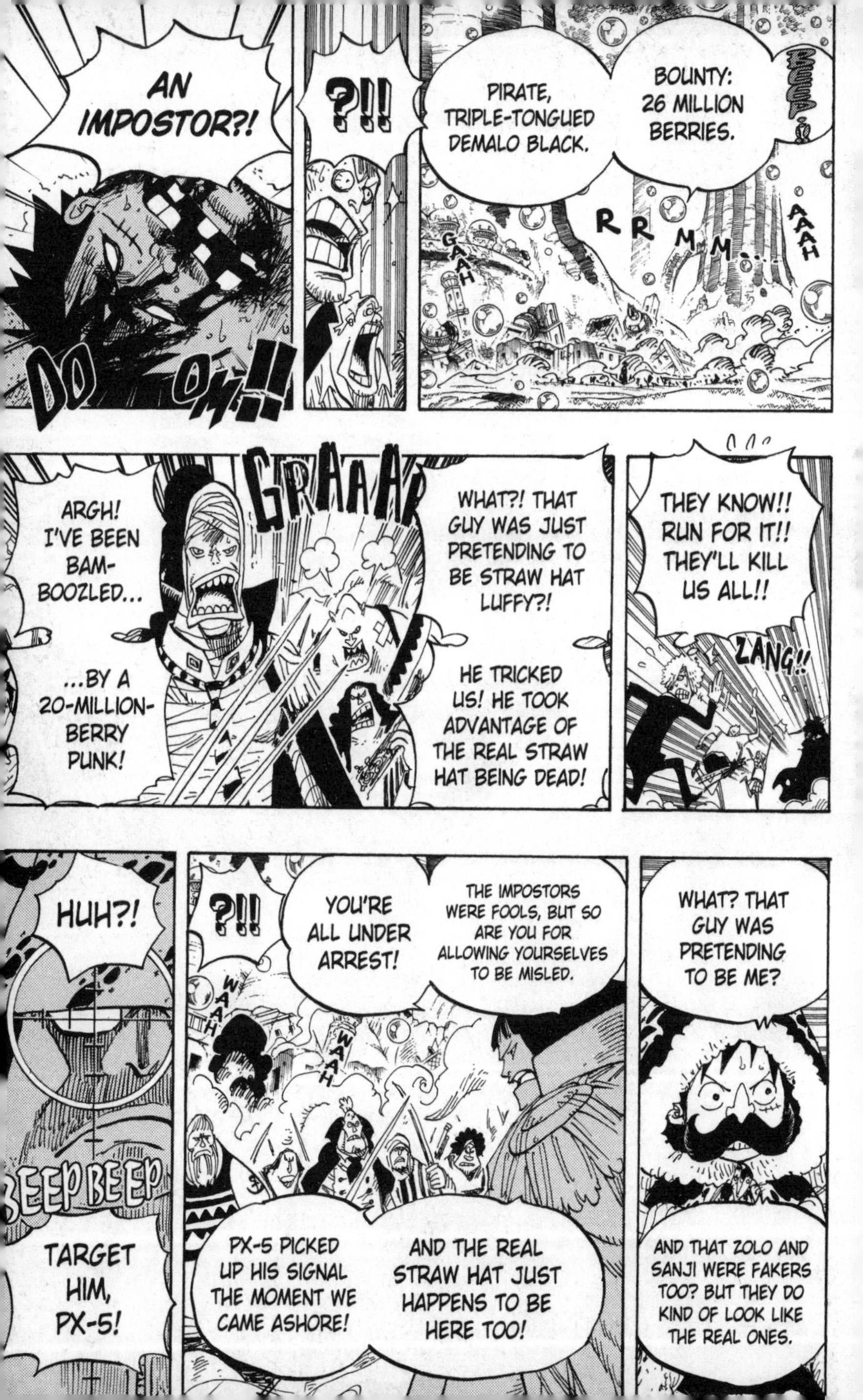
BOUNTY: 26 MILLION BERRIES.
PIRATE, TRIPLE-TONGUED DEMALO BLACK.
AAAH
RRMMM...
GAAH
?!!
AN IMPOSTOR?!
DOOM!!
THEY KNOW!! RUN FOR IT!! THEY'LL KILL US ALL!!
ZANG!!
WHAT?! THAT GUY WAS JUST PRETENDING TO BE STRAW HAT LUFFY?!
HE TRICKED US! HE TOOK ADVANTAGE OF THE REAL STRAW HAT BEING DEAD!
ARGH! I'VE BEEN BAM-BOOZLED...
...BY A 20-MILLION-BERRY PUNK!
WHAT? THAT GUY WAS PRETENDING TO BE ME?
AND THAT ZOLO AND SANJI WERE FAKERS TOO? BUT THEY DO KIND OF LOOK LIKE THE REAL ONES.
THE IMPOSTORS WERE FOOLS, BUT SO ARE YOU FOR ALLOWING YOURSELVES TO BE MISLED.
YOU'RE ALL UNDER ARREST!
?!!
WAAAH
WAAAH
AND THE REAL STRAW HAT JUST HAPPENS TO BE HERE TOO!
PX-5 PICKED UP HIS SIGNAL THE MOMENT WE CAME ASHORE!
HUH?!
BEEP BEEP
TARGET HIM, PX-5!

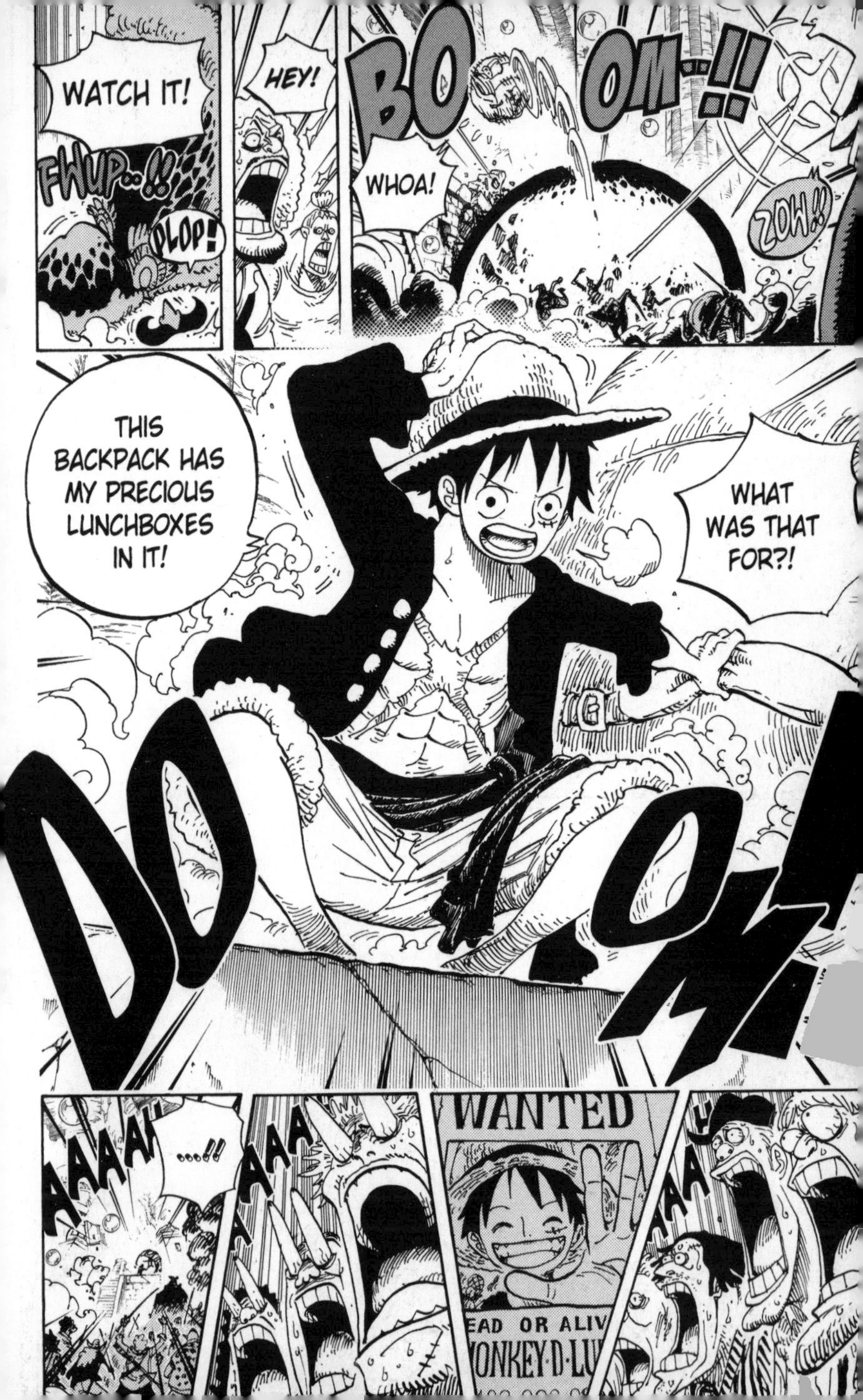
BO
OM!!
ZOW!!
WHOA!
HEY!
WATCH IT!
FWUP!!
PLOP!
WHAT WAS THAT FOR?!
THIS BACKPACK HAS MY PRECIOUS LUNCHBOXES IN IT!
AA
WANTED
EAD OR ALIV
ONKEY·D·LU
AA
AAAA
...!!

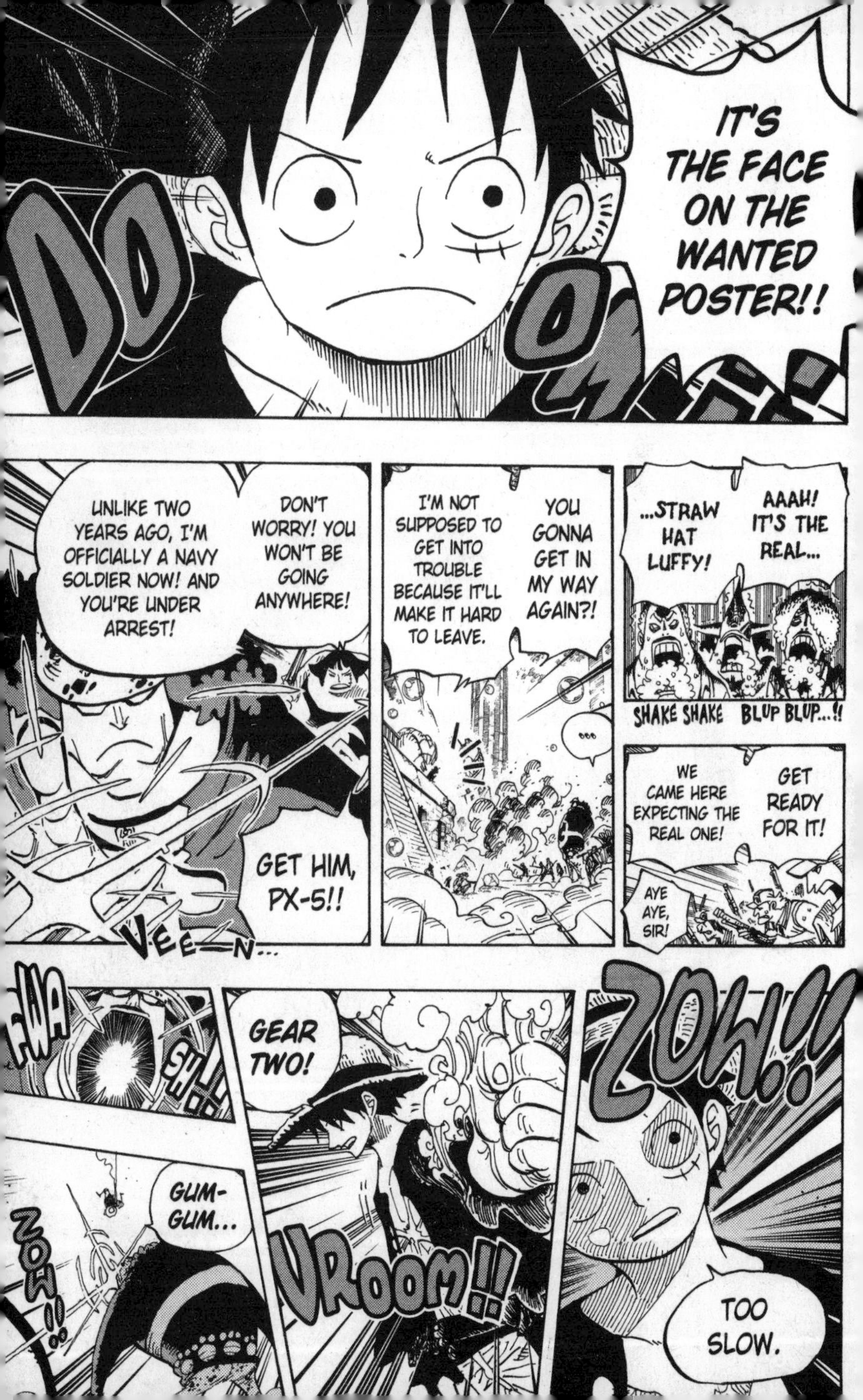
DOOM
IT'S THE FACE ON THE WANTED POSTER!!
AAAH! IT'S THE REAL...
...STRAW HAT LUFFY!
BLUP BLUP...!!
SHAKE SHAKE
GET READY FOR IT!
WE CAME HERE EXPECTING THE REAL ONE!
AYE AYE, SIR!
YOU GONNA GET IN MY WAY AGAIN?!
I'M NOT SUPPOSED TO GET INTO TROUBLE BECAUSE IT'LL MAKE IT HARD TO LEAVE.
...
DON'T WORRY! YOU WON'T BE GOING ANYWHERE!
UNLIKE TWO YEARS AGO, I'M OFFICIALLY A NAVY SOLDIER NOW! AND YOU'RE UNDER ARREST!
GET HIM, PX-5!!
VEE—N...
ZOOM!!
TOO SLOW.
GEAR TWO!
VROOM!!
FWA
GUM-GUM...
ZOOM!!

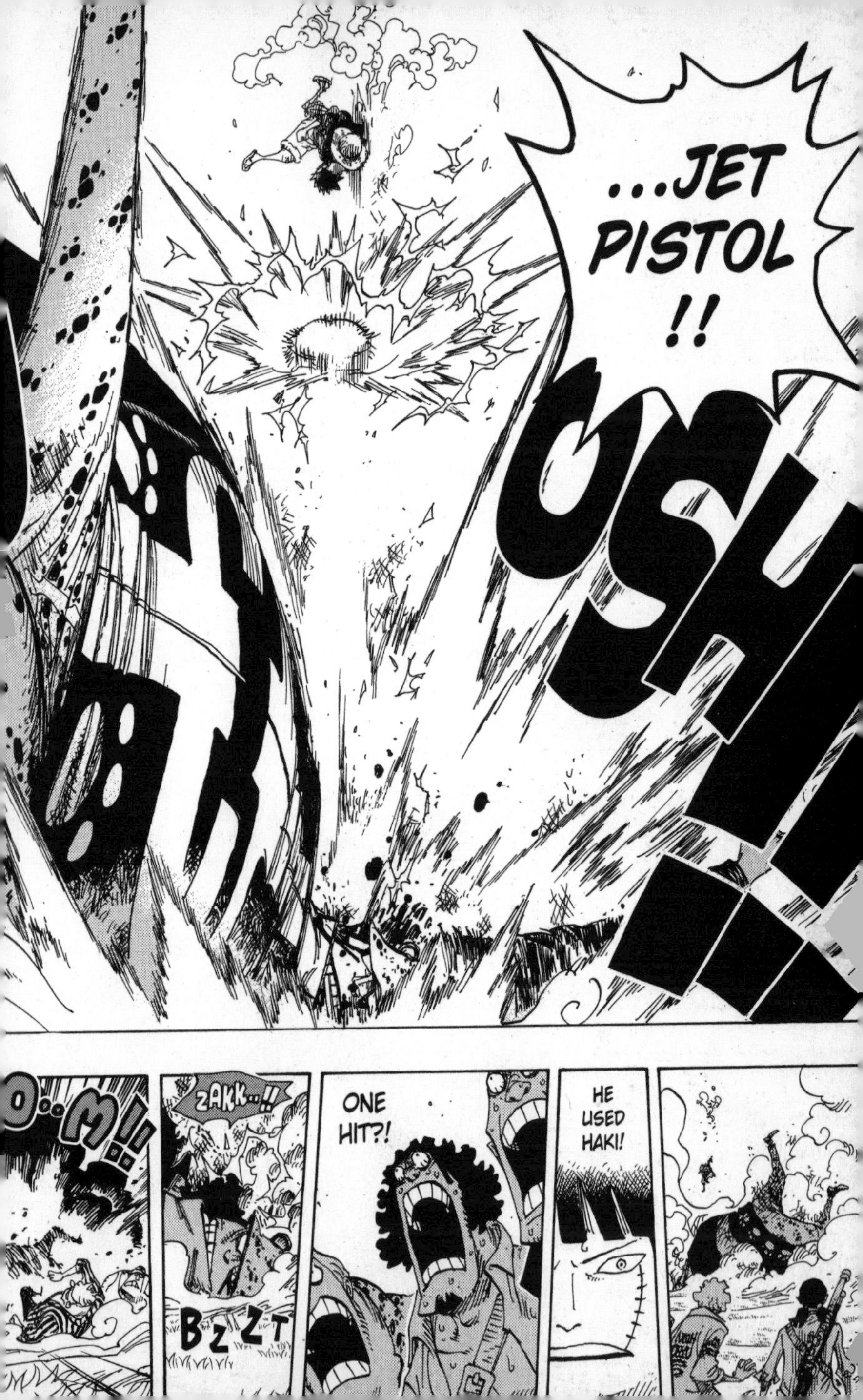
...JET PISTOL !!
HE USED HAKI!
ONE HIT?!
ZAKK..!!
BZZT

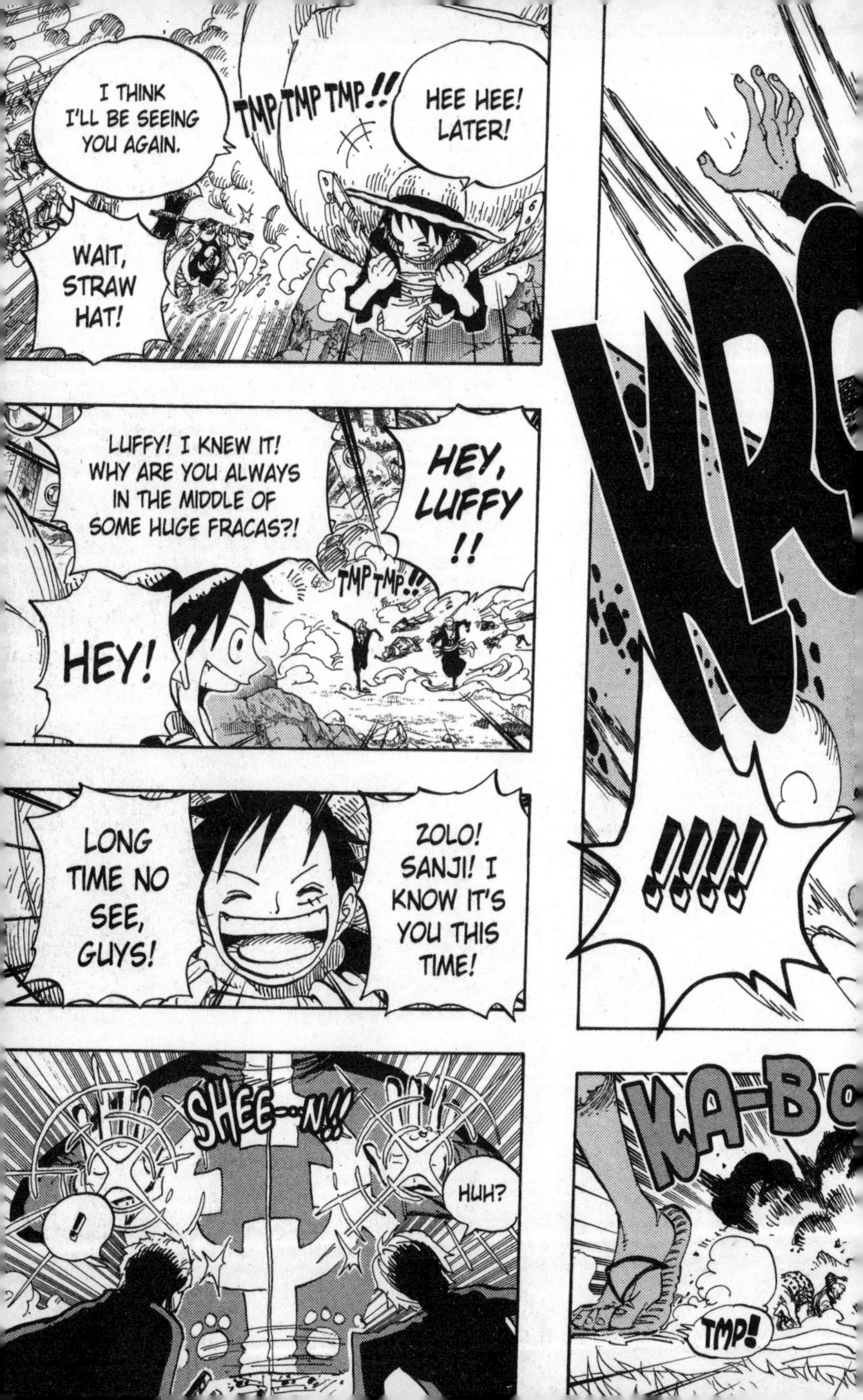
KRS
!!!!
HEE HEE! LATER!
TMP TMP TMP!!
I THINK I'LL BE SEEING YOU AGAIN.
WAIT, STRAW HAT!
HEY, LUFFY !!
LUFFY! I KNEW IT! WHY ARE YOU ALWAYS IN THE MIDDLE OF SOME HUGE FRACAS?!
TMP TMP!!
HEY!
ZOLO! SANJI! I KNOW IT'S YOU THIS TIME!
LONG TIME NO SEE, GUYS!
KA-BO
TMP!
SHEE--N!!
HUH?
!

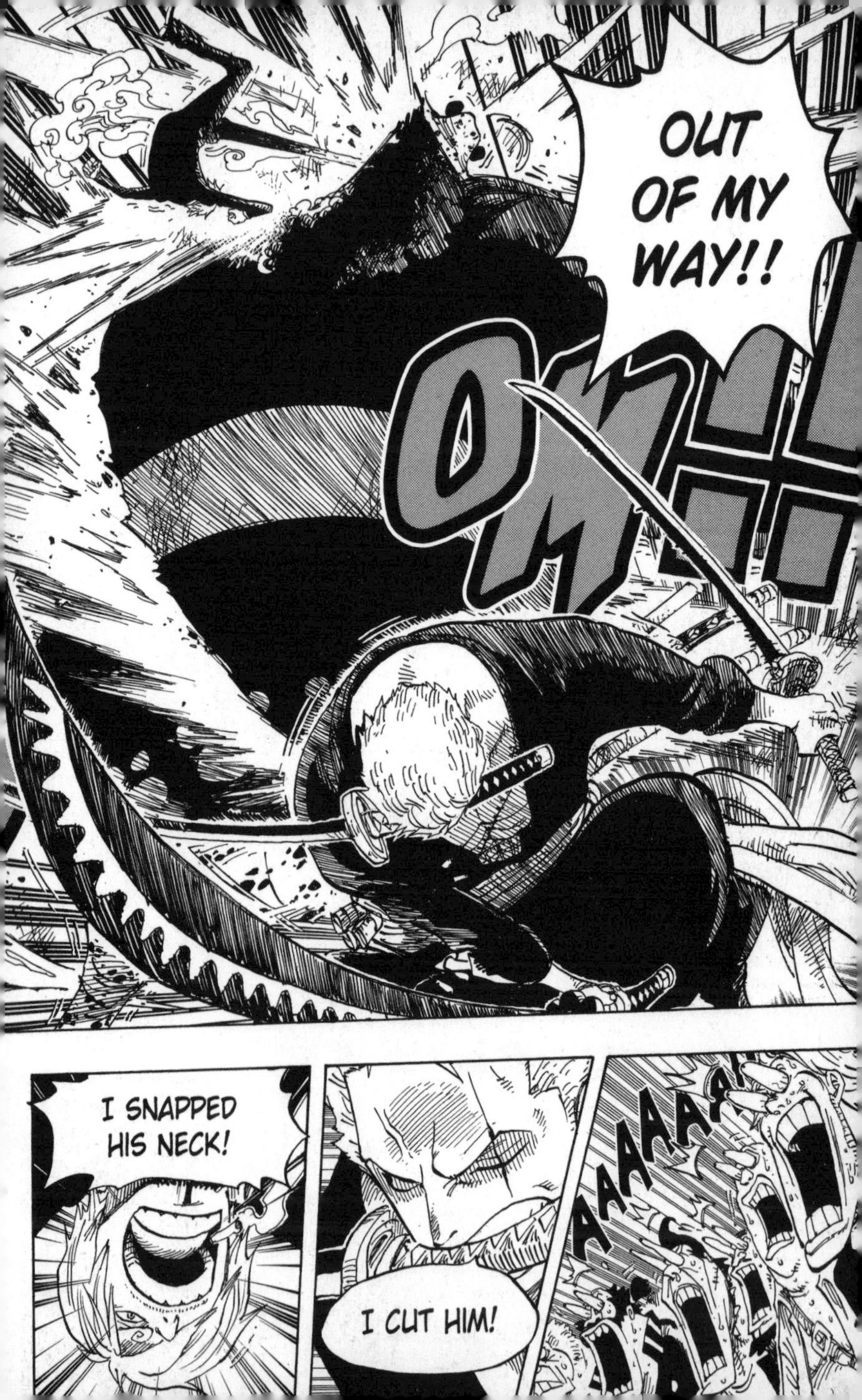
OUT OF MY WAY!!
AAAAAAA
I CUT HIM!
I SNAPPED HIS NECK!

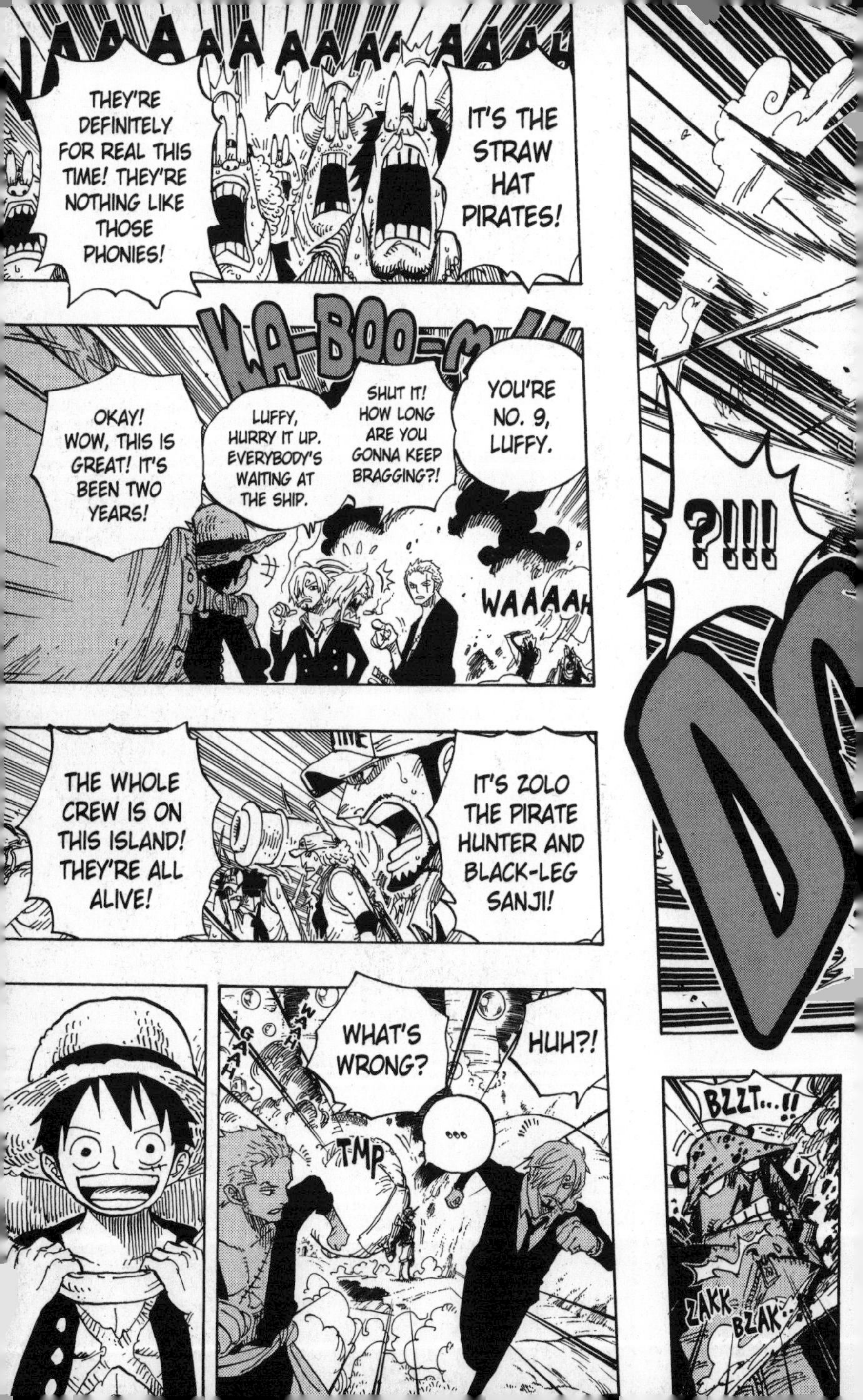
?!!!
AAAAAAAAAAAA
IT'S THE STRAW HAT PIRATES!
THEY'RE DEFINITELY FOR REAL THIS TIME! THEY'RE NOTHING LIKE THOSE PHONIES!
KA-BOO-M!!
YOU'RE NO. 9, LUFFY.
SHUT IT! HOW LONG ARE YOU GONNA KEEP BRAGGING?!
LUFFY, HURRY IT UP. EVERYBODY'S WAITING AT THE SHIP.
OKAY! WOW, THIS IS GREAT! IT'S BEEN TWO YEARS!
WAAAAH
IT'S ZOLO THE PIRATE HUNTER AND BLACK-LEG SANJI!
THE WHOLE CREW IS ON THIS ISLAND! THEY'RE ALL ALIVE!
BZZT...!!
ZAKK
BZAK...
HUH?!
WHAT'S WRONG?
WAAH
GAAH
...
TMP

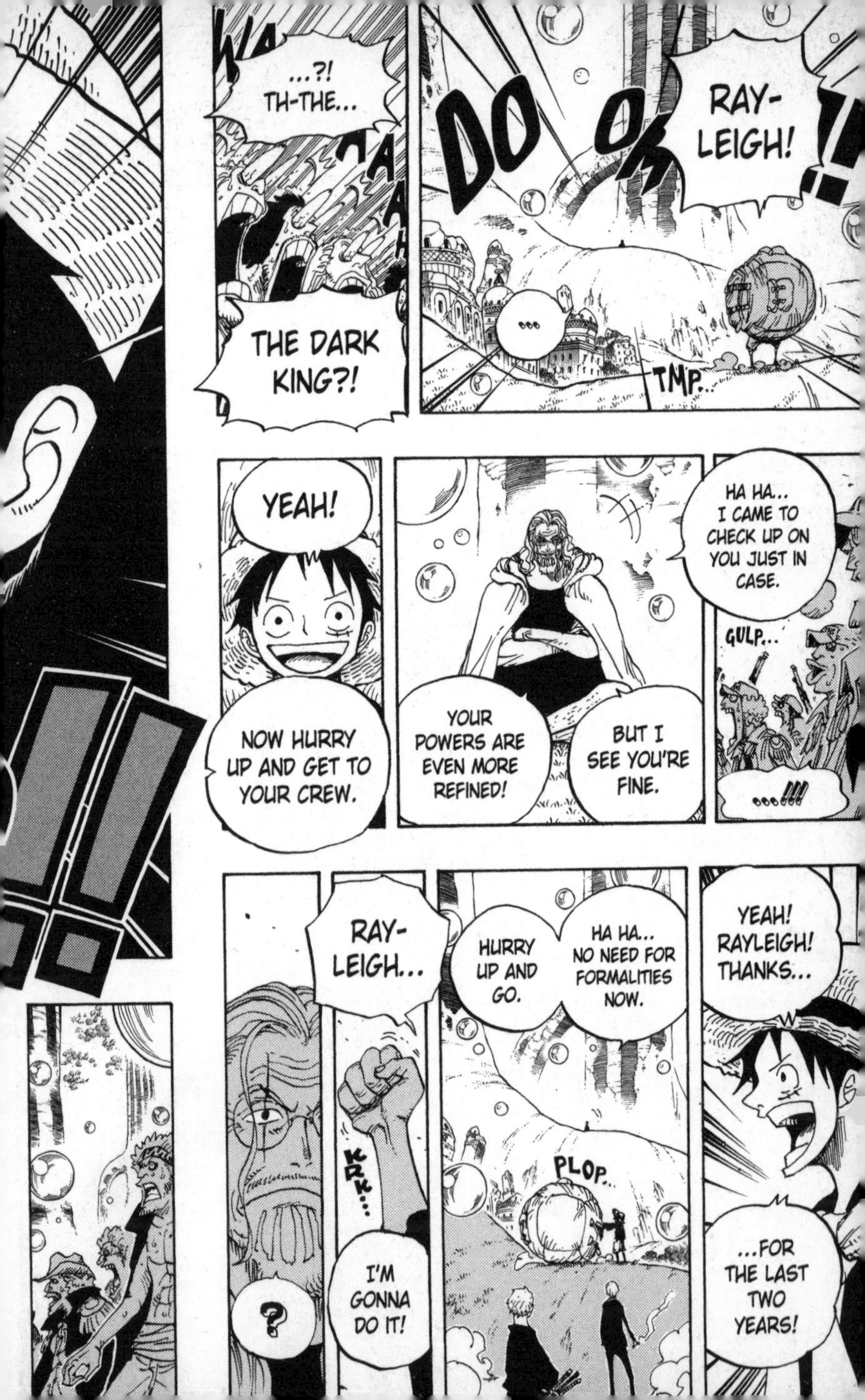
RAY-LEIGH!!
DOOM
...
TMP...
...?! TH-THE...
THE DARK KING?!
HA HA... I CAME TO CHECK UP ON YOU JUST IN CASE.
GULP...
...!!!
BUT I SEE YOU'RE FINE.
YOUR POWERS ARE EVEN MORE REFINED!
YEAH!
NOW HURRY UP AND GET TO YOUR CREW.
YEAH! RAYLEIGH! THANKS...
...FOR THE LAST TWO YEARS!
HA HA... NO NEED FOR FORMALITIES NOW.
HURRY UP AND GO.
PLOP...
RAY-LEIGH...
KRK...
I'M GONNA DO IT!
?

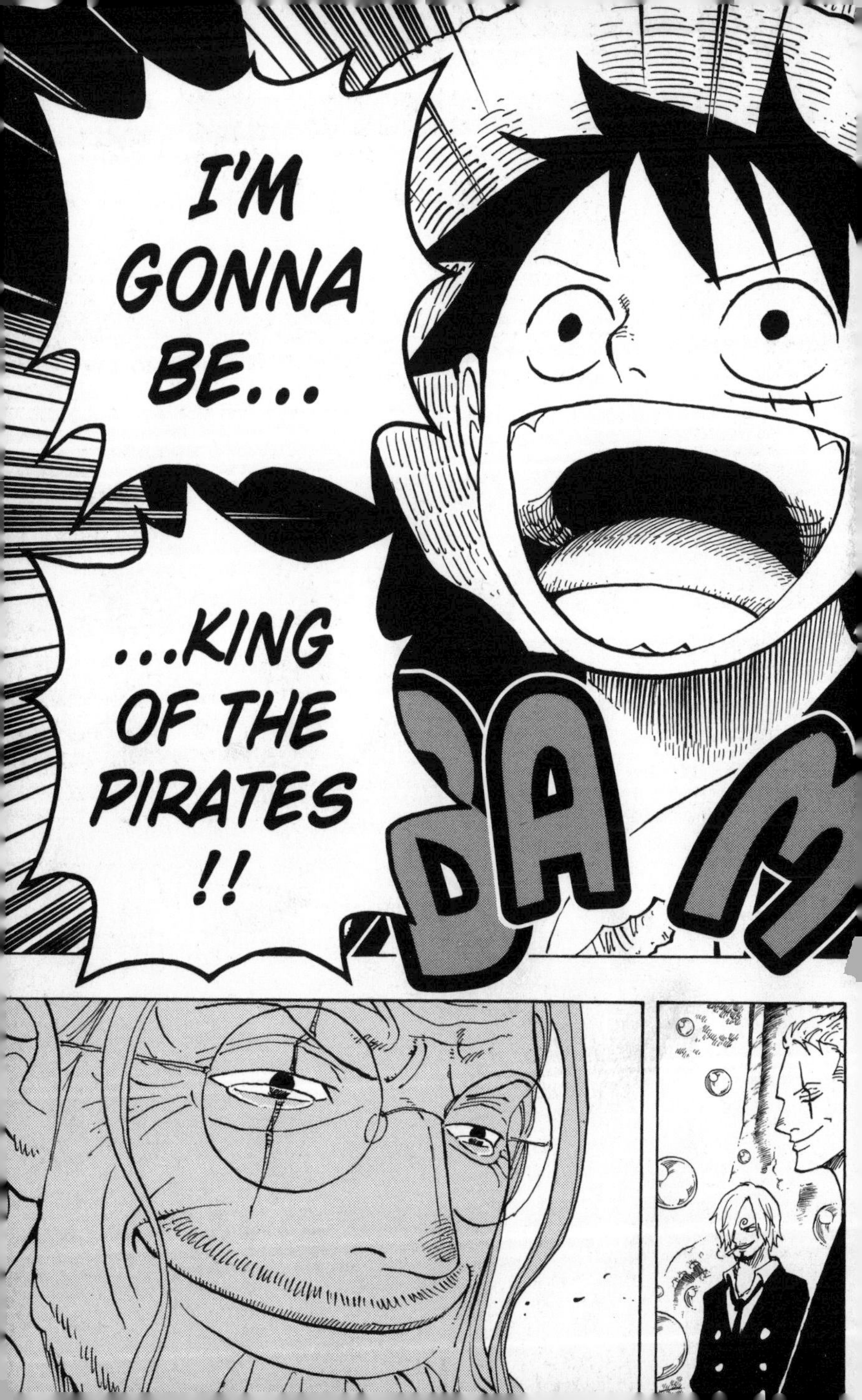
I'M GONNA BE...
...KING OF THE PIRATES!!
BAM

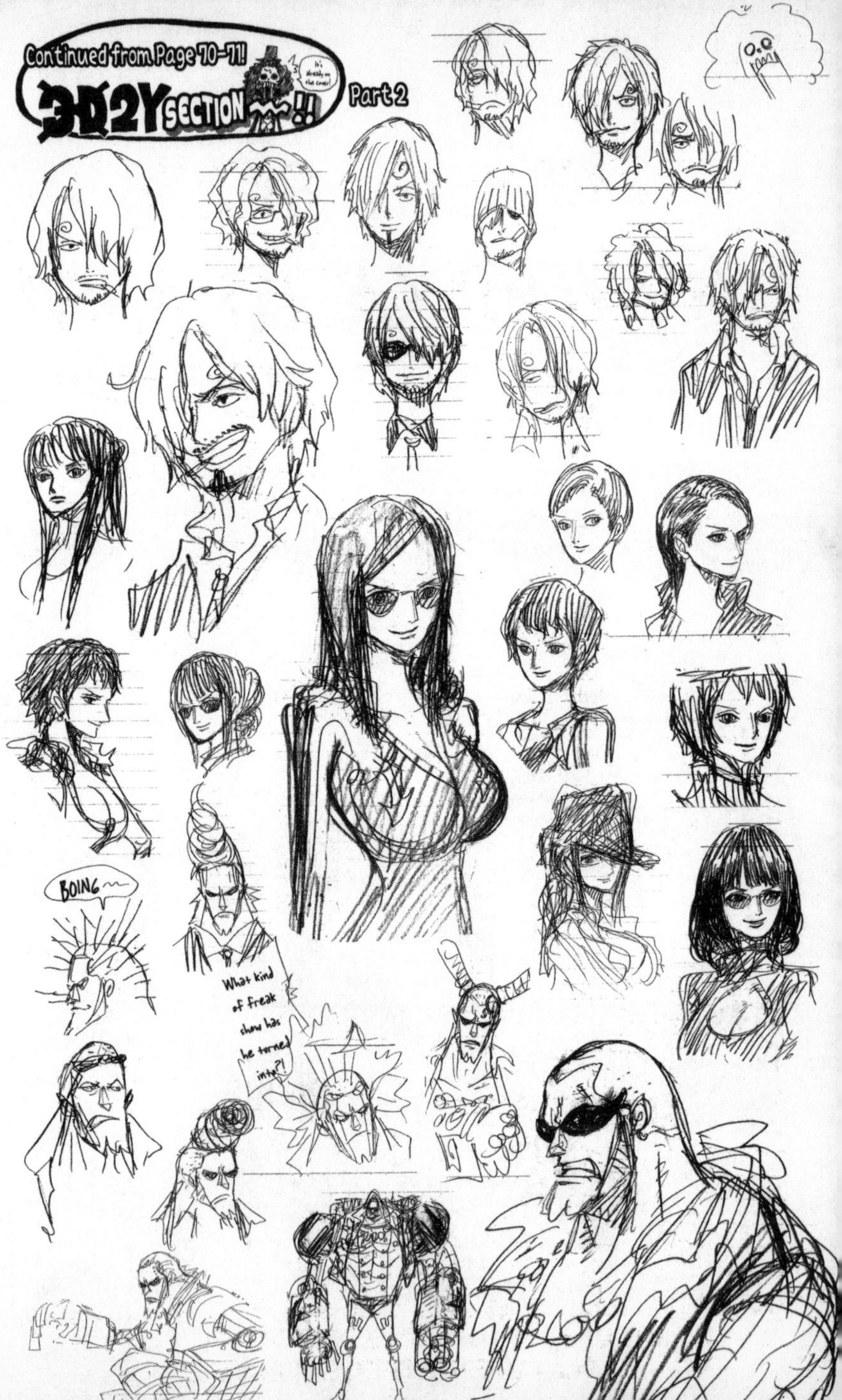
Continued from Page 70-71!
3D2Y SECTION~!!
It's already on the cover!
Part 2
BOING~
What kind of freak show has he turned into?!

Chapter 602:
DOWNWARD HO!

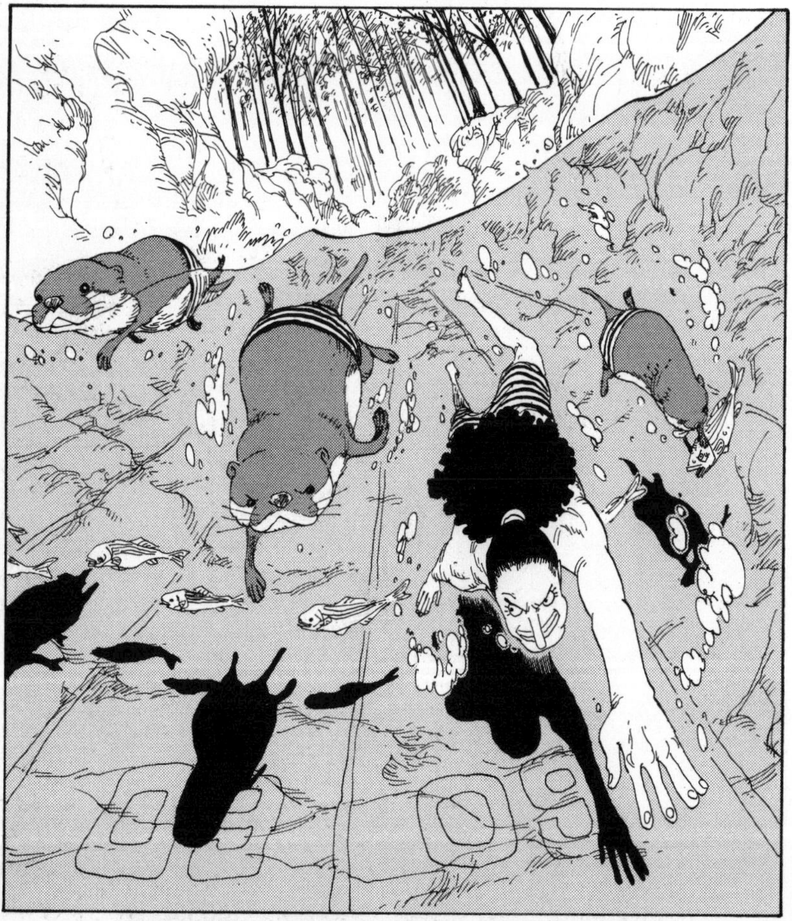

REQUEST: "USOPP RACING WITH OTTERS"
BY TEA CEREMONY CLUB PRESIDENT

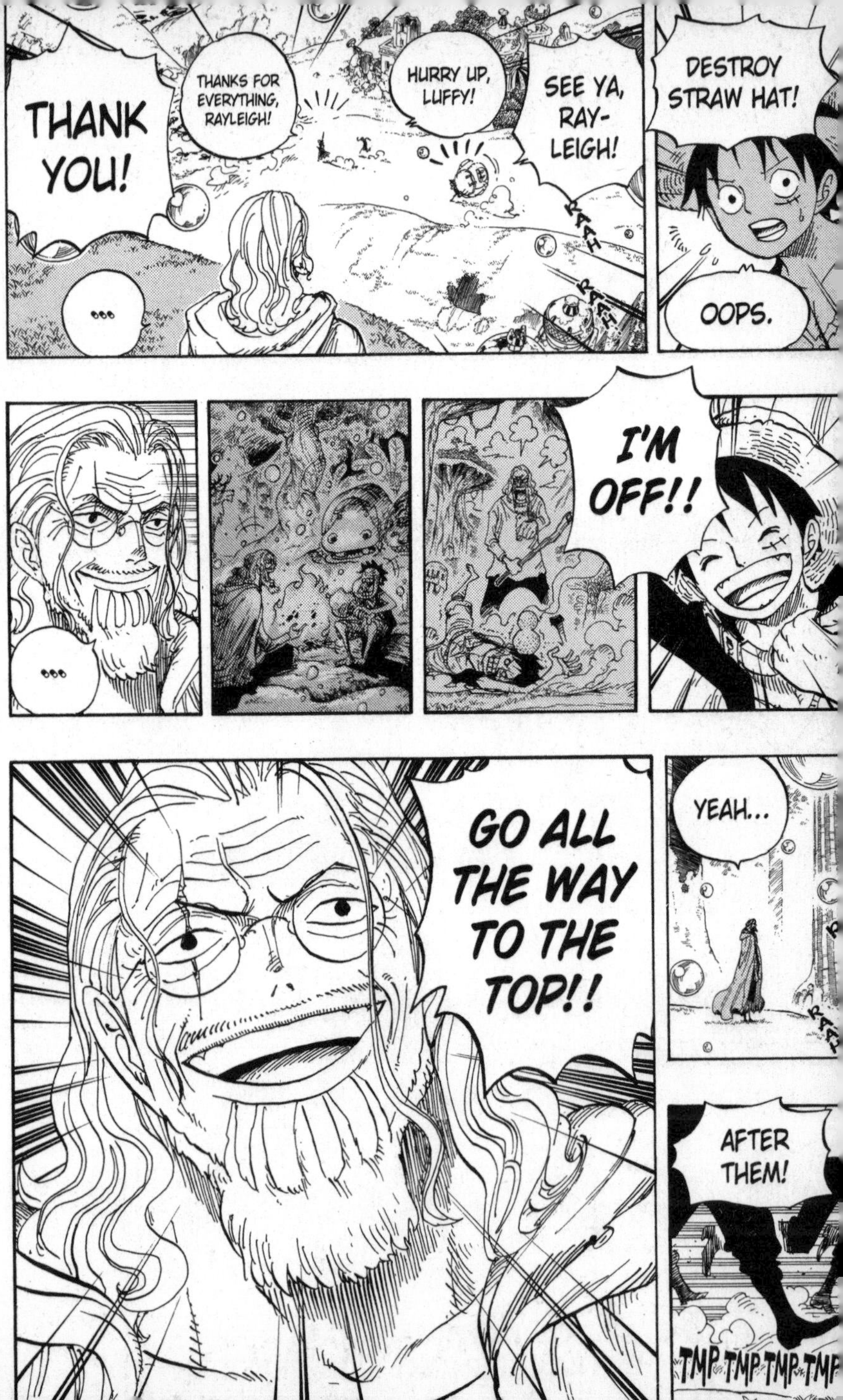
DESTROY STRAW HAT!
OOPS.
SEE YA, RAY- LEIGH!
RAAH
RAAH
HURRY UP, LUFFY!
THANKS FOR EVERYTHING, RAYLEIGH!
THANK YOU!
...
I'M OFF!!
...
YEAH...
AFTER THEM!
TMP TMP TMP TMP
GO ALL THE WAY TO THE TOP!!

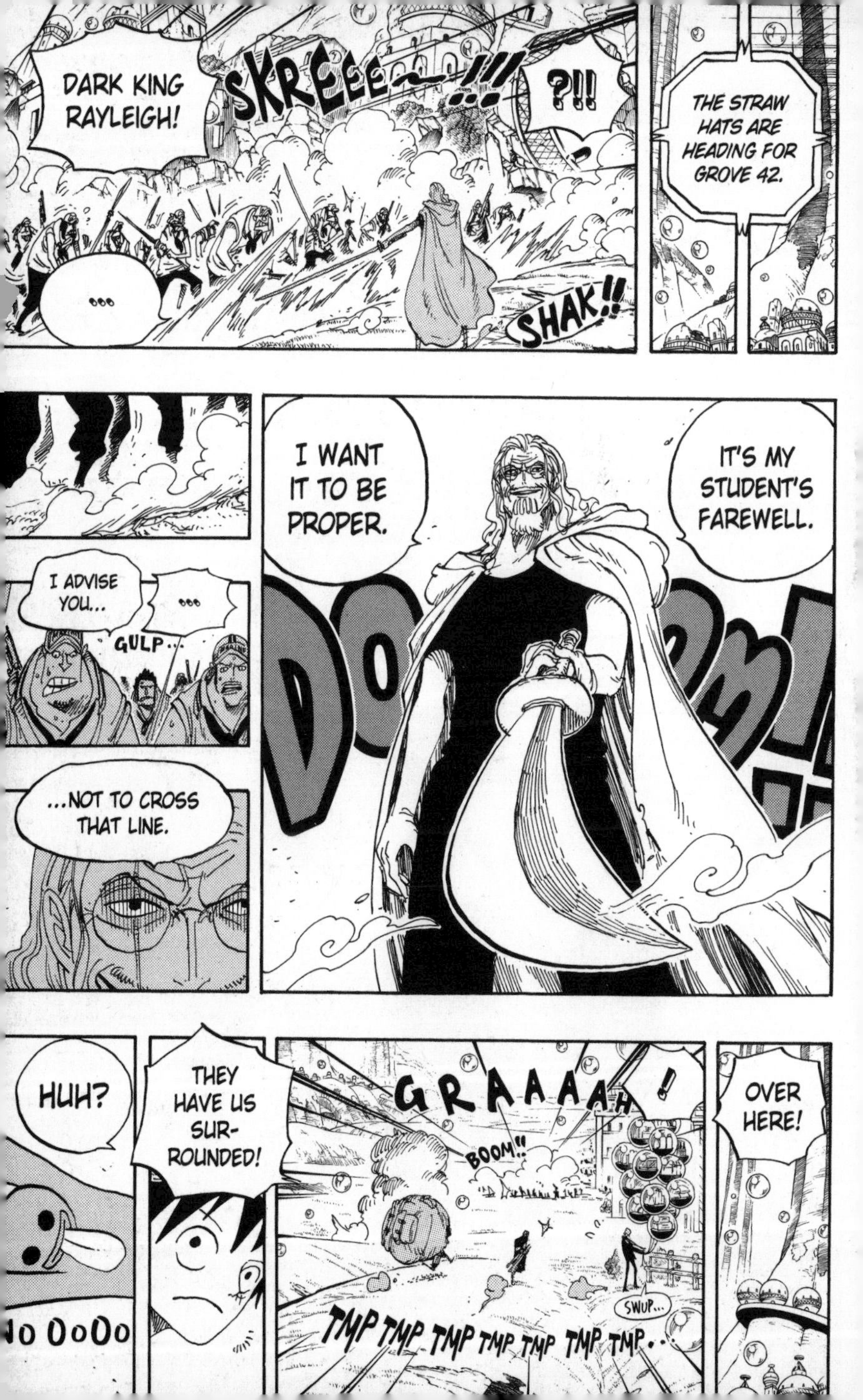
THE STRAW HATS ARE HEADING FOR GROVE 42.
?!!
SKREEE~!!!
DARK KING RAYLEIGH!
SHAK!!
...
IT'S MY STUDENT'S FAREWELL.
I WANT IT TO BE PROPER.
DOOM!!
I ADVISE YOU...
...
GULP...
...NOT TO CROSS THAT LINE.
OVER HERE!
GRAAAAH!
BOOM!!
SWUP...
TMP TMP TMP TMP TMP TMP TMP...
THEY HAVE US SUR-ROUNDED!
HUH?

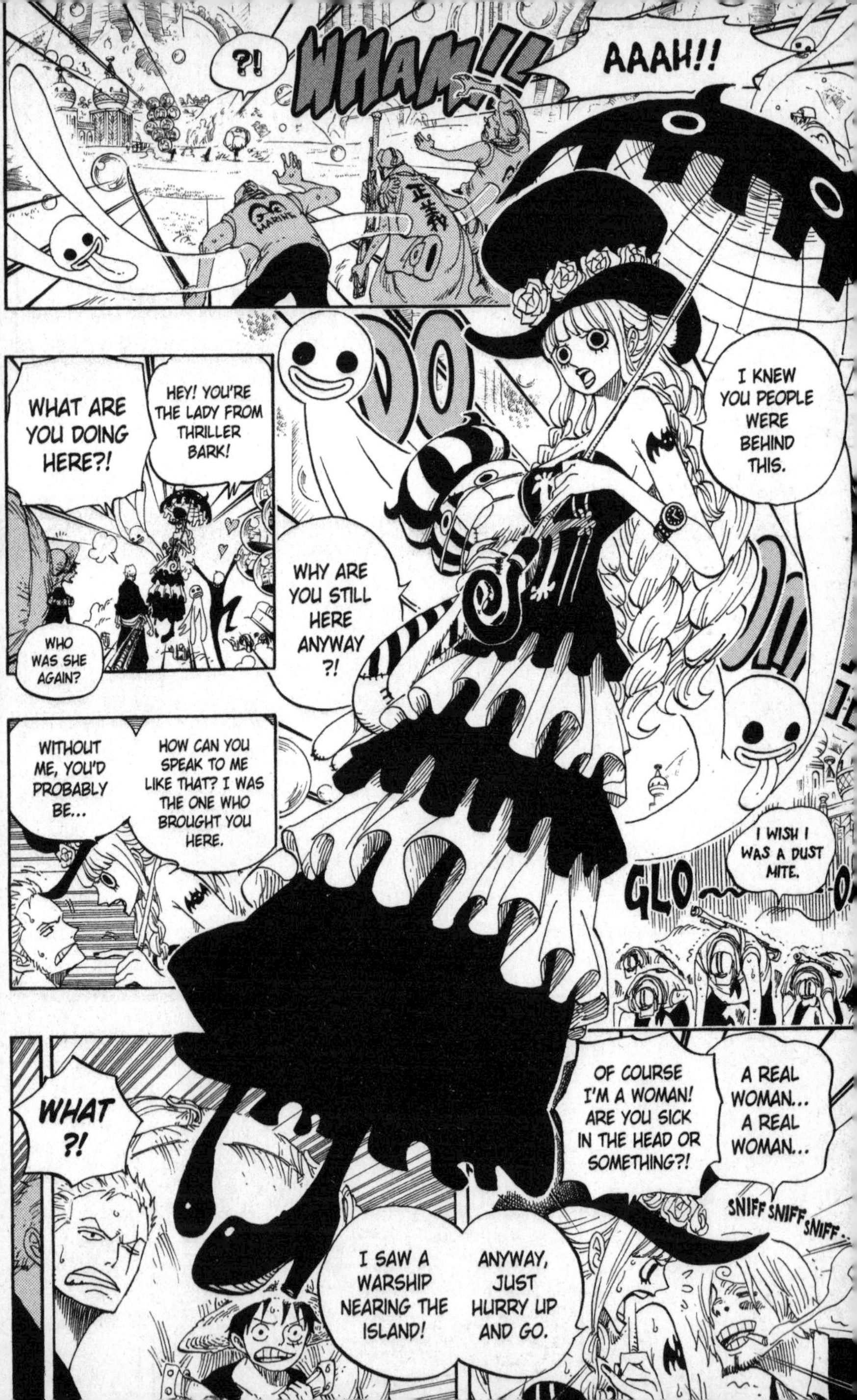
AAAH!!
WHAM!!
?!
I KNEW YOU PEOPLE WERE BEHIND THIS.
WHY ARE YOU STILL HERE ANYWAY ?!
HEY! YOU'RE THE LADY FROM THRILLER BARK!
WHAT ARE YOU DOING HERE?!
WHO WAS SHE AGAIN?
I WISH I WAS A DUST MITE.
GLO~~O
HOW CAN YOU SPEAK TO ME LIKE THAT? I WAS THE ONE WHO BROUGHT YOU HERE.
WITHOUT ME, YOU'D PROBABLY BE...
A REAL WOMAN... A REAL WOMAN...
SNIFF SNIFF SNIFF...
OF COURSE I'M A WOMAN! ARE YOU SICK IN THE HEAD OR SOMETHING?!
WHAT ?!
ANYWAY, JUST HURRY UP AND GO.
I SAW A WARSHIP NEARING THE ISLAND!

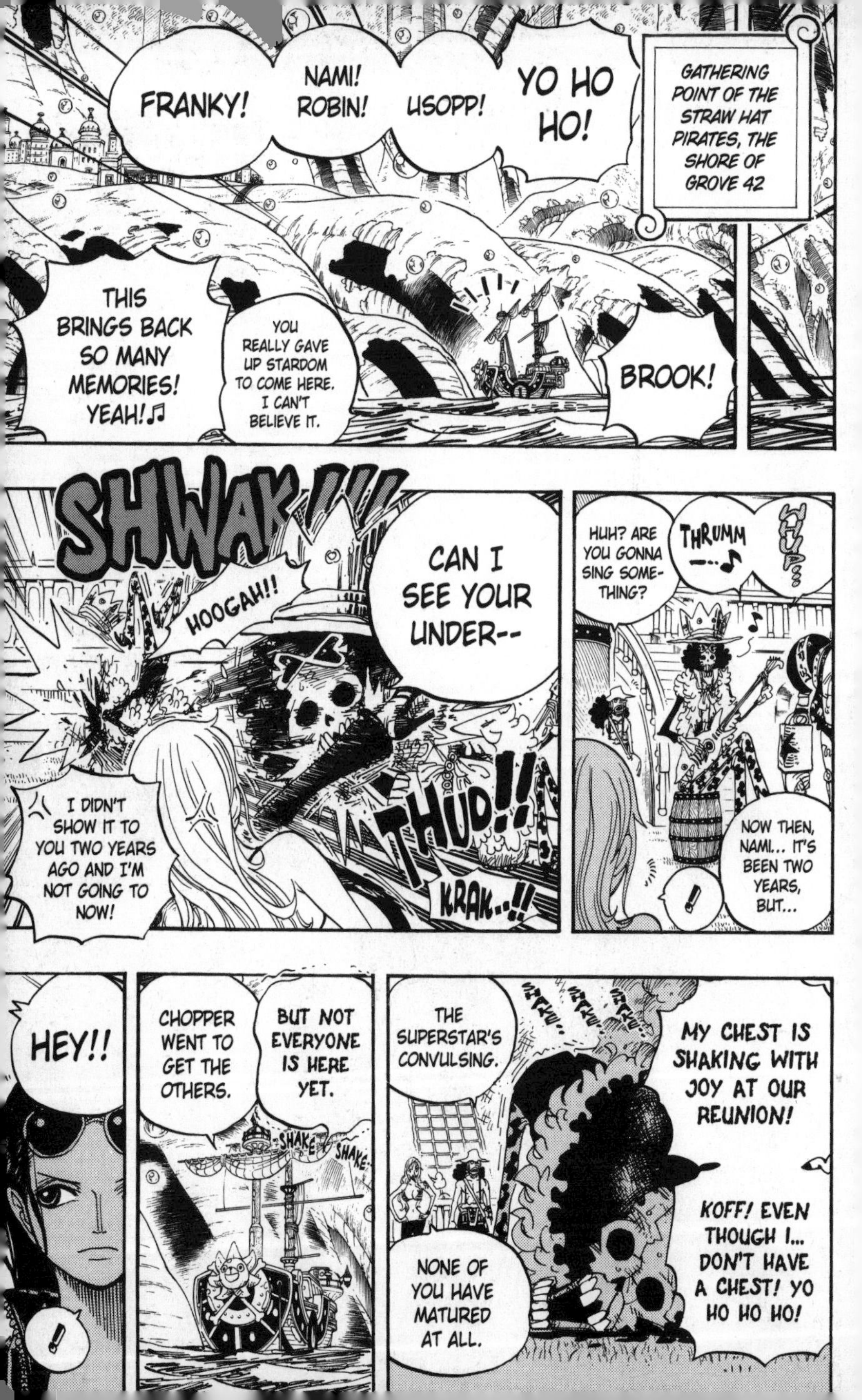
GATHERING POINT OF THE STRAW HAT PIRATES, THE SHORE OF GROVE 42
YO HO HO!
USOPP!
NAMI! ROBIN!
FRANKY!
BROOK!
YOU REALLY GAVE UP STARDOM TO COME HERE. I CAN'T BELIEVE IT.
THIS BRINGS BACK SO MANY MEMORIES! YEAH!♫
THRUMM —..♪
HUH? ARE YOU GONNA SING SOME-THING?
NOW THEN, NAMI... IT'S BEEN TWO YEARS, BUT...
!
CAN I SEE YOUR UNDER--
SHWAK!!!
HOOGAH!!
THUD!!
KRAK..!!
I DIDN'T SHOW IT TO YOU TWO YEARS AGO AND I'M NOT GOING TO NOW!
MY CHEST IS SHAKING WITH JOY AT OUR REUNION!
SHAKE.. SHAKE.. SHAKE..
THE SUPERSTAR'S CONVULSING.
KOFF! EVEN THOUGH I... DON'T HAVE A CHEST! YO HO HO!
NONE OF YOU HAVE MATURED AT ALL.
BUT NOT EVERYONE IS HERE YET.
CHOPPER WENT TO GET THE OTHERS.
SHAKE SHAKE
HEY!!
!

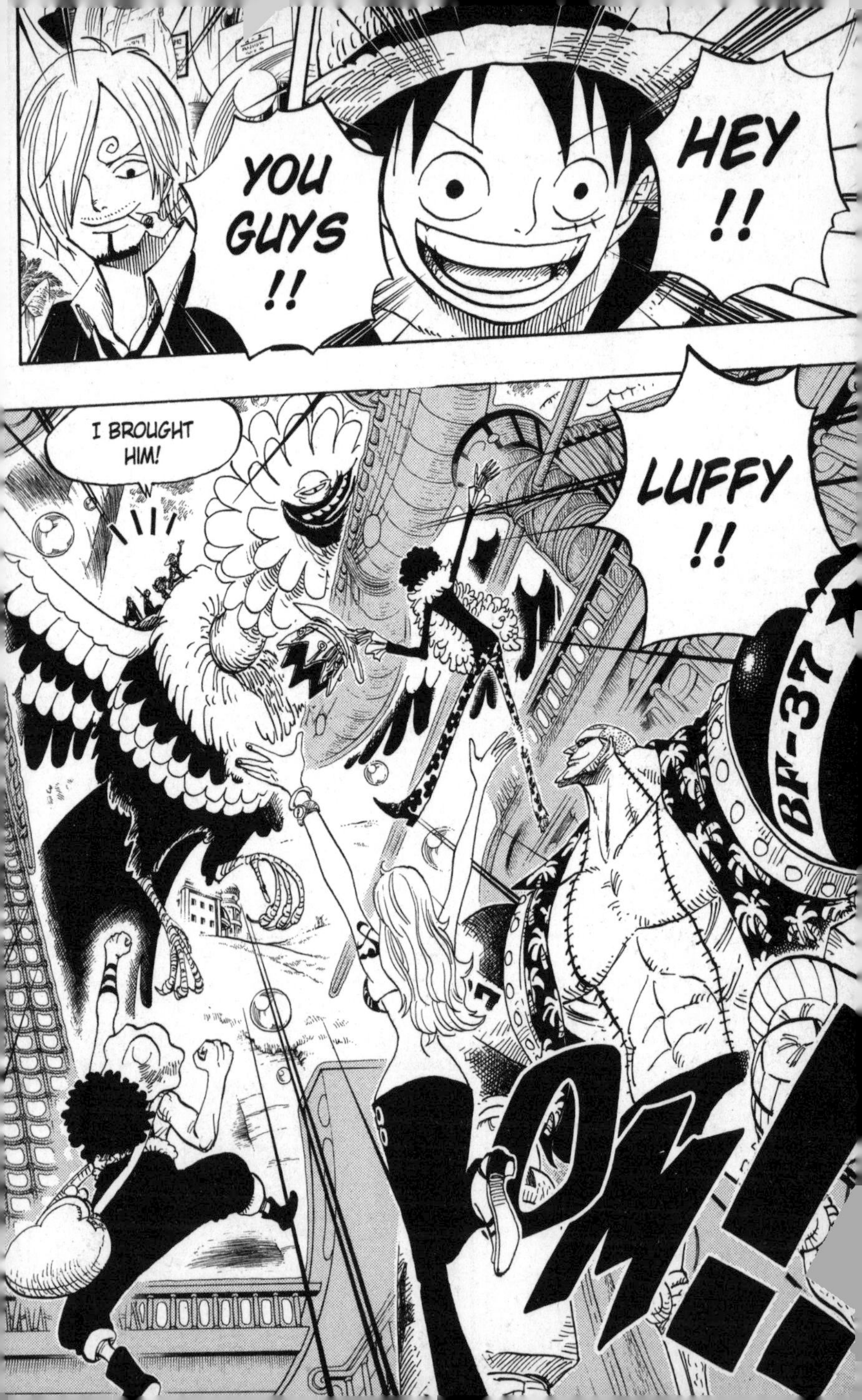
HEY !!
YOU GUYS !!
LUFFY !!
BF-37
I BROUGHT HIM!

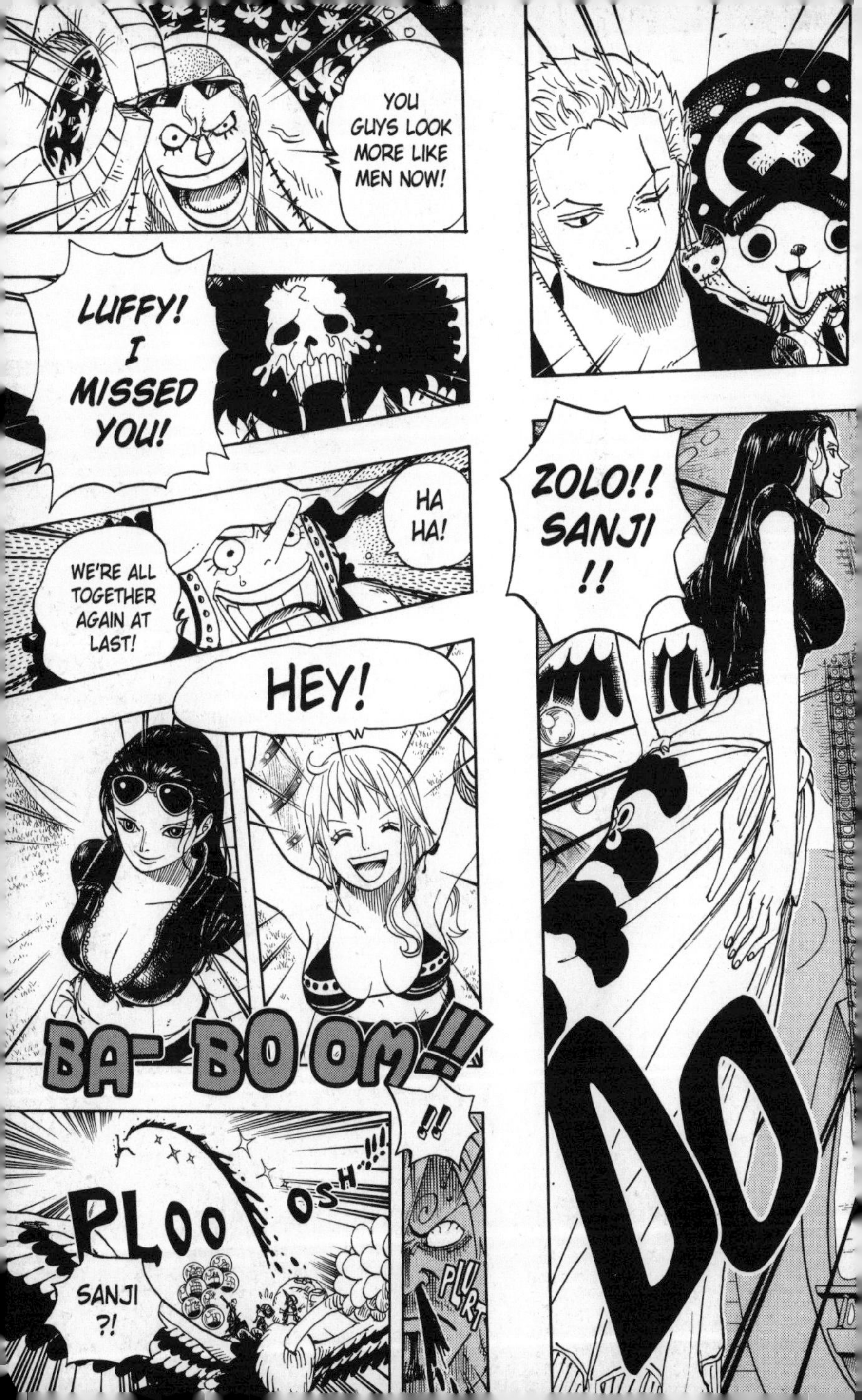
YOU GUYS LOOK MORE LIKE MEN NOW!
ZOLO!! SANJI!!
DO
LUFFY! I MISSED YOU!
HA HA!
WE'RE ALL TOGETHER AGAIN AT LAST!
HEY!
BA-BOOM!!
!!
PLOOSH!!!
PLURT
SANJI?!

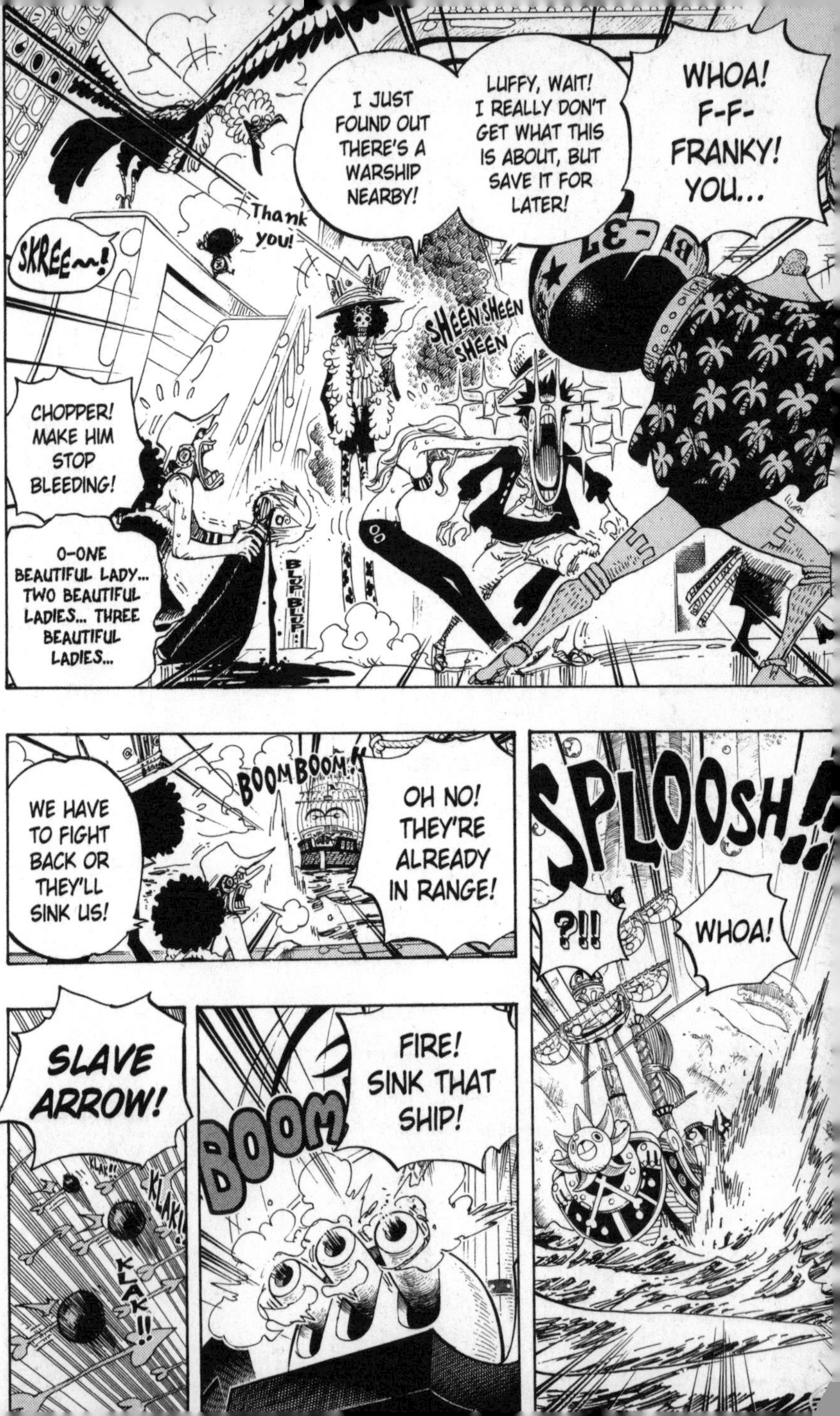
WHOA! F-F-FRANKY! YOU...
LUFFY, WAIT! I REALLY DON'T GET WHAT THIS IS ABOUT, BUT SAVE IT FOR LATER!
I JUST FOUND OUT THERE'S A WARSHIP NEARBY!
SHEEN SHEEN SHEEN
Thank you!
SKREE~~!
CHOPPER! MAKE HIM STOP BLEEDING!
O-ONE BEAUTIFUL LADY... TWO BEAUTIFUL LADIES... THREE BEAUTIFUL LADIES...
BLUP BLUP
SPLOOSH!!
WHOA!
?!!
OH NO! THEY'RE ALREADY IN RANGE!
BOOM BOOM
WE HAVE TO FIGHT BACK OR THEY'LL SINK US!
FIRE! SINK THAT SHIP!
BOOM
SLAVE ARROW!
KLAK!!
KLAK!!

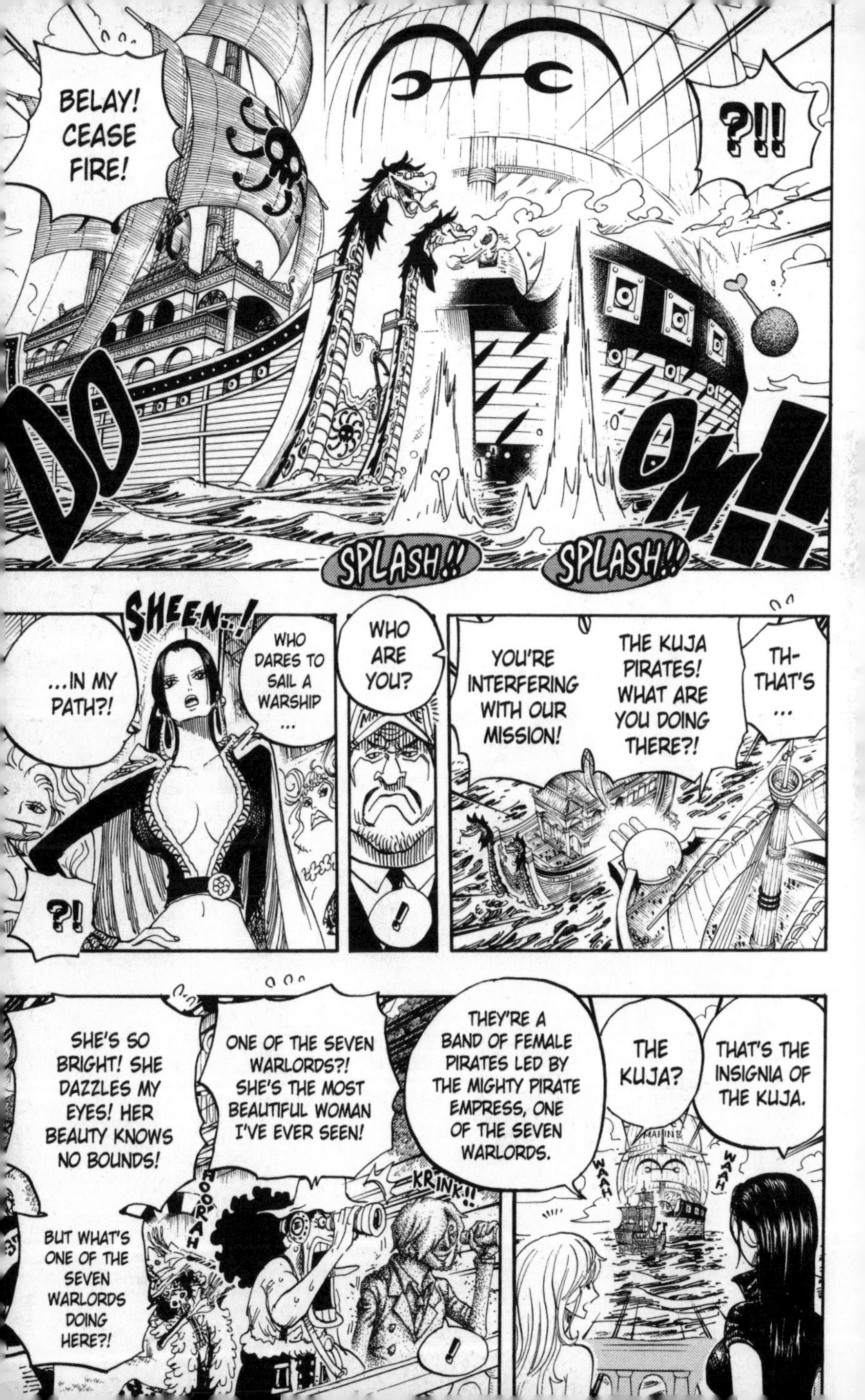
?!!
BELAY! CEASE FIRE!
DOOM!!
SPLASH!!
SPLASH!!
TH-THAT'S...
THE KUJA PIRATES! WHAT ARE YOU DOING THERE?!
YOU'RE INTERFERING WITH OUR MISSION!
WHO ARE YOU?
!
SHEEN..!
WHO DARES TO SAIL A WARSHIP...
...IN MY PATH?!
?!
THAT'S THE INSIGNIA OF THE KUJA.
THE KUJA?
WAAH
WAAH
THEY'RE A BAND OF FEMALE PIRATES LED BY THE MIGHTY PIRATE EMPRESS, ONE OF THE SEVEN WARLORDS.
KRINK!!
ONE OF THE SEVEN WARLORDS?! SHE'S THE MOST BEAUTIFUL WOMAN I'VE EVER SEEN!
SHE'S SO BRIGHT! SHE DAZZLES MY EYES! HER BEAUTY KNOWS NO BOUNDS!
HOORAH
BUT WHAT'S ONE OF THE SEVEN WARLORDS DOING HERE?!
!

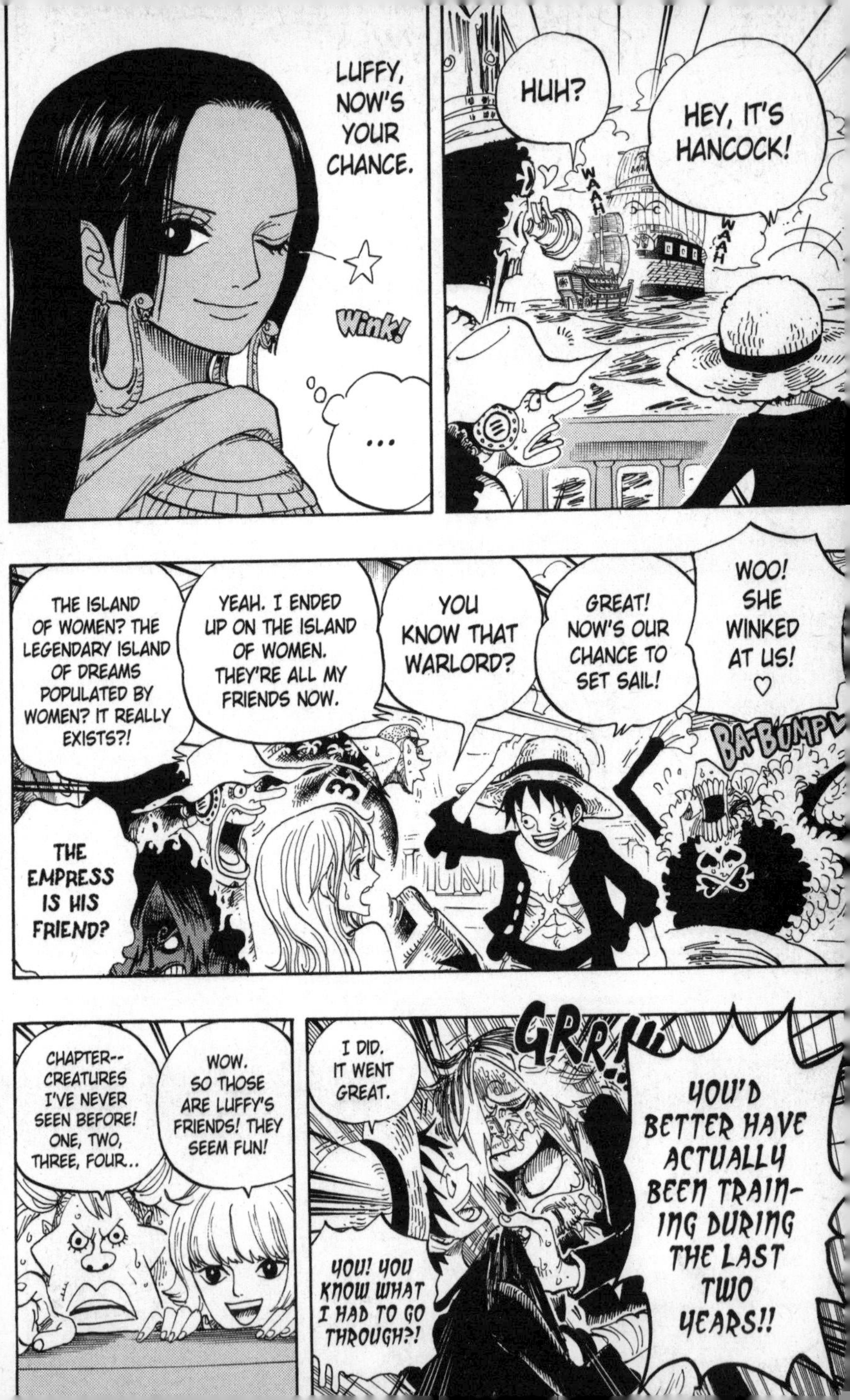
HEY, IT'S HANCOCK!
HUH?
WAAH
WAAH
LUFFY, NOW'S YOUR CHANCE.
Wink!
...
WOO! SHE WINKED AT US! ♥
BA-BUMP
GREAT! NOW'S OUR CHANCE TO SET SAIL!
YOU KNOW THAT WARLORD?
YEAH. I ENDED UP ON THE ISLAND OF WOMEN. THEY'RE ALL MY FRIENDS NOW.
THE ISLAND OF WOMEN? THE LEGENDARY ISLAND OF DREAMS POPULATED BY WOMEN? IT REALLY EXISTS?!
THE EMPRESS IS HIS FRIEND?
GRR!!
YOU'D BETTER HAVE ACTUALLY BEEN TRAINING DURING THE LAST TWO YEARS!!
I DID. IT WENT GREAT.
YOU! YOU KNOW WHAT I HAD TO GO THROUGH?!
WOW. SO THOSE ARE LUFFY'S FRIENDS! THEY SEEM FUN!
CHAPTER-- CREATURES I'VE NEVER SEEN BEFORE! ONE, TWO, THREE, FOUR..

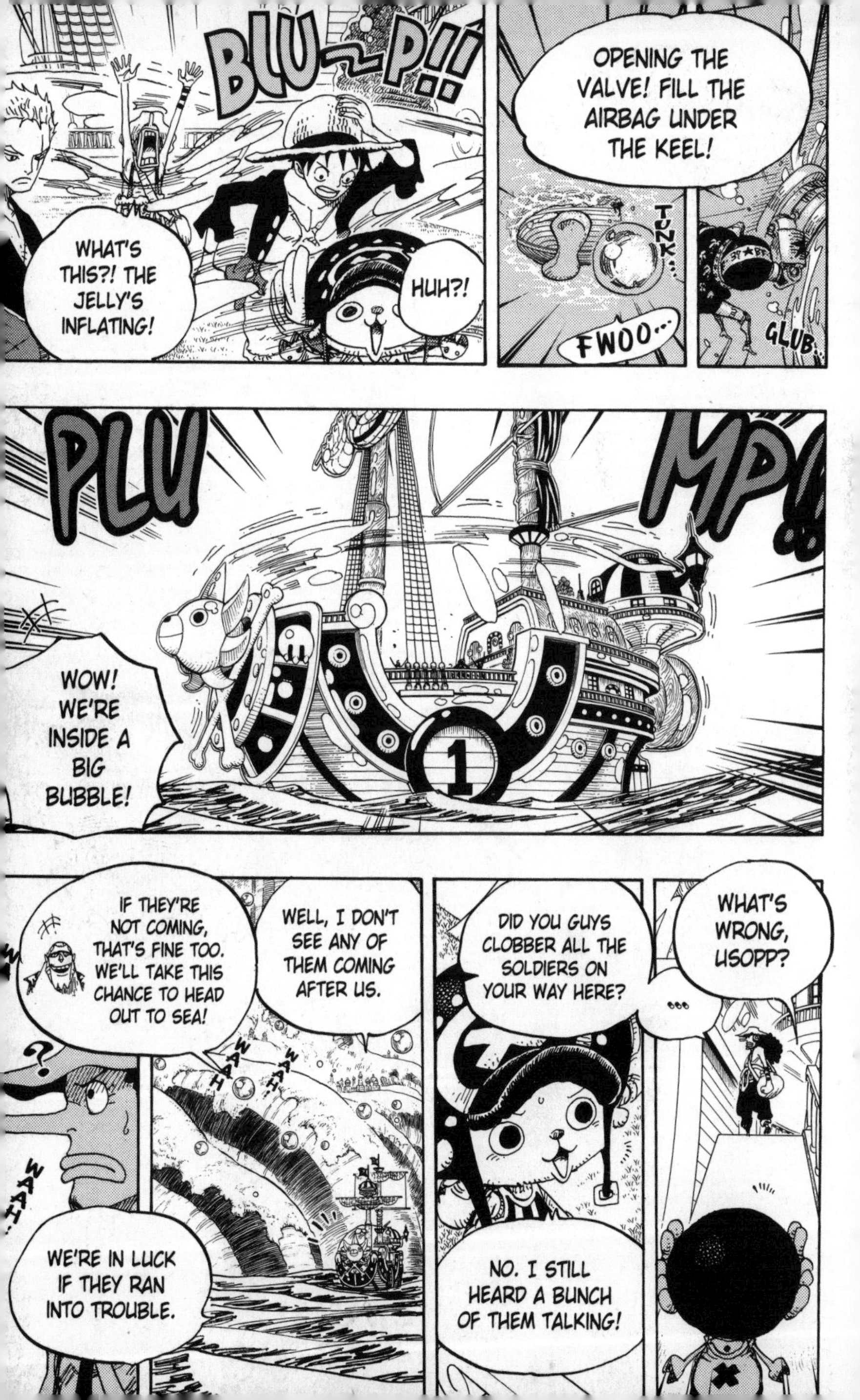
OPENING THE VALVE! FILL THE AIRBAG UNDER THE KEEL!
TUNK...
FWOO...
GLUB...
BLU~P!!
HUH?!
WHAT'S THIS?! THE JELLY'S INFLATING!
PLUMP!!
WOW! WE'RE INSIDE A BIG BUBBLE!
WHAT'S WRONG, USOPP?
...
DID YOU GUYS CLOBBER ALL THE SOLDIERS ON YOUR WAY HERE?
NO. I STILL HEARD A BUNCH OF THEM TALKING!
WELL, I DON'T SEE ANY OF THEM COMING AFTER US.
IF THEY'RE NOT COMING, THAT'S FINE TOO. WE'LL TAKE THIS CHANCE TO HEAD OUT TO SEA!
WAAH
WAAH
WAAH
WE'RE IN LUCK IF THEY RAN INTO TROUBLE.

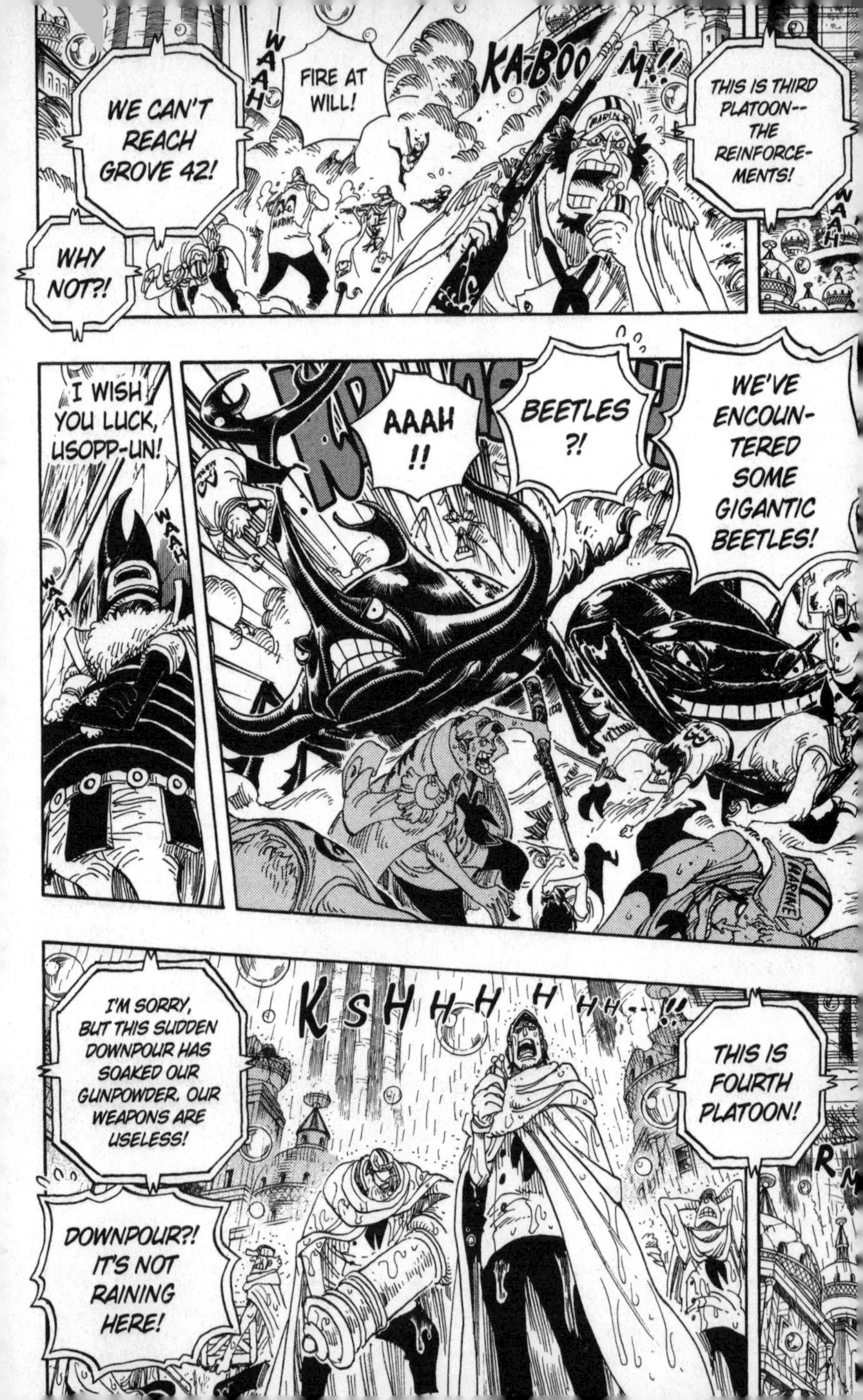
THIS IS THIRD PLATOON-- THE REINFORCEMENTS!
WAAH
KA-BOOM!!
FIRE AT WILL!
WAAH
WE CAN'T REACH GROVE 42!
WHY NOT?!
WE'VE ENCOUNTERED SOME GIGANTIC BEETLES!
BEETLES?!
AAAH!!
WAAH
I WISH YOU LUCK, USOPP-UN!
WAAH
WAAH
THIS IS FOURTH PLATOON!
KSHHHHHH...!!
I'M SORRY, BUT THIS SUDDEN DOWNPOUR HAS SOAKED OUR GUNPOWDER. OUR WEAPONS ARE USELESS!
DOWNPOUR?! IT'S NOT RAINING HERE!

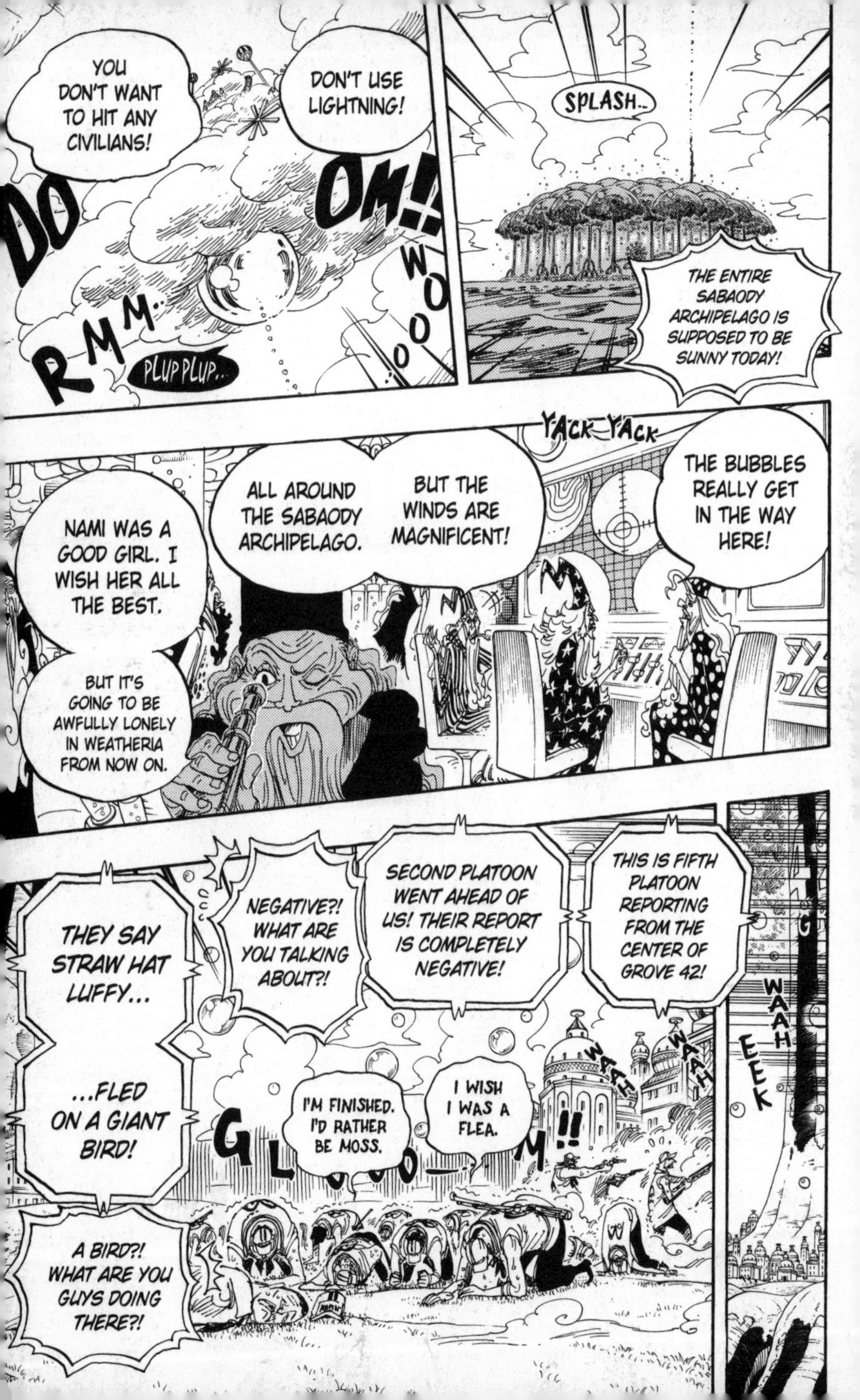
SPLASH..
THE ENTIRE SABAODY ARCHIPELAGO IS SUPPOSED TO BE SUNNY TODAY!
DON'T USE LIGHTNING!
YOU DON'T WANT TO HIT ANY CIVILIANS!
DOOM!!
WOOOO
RMM..
PLUP PLUP..
YACK YACK
THE BUBBLES REALLY GET IN THE WAY HERE!
BUT THE WINDS ARE MAGNIFICENT!
ALL AROUND THE SABAODY ARCHIPELAGO.
NAMI WAS A GOOD GIRL. I WISH HER ALL THE BEST.
BUT IT'S GOING TO BE AWFULLY LONELY IN WEATHERIA FROM NOW ON.
WAAH
EEK
THIS IS FIFTH PLATOON REPORTING FROM THE CENTER OF GROVE 42!
SECOND PLATOON WENT AHEAD OF US! THEIR REPORT IS COMPLETELY NEGATIVE!
NEGATIVE?! WHAT ARE YOU TALKING ABOUT?!
THEY SAY STRAW HAT LUFFY...
...FLED ON A GIANT BIRD!
A BIRD?! WHAT ARE YOU GUYS DOING THERE?!
WAAH
WAAH
I WISH I WAS A FLEA.
I'M FINISHED. I'D RATHER BE MOSS.
GLOOOM!!

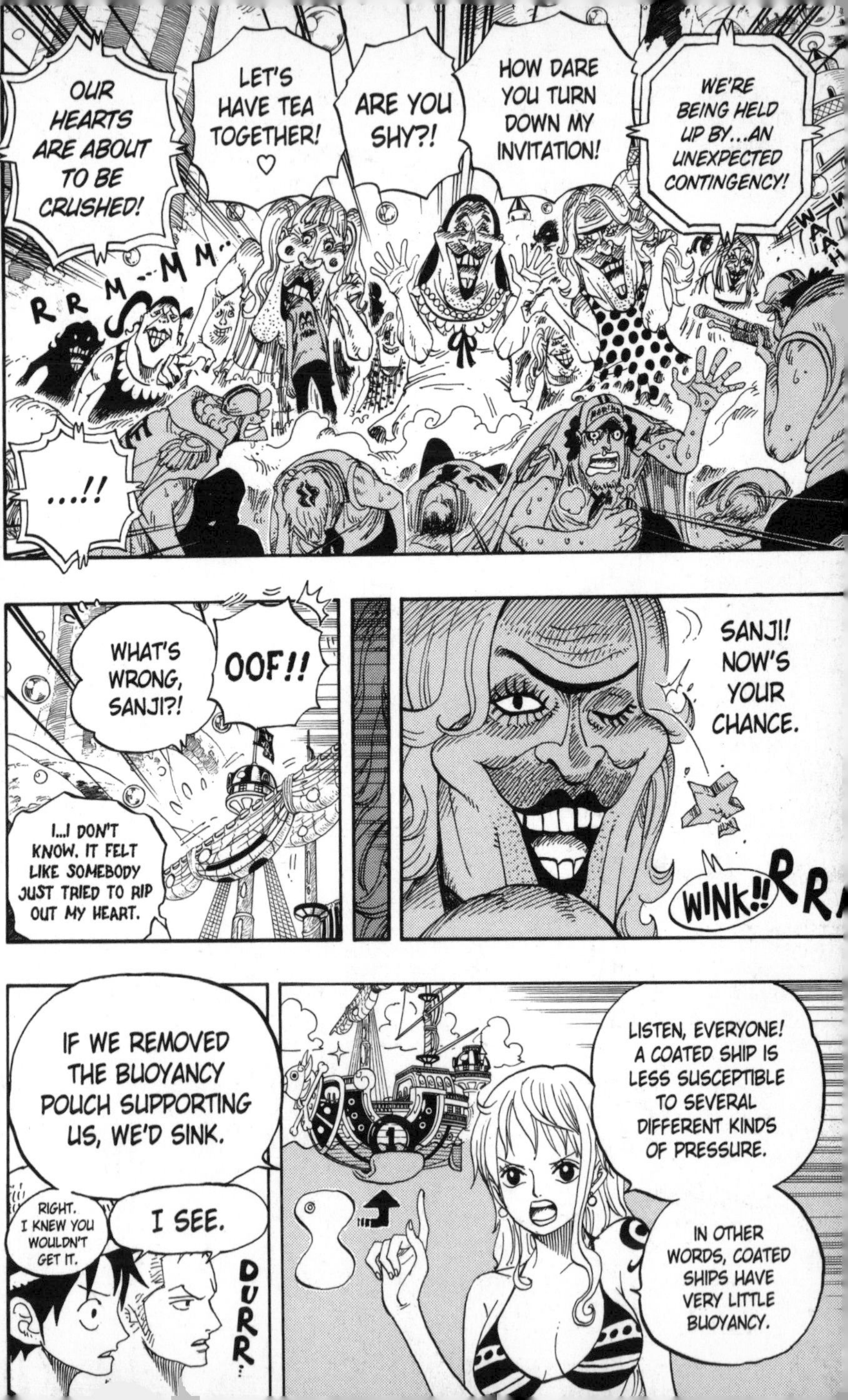
WE'RE BEING HELD UP BY...AN UNEXPECTED CONTINGENCY!
HOW DARE YOU TURN DOWN MY INVITATION!
ARE YOU SHY?!
LET'S HAVE TEA TOGETHER! ♡
OUR HEARTS ARE ABOUT TO BE CRUSHED!
RRM--MM..
...!!
SANJI! NOW'S YOUR CHANCE.
WINK!!
OOF!!
WHAT'S WRONG, SANJI?!
I...I DON'T KNOW. IT FELT LIKE SOMEBODY JUST TRIED TO RIP OUT MY HEART.
LISTEN, EVERYONE! A COATED SHIP IS LESS SUSCEPTIBLE TO SEVERAL DIFFERENT KINDS OF PRESSURE.
IN OTHER WORDS, COATED SHIPS HAVE VERY LITTLE BUOYANCY.
IF WE REMOVED THE BUOYANCY POUCH SUPPORTING US, WE'D SINK.
I SEE.
RIGHT. I KNEW YOU WOULDN'T GET IT.
DURR...

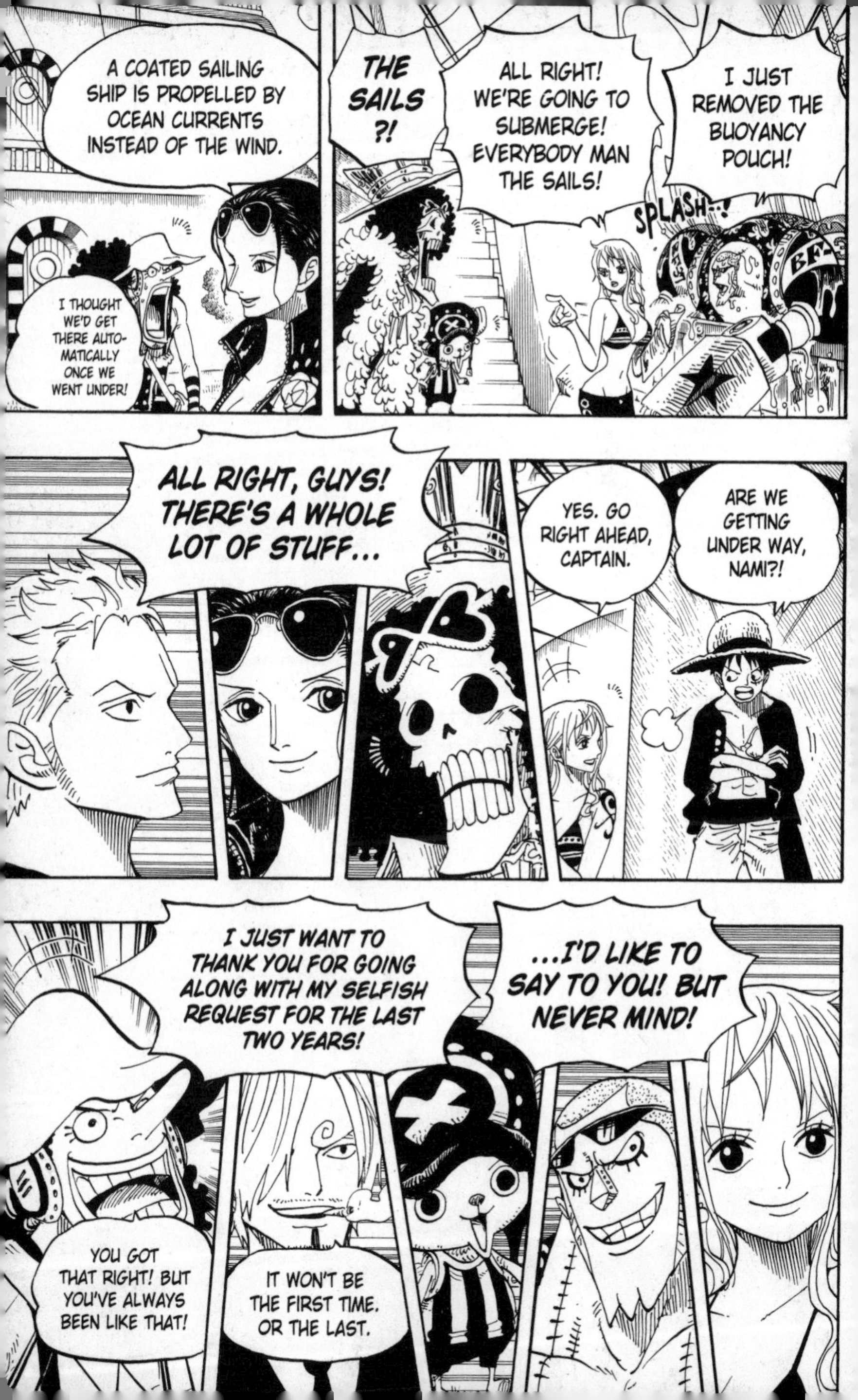
I JUST REMOVED THE BUOYANCY POUCH!
SPLASH..!
ALL RIGHT! WE'RE GOING TO SUBMERGE! EVERYBODY MAN THE SAILS!
THE SAILS?!
A COATED SAILING SHIP IS PROPELLED BY OCEAN CURRENTS INSTEAD OF THE WIND.
I THOUGHT WE'D GET THERE AUTO-MATICALLY ONCE WE WENT UNDER!
ARE WE GETTING UNDER WAY, NAMI?!
YES. GO RIGHT AHEAD, CAPTAIN.
ALL RIGHT, GUYS! THERE'S A WHOLE LOT OF STUFF...
I JUST WANT TO THANK YOU FOR GOING ALONG WITH MY SELFISH REQUEST FOR THE LAST TWO YEARS!
...I'D LIKE TO SAY TO YOU! BUT NEVER MIND!
IT WON'T BE THE FIRST TIME. OR THE LAST.
YOU GOT THAT RIGHT! BUT YOU'VE ALWAYS BEEN LIKE THAT!

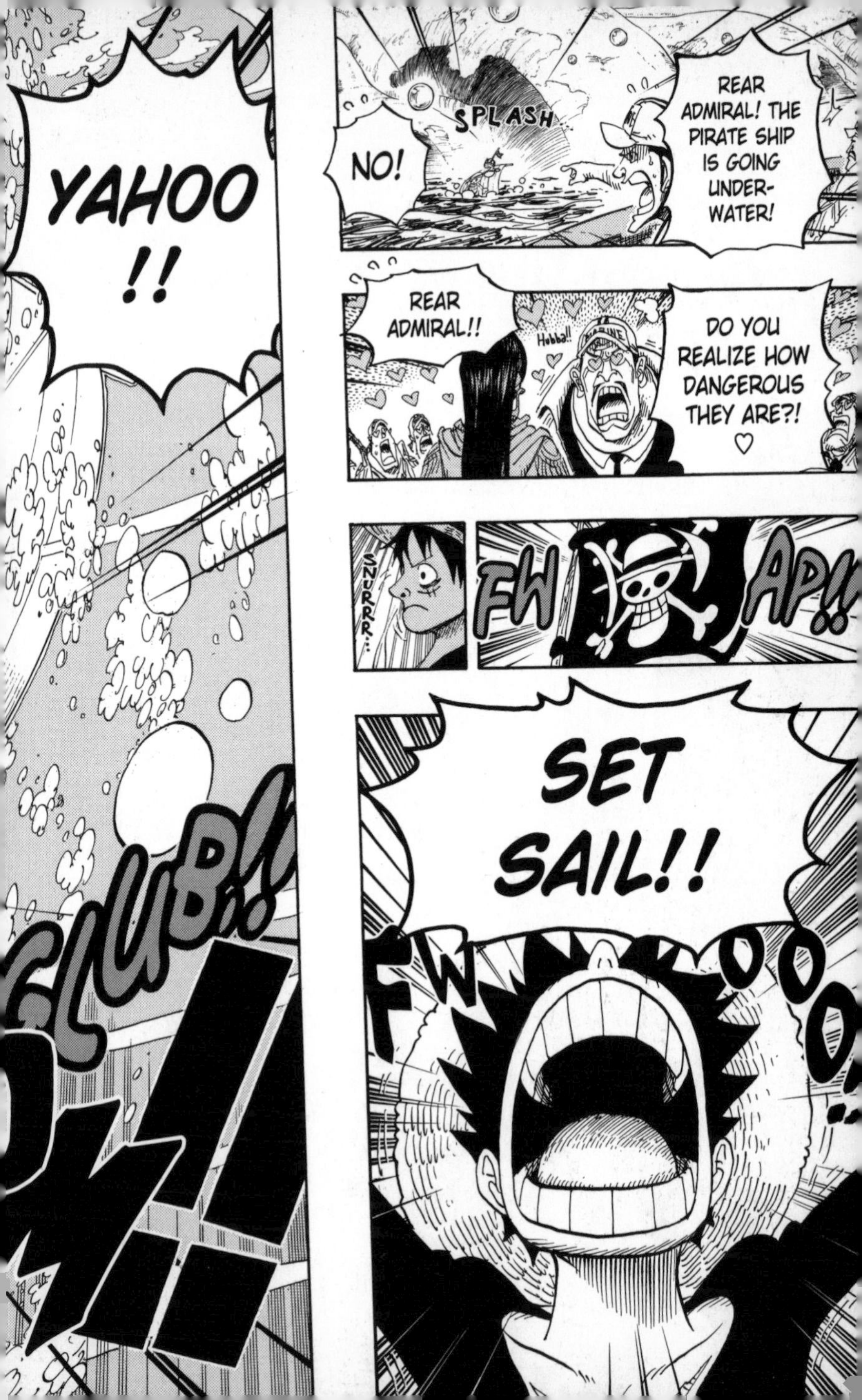
REAR ADMIRAL! THE PIRATE SHIP IS GOING UNDER-WATER!
SPLASH
NO!
DO YOU REALIZE HOW DANGEROUS THEY ARE?! ♡
Hobba!!
REAR ADMIRAL!!
FWAP!!
SNURRR...
SET SAIL!!
YAHOO!!
GLUB!!

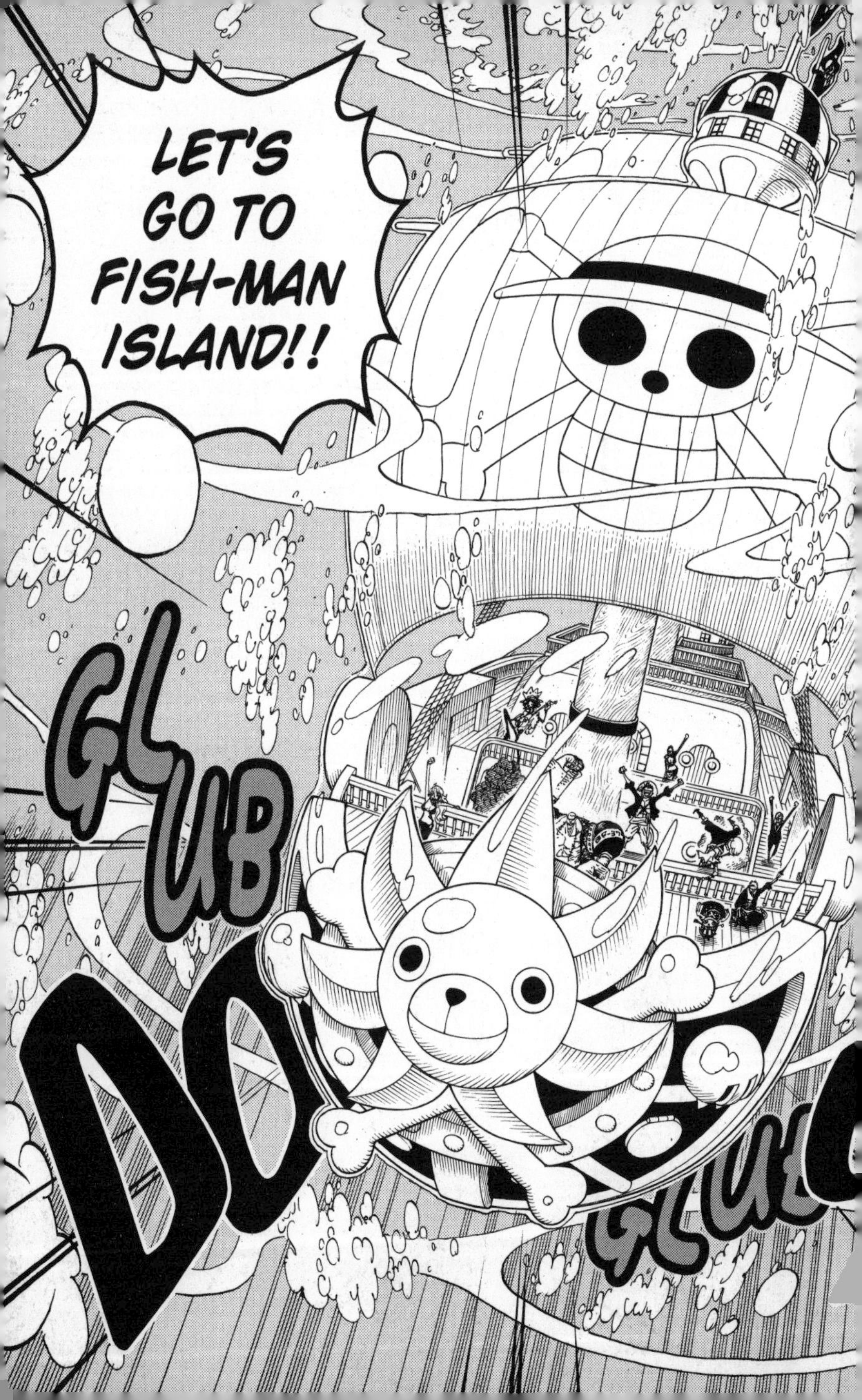
LET'S GO TO FISH-MAN ISLAND!!
GLUB
DO

FRANKY'S VOICE ACTOR, KAZUKI YAO!

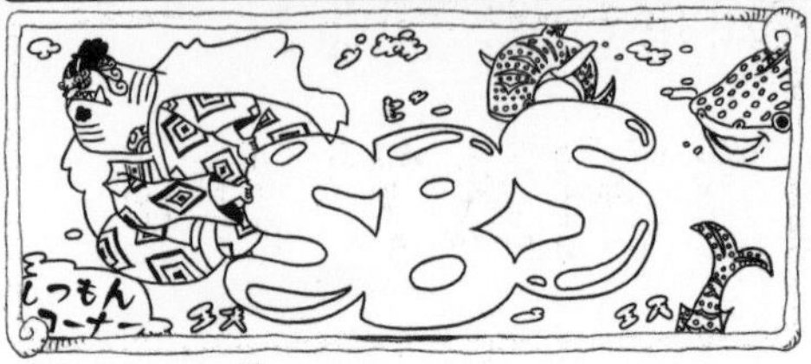
SBS

(Shota Masubuchi, Tochigi)

SBS Question Corner

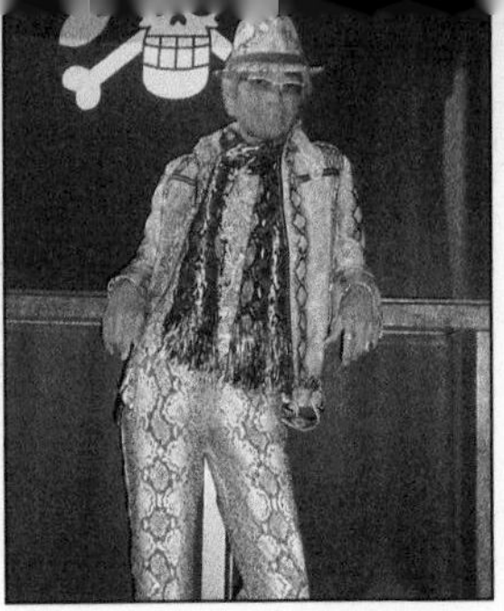

HDYD! (How Do you do!)

Wow, it's the eighth one already. We have quite the lively guest this time around. Since I was little, I tended to get interested in weird things, so he was actually the first voice actor I hung out with! Yes, this weird guy used to be an idol voice actor! All the weirdos of One Piece are played by him! Django! Mr. 2 Bon Clay are all him!

He's also the voice of Franky! Kazuki Yao! In the house!

Oda(O): Okay, please come in, Yao.

Yao(Y): Hi, I wrapped myself up completely in snakeskin. From top to bottom. Every night at the Minato District, I take some tequila and BEEP!!

O: Hey! We can't air that! I'll have to take that part out later! Man, you're scary!

Y: I'm actually the one with the most common sense around here.

O: How?! Anyway, let's move on. If you have so much common sense, do you know what SBS stands for?

Y: Of course. man. (S)uck on some (B)oobs (S)oon!

O: Don't! Get out of here! O-Oh, excuse me. I don't know what came over me.

Y: Yeah, you need to calm down, Eiichiro.

O: Shut up! Whose fault do you think it is?! Oh, excuse me. Anyway, we have a lot of letters, so let's move on with the SBS.

Y: Yeah! Bring it on! And bring some booze!

O: You're going to do it while drinking?!

Yao's SBS will continue on page 200!

PREVIEW FOR NEXT VOICE ACTOR'S SBS

Next will be our very last Voice Actor SBS! And it will be this person who will take the last spot!

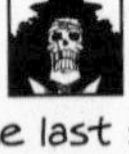

Brook (Cho)

Take your best shot at Cho! It'll be the last so make sure you have no regrets!

Chapter 603:

KEEP THAT IN MIND

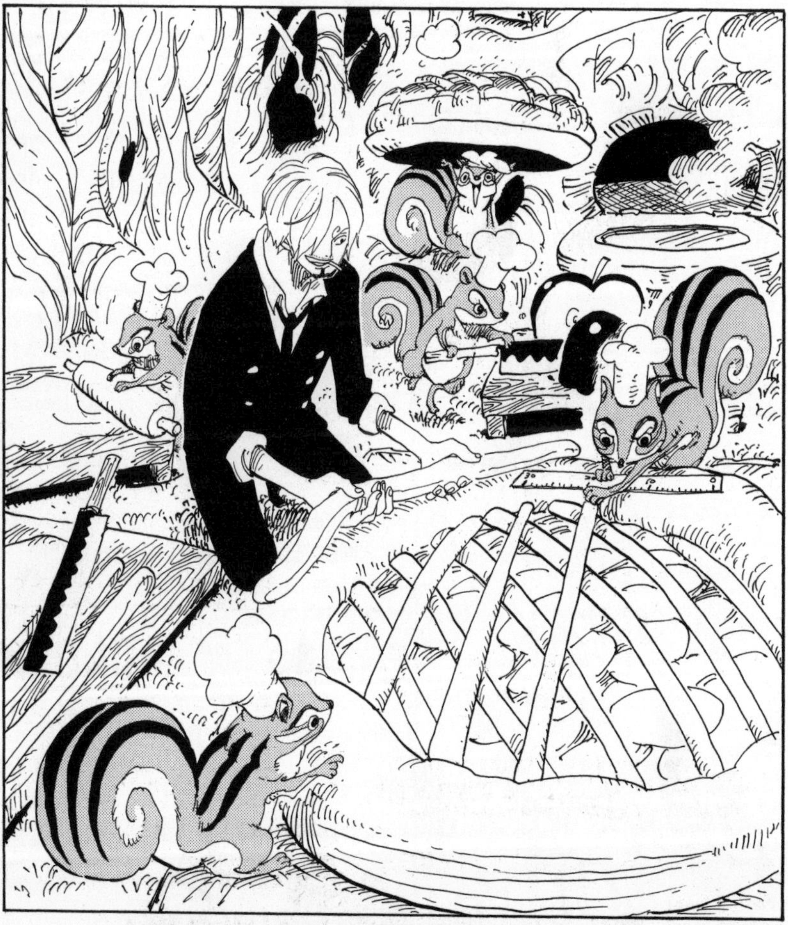

REQUEST: "SANJI AND CUTE SQUIRRELS MAKING PIE TOGETHER" BY NSC HAYAO

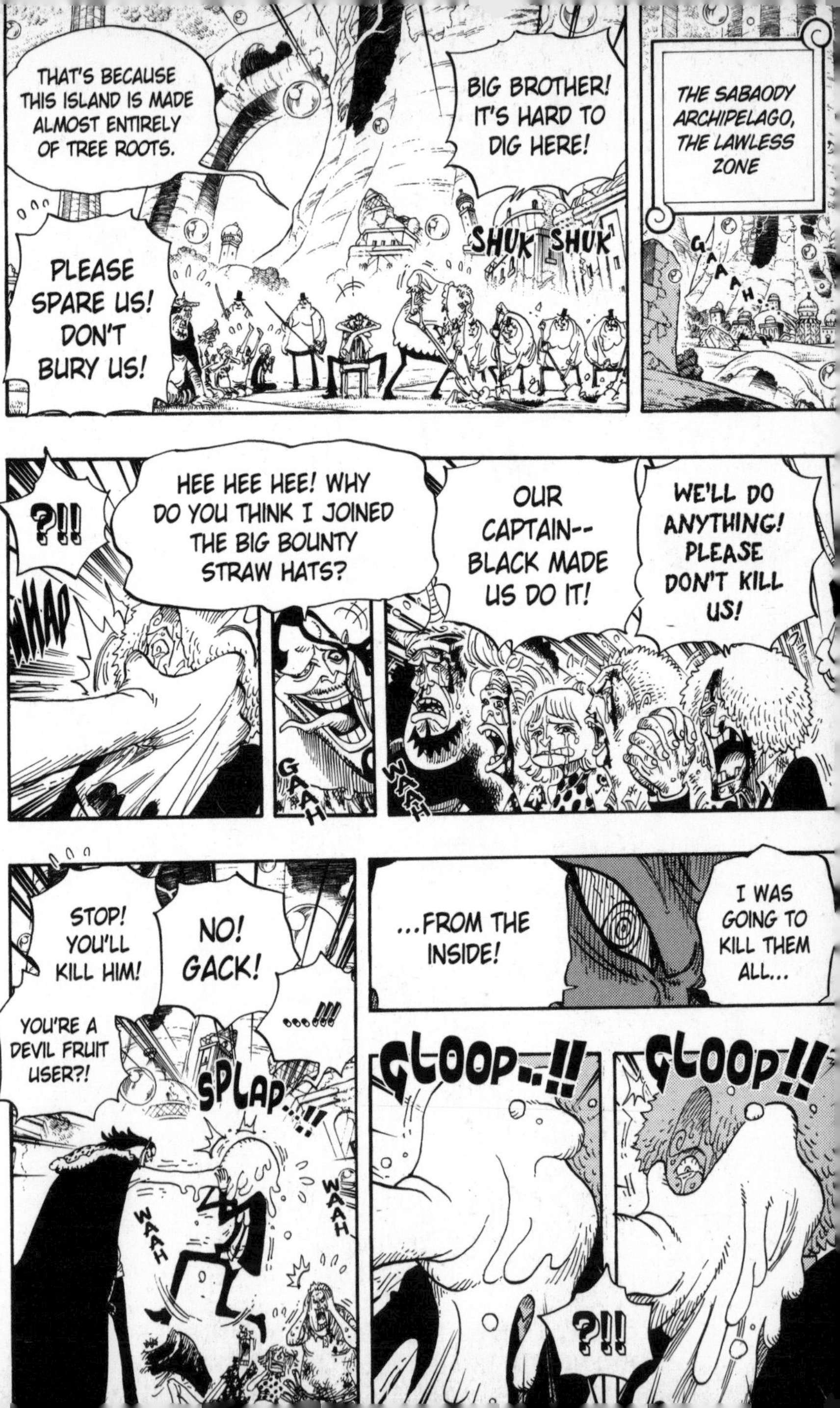
THE SABAODY ARCHIPELAGO, THE LAWLESS ZONE
GAAAH
BIG BROTHER! IT'S HARD TO DIG HERE!
SHUK SHUK
THAT'S BECAUSE THIS ISLAND IS MADE ALMOST ENTIRELY OF TREE ROOTS.
PLEASE SPARE US! DON'T BURY US!
WE'LL DO ANYTHING! PLEASE DON'T KILL US!
OUR CAPTAIN-- BLACK MADE US DO IT!
WAAH
HEE HEE HEE! WHY DO YOU THINK I JOINED THE BIG BOUNTY STRAW HATS?
GAAH
?!!
WHAP
I WAS GOING TO KILL THEM ALL...
...FROM THE INSIDE!
GLOOP!!
GLOOP..!!
?!!
NO! GACK!
STOP! YOU'LL KILL HIM!
...!!!
YOU'RE A DEVIL FRUIT USER?!
SPLAP..!!
WAAH
WAAH

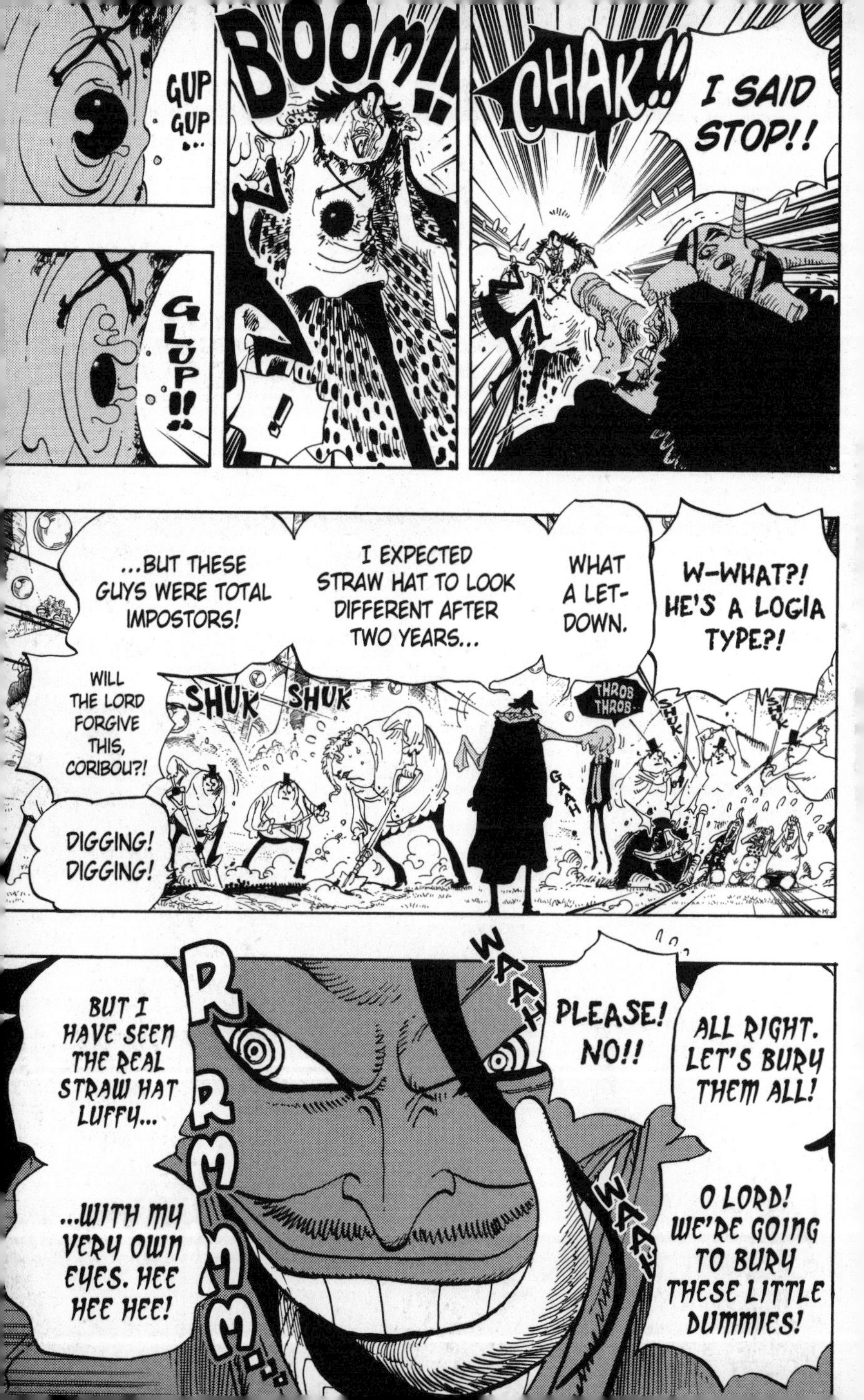
CHAK!!
I SAID STOP!!
BOOM!!
!
GUP GUP...
GLUP!!
W-WHAT?! HE'S A LOGIA TYPE?!
WHAT A LET-DOWN.
I EXPECTED STRAW HAT TO LOOK DIFFERENT AFTER TWO YEARS...
...BUT THESE GUYS WERE TOTAL IMPOSTORS!
THROB THROB
SHUK
GAAH
SHUK SHUK
WILL THE LORD FORGIVE THIS, CORIBOU?!
DIGGING! DIGGING!
ALL RIGHT. LET'S BURY THEM ALL!
PLEASE! NO!!
WAAH
O LORD! WE'RE GOING TO BURY THESE LITTLE DUMMIES!
WAAH
RRMMMM...
BUT I HAVE SEEN THE REAL STRAW HAT LUFFY...
...WITH MY VERY OWN EYES. HEE HEE HEE!

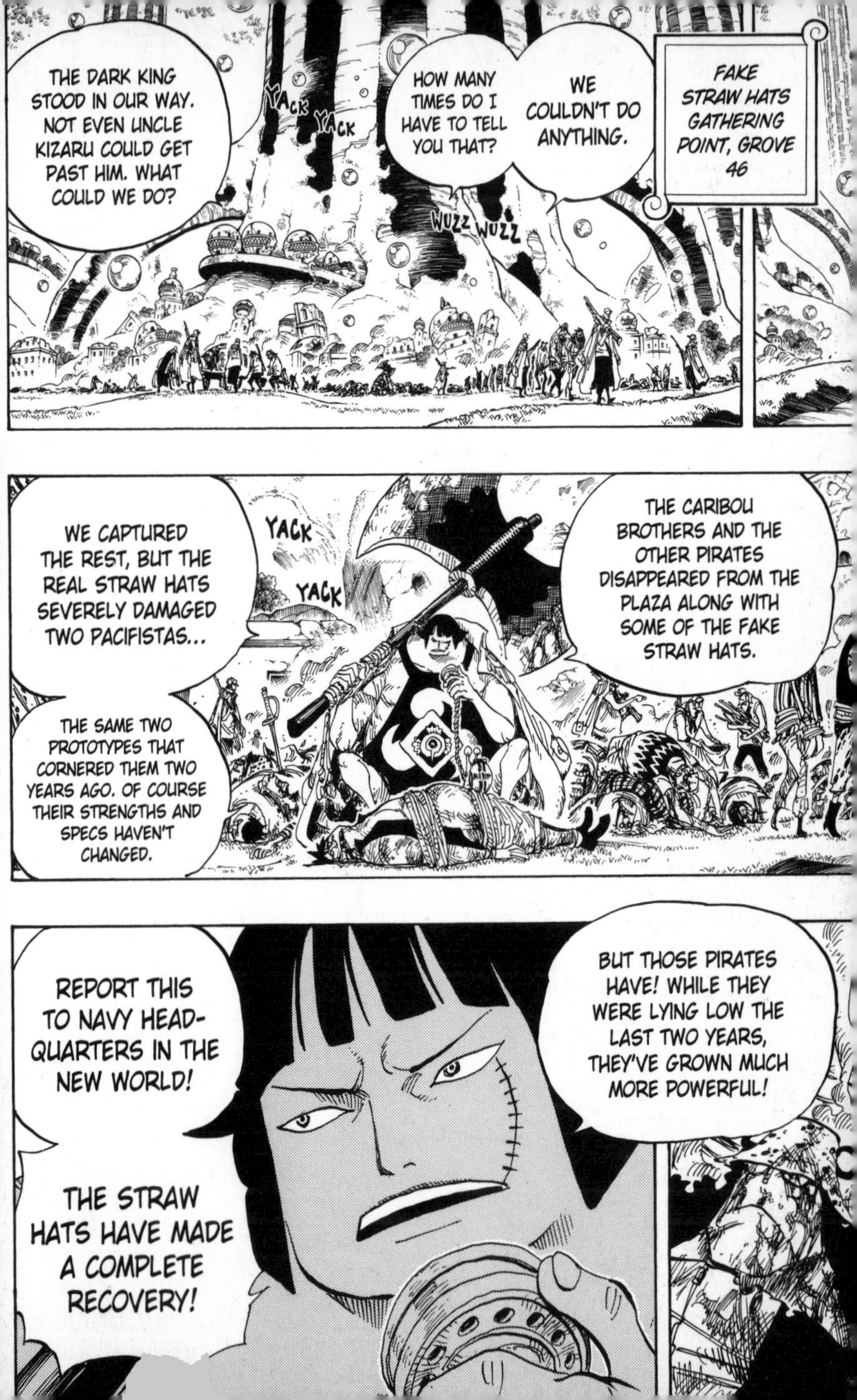
FAKE STRAW HATS GATHERING POINT, GROVE 46
WE COULDN'T DO ANYTHING.
HOW MANY TIMES DO I HAVE TO TELL YOU THAT?
YACK YACK
THE DARK KING STOOD IN OUR WAY. NOT EVEN UNCLE KIZARU COULD GET PAST HIM. WHAT COULD WE DO?
WUZZ WUZZ
THE CARIBOU BROTHERS AND THE OTHER PIRATES DISAPPEARED FROM THE PLAZA ALONG WITH SOME OF THE FAKE STRAW HATS.
YACK
YACK
WE CAPTURED THE REST, BUT THE REAL STRAW HATS SEVERELY DAMAGED TWO PACIFISTAS...
THE SAME TWO PROTOTYPES THAT CORNERED THEM TWO YEARS AGO. OF COURSE THEIR STRENGTHS AND SPECS HAVEN'T CHANGED.
BUT THOSE PIRATES HAVE! WHILE THEY WERE LYING LOW THE LAST TWO YEARS, THEY'VE GROWN MUCH MORE POWERFUL!
REPORT THIS TO NAVY HEAD-QUARTERS IN THE NEW WORLD!
THE STRAW HATS HAVE MADE A COMPLETE RECOVERY!

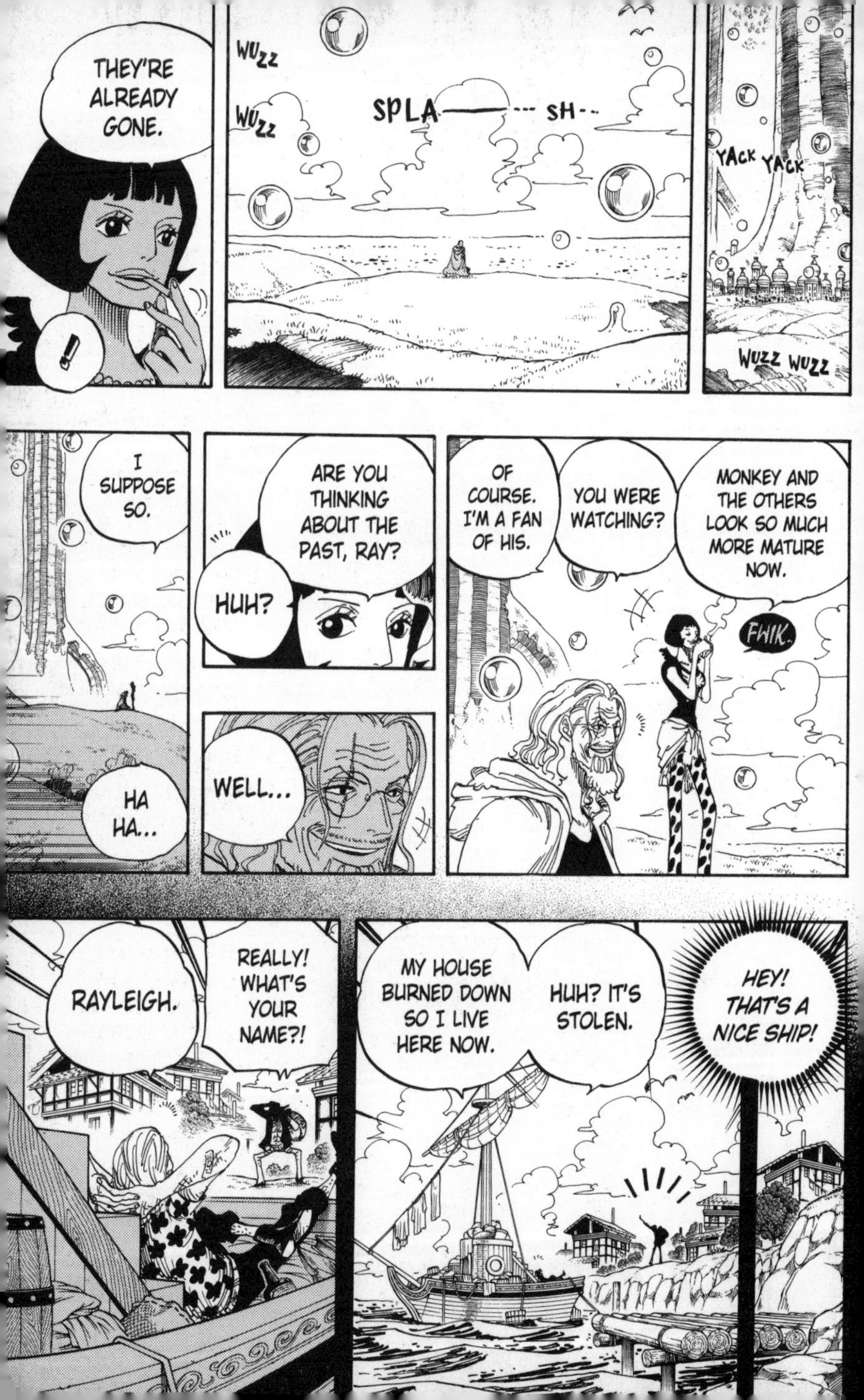
YACK YACK
WUZZ WUZZ
WUZZ
WUZZ
SPLA——--- SH--
THEY'RE ALREADY GONE.
!
MONKEY AND THE OTHERS LOOK SO MUCH MORE MATURE NOW.
FWIK.
YOU WERE WATCHING?
OF COURSE. I'M A FAN OF HIS.
ARE YOU THINKING ABOUT THE PAST, RAY?
HUH?
WELL...
I SUPPOSE SO.
HA HA...
HEY! THAT'S A NICE SHIP!
HUH? IT'S STOLEN.
MY HOUSE BURNED DOWN SO I LIVE HERE NOW.
REALLY! WHAT'S YOUR NAME?!
RAYLEIGH.

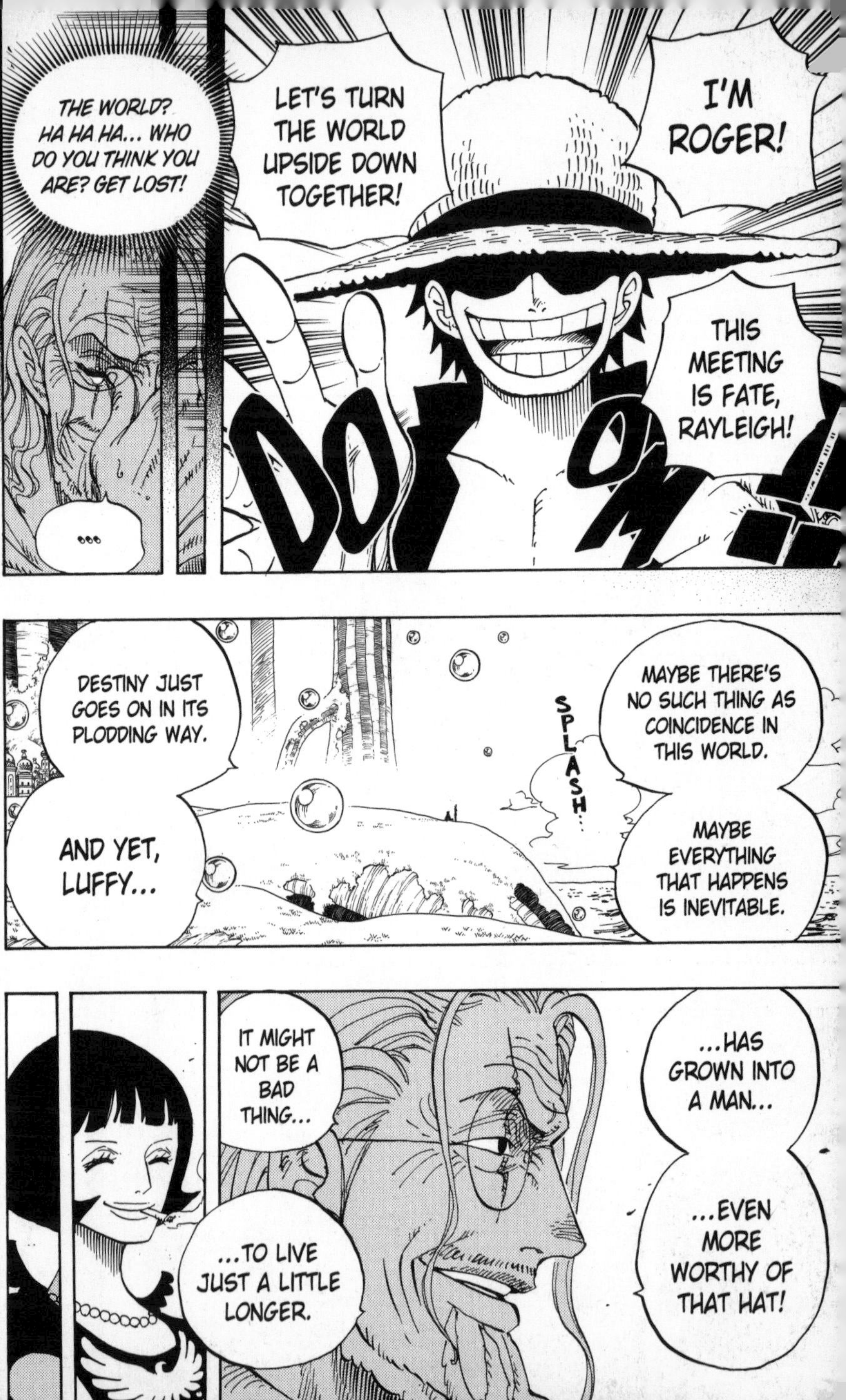
I'M ROGER!
LET'S TURN THE WORLD UPSIDE DOWN TOGETHER!
THIS MEETING IS FATE, RAYLEIGH!
DOOM!!
THE WORLD? HA HA HA... WHO DO YOU THINK YOU ARE? GET LOST!
...
MAYBE THERE'S NO SUCH THING AS COINCIDENCE IN THIS WORLD.
MAYBE EVERYTHING THAT HAPPENS IS INEVITABLE.
SPLASH...
DESTINY JUST GOES ON IN ITS PLODDING WAY.
AND YET, LUFFY...
...HAS GROWN INTO A MAN...
...EVEN MORE WORTHY OF THAT HAT!
IT MIGHT NOT BE A BAD THING...
...TO LIVE JUST A LITTLE LONGER.

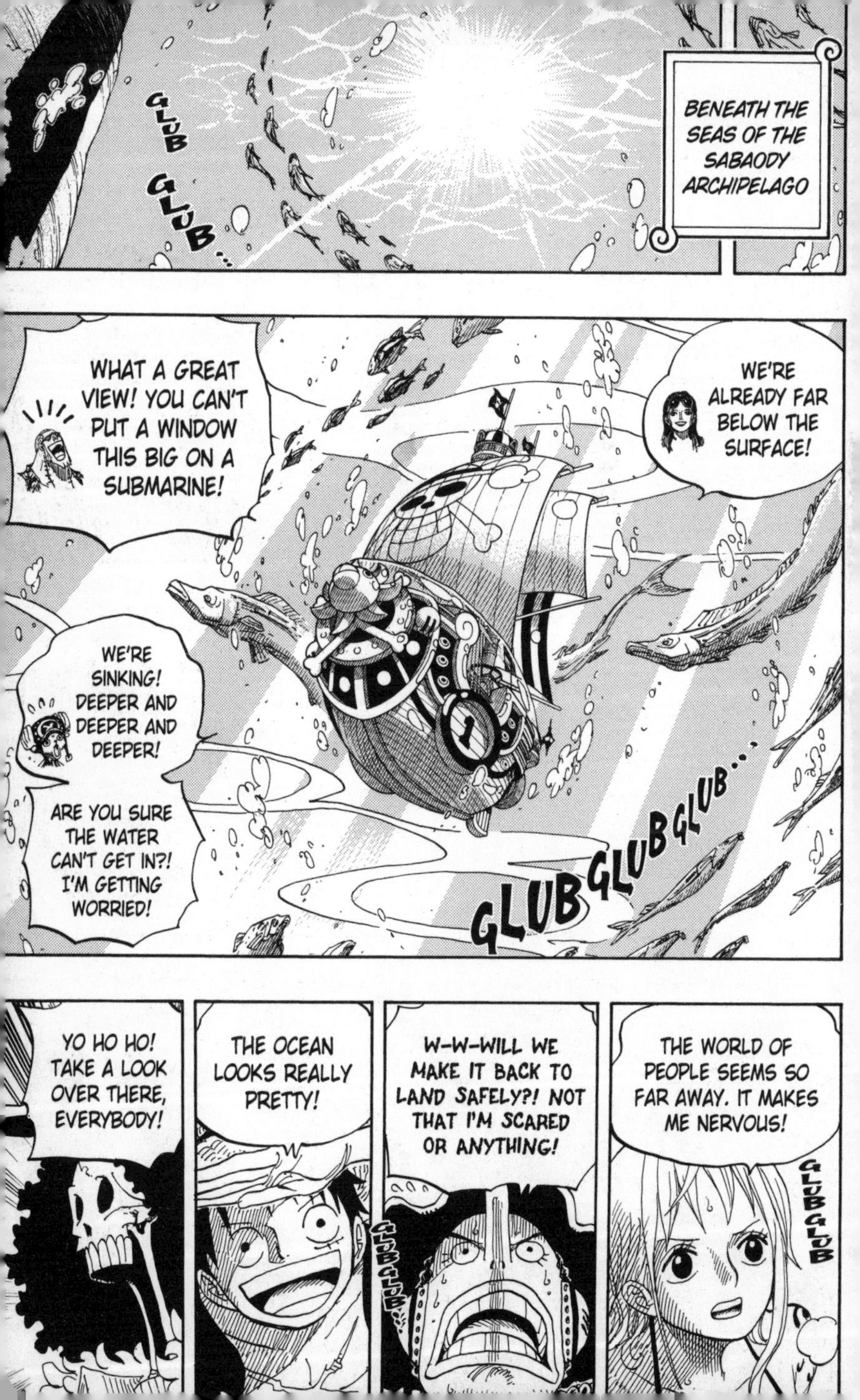
BENEATH THE SEAS OF THE SABAODY ARCHIPELAGO
GLUB GLUB...
WE'RE ALREADY FAR BELOW THE SURFACE!
WHAT A GREAT VIEW! YOU CAN'T PUT A WINDOW THIS BIG ON A SUBMARINE!
GLUB GLUB GLUB GLUB...
WE'RE SINKING! DEEPER AND DEEPER AND DEEPER!
ARE YOU SURE THE WATER CAN'T GET IN?! I'M GETTING WORRIED!
THE WORLD OF PEOPLE SEEMS SO FAR AWAY. IT MAKES ME NERVOUS!
GLUB GLUB
W-W-WILL WE MAKE IT BACK TO LAND SAFELY?! NOT THAT I'M SCARED OR ANYTHING!
GLUB GLUB...
THE OCEAN LOOKS REALLY PRETTY!
YO HO HO! TAKE A LOOK OVER THERE, EVERYBODY!

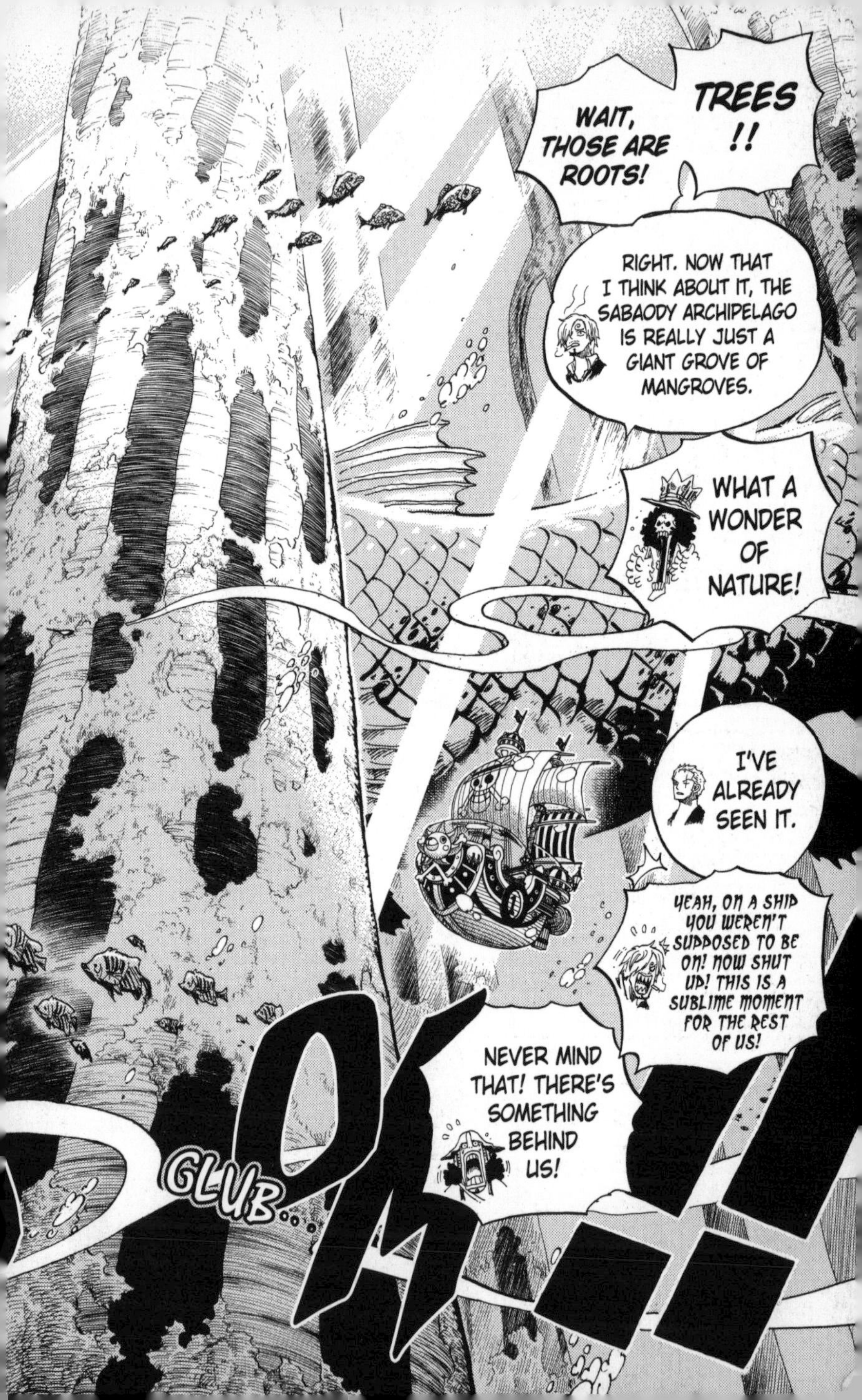
TREES!!
WAIT, THOSE ARE ROOTS!
RIGHT. NOW THAT I THINK ABOUT IT, THE SABAODY ARCHIPELAGO IS REALLY JUST A GIANT GROVE OF MANGROVES.
WHAT A WONDER OF NATURE!
I'VE ALREADY SEEN IT.
YEAH, ON A SHIP YOU WEREN'T SUPPOSED TO BE ON! NOW SHUT UP! THIS IS A SUBLIME MOMENT FOR THE REST OF US!
NEVER MIND THAT! THERE'S SOMETHING BEHIND US!
GLUB...

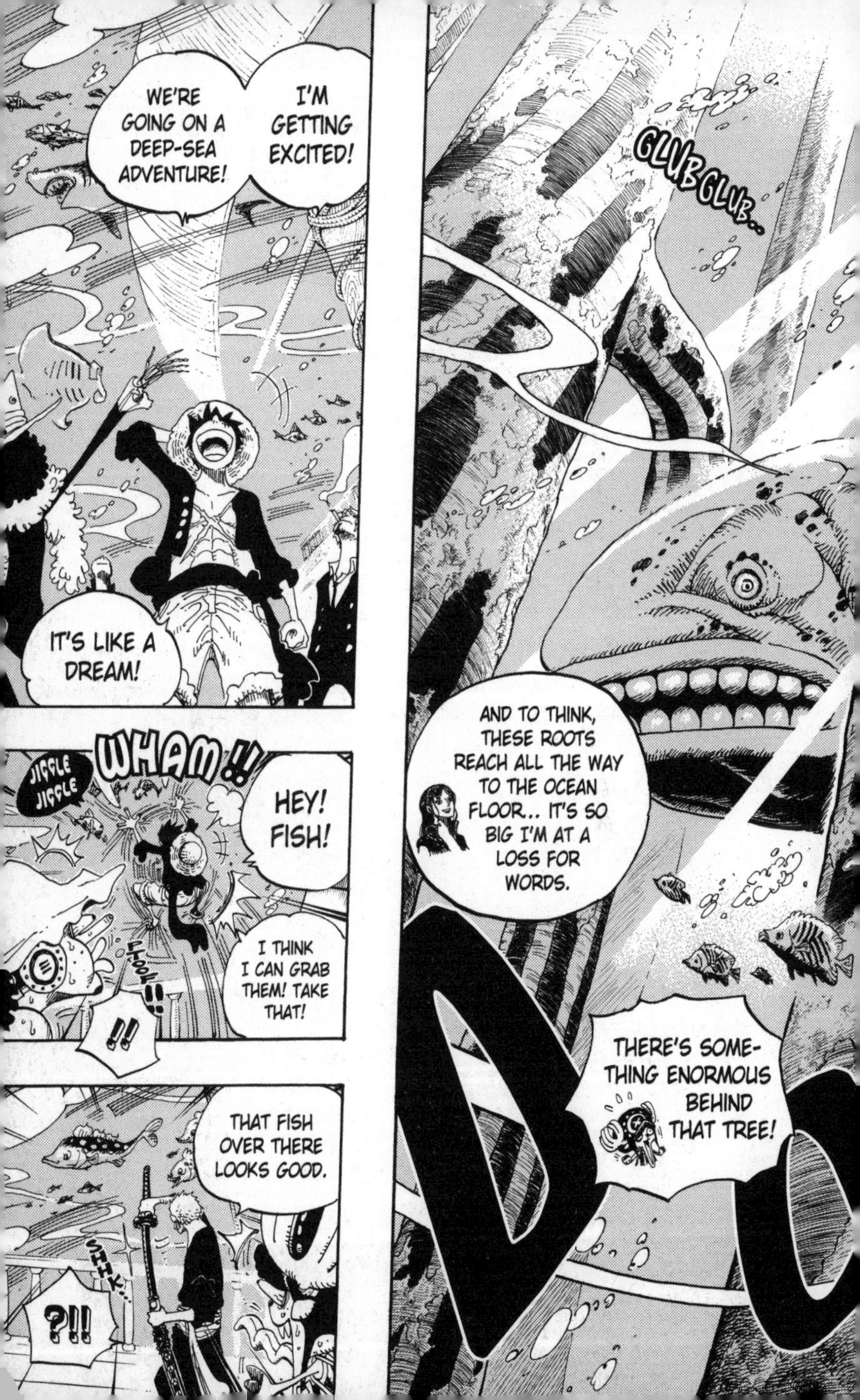
GLUB GLUB...
AND TO THINK, THESE ROOTS REACH ALL THE WAY TO THE OCEAN FLOOR... IT'S SO BIG I'M AT A LOSS FOR WORDS.
THERE'S SOME-THING ENORMOUS BEHIND THAT TREE!
I'M GETTING EXCITED!
WE'RE GOING ON A DEEP-SEA ADVENTURE!
IT'S LIKE A DREAM!
HEY! FISH!
WHAM!!
JIGGLE JIGGLE
I THINK I CAN GRAB THEM! TAKE THAT!
FLOOF!!
!!
THAT FISH OVER THERE LOOKS GOOD.
SHHK...
?!!

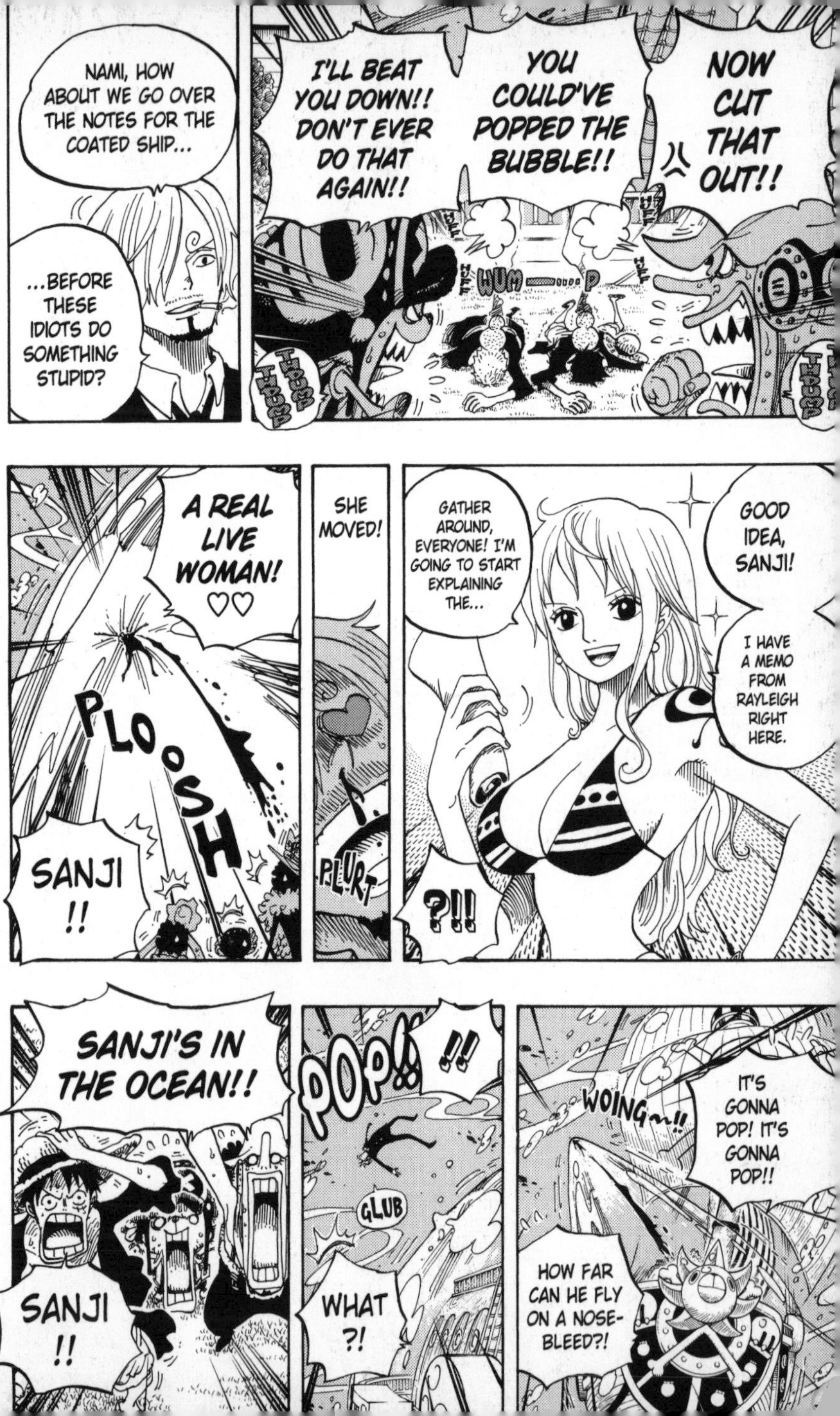
NOW CUT THAT OUT!!
YOU COULD'VE POPPED THE BUBBLE!!
I'LL BEAT YOU DOWN!! DON'T EVER DO THAT AGAIN!!
THUMP
HUFF
WUM—P
THUMP THUMP
NAMI, HOW ABOUT WE GO OVER THE NOTES FOR THE COATED SHIP...
...BEFORE THESE IDIOTS DO SOMETHING STUPID?
GOOD IDEA, SANJI!
I HAVE A MEMO FROM RAYLEIGH RIGHT HERE.
GATHER AROUND, EVERYONE! I'M GOING TO START EXPLAINING THE...
?!!
SHE MOVED!
PLURT
A REAL LIVE WOMAN! ♡♡
PLOOSH
SANJI!!
IT'S GONNA POP! IT'S GONNA POP!!
WOING~~!!
HOW FAR CAN HE FLY ON A NOSE-BLEED?!
POP!!
!!
GLUB
WHAT?!
SANJI'S IN THE OCEAN!!
SANJI!!

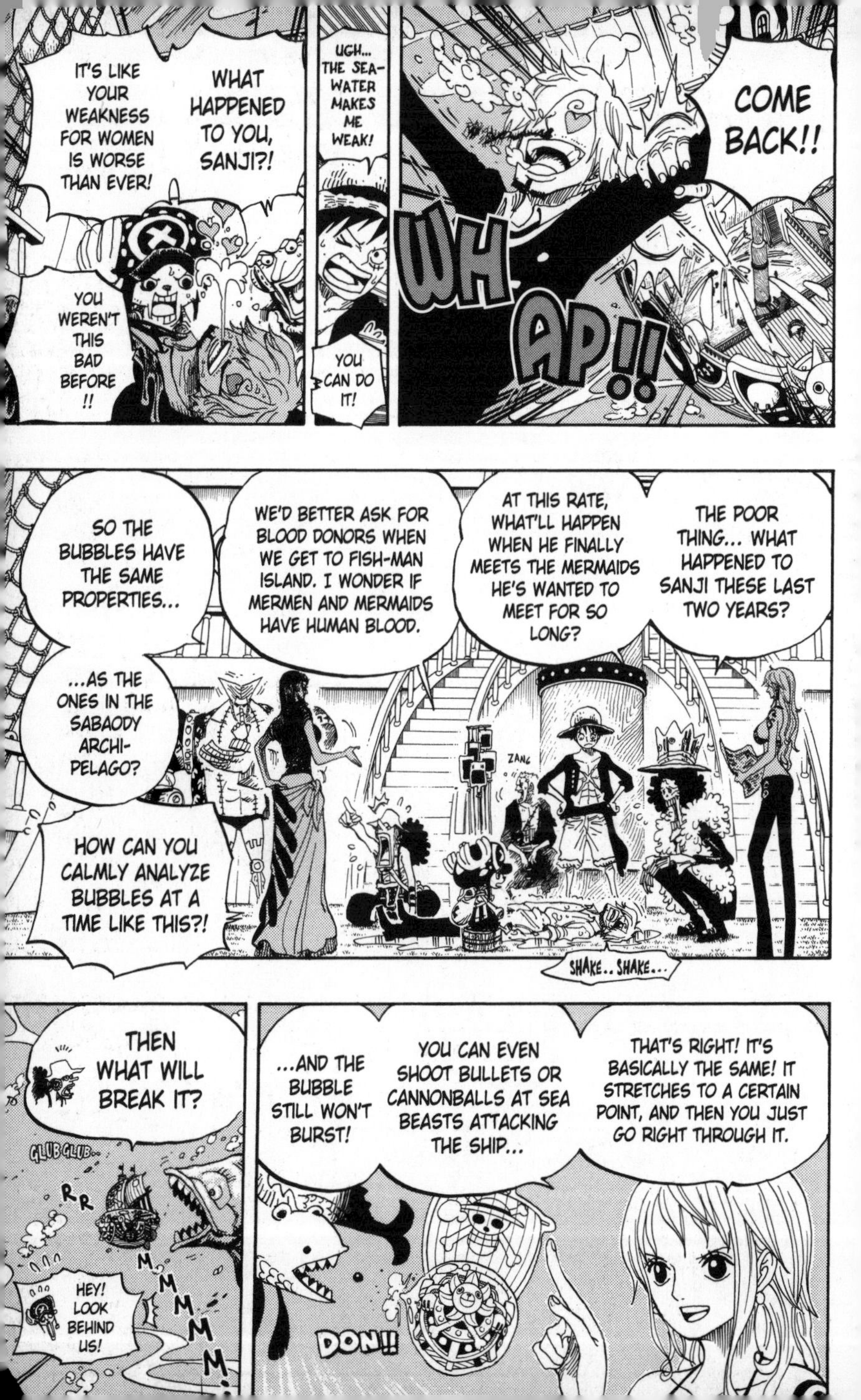
COME BACK!!
WHAP!!
UGH... THE SEA-WATER MAKES ME WEAK!
YOU CAN DO IT!
WHAT HAPPENED TO YOU, SANJI?!
IT'S LIKE YOUR WEAKNESS FOR WOMEN IS WORSE THAN EVER!
YOU WEREN'T THIS BAD BEFORE !!
THE POOR THING... WHAT HAPPENED TO SANJI THESE LAST TWO YEARS?
AT THIS RATE, WHAT'LL HAPPEN WHEN HE FINALLY MEETS THE MERMAIDS HE'S WANTED TO MEET FOR SO LONG?
WE'D BETTER ASK FOR BLOOD DONORS WHEN WE GET TO FISH-MAN ISLAND. I WONDER IF MERMEN AND MERMAIDS HAVE HUMAN BLOOD.
SO THE BUBBLES HAVE THE SAME PROPERTIES...
...AS THE ONES IN THE SABAODY ARCHI-PELAGO?
ZANG
HOW CAN YOU CALMLY ANALYZE BUBBLES AT A TIME LIKE THIS?!
SHAKE.. SHAKE...
THAT'S RIGHT! IT'S BASICALLY THE SAME! IT STRETCHES TO A CERTAIN POINT, AND THEN YOU JUST GO RIGHT THROUGH IT.
YOU CAN EVEN SHOOT BULLETS OR CANNONBALLS AT SEA BEASTS ATTACKING THE SHIP...
...AND THE BUBBLE STILL WON'T BURST!
DON!!
THEN WHAT WILL BREAK IT?
GLUB GLUB..
RR
MMMMM
HEY! LOOK BEHIND US!

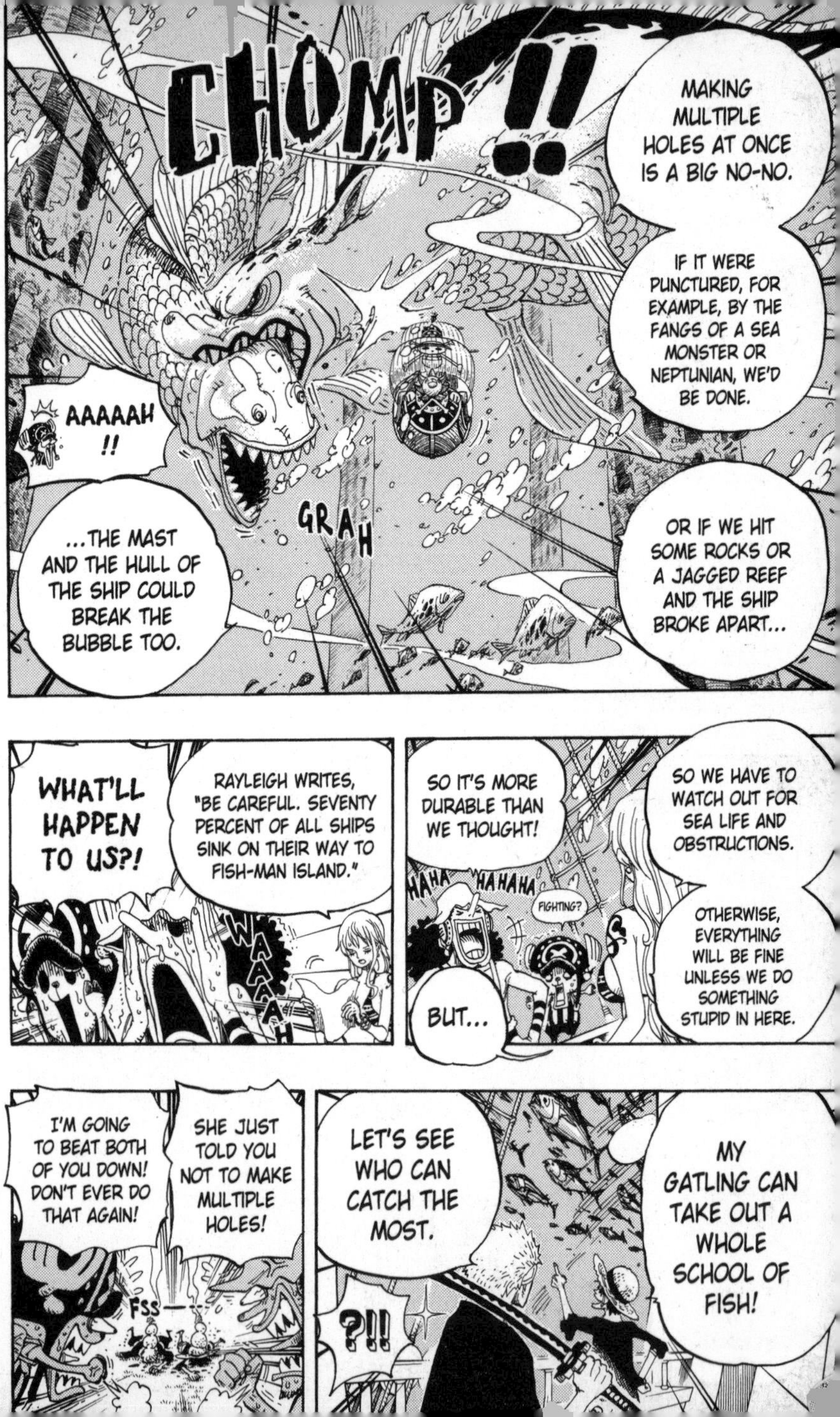
MAKING MULTIPLE HOLES AT ONCE IS A BIG NO-NO.
CHOMP!!
IF IT WERE PUNCTURED, FOR EXAMPLE, BY THE FANGS OF A SEA MONSTER OR NEPTUNIAN, WE'D BE DONE.
AAAAAH!!
OR IF WE HIT SOME ROCKS OR A JAGGED REEF AND THE SHIP BROKE APART...
GRAH
...THE MAST AND THE HULL OF THE SHIP COULD BREAK THE BUBBLE TOO.
SO WE HAVE TO WATCH OUT FOR SEA LIFE AND OBSTRUCTIONS.
SO IT'S MORE DURABLE THAN WE THOUGHT!
HAHA HAHAHA
FIGHTING?
OTHERWISE, EVERYTHING WILL BE FINE UNLESS WE DO SOMETHING STUPID IN HERE.
BUT...
RAYLEIGH WRITES, "BE CAREFUL. SEVENTY PERCENT OF ALL SHIPS SINK ON THEIR WAY TO FISH-MAN ISLAND."
WHAT'LL HAPPEN TO US?!
WAAAAAH
MY GATLING CAN TAKE OUT A WHOLE SCHOOL OF FISH!
LET'S SEE WHO CAN CATCH THE MOST.
?!!
SHE JUST TOLD YOU NOT TO MAKE MULTIPLE HOLES!
I'M GOING TO BEAT BOTH OF YOU DOWN! DON'T EVER DO THAT AGAIN!
FSS

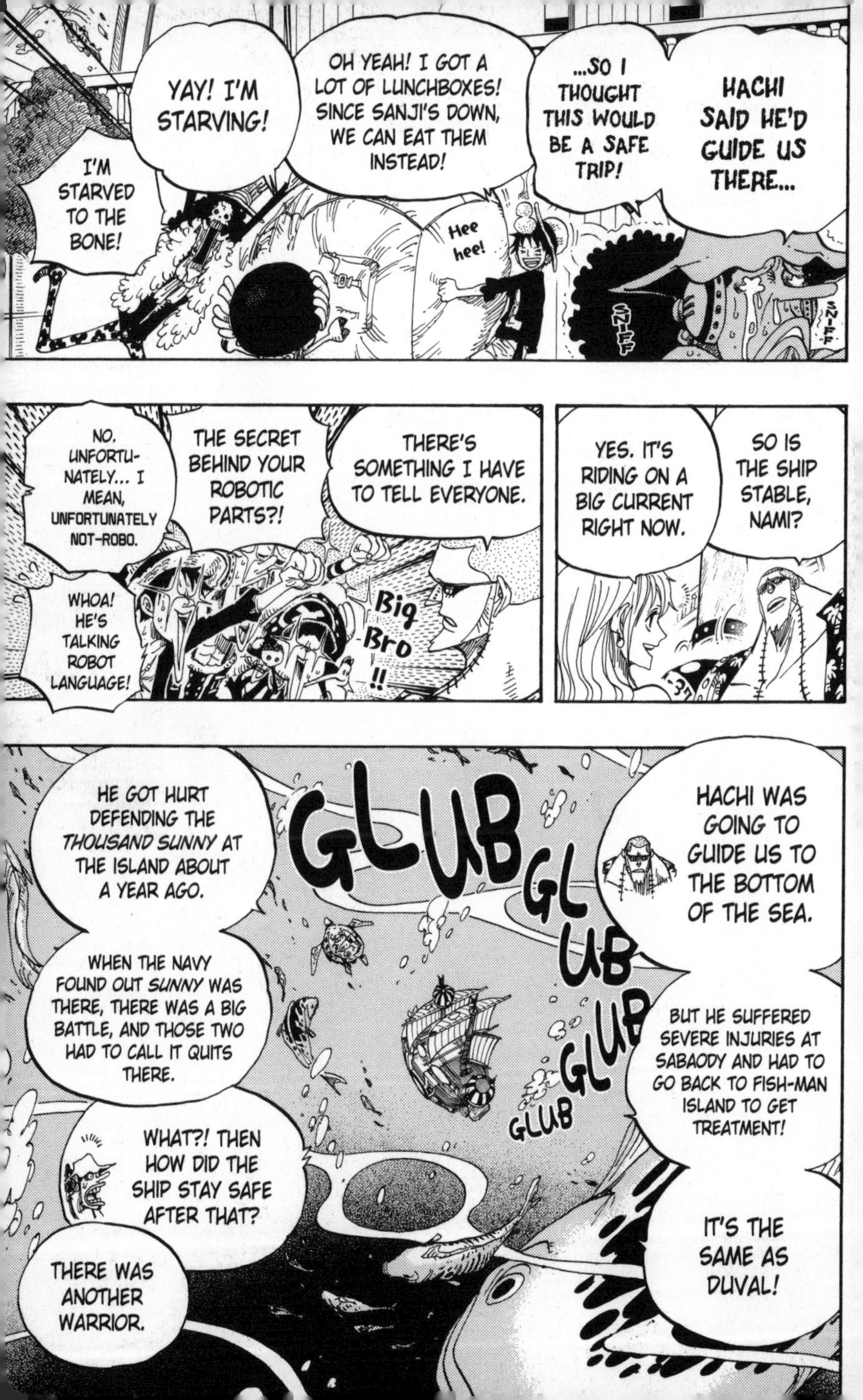
HACHI SAID HE'D GUIDE US THERE...
SNIFF
SNIFF
...SO I THOUGHT THIS WOULD BE A SAFE TRIP!
Hee hee!
OH YEAH! I GOT A LOT OF LUNCHBOXES! SINCE SANJI'S DOWN, WE CAN EAT THEM INSTEAD!
YAY! I'M STARVING!
I'M STARVED TO THE BONE!
SO IS THE SHIP STABLE, NAMI?
YES. IT'S RIDING ON A BIG CURRENT RIGHT NOW.
THERE'S SOMETHING I HAVE TO TELL EVERYONE.
THE SECRET BEHIND YOUR ROBOTIC PARTS?!
Big Bro!!
NO. UNFORTU-NATELY... I MEAN, UNFORTUNATELY NOT-ROBO.
WHOA! HE'S TALKING ROBOT LANGUAGE!
HACHI WAS GOING TO GUIDE US TO THE BOTTOM OF THE SEA.
BUT HE SUFFERED SEVERE INJURIES AT SABAODY AND HAD TO GO BACK TO FISH-MAN ISLAND TO GET TREATMENT!
IT'S THE SAME AS DUVAL!
GLUB GLUB GLUB GLUB GLUB
HE GOT HURT DEFENDING THE *THOUSAND SUNNY* AT THE ISLAND ABOUT A YEAR AGO.
WHEN THE NAVY FOUND OUT *SUNNY* WAS THERE, THERE WAS A BIG BATTLE, AND THOSE TWO HAD TO CALL IT QUITS THERE.
WHAT?! THEN HOW DID THE SHIP STAY SAFE AFTER THAT?
THERE WAS ANOTHER WARRIOR.

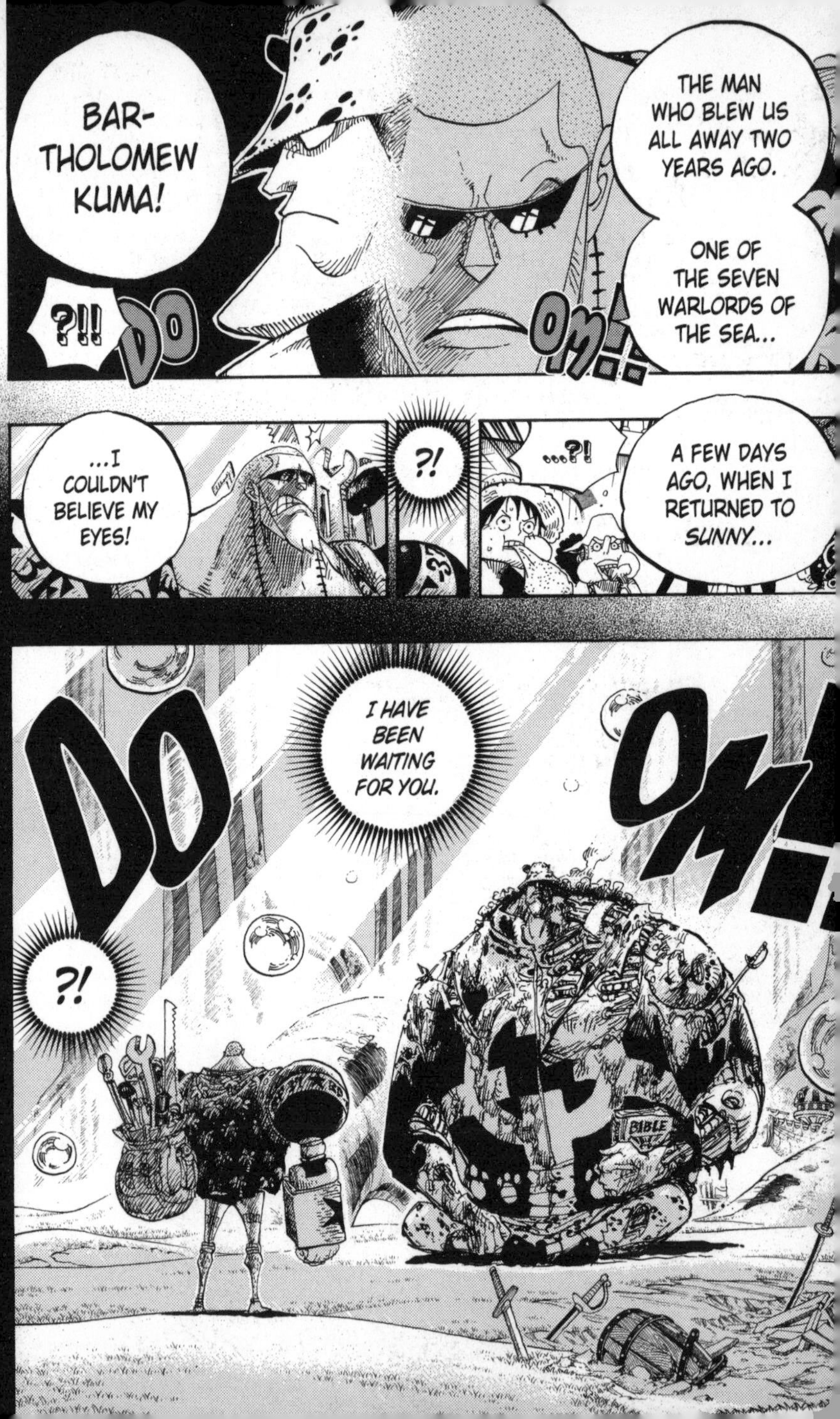
THE MAN WHO BLEW US ALL AWAY TWO YEARS AGO.
ONE OF THE SEVEN WARLORDS OF THE SEA...
DO OM!!
BAR-THOLOMEW KUMA!
?!!
A FEW DAYS AGO, WHEN I RETURNED TO SUNNY...
...?!
?!
...I COULDN'T BELIEVE MY EYES!
DO OM!!
I HAVE BEEN WAITING FOR YOU.
?!
BIBLE

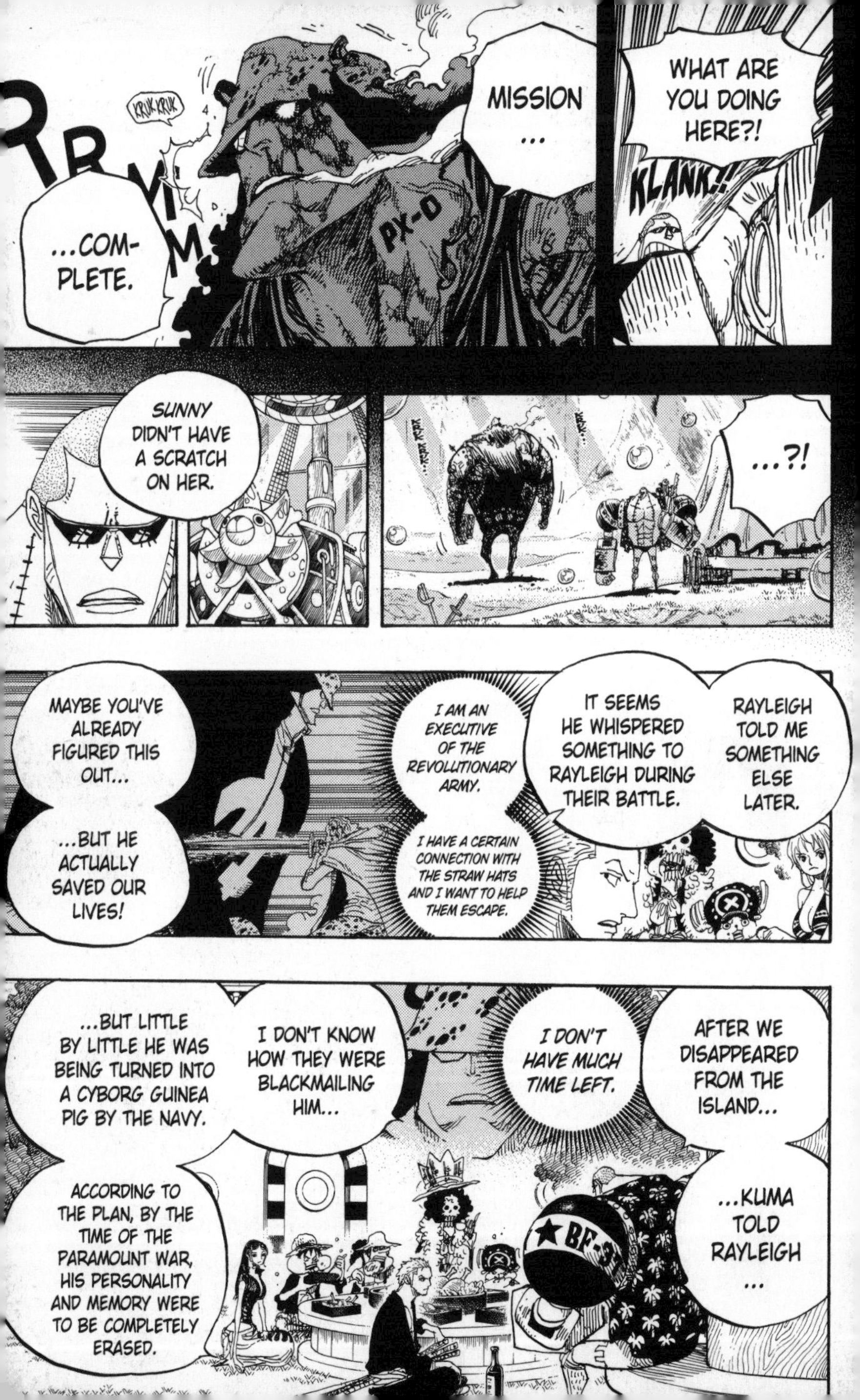
WHAT ARE YOU DOING HERE?!
KLANK!!
KRUK KRUK
MISSION ...
...COM-PLETE.
...?!
SUNNY DIDN'T HAVE A SCRATCH ON HER.
RAYLEIGH TOLD ME SOMETHING ELSE LATER.
IT SEEMS HE WHISPERED SOMETHING TO RAYLEIGH DURING THEIR BATTLE.
I AM AN EXECUTIVE OF THE REVOLUTIONARY ARMY.
I HAVE A CERTAIN CONNECTION WITH THE STRAW HATS AND I WANT TO HELP THEM ESCAPE.
MAYBE YOU'VE ALREADY FIGURED THIS OUT...
...BUT HE ACTUALLY SAVED OUR LIVES!
AFTER WE DISAPPEARED FROM THE ISLAND...
...KUMA TOLD RAYLEIGH ...
I DON'T HAVE MUCH TIME LEFT.
I DON'T KNOW HOW THEY WERE BLACKMAILING HIM...
...BUT LITTLE BY LITTLE HE WAS BEING TURNED INTO A CYBORG GUINEA PIG BY THE NAVY.
ACCORDING TO THE PLAN, BY THE TIME OF THE PARAMOUNT WAR, HIS PERSONALITY AND MEMORY WERE TO BE COMPLETELY ERASED.

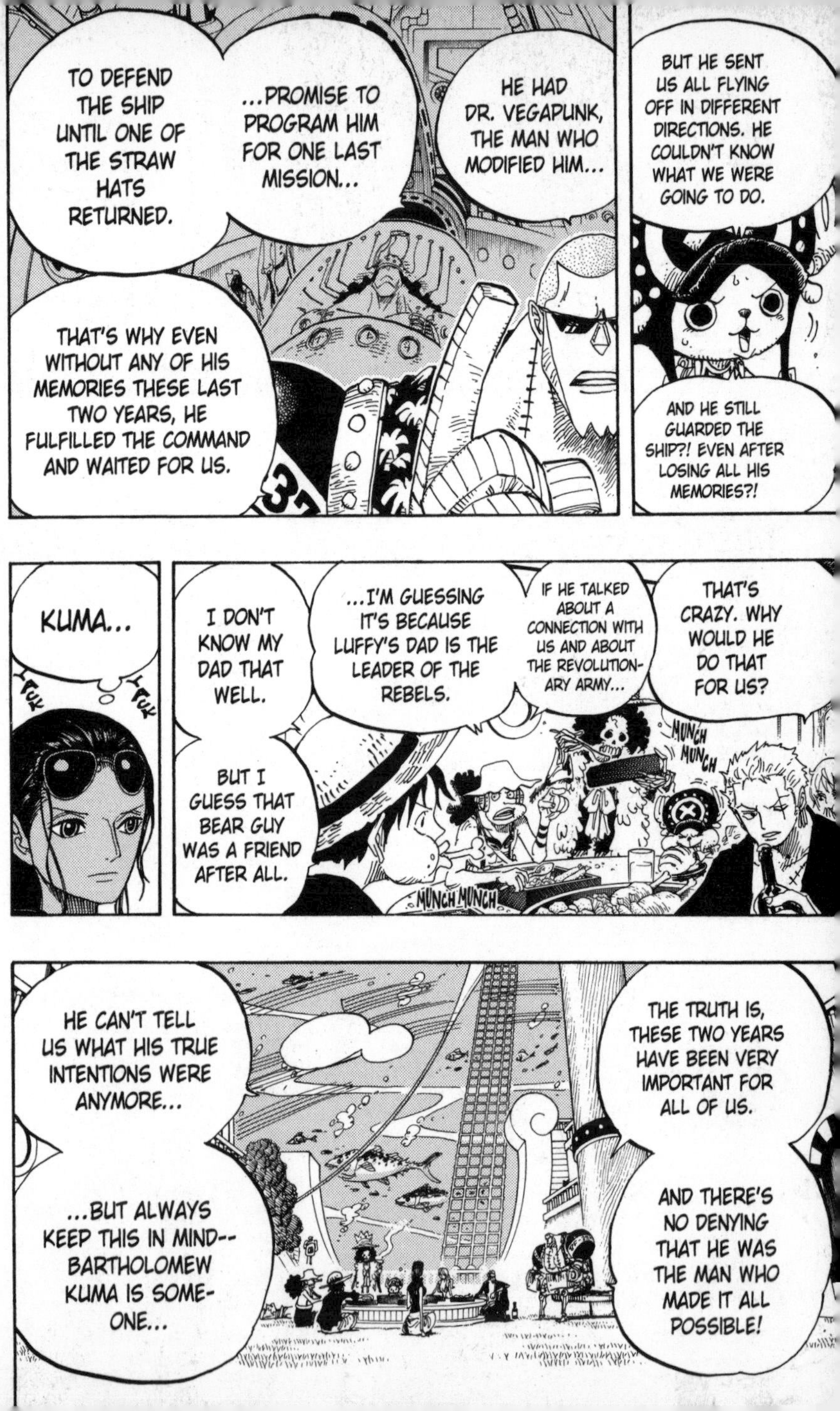
BUT HE SENT US ALL FLYING OFF IN DIFFERENT DIRECTIONS. HE COULDN'T KNOW WHAT WE WERE GOING TO DO.
AND HE STILL GUARDED THE SHIP?! EVEN AFTER LOSING ALL HIS MEMORIES?!
HE HAD DR. VEGAPUNK, THE MAN WHO MODIFIED HIM...
...PROMISE TO PROGRAM HIM FOR ONE LAST MISSION...
TO DEFEND THE SHIP UNTIL ONE OF THE STRAW HATS RETURNED.
THAT'S WHY EVEN WITHOUT ANY OF HIS MEMORIES THESE LAST TWO YEARS, HE FULFILLED THE COMMAND AND WAITED FOR US.
THAT'S CRAZY. WHY WOULD HE DO THAT FOR US?
IF HE TALKED ABOUT A CONNECTION WITH US AND ABOUT THE REVOLUTION-ARY ARMY...
MUNCH MUNCH
...I'M GUESSING IT'S BECAUSE LUFFY'S DAD IS THE LEADER OF THE REBELS.
I DON'T KNOW MY DAD THAT WELL.
BUT I GUESS THAT BEAR GUY WAS A FRIEND AFTER ALL.
MUNCH MUNCH
KUMA...
THE TRUTH IS, THESE TWO YEARS HAVE BEEN VERY IMPORTANT FOR ALL OF US.
AND THERE'S NO DENYING THAT HE WAS THE MAN WHO MADE IT ALL POSSIBLE!
HE CAN'T TELL US WHAT HIS TRUE INTENTIONS WERE ANYMORE...
...BUT ALWAYS KEEP THIS IN MIND-- BARTHOLOMEW KUMA IS SOME-ONE...

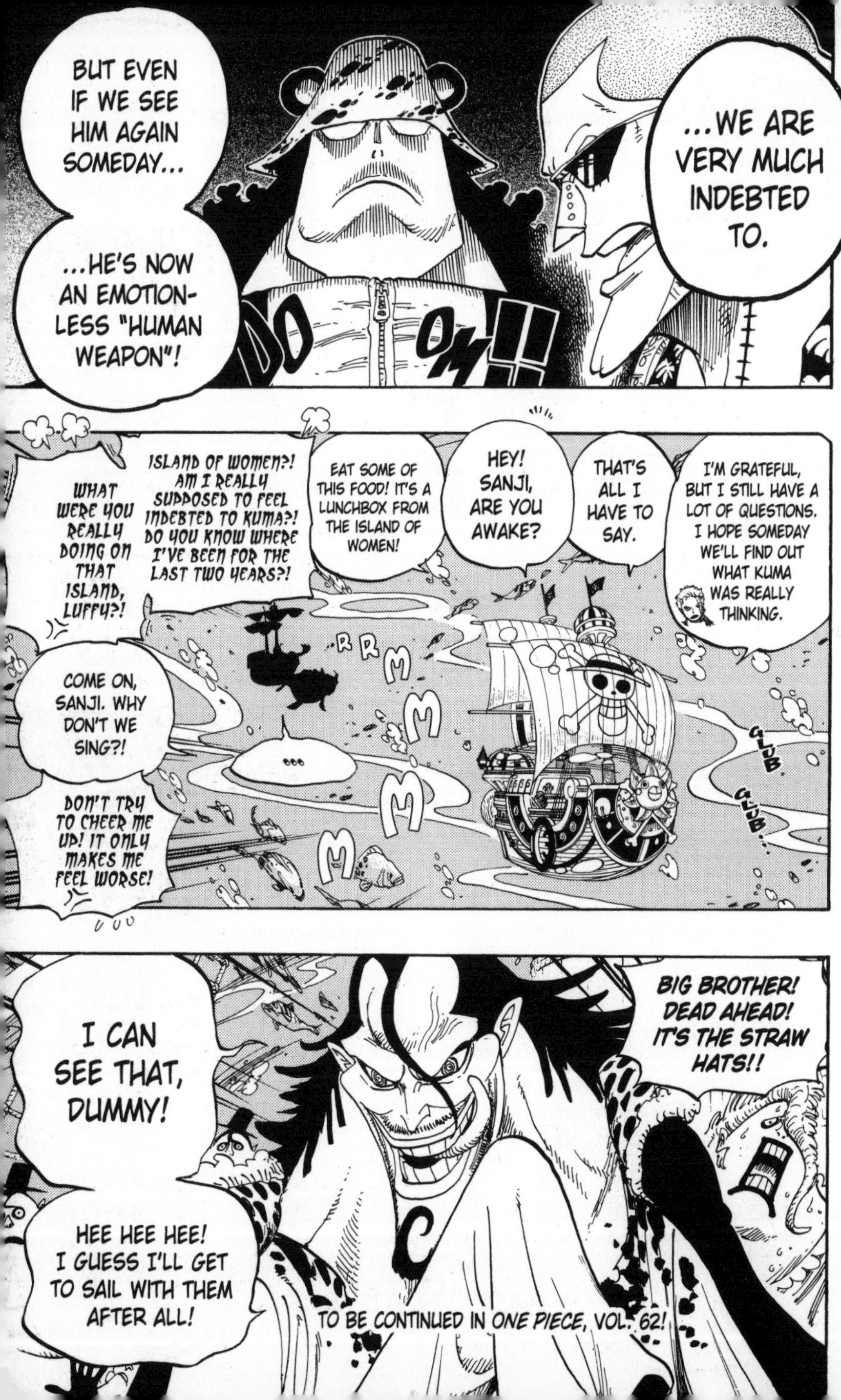
...WE ARE VERY MUCH INDEBTED TO.
BUT EVEN IF WE SEE HIM AGAIN SOMEDAY...
...HE'S NOW AN EMOTION-LESS "HUMAN WEAPON"!
DOOM!!
I'M GRATEFUL, BUT I STILL HAVE A LOT OF QUESTIONS. I HOPE SOMEDAY WE'LL FIND OUT WHAT KUMA WAS REALLY THINKING.
THAT'S ALL I HAVE TO SAY.
HEY! SANJI, ARE YOU AWAKE?
EAT SOME OF THIS FOOD! IT'S A LUNCHBOX FROM THE ISLAND OF WOMEN!
ISLAND OF WOMEN?! AM I REALLY SUPPOSED TO FEEL INDEBTED TO KUMA?! DO YOU KNOW WHERE I'VE BEEN FOR THE LAST TWO YEARS?!
WHAT WERE YOU REALLY DOING ON THAT ISLAND, LUFFY?!
GLUB GLUB...
RRMMMMM
COME ON, SANJI. WHY DON'T WE SING?!
DON'T TRY TO CHEER ME UP! IT ONLY MAKES ME FEEL WORSE!
BIG BROTHER! DEAD AHEAD! IT'S THE STRAW HATS!!
I CAN SEE THAT, DUMMY!
HEE HEE HEE! I GUESS I'LL GET TO SAIL WITH THEM AFTER ALL!
TO BE CONTINUED IN ONE PIECE, VOL. 62!

OUR VERY OWN SHIPWRIGHT, KAZUKI YAO!

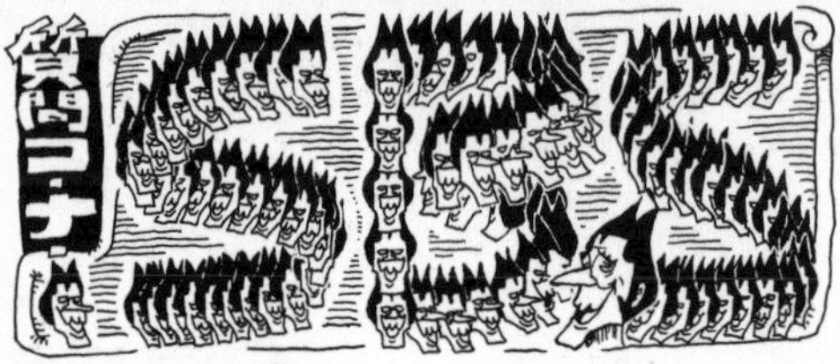

(Oba-san, Ehime)

SBS Question Corner

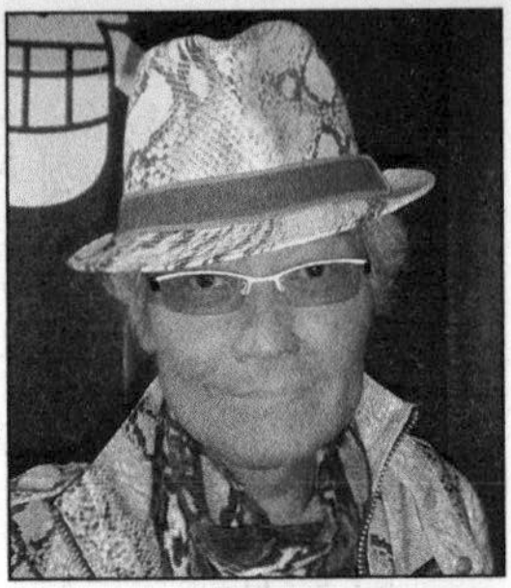

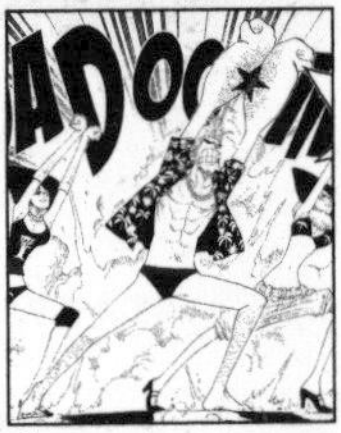

Reader (Q): I have a question for Kazuki Yao.

Are you super this week?

--Shining Butter

Yao (Y): Yes! I'm super, super, super this week.

Q: When you chug cola, what comes out of your mouth later?

--Bz Mania

A: A shout from my soul.

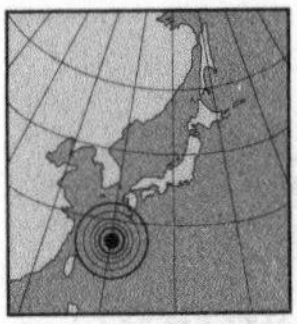

Q: After moving north through Japan, will Hurricane Franky turn into a pervert low-pressure system?

--Bacchon III

A: No. It'll maintain 1000 hectopascals and go around the world, later turning into a super pervert.

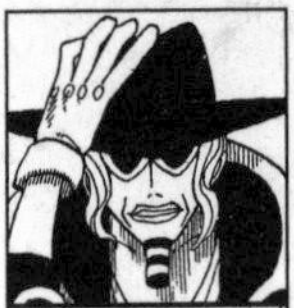

Q: Franky, Bon Clay, or Django. Which one is closest to your own personality? ⌒□⌒

--Kagakkonotokko

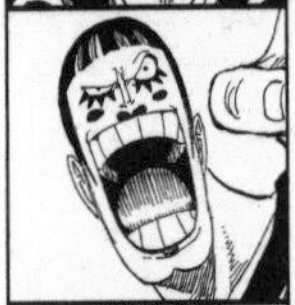

A: I have something in common with all of them. Like I'm always wearing sunglasses and regular glasses, I like cross-dressers, and I'm always wearing nothing but my underwear at home.

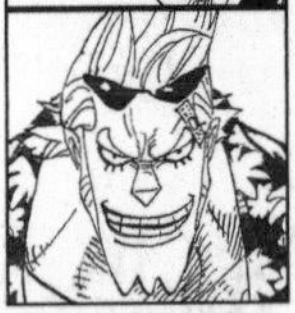

Q: Hello, Yao! You used to play enemy characters. How did you feel when you found out you'd be playing Franky?

--Tarao

A: I thought, I'm finally a friend!

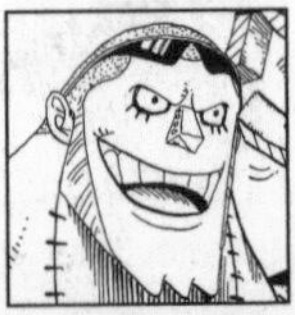

Q: You've played Django, Mr. 2, Franky and many other roles in *One Piece*. But out of all of them, which one did you think was the most fun?

--Tamitami

A: To be honest, Bon Clay. But I can't wait to play the new Franky too.

Q: Do you like younger girls? Be honest with me. How low can you go? What do you **really** think?

A: I can go up or down. On the low end, I like Mana Ashida. If you want to go high, I can go with Miyoko Aso who plays Fune's voice (from Sazae-san). But right now, the perfect one for me is Mirai Shida!

Q: Please tell me your favorite drink and snack.

--Igaguri

A: Past Bourbon & Parliament,
Now Wheat shochu & karasumi

Q: I have a question. How do you say Franky's "Super!"? My friend and I tried to imitate it, but we can't seem to get it right. (LOL) It just becomes an ordinary "super." Can you give us any pointers? ♡

--Holmes ☆ San

A: You take a deep breath and suck in all the evil energy there is the world, filter all of that in your body, and expel it out with a **"Super!"** as hard as you can

Q: Franky seems to have the fashion sense of a pervert, but what about you? If you do, take this! "I give you a ton of speedos!" Don't be shy.

--Tonbanshingi ♡ Chopper

A: I love it. I'll be waiting for those speedos. If you got some miniskirts, I'll take them too!

Q: I have a question! Was there anything you were embarrassed by when playing the voice of Franky?

--P

A: No way! No one is like that!
You can't do this job if you get embarrassed by anything!

Q: Why kind of character do you want to play next?

--Kazumi S-aki

A: I want to play a cool and quiet handsome type. Or a tiny village elder.

Q: If you would like, tell me a youthful mistake you made, just like Franky.

--Carp

A: I could tell you, but it's so obscene, it might not go into print... Oh, well. I'll tell you. You see, about ten years ago...

Oda: H-Hold on! Yao! What are you trying to talk about?! Don't talk about obscene stuff here! Young kids could be reading!

Yao: Come on. It'll be fine.

Oda: No! This volume might be canceled!?

Yao: You see, ten years ago I was at Shinjuku and

Oda: See you next time.

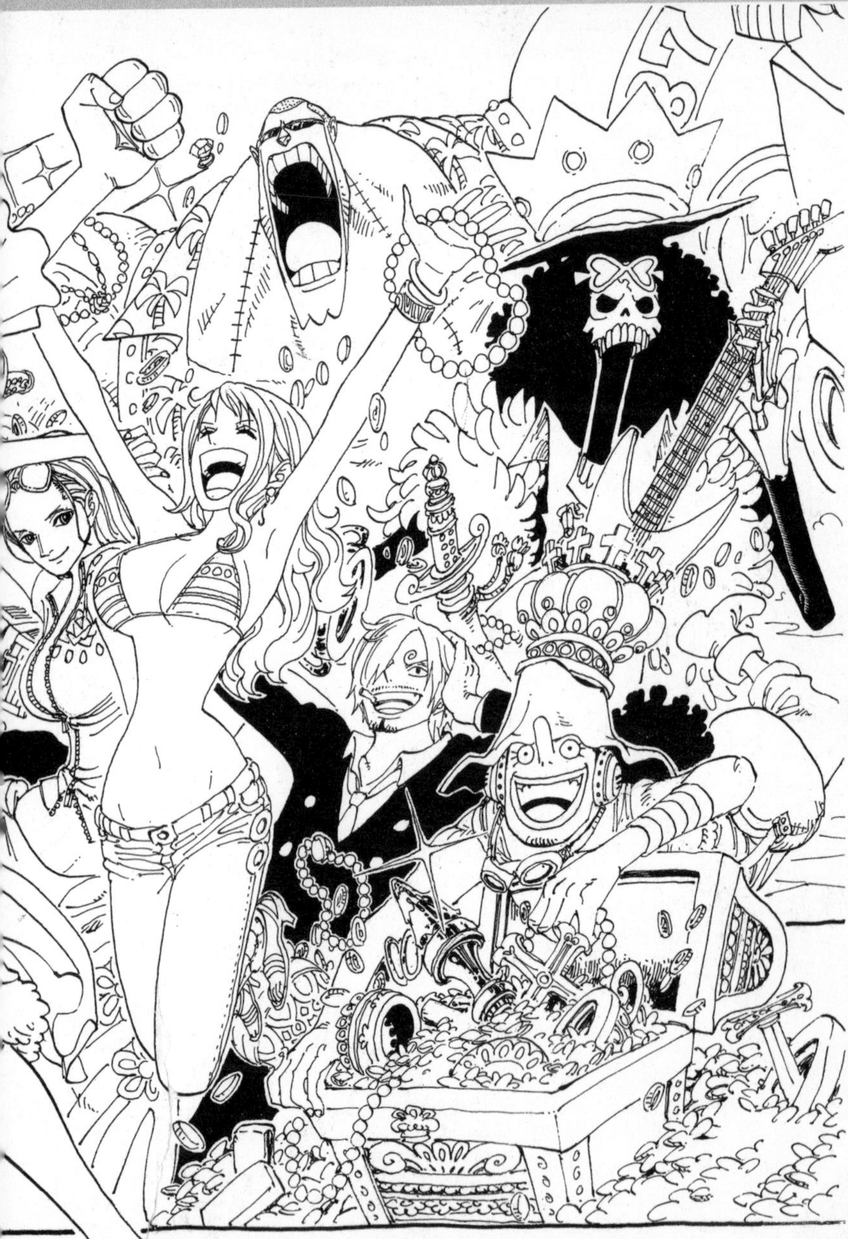

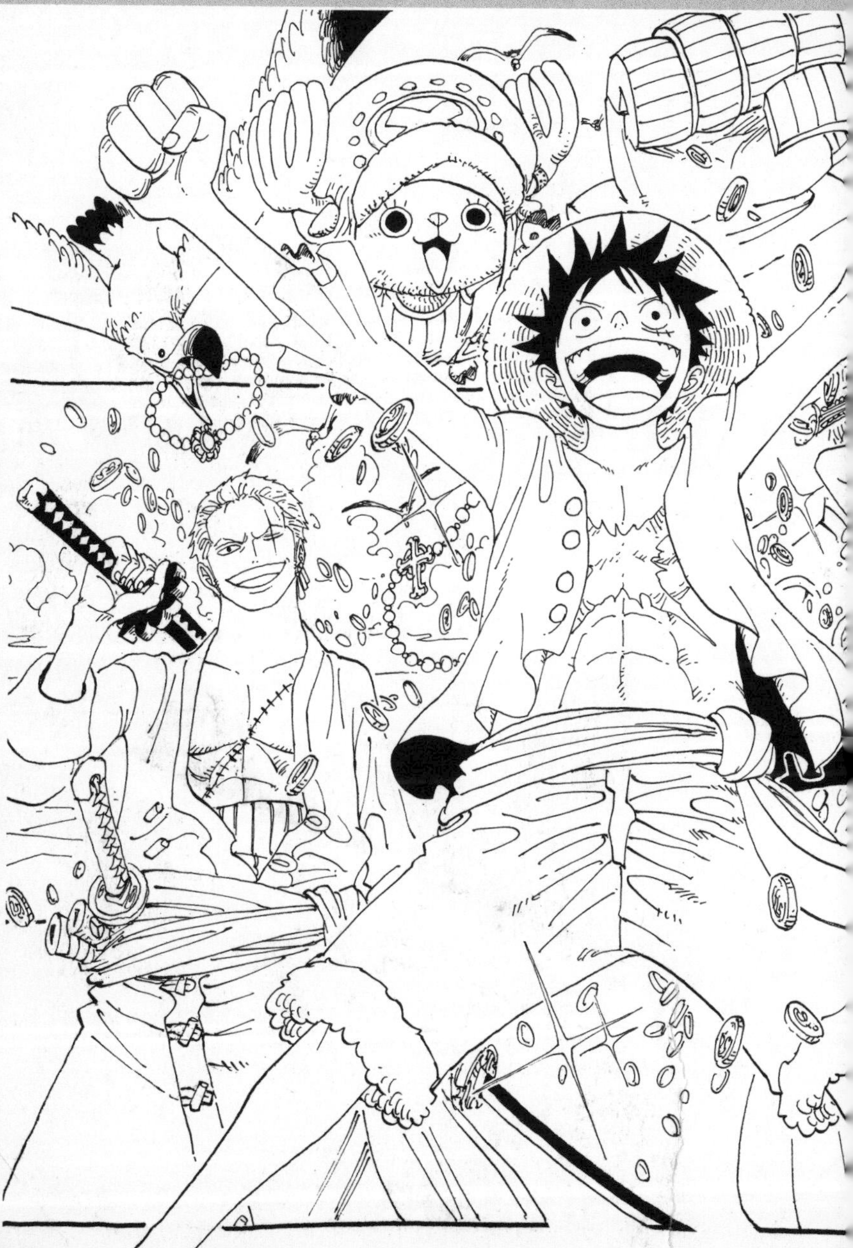

COMING NEXT VOLUME:

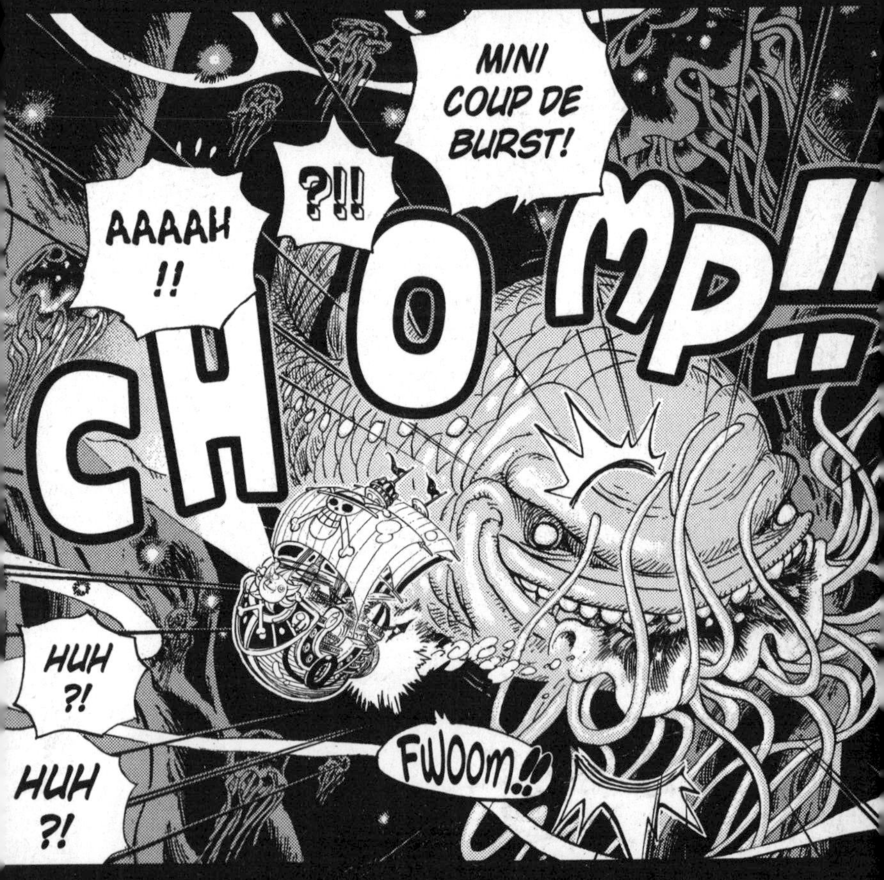
MINI COUP DE BURST!
?!!
AAAAH !!
CHOMP!!
HUH ?!
HUH ?!
FWOOM!!

As the Straw Hat crew dives underwater, they encounter one danger after another. As if vicious pirates weren't bad enough, how will they contend with the giant sea beasts?! And when they finally make it to Fish-Man Island, can Sanji survive coming face to face with a beautiful mermaid...?

ON SALE MAY 2012!

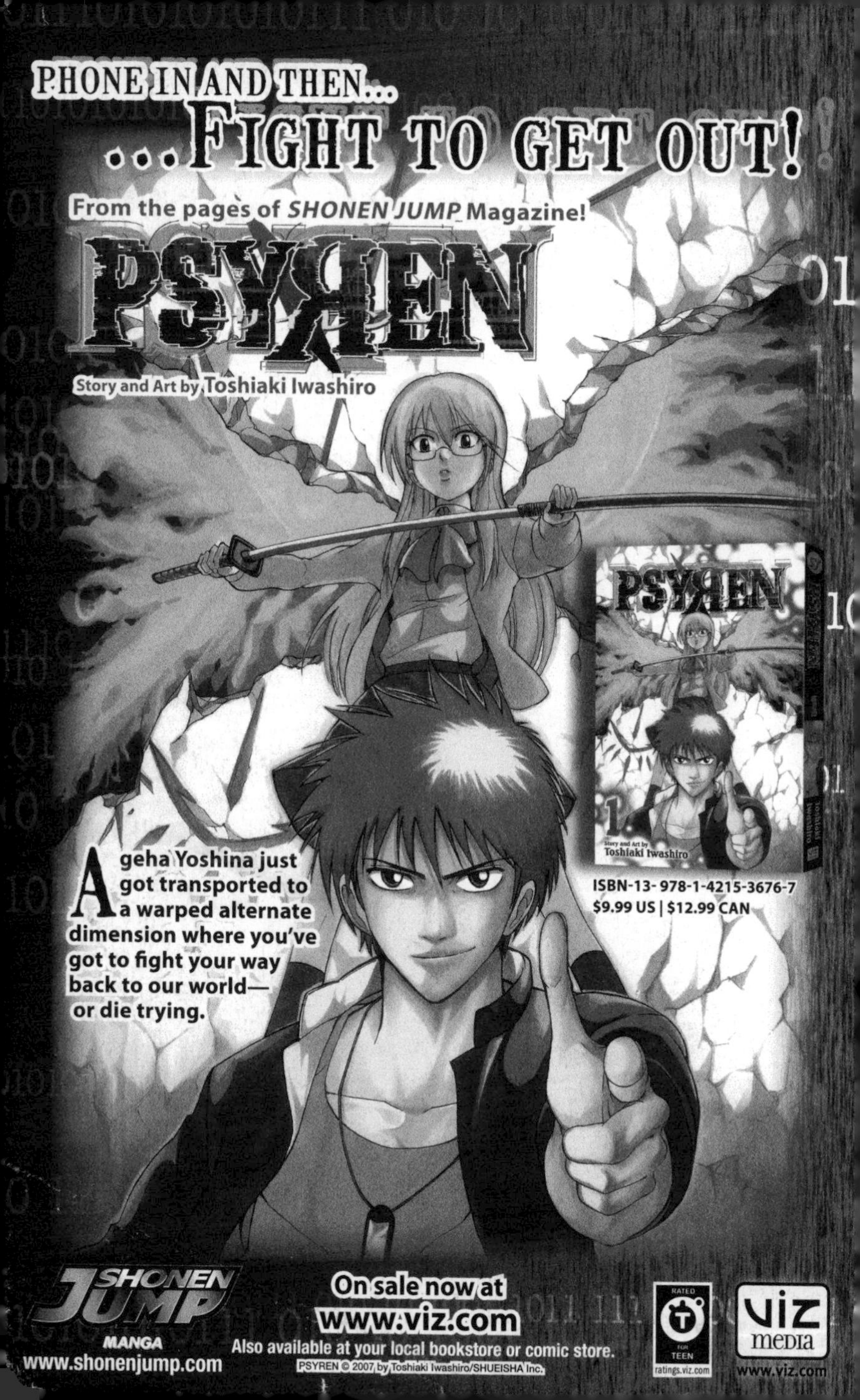
PHONE IN AND THEN...
...FIGHT TO GET OUT!
From the pages of SHONEN JUMP Magazine!
PSYREN
Story and Art by Toshiaki Iwashiro
Ageha Yoshina just got transported to a warped alternate dimension where you've got to fight your way back to our world—or die trying.
PSYREN
1
Story and Art by Toshiaki Iwashiro
ISBN-13- 978-1-4215-3676-7
$9.99 US | $12.99 CAN
SHONEN JUMP
MANGA
www.shonenjump.com
On sale now at
www.viz.com
Also available at your local bookstore or comic store.
PSYREN © 2007 by Toshiaki Iwashiro/SHUEISHA Inc.
RATED T FOR TEEN
ratings.viz.com
viz media
www.viz.com

BAKUMAN。

STORY BY TSUGUMI OHBA
ART BY TAKESHI OBATA

From the creators of *Death Note*

The mystery behind manga making REVEALED!

Average student Moritaka Mashiro enjoys drawing for fun. When his classmate and aspiring writer Akito Takagi discovers his talent, he begs to team up. But what exactly does it take to make it in the manga-publishing world?

Bakuman., Vol. 1
ISBN: 978-1-4215-3513-5
$9.99 US / $12.99 CAN *

Manga on sale at store.viz.com

Also available at your local bookstore or comic store

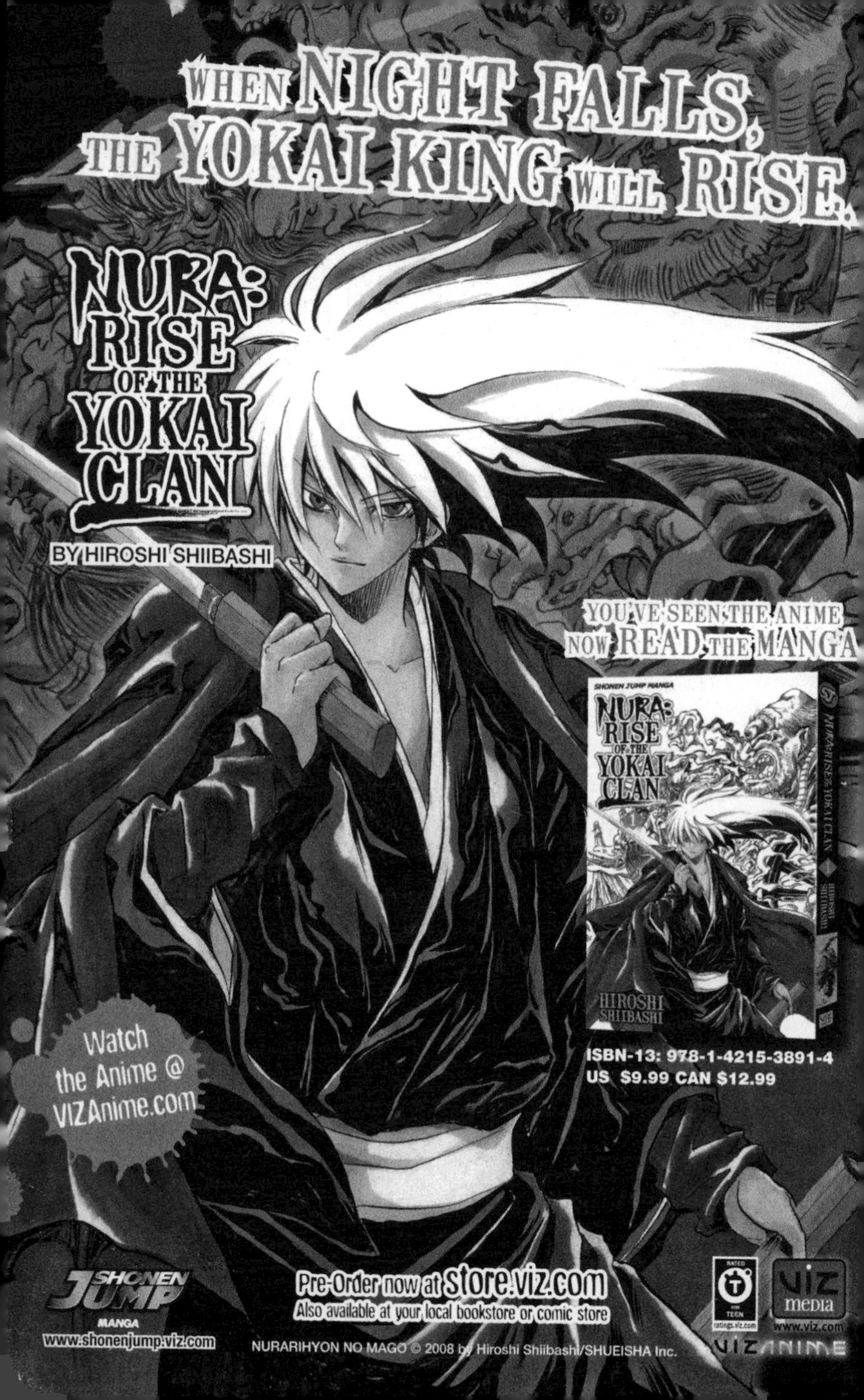
WHEN NIGHT FALLS, THE YOKAI KING WILL RISE.
NURA: RISE OF THE YOKAI CLAN
BY HIROSHI SHIIBASHI
YOU'VE SEEN THE ANIME NOW READ THE MANGA
SHONEN JUMP MANGA
NURA: RISE OF THE YOKAI CLAN
HIROSHI SHIIBASHI
ISBN-13: 978-1-4215-3891-4
US $9.99 CAN $12.99
Watch the Anime @ VIZAnime.com
SHONEN JUMP MANGA
www.shonenjump.viz.com
Pre-Order now at store.viz.com
Also available at your local bookstore or comic store
RATED T FOR TEEN
ratings.viz.com
viz media
www.viz.com
NURARIHYON NO MAGO © 2008 by Hiroshi Shiibashi/SHUEISHA Inc.
VIZANIME

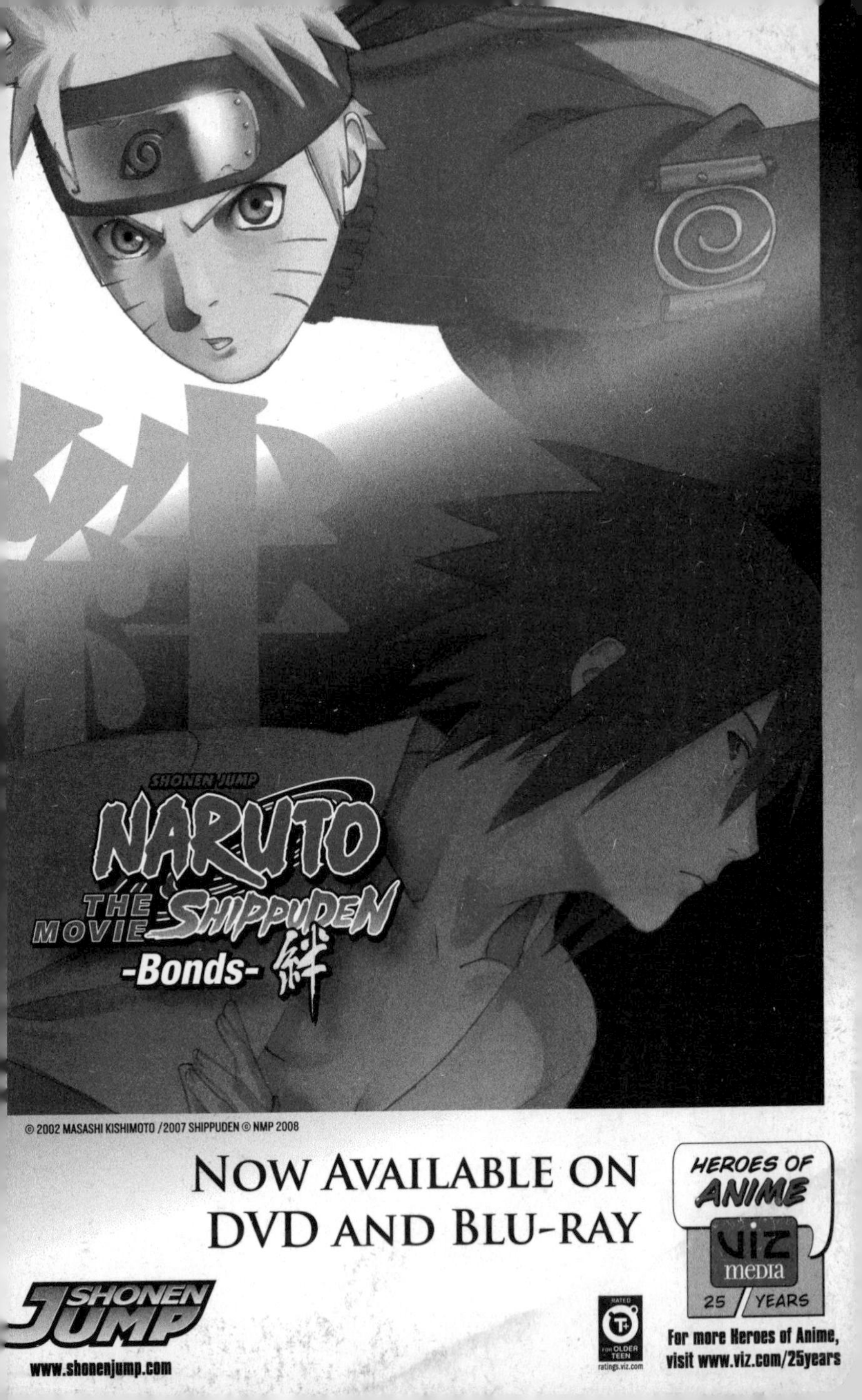
SHONEN JUMP
NARUTO
THE MOVIE SHIPPUDEN
-Bonds- 絆